UNCERTAIN AMERICANS

UNCERTAIN AMERICANS
readings in ethnic history

edited by

LEONARD DINNERSTEIN and FREDERIC COLE JAHER
University of Arizona   University of Illinois, Urbana

New York • Oxford University Press • 1977

for
Andrew and Julie Dinnerstein
and
Diane and David Jaher

Preface

Today the American people regard with considerable ambivalence the plight of their deprived minorities. These clashing feelings arise from traditional attachments to equality and justice which conflict with a long history of racial repression and hostility. During the past decade unprecedented amounts of public and private assistance have been offered to ease the dispossessed into the middle-class world. Yet a growing number of Americans feel that not only has too much been done too soon for certain minorities, but also that members of Caucasian ethnic groups who shared the deprivations of many blacks, Indians, and Hispanics were being totally ignored by the media, the government, and the liberal reformers and intellectuals.

White ethnics, especially Italians, Poles, and others of Slavic descent, made significant efforts to publicize their presence. Members of many of these groups also believed that they, too, should have received governmental largesse and sympathetic treatment in newspapers and on television. Their very presence, as well as the enunciation of their concerns, reminds us of the persistence of the minority "problem" in the United States and shows us how difficult it is to maintain both ethnic diversity and national unity—and, more important, to root out injustice toward any group. Our purpose in preparing this revised edition of *The Aliens* (originally published in 1970) is to explore the history of minority groups from colonial times to the present day in order to comprehend and communicate a vital aspect of the national existence—the experience of America's ethnic groups.

In varying degrees, depending upon approximation to the Anglo-Saxon ideal, ethnic minorities have been considered foreign even when native-born. Jews, for example, have adapted to, and absorbed, middle-class standards and values, yet latent anti-Semitism continues. Many blacks, Mexicans, and Italians, to name three others, have also moved up the socioeconomic ladder without erasing the stereotypical impressions others have of their groups. And any indication of attachment to a foreign language or heritage is seen by "Americans" as vindication of their belief that "they" (and the group being judged differs from region to region) will never really become "Americans." For convenience, then, we designate as ethnic minorities all groups of non-English origin. Included in our working definition are peoples of different national backgrounds such as the Scots, the Irish, the Welsh, and the Germans; of different racial origins such as the blacks, the Indians, and the Orientals; and religious minorities such as the Jews and the Catholics.

We emphasize the harsher aspects of minority group experiences in the United States, for we feel that the conflicts and frustrations of minority life in America have often been minimized or overlooked. Students of American history are too frequently ignorant of the humiliating conditions endured by these people. Although most minorities achieved, with varying degrees of difficulty, homogenized middle-class American goals, we feel that it is equally instructive and accurate to emphasize the struggle and cost of this process and to indicate where the outcome has been exclusion and failure rather than acceptance and accomplishment. Although we have included articles representing various aspects of minority life, our emphasis on struggle and ordeal reveals our concern to uncover past and present group conflicts in American society, for only when the background to the struggle is known, can the situation of now be dealt with intelligently and effectively.

Since the early 1970s the revival of ethnic identification has been conspicuously in the news. We believe that this is only a passing fad. Fortunately or unfortunately, depending upon the point of view, most educated members of ethnic groups in the United States want to be fully accepted by the dominant elements of society. Public education subverts ethnic cohesion. Like Eliza of *Pygmalion* and *My Fair Lady,* who could not return to the status of flower girl once she had become a lady, members of ethnic groups educated in American colleges and universities can no longer return to, or be completely comfortable in, the ghettos where they may have grown up. Members of white ethnic groups may sustain an attachment to their old friends and relatives, religious heritage, traditional foods and holidays, and their own cultural attributes, but in about two or three generations social and economic mobility make the descendants of most white ethnics more similar to other Americans than to their ancestors who left Europe, Asia, or Latin America. It is the fact of cultural similarity with most other Americans that we hope to project in this book: we think it important for all Americans to be familiar with the heritage of their neighbors and fellow citizens and to recognize that the initial experiences of most minority groups bore more similarities than differences when set beside their own.

A number of people have helped us prepare this book. David M. Reimers and Roger L. Nichols made bibliographical suggestions, Ruth Ash and Dorothy Donnelly provided secretarial assistance, and Wiladene Stickel typed the revised manuscript copy.

Leonard Dinnerstein
Frederic Cople Jaher

University of Arizona
University of Illinois, Urbana
May 1976

Contents

4 ETHNIC MINORITIES IN CONTEMPORARY AMERICA   271

UNCERTAIN
AMERICANS

Introduction

America was created and shaped by successive waves of migrants. First a recently discovered outpost of the great age of European exploration and colonization, inhabited primarily by tribes of Indians, the new land quickly attracted people from Europe. They later brought shiploads of chained Africans. When the series of great migrations ended in the 1920s over thirty-five million foreigners had come to the United States. Democracy and capitalism, the core of the American social system, were implanted, sustained, and expanded largely through the migrants' strong backs, quick minds, and grim determination.

Yet newcomers have rarely received a warm reception. The inscription on the Statue of Liberty in the harbor of New York City begins:

Give me your tired, your poor,
Your huddled masses yearning to breathe free

but many Americans throughout history have rejected people with alien cultures. At one time French Huguenots, Scotch-Irish, and Germans received the scorn and maltreatment that are visited upon blacks, Indians, and Spanish-speaking Americans today.

Because of a predominantly English heritage in the colonial period, the United States, a country of many peoples, often has evaluated its varied citizenry by a single standard: white, Anglo-Saxon, middle-class Protestantism. Although popular rhetoric glorified the country as a melting pot of different peoples, in actuality this has meant melting diversity into conformity with Anglo-Saxon characteristics. Those unable or unwilling to accomplish the transformation have suffered varying degrees of abuse and ostracism because middle-class America demands conformity before it gives acceptance.

Despite confidence in their Anglo-Saxon superiority, the British adopted liberal immigration policies for their New World colonies because mercantilism, the prevailing economic system which shaped English policy in the seventeenth and eighteenth centuries, identified national power with imperial domain. Colonies were thought necessary to relieve the mother country of overpopulation and to create a favorable balance of trade by providing a source of cheap raw materials and a market for domestic exports. Britain encouraged European emigration to North America. English policy, aimed at increasing

3

permanent agricultural settlement, differed from the strategy of France and Spain, which used colonies as trading posts rather than large permanent markets. Uninterested in agricultural settlement, France and Spain restricted entry to those Catholics who would accept centralized direction from the throne.

Revolution and restoration of the monarchy in England left the colonies to their own devices until the 1660s. Although intervention thereafter increased, the policy of salutary neglect persisted until 1763. Consequently, immigration policy emanated from provincial needs rather than from specifically English interests or the global considerations of empire. Settlers were needed to populate the hinterland, subdue the frontier, resist Indians or French and Spanish competitors, and further the growth of trade and agriculture. Through a large part of the seventeenth century it seemed that the demand for newcomers could be satisfied by English immigrants alone. Widespread unemployment, religious persecution, and political unrest brought a considerable number of Englishmen to these shores. After 1660 internal tranquility and improved living conditions curbed emigration from England, but religious, political, and economic grievances continued to draw other nationalities, chiefly Scotch Irish, Germans, French Huguenots, Scandinavians, and Dutch. They found few obstacles to settlement in English provinces because the need for manpower outpaced the labor supply. The labor scarcity resulted in enforced importation of blacks and encouraged the development of slave labor.

Despite the need for new settlers English colonials had mixed feelings about foreign arrivals. Anglo-Saxon mobs attacked Huguenots in Frenchtown, Rhode Island, and destroyed a Scotch Irish frontier settlement in Worcester, Massachusetts. Virginia in 1699 instituted a fifteen shilling tax on servants coming from anywhere except England and Wales; Pennsylvania in 1729 imposed a forty shilling tax on foreigners (Irishmen paid only twenty shillings), but dropped it the next year after protests from Germans in the colony; and Rhode Island in 1729 required ship captains to post bonds for all persons who had not embarked from the British Isles.

Germans and Scotch Irish, with Indians and blacks the largest ethnic minorities in colonial times, suffered many of the abuses historically associated with American minority groups. Southern planters contemptuously stereotyped the German farmer as a "boorish peasant, close-fisted, ignorant, rude in his manners, outlandish in his dress." Germans attempted to maintain their own language and customs in Pennsylvania and the South but social pressures forced second- and third-generation settlers to anglicize. In one tale a self-conscious German addressed a compatriot who had spoken German, "O, gay vay mit your Deutsch; you know I besser English." Striving for acceptance, many Germans claimed English, French, or Scotch heritage to elevate their social status. The Scotch-Irish endured similar criticism from colonials of English extraction. They were considered "clannish, contentious, and hard to get along with." Ethnic conflict was not restricted to difficulties between those of English stock and other races and nationalities. Quarrels over land and juxtaposition of groups with different cultures led to disputes between recently arrived minorities, as in the case of the Germans and Scotch-Irish on Pennsylvania's frontier in the eighteenth century.

Non-English immigrants suffered mild and temporary difficulties compared to those of Indians and blacks. Within three generations Germans and Scotch-Irish dropped their "foreign" characteristics, assimilated to the dominant culture, and disappeared (except for a few German settlements in Pennsylvania) as distinct ethnic groups. Red men and black men were not as readily incorporated into the larger community. By the 1670s the English provinces, now expanding beyond the eastern seaboard, confronted Indians resentful of repreated encroachments upon their land. A number of wars ensued. King Philip's War (1675–76) between five Indian tribes and the New England Federation was the bloodiest of these early conflicts. By the end of the struggle one out of every sixteen settlers of military age in New England had been killed, twelve towns totally destroyed, and half the towns suffered damage. More historically noteworthy than the casualties, the conflict ended attempts to Christianize the Indians.

The pattern of black slavery became fixed until emancipation in 1865. The process of bondage for blacks was worked out early in American history: seizure in native Africa; brutal passage to the western hemisphere; enslavement in America perpetuated by total control over individual and family life. By the 1640s and '50s scattered Virginia records show marked differences in treatment between black and white servants: blacks received severer penalties for running away, miscegenation became a criminal act, black bondsmen could not bear firearms and were listed as tithables. Court cases of these years indicated that life servitude already existed for Afro-Americans. During the 1660s Virginia formulated the first slave code. The process of enslavement evolved similarly in Maryland. South Carolina, settled later, skipped the preliminaries by providing for slavery in its fundamental constitution of 1669.

In the North, where slavery was not rooted in the economic system, most bondsmen acted as household servants or coworkers. Under these conditions black servitude was on a smaller, less formal scale. But slave revolts in New York City in 1712 and 1741 indicate that blacks also found the system humiliating and oppressive in the North. New England, except for Rhode Island, had fewer slaves than any other region. In 1700, blacks numbered 1,000 out of a population of approximately 90,000 in Massachusetts, Connecticut, Rhode Island, and New Hampshire. Economically independent of slave labor and inhabited by relatively few bondsmen, this region enacted the mildest servitude regulations. But even these restrictions were confining and humiliating: slaves could not strike white men or appear on the streets after 9 P.M.; they could not buy liquor; and they could be bought or sold at the owner's wish. Unlike southern slaves, however, northern slaves frequently owned property, testified against whites, and learned to read and write.

America's growth in wealth, territory, and power resulted in disaster for Indians and blacks. After the colonies separated from Great Britain, land-hungry Americans encroached upon Indian territory once protected by the British to foster imperial harmony and enhance the fur trade. When Indians resisted the white men's expansion or sought to reoccupy their old hunting grounds, they were beaten back. From 1790–96 five-sixths of the federal government expenditure went into the Indian war in the Northwest territory as northern tribes vainly attempted to halt white pioneers at the Ohio River. Under the leadership of the Shawnee chief Tecumseh the Indians organized their most determined resistance against the advance of white settlers into the Old Northwest. But General William Henry Harrison's army destroyed the tribal confederacy at the battle of Tippecanoe, Indiana, in 1811. As white Americans relentlessly moved westward conflicts with Indians continually recurred. Some Indians unsuccessfully fought while others yielded to the inevitable and moved westward peacefully; eventually all of those tribes not completely destroyed moved northward to Canada or else accepted a restricted life on reservations.

Hopes for blacks improved after America emerged victorious from the Revolutionary War with Great Britain. The widespread belief in the Enlightenment philosophy of the rights of man and natural equality inspired emancipation legislation in the 1780s in Massachusetts, Rhode Island, New York, and New Jersey. In the Upper South, a number of Virginians and North Carolinians also spoke out boldly for manumission but the state legislatures rejected the necessary statutes. A few years later the growth of the textile industry in the United States and Great Britain created a large demand for raw cotton and advocates of emancipation diminished in number. Eli Whitney's cotton gin by facilitating the gathering of short staple upland cotton revitalized the plantation system. Northern merchants and manufacturers who profited from cotton raw materials and exports said little about what southerners called the "peculiar institution."

Between 1800 and the Civil War, blacks, whether in the North or South, slave or free, steadily lost civil and human rights. Through conquest and legislative compromise, slavery expanded into new areas. In many of the new slave states, for example, Louisiana and Mississippi, climate and the rawness of frontier capitalism made bondage more onerous. In the Upper South being sold "down the river" to the recently settled cotton lands was a form of control used to threaten or eliminate troublesome bondsmen. But even in the mellower regions, slavery's profitability and expansion worsened the conditions of bondage. States passed laws making it virtually impossible to free slaves, prohibited or curtailed bondsmen's movements, and forced free blacks to leave or accept a constrained existence.

In the "free North" blacks' status also deteriorated. By 1860 only Massachusetts, New Hampshire, Vermont, and Maine allowed them to vote on an equal footing with whites. The Old Northwest, Ohio, Indiana, and Illinois, influenced by large numbers of southern settlers, constitutionally restricted black immigration. In the Far West California prohibited them from testifying against white men and Oregon prohibited them from holding real estate, making contracts, or initiating lawsuits. In Northern cities, for example Boston and New York, custom and law segregated neighborhoods, schools, and transportation. Competition between the older black enclaves and newly arrived ethnic groups for low-paying manual labor jobs and marginal housing resulted in racial conflict in Northern cities. During the 1830s and '40s race riots broke out in Philadelphia, New York, Pittsburgh, Cincinnati, and other areas where black men were excluded from the more remunerative skilled trades.

Slaves were the chief source of manual labor for southern planter-capitalists. In the North and the Far West by the 1830s large numbers of migrants from Europe and Asia provided mercantile and industrial capitalists with fresh sources of labor. Irish Catholics on the East Coast and Chinese on the West worked in construction and railroad gangs. In New England textile towns Irish immigrants replaced native-born farm girls in cotton cloth factories. When not directly employed in the industrial system, the Irish sought domestic service as coachmen or maids. Nativist bigotry and lack of urban industrial experience restricted the Irish and Chinese to those odd jobs which needed strong backs rather than sophisticated skills.

Many impoverished Irish and Chinese immigrants remained in ports of disembarkation like Philadelphia, Boston, New York, and New Orleans, but others made their way inland. Both groups worked on the railroads. The Irish also served as menials, dug canals and tunnels, and were important factors in the construction industry in cities like New Orleans, San Francisco, Philadelphia, Chicago, Milwaukee, and Detroit. The Chinese went first to the California mines, then did laundry, owned restaurants, entered agricultural service, and worked as both miners and menials along the West Coast and in the Rocky Mountain area. The Scandinavians, and Germans who did not remain in the urban areas of the East, moved out into middle America. Communities of Swedish and Norwegian pioneers tilled the soil in Illinois, Wisconsin, Minnesota, Iowa, and the Dakotas. Germans went to all of those states as well as numerous others. They bought land throughout the Midwest and in Texas. Some Germans went to southern cities like Memphis, Charleston, Nashville, New Orleans, and Louisville, but more found homes in New York, Philadelphia, Chicago, Milwaukee, Cincinnati, and St. Louis. These cities, points of exchange between East and West, grew with the settlement of their back country and with developing interregional commerce. The Germans, too, prospered as skilled tailors, carpenters, mechanics, brewers, and bankers or small shopkeepers.

Americans stereotyped the foreign born. Swedes and Finns, for example, were deemed stolid, honorable sons of the soil. Germans had a mixed reputation. Although respected for enterprise, industry, and commerical success, they were criticized as boorish beer swillers who clung to their native language and violated the American sabbath by drinking, gaming, and other forms of un-Christian carousal. Social views, as well as personal habits, drew hostility from native Americans. The revolution-tainted ''1848ers'' were attacked for abolitionism and atheism. Opposition toward Germans reached such a peak in the state of New York in the 1850s that the legislature refused to charter a Turnverein Association for fear that the social club was an anarchist nest.

On the West Coast, California, which repressed Chinese, Indians, blacks, Hawaiians, South Americans, Mexicans, and Frenchmen, stands out as the archetypal nativist state. Frontier violence, land hunger, squabbles over mineral rights, and the presence of a large number of southerners (nearly a third of the population in the middle of the nineteenth century) contributed to California's hostility toward minority groups. Chinese, along with Indians and blacks, were barred from voting by the 1848 state constitution, denied legal protection when driven from gold stakes, forbidden to testify in state courts, and plundered with impunity. The 150,000 ''Digger'' Indians, a peaceful, pastoral people, if picked up as vagrants (white law enforcers defined vagrancy arbitrarily), were fined and/or sold for a maximum term of four months' slave labor (minors could be sentenced to terms of servitude lasting until they were 30 years of age) and driven from their homes or murdered by gold rush miners. The San Francisco *Californian* epitomized the region's ethnic bigotry in a March 15, 1848, statement: ''We desire only a white population in California.''

Californians were not the only Americans who viewed the United States as a white man's country. The attitude that the West Coasters expressed so bluntly eventually led to repressive and exclusive national legislation. Unlike Indians and blacks, the Chinese could very easily be kept out. In 1882 the United States Congress suspended Chinese immigration for ten years and forbade the naturalization of Orientals already in the country.

Repeated resistance to Chinese entry culminated in 1924 when Congress excluded all Orientals. A generation later this policy was repudiated; the Immigration Act of 1965 eliminated ethnic origins as a qualifying factor for newcomers.

Regulating the presence of Indians and blacks presented different problems. The former were the true natives and could not be barred. But they could be slaughtered and put in reservations. The period between the Civil War and the battle of Wounded Knee in 1892 marked the most ferocious Indian wars. White Americans continually pushed westward. The government in Washington tore up and renegotiated peace treaties which guaranteed Indians the right to land in what subsequently became Nebraska, the Dakotas, Montana, Wyoming, Oklahoma, and other western states.

Some white Americans were concerned with the "Indian problem" and sought ways to solve it. Unfortunately their efforts were directed by misguided notions of reform which, as in other reform activities of the period, meant enforcing white middle-class standards. The United States government set up an Indian Bureau, ostensibly to supervise and train Indians for useful work in American society, and Congress appropriated the necessary sums for mechanical and agricultural education. The "good" intentions of some Congressmen, however, rarely affected the insipid or brutal policies of the Indian agents, who too often were ill-fitted for their supervisory positions. Even if the personnel had been humane, the disruption of tribal culture caused by the new policy added to the Indians' already anguished existence. The Dawes Severalty Act of 1887 provided for the dissolution of the Indian tribes as legal entities and the distribution of tribal lands among individual members. It also stipulated that Indians should become American citizens by 1906. Congress, however, did not grant the Indians citizenship until 1924.

While native-born ethnic minorities struggled to acculturate themselves, the arrival of new groups of European, Asian, and Latin-American immigrants intensified national tensions. The industrial revolution spawned the growth of cities and created millions of unskilled jobs. Into this gap flowed Italians, eastern Europeans, Jews, Hungarians, Greeks, Japanese, Mexicans, and Caribbean blacks. Like earlier arrivals they sought opportunities and peaceful communities.

Heretofore, northern and western Europeans with fair skin, blond hair, and blue eyes had provided the bulk of America's foreign born. Except for the Irish, they were mainly Protestants searching for farmland. Beginning in the 1880s, however, swarthy types from more alien cultures predominated among the newcomers. Southern and eastern Europeans, frequently Jews and Roman or Greek Catholics, lacked the capital that many German and Scandinavian migrants had possessed and remained in the coastal cities upon arrival. Others, either helped by relatives or recruited at the dock by scouts for large employers, flocked to the mining and manufacturing communities in Illinois, Pennsylvania, Ohio, and Indiana, where work could be found that required neither skills nor knowledge of English. They toiled at the most menial, back-breaking tasks for abominably low wages and lived in crowded, unhealthy tenements or shanties.

The prospects of "alien hordes" overrunning the United States upset many Americans of older lineage. A Progressive journalist, Burton J. Hendrick, began an article in 1913 with the prediction that in less than 100 years "the United States will be peopled chiefly by Slavs, negroes [sic], and Jews." Two years earlier a writer in the *Popular Science Monthly* had warned that if too many Jews entered the United States, "We shall lose our inherited Anglo-Saxon ideals, and instead of a perfect amalgamation, we shall confront the danger of a complete racial substitution.''

Renowned members of the American intelligentsia twisted new scientific theories to support concepts of racial inferiority. The historian-politician Henry Cabot Lodge supported legislation in Congress which would have effectively barred most of the ''new immigrants'' from entering this country. Political scientist John W. Burgess wrote treatises glorifying Anglo-Saxons and debasing blacks and Orientals. And University of Wisconsin sociologist E. A. Ross devoted reams of paper to glorifying the ''innate ethical endowment'' of northern Europeans while castigating Slavs for being ''noisome and repulsive'' and Italians for being unable ''to take rational care of themselves.''

Anxieties about foreigners supplanting ''real'' Americans stimulated the establishment of organizations like the Immigration Restriction League whose views were advertised by their names. Beginning in the 1890s various groups of patriotic societies, laborers, and politicians from the South and the West who did not have to worry about any ethnic voters agitated for a more restrictive policy. The culmination of these efforts came in 1924 when Congress severely limited further immigration from Europe and all but excluded Africans and Orientals. Latin Americans were exempt from this statute.

The barring of further large-scale immigration from Europe and Asia hastened the process of assimilating European immigrants. But animosity continued toward those whose skin pigmentations were darker than the Europeans'. Blacks, Indians, Orientals, and many Spanish-speaking citizens bore and still bear incomparably different burdens from American Caucasians. The difference lies in the crucial distinction between race and nationality. Americans of European extraction have always considered darker complexioned minorities genetically inferior to themselves.* For Caucasians, at least legally, until the late nineteenth century America had lived up to its ideal as a refuge for the oppressed from other lands. But from their first associations with settlers of Anglo-Saxon or other European origins, yellow men, red men, brown men, and black men were treated as servants, slaves, and savages, and aroused hostility, fear, and contempt in the dominant culture. While others have suffered similar humiliations and deprivations, they have not endured such prolonged and severe hardships.

Since World War II discrimination against Americans of Oriental extraction has subsided. Chiefly confined to the West Coast, repression of the Chinese and Japanese persisted despite a favorable image of Orientals as industrious, courteous, and cultured. In the 1930s, for example, ''Charlie Chan'' (Chinese) and ''Mr. Moto'' (Japanese) appeared as highly honorable and sophisticated movie detective heroes. With victory over Japan in the Second World War and a deepening sensitivity to and rejection of bigotry, these positive stereotypes encouraged the acceptance of Chinese- and Japanese-Americans.

Another group victimized by white Americans is the Spanish-speaking minority in Colorado, Texas, New Mexico, Arizona, and California. Characterized in 1950 as ''the least known, the least sponsored, and the least vocal large minority group in the nation,'' the Spanish-speaking Americans are, in a sense, both the oldest and newest of minorities. As long ago as 1598 they founded villages in what is now the state of New Mexico. After

*See chapters 1 and 2 in Winthrop Jordan, *White Over Black* (Chapel Hill: University of North Carolina Press, 1968); see also Louis Ruchames, ''The Sources of Racial Thought in Colonial America,'' *Journal of Negro History*, LII (1967), 251–77.

the Mexican-American War ended in 1848 about 75,000 residents of the Southwest and Far West found that their lands had been ceded to the United States. Some of these people returned to Mexico but most remained in their homes. Few were prosperous; most were downtrodden and their descendants have remained so. Another group of Mexican-Americans in the southwest crossed the Texas-Mexico border as itinerant laborers (those who waded across the Rio Grande illegally were known as "wetbacks"). Some of the newcomers have remained in the United States. The recent settlers are considered inferior by most white Americans (or "Anglos" as they are referred to in the Southwest) because of their mixed black, Indian, and Spanish ancestry. Reinforcing Anglo prejudices are the poverty-ridden communities in which unskilled Mexican-Americans live. A Texas farmer described conventional Anglo attitudes when he said: "You can't mix with a Mexican and hold his respect. It's like the nigger; as long as you keep him in his place he is all right."

On the East Coast the Puerto Ricans, another Latin American minority, began to arrive on the mainland after World War I but their presence in large numbers did not arouse concern until after World War II. They have also suffered racial slurs and an impoverished existence. Like many before them they came primarily for the job opportunities available to them. In 1959 more than 95 percent of the Puerto Ricans lived in New York City (there are now colonies in Bridgeport, Connecticut; Newark, New Jersey; Philadelphia; Rochester, New York; and Chicago). An overwhelming number replaced Jews and Italians at unskilled and semiskilled occupations in the garment industry.

In the Southwest and Far West the Mexican-American minority has received considerable attention during the past decade or so. Although 80 percent of these people now live in urban areas, awareness of their circumstances has risen largely because the media has publicized the plight of the agricultural workers, especially in California. The campaigns of César Chavez to organize farm laborers and the representational struggle between his union, the United Farm Workers, and the Teamsters have highlighted Chicano problems. In the 1960s Reies López Tijerina ranked second only to Chavez among Mexican-American leaders seeking to redress Chicano grievances. Tijerina inaugurated the Alianza Federal de Mercedes (the Federal Alliance of Land Grants) in 1963 to regain for his people the lands he charged that Anglos stole from the ancestors of Mexican-Americans in violation of the Treaty of Guadalupe Hidalgo. In pursuit of this cause Tijerina and his followers have engaged in massive acts of civil disobedience that brought a two-year prison term to the Alianza founder. The movement for Chicano justice, exemplified by these figures and their organizations, has led within the last decade to the formation of several associations, chiefly the Brown Berets, the Mexican-American Youth Organization, and a Congress of Mexican-American Unity representing 200 different Chicano agencies, dedicated to the struggle for the rights of this ethnic minority.

Another regional minority is the Indians, now located mainly in the Southwest and north central states, and also, after years of neglect, receiving widespread publicity. The conflicts between the American Indian Movement (AIM) and more conservative tribal figures allied with the Bureau of Indian Affairs have focused on militant demands for the return of land illegally taken by treaty violations and on the 1974 war between the AIM faction and local Indian officials at Wounded Knee, a Sioux reservation in North Dakota. The recent upsurges of Chicanos and Indians may yet encourage a bid from the Eskimos, America's forgotten minority, for more equitable treatment. The country's need for oil, which motivated the current construction of the Alaskan pipeline, is integrating that state into the national economy and undoubtedly will intensify dislocations in Eskimo life and may arouse that impoverished regional minority to the kind of actions that draw the attention of their fellow Americans to their plight.

The newly awakened militancy of other ethnic groups has been in part prompted by the rising consciousness of the blacks. White oppression of blacks has created the most basic, severe, and enduring problems in ethnic relations in the United States. No other ethnic group in the United States has ever been subjected to prolonged enslavement or to the frustrations, disappointments, and humiliations that the black man has borne for more than three centuries. The Civil War formally freed the slave but white America kept his descendants in a subordinate position. Consequently the nineteenth-century black man had little opportunity for education or advancement. In 1895 Booker T. Washington advised his race to become self-dependent and prove to whites that they were worthy of equality. To foster this responsibility Washington advocated industrial education. If blacks would learn skilled trades they would be able to care for themselves, he reasoned, even though manual training would keep them out of the middle class and in continued subordination to whites.

After 1900 persisting repression and poverty convinced a younger generation of blacks that accommodation had failed. The Niagara Movement, founded by William E. B. Du Bois in 1905, demanded ''the abolition of all caste distinctions based simply on race and color.'' Its members opposed school segregation in Philadelphia and Chicago and brought suits against railroad segregation. In 1909 most of the members of the Niagara Movement, along with liberal whites, established the National Association for the Advancement of Colored People (NAACP), an organization dedicated to securing racial equality. In 1915 the NAACP brought suit in the Supreme Court against southern disfranchisement of blacks, thus beginning the long legal struggle for civil rights.

The high point in the drive for equality was reached in the 1950s and early 1960s when a series of legislative and judicial actions apparently guaranteed equal civil rights and heralded the end of segregation in education, housing, and jobs. These victories were largely the result of a combination of tactics by different black organizations. The NAACP fought for civil rights through the courts and by encouraging influential white liberals to bring political pressure on all levels of government. The Congress of Racial Equality (CORE), the Southern Christian Leadership Conference (SCLC), and the Student Nonviolent Coordinating Committee (SNCC), composed of the younger, postwar generation of whites and blacks and inspired by Martin Luther King's successful boycott of the segregated Montgomery, Alabama, bus system in 1955–56, turned to direct action through sit-ins and voter registration.

Not all blacks believed that integration would solve America's race dilemma, however. Marcus Garvey, founder in 1914 of the Universal Negro Improvement Association (UNIA), contended that whites would remain bigoted; consequently the black must develop ''a distinct racial type of civilization of his own and . . . work out his salvation in his motherland, all to be accomplished under the stimulus and influence of the slogan, 'Africa for the Africans,' at home and abroad.'' To implement this vision, Garvey urged blacks to support business and the UNIA organized groceries, restaurants, laundries, and a printing plant. Garvey emphasized the African part and declared that God and Christ were black.

A generation later the Black Muslims under the leadership of Elijah Muhammad and

Malcolm X emerged as the leading black nationalist movement. Through appealing to middle-class Puritanism and race pride, the Muslims rehabilitated a number of black addicts and criminals. At first their message of white hatred and talk of violence aided the civil rights movement by making integration a desirable alternative to whites. However, black nationalism gained adherents as black family income failed to keep pace with that of whites. When black unemployment continued to rise and de facto segregation in schools and neighborhoods increased despite legislation to the contrary additional followers hopped on the bandwagon. CORE and SNCC rejected the integrationism of the early 1960s to demand black control over black communities and over the civil rights movement. New leaders like Stokely Carmichael and H. Rap Brown challenged the older, leading integrationists, Bayard Rustin, A. Philip Randolph, and even Martin Luther King, Jr. Rifts opened between the new militants and traditional civil rights organizations like the NAACP and the National Urban League.

During the 1960s the growth of militant separatism, the ghetto riots, and the tendency of the Black Panthers and other elements of the black community to become involved in violent confrontations with the white establishment occurred at a time of unprecedented emphasis on civil rights and improvement in political, vocational, and educational opportunities. Although most blacks still desired to become accepted as full-fledged Americans and the majority then regarded the late Martin Luther King, Jr., as their most beloved leader, racial friction intensified. Initial advancement raised black expectations and the slow pace of their fulfillment aggravated long-standing frustrations. Conversely, most whites for the past twenty years have thought that the blacks were "moving too fast" and had obtained too much outside help in their progress toward equality. Black resentment combined with white anxiety and mutual hostility have created the present impasse.

Since the apex of the late 1960s black gains in education, desegregation, and income have turned into losses. Presidents Richard Nixon and Gerald Ford have been less aggressive than the Johnson administration in taking action to implement civil rights legislation. After 1970 the median income gap between black and white families has increased at a rate of 1 percent a year. Since 1973 the proportion of black college students has diminished. Residential and school segregation, outside the rural South, has expanded despite laws and judicial decisions in favor of integration. Several recent events have highlighted these reversals. In *Milliken* v. *Bradley* (1974) the Supreme Court ruled that school districts across city-suburb boundaries did not have to transfer students in order to achieve school desegregation. In 1975 Professor James S. Coleman, author of the influential 1966 U. S. Civil Rights Commission-sponsored report, *Equality of Educational Opportunity*, which supported educational desegregation, changed his mind and argued that government-enforced busing promoted the white flight from the cities, thus increasing segregation. Ironically, in the face of these developments the civil rights movement and black militancy have actually declined. College students, generally less activistic than in the 1960s, no longer work as vigorously for racial equality. The urban riots have not recurred since the 1968 confrontations in Washington, D.C., and Chicago. The Black Panthers have turned away from revolutionary rhetoric to emphasize social welfare programs in the slums and to enter one of their leaders in the 1974 Oakland, California, mayoralty election. And in 1975 the Black Muslims began to admit whites into their organization.

Ethnic minorities display a mixed response of assimilation and alienation in their relations to contemporary America. The European nationalities have largely been absorbed into the host culture. The 1965 immigration act eliminated racial barriers and redefined the quota system to favor close relatives of Americans and foreigners with skills needed in the United States. As a result, more Asians than Europeans have been coming to the United States in the 1970s and the ghettos of the Germans, Irish, Slavs, and Jews have virtually been eliminated. The children and grandchildren of the Europeans have forgotten or never learned the old-country customs and language. The native-born no longer speak the tongue of their ancestors, and the immigrant theater, newspapers, and benevolent societies are moribund. Government agencies have now replaced ethnic associations in helping immigrants and refugees.

Religious differences, so marked between newly arrived devout Catholics, conservative Protestants from Germany and Scandinavia, and orthodox Jews, have appreciably lessened in the liberal and reform versions of these faiths and in the current ecumenical spirit. The nationality parish, once a burning issue for the Catholic Church, has gradually lost intensity, and sectarian unity is replacing the ethnic divisions in American Lutheranism. Intermarriage, that most intimate sign of ethnic assimilation, is also spreading. Eighty percent of the Protestants, 84 percent of the Catholics, and 94 percent of the Jews married within their respective religions in 1940. Investigations in the 1960s revealed that about one in three Jews and Catholics were choosing spouses from different faiths. Similar trends occurred in marriages among different nationality groups. A study of New Haven, Connecticut, showed that, in 1870, 91 percent of the ethnic minorities in that city married within the nationality group compared with 63 percent in 1940. The rate of ethnic group intermarriage increased with longevity in the United States. During the 1960s only about 40 percent of the Irish and Germans (old immigrant groups) wedded other Irish or Germans, 60 percent of the Italians and Poles (new immigrant groups) married endogamously, and Mexican-Americans and Puerto Ricans rarely married outside their own enclave. Americans whose parents, grandparents, or great-grandparents originated in Europe, along with Orientals, have also climbed from low occupational, educational, and income levels to respectable statuses of vocation and wealth. In the cases of the Jews, Japanese, Germans, and Scandinavians they have achieved and even surpassed the plateau reached by their fellow citizens of Anglo-American stock.

Other minorities, as reflected in the contemporary experiences of Chicanos, blacks, and Indians, still encounter difficulties in American society, and the result of their deprivation and exclusion is the ethnic friction that continues to constitute a fundamental source of national conflict. But the more fortunate nationalities also are growing more aggressive in protecting themselves from what they perceive as threats against their status or rights. Although their militancy stems partly from the black, red, and brown power movements, it arises also from long-standing grievances and insecurities regarding their place in America. B'nai B'rith's Anti-Defamation League (founded 1913) continues its vigilance against anti-Semitism, and Meir Kahane's Jewish Defense League (founded 1968) opposes the goal of assimilation and militantly agitates for Jewish nationalism. The founding of the Italian-American Civil Rights League in 1970 to protest alleged insults to Italian-Americans in the public media and unfair treatment by such law enforcement agencies as the Federal Bureau of Investigation shows yet another minority's intensified concern for its position in American society.

Regrettably, as occurred throughout the history of ethnic minorities in the United States, this latest drive for respect and equality often is aimed at other ethnic enclaves as well as at traditional racial and nationality prejudices. Several black civil rights organizations in the 1960s, for example CORE, barred whites from membership and recent confrontations among ethnic minorities, chiefly between blacks and Irish, Italian, Slavic, and Jewish communities in such cities as Boston and New York over the means and sometimes the goals of integration in schools, neighborhoods, and the civil service bureaucracies, indicate that racial and ethnic problems continue to plague America.

SELECTED BIBLIOGRAPHY

After each sectional introduction are a number of items which should be of interest to those who want to know more about minorities in the United States. We have made no attempt to be exhaustive in our coverage; we are merely listing one or two titles which broadly cover the different groups. Most of our suggestions contain significant bibliographical essays which might be pursued with profit by the interested student.

For brief surveys of the immigrants from Europe, Asia, and Latin America see Leonard Dinnerstein and David M. Reimers, *Ethnic Americans: A History of Immigration and Assimilation* (New York: Dodd, Mead, 1975), and Maldwyn Jones, *American Immigration* (Chicago: University of Chicago Press, 1960). Oscar Handlin's *The Uprooted* (Boston: Little, Brown, 1951) is an impressionistic and moving evocation of the immigrant experience during the mass migration from Europe to the United States.

Two groups that are covered in all of our sections are the Indians and the blacks. It would be impossible to list even the most prominent of the works on each group, but on the Indians one might begin with Wilcomb E. Washburn, *The Indian in America* (New York: Harper & Row, 1975), and Roger L. Nichols and George R. Adams, editors, *The American Indian* (Waltham, Mass.: Xerox, 1971). An excellent short history of the black experience may be found in Elliott Rudwick and August Meier, *From Plantation to Ghetto* (2nd edition; New York: Hill and Wang, 1970).

1

THE COLONIAL ERA

Ethnic conflict in America began well before the first white settlements of the sixteenth century; Indian tribes with conflicting culutres and interests battled each other repeatedly. With the arrival of Spanish, French, British, Dutch, and Swedish immigrants came additional struggles. Missionaries tried to convert Indians, Congregationalists banished Quakers from Massachusetts Bay, and territorial squabbles among the French, Spanish, and British occurred over land, the fur trade, and ultimately the destiny of the continent.

For most of the seventeenth-century English-speaking groups concentrated in New England and Virginia; Dutch and Swedes settled along the Hudson and Delaware Rivers; Germans established themselves in Pennsylvania; and French Huguenots made their homes in the infant cities of Charleston, Philadelphia, New York, and environs. The British settlers came in greater numbers and they came to stay. Except for the relatively small numbers of Huguenots and German Pietists, there were no intense religious controversies in other European countries that would impel, as they did the Pilgrims, Puritans, and Quakers in England, great numbers toward permanent emigration. Immigrants from other nations either accepted British rule or were too weak to challenge British sovereignty. When large numbers of Germans emigrated to the New World in the eighteenth century, they settled in areas already governed by the English. While Pennsylvania, Plymouth, Massachusetts Bay, Virginia, and the Carolinas became sites of permanent settlement, the Dutch, Spanish, and French enclaves were mostly armed trading posts intended for quick profit through commerce. By the eighteenth century, when colonization replaced trade as the primary reason for New World establishments, the English were far ahead of their rivals, the French, in the strength and sophistication of their settlements.

During the first seventy-five years of the eighteenth century the Scotch-Irish constituted the largest immigrant group from the British Isles. They had been driven out of Ulster and Scotland by depression in the linen industry and by enclosure of farming and grazing acreage which made small farmers landless. (Large landowners would consolidate smaller properties in order to gain profits and efficiency of large-scale farming.) Most migrants, too poor to pay their own way, came as indentured servants, selling their labor for a number of years in return for free transportation to the colonies. The majority of these, after working out their passage, drifted into the cities where they became unskilled laborers. But many ex-servants and the larger proportion of those wealthy enough not to have to mortgage their first years in the new country sought the frontier where land was most easily and cheaply acquired, or became (with little training) physicians, lawyers, and merchants in Boston, New York, and other colonial cities. The Scotch-Irish were most in evidence on the frontiers of Pennsylvania, New York, Virginia, Georgia, and the Carolinas. Their unpolished manners, evangelical religion, lack of education, demands for protection against the French and Indians, and opposition to the Eastern religious, political, and social establishment raised hackles in Tidewater Virginia, Charleston, New York City, and Philadelphia. Pennsylvania Quakers labeled them a "pernicious and pugnacious people." "Poverty, wretchedness, misery, and want are become almost universal among them," commented a writer in *The Pennsylvania Gazette* in 1729. At the same time that they received such condemnation Scotch-Irish were welcomed for expanding settlement and acting as a buffer against hostile Indians, French, and Spanish.

Another large outpouring of immigrants came from the German states in central Europe. They included Moravian Pietists, who came primarily because of religious persecution, as well as Lutherans and members of the German Reformed Church who sought greater economic opportunities in the New World. Unlike the Scotch-Irish they usually settled behind the edge of the frontiers. The reputedly thrifty and diligent Germans made more efficient and prosperous farmers than the Ulsterites on the frontiers. By 1766 enclaves of German farmers dotted Pennsylvania as well as the Cumberland and Shenandoah Valleys of Maryland and Virginia.

African slaves, the third largest migrant group, first made their appearance in sixteenth-century Spanish colonies. For economic and philosophical reasons colonists preferred black bondsmen to captive Indian labor. The image of the noble red man, God's innocent child of nature, generated a certain reluctance to enslave the native population. Moreover, the Indians, remaining in their native habitat, were considerably more intractable than Africans, cut off from their culture. Or perhaps more importantly the Indian population, decimated by its contact with European civilization, proved insufficient to fulfill the expanding labor demands of the colonial settlements.

After 1697, with the end of the Royal African Company's monopoly on the slave trade, the importation of blacks increased tremendously. During the eighteenth century approximately 200,000 arrived in America. Ninety percent of them went to the South, a region more suited to slavery than the North because of its larger land holdings. Slave labor, the existence of few cities, and pre-emption of the best land by large planters discouraged other types of immigration as white newcomers found better opportunities for land and labor in the North. The South's failure to attract the white foreign-born, a disability partly attributable to the slave system, continued into the twentieth century and left the section dependent upon bondsmen for its labor supply and more completely committed to a plantation economy.

Although there were relatively few white immigrants, the existence of large numbers of blacks (two-fifths of the population of Virginia, one-third that of North Carolina and Maryland, more than one-third that of Georgia, and nearly two-thirds that of South Carolina) made the colonial South less ethnically homogeneous than New England. New England, partly due to the greater economic opportunities in the Middle Colonies, and partly due to the aloofness of the first-generation Puritans, who wished to prevent "contamination" of Massachusetts Bay Colony by alien sects, remained the most ethnically uniform region. In the Middle Colonies, however, settlers of English extraction comprised only about one-half the total population. New York City, with its polyglot citizenry, and Pennsylvania, with its large English, German, and Scotch-Irish settlements, are the most notable examples of the ethnic mixture in the region.

Labor shortages, the need for frontier defense against the French, Spanish, and Indians, availability of land, and the desire of colonies to advance settlement and develop resources guaranteed a generally favorable reception for Protestant newcomers. Colonists used a variety of strategies to attract European emigrants: Virginia and Maryland gave land to those who brought over settlers (the "head right" system, in which a man had the right to claim an additional fifty acres for each person or head that he brought over); some legislatures exempted immigrants from taxes or debt action for specified periods of time; others provided new arrivals with free land or tools; most enacted easy naturalization laws. William Penn undertook a vigorous advertising campaign to entice migrants while Massachusetts employed immigration agents and offered bounties to defray the costs of ocean passage.

Despite these lures ethnic conflicts that would someday reverse the generally proimmigration attitudes of colonial times are revealed in the restrictions and hostility directed toward some of the newcomers. Most colonies levied head taxes on Roman Catholics, paupers, and felons; New Englanders shunned Quakers and Scotch-Irish; hostility flared between the Germans and Scotch-Irish settled near each other; Pennsylvania English manifested contempt for Pennsylvania Germans (Benjamin Franklin called them "Palatine Boors"); and prejudice against blacks and Indians pervaded all of the colonies.

Ethnic groups in the few cities assimilated more rapidly into the dominant English culture than those in the more isolated rural settlements. In New York City, by the beginning of the eighteenth century, the Dutch families remaining from New Netherland days succumbed completely to anglicizing while their upstate cousins still worshiped in the ritual and spoke in the tongue of the old country.

Well before independence fundamental aspects of the American creed appeared. On the eve of revolution the colonies established themselves as a land of refuge and opportunity for Europeans and as a place of oppression for blacks and Indians. The need for labor overcame prejudices against the admission of prisoners, blacks, Catholics, and non-English Europeans and ethnic conflict did not then seriously disturb the development of white America. The European-born established their own communities or assimilated into the dominant culture. America would change greatly in the century after independence but the pattern of ethnic friction and assimilation fixed in colonial times remained remarkably constant.

SELECTED BIBLIOGRAPHY

Two excellent accounts of Indian-white relations in colonial America are Gary B. Nash, *Red, White, and Black: The Peoples of Early America* (Englewood Cliffs, N. J.: Prentice-Hall, 1974), and Richard S. Slotkin, *Regeneration Through Violence: The Mythology of the American Frontier, 1600–1860* (Middletown, Conn.: Wesleyan University Press, 1974). Winthrop D. Jordan, *White Over Black* (Chapel Hill: University of North Carolina Press, 1968), explores the origins of American racism and the beginnings of slavery; an abridged version was published under the title *The White Man's Burden* (New York: Oxford University Press, 1974); Gerald W. Mullin, *Flight and Rebellion: Slave Resistance in Eighteenth Century Virginia* (Oxford University Press, 1972), and Edmund S. Morgan, *American Slavery, American Freedom: The Ordeal of Colonial Virginia* (New York: W. W. Norton and Co., 1975), concentrate on one state but their findings have broader implications than their titles might suggest.

Little has been written about colonial Germans in recent times but Albert B. Faust's *The German Element in the United States* (2 vols.; Boston: Houghton Mifflin, 1909) and Lucy Forney Bittinger's *The Germans in Colonial Times* (Philadelphia: J. B. Lippincott, 1901) are still useful.

On the Scotch-Irish see Henry Jones Ford's *The Scotch-Irish in America* (3rd ed.; Hamden, Conn.: Archon Books, 1966) and James G. Leyburn's *The Scotch-Irish* (Chapel Hill: University of North Carolina Press, 1962), which also contains a superb bibliography. On the Scots see Ian Charles Cargill Graham, *Colonists from Scotland: Emigration to North America, 1707–1783* (Ithaca, N.Y.: Cornell University Press, 1956).

The enterprising student will find an almost unexplored area if he surveys the history of Huguenots in colonial America. Arthur H. Hirsch's *The Huguenots of Colonial South Carolina* (2nd ed.; Hamden, Conn.: Archon Books, 1962); James L. Bugg Jr.'s "The

French Huguenot Frontier Settlement of Manakin Town,'' *Virginia Magazine of History and Biography,* 61 (1953), 359–94; and Esther Bernon Carpenter's "The Huguenot Influence in Rhode Island,'' Rhode Island Historical Society *Proceedings,* 1865–1886, pp. 46–74, are among the few items extant.

Indian Cultural Adjustment
to European Civilization

NANCY OESTREICH LURIE

The dismal history of the Indians in this nation was foreshadowed in their first encounter with a permanent American settlement. Nancy Lurie's account of Indian contact with the Jamestown colonists, taking place in Virginia between 1607 and 1646, indicates that interactions between these peoples were primarily based on exploitation, coercion, and brutal repression, a nexus only slightly relieved by occasional attitudes of mutual respect and paternalism. Her examination of the relationship between the native Americans and the transplanted Englishmen is considerably enhanced by showing that the same ignoble and positive impulses existed on both sides, that red and white relationships were influenced by intertribal conflicts, that the natives looked upon the original Jamestown settlement as an unimportant outpost, that for valid reasons the Indians rejected the anthropomorphic vision of technological and moral superiority that the immigrants claimed for themselves, and that the practical experiences of the new settlers gave them a glimmering recognition that the Indians were their equals. An indication of the latter feeling was the marriage between the daughter of the chief of the Powhatan Confederacy and an early Virginian. Finally, Lurie successfully shows how, within forty years, relations between the Indians and the whites changed drastically as the balance of power shifted from the former to the latter.

... During much of the sixteenth century Europeans were active in regions immediately adjacent to Virginia and possibly in Virginia itself. Their activity was often associated with violence, and there was sufficient time for rumors concerning them to have reached the Virginia natives before any direct contacts were made. By the time the English attempted to found colonies on the east coast toward the close of the sixteenth century, they encountered difficulties which may have been more than the simple result of European inexperience in developing techniques for survival in the New World. Raleigh's enterprise, for example, may have been singularly ill-timed. A general unrest in Indian-white relationships marked the period from 1577 to 1597 in the Carolina region where Raleigh's followers chose to remain. Pemisipan, a Secotan chief who attempted to

From James O. Smith, ed., *Seventeenth Century America* (University of North Carolina Press, 1959), pp. 33–60. Reprinted by permission of the publisher and the Institute of Early American History and Culture.

organize opposition to the British in 1585, could hardly have been blamed if he saw a curious similarity to accounts he may have heard concerning the Spanish when, for the trifling matter of the theft of a silver cup, the English burned the corn and destroyed the buildings at his village of Aquascogoc.

The later events at Cape Henry, the first landfall of the Jamestown colonists, suggest that the immediate hostility expressed by the Indians was inspired by fear of reprisals for the fate of Raleigh's colony. The Indians who attacked the English belonged to the Chesapeake tribe, immediately adjacent to the tribes with whom Permisipan conspired. It is also possible, as James Mooney implies, that by 1607 the Virginia Indians evaluated any sudden appearance of Europeans as evil and took immediate measures to repel them. However, this view oversimplifies several important factors. Long before any Europeans arrived at Jamestown, the Indians had been fighting over matters of principle important to them, such as possession of land and tribal leadership. If they were aware of the fate of other Indians at the hands of Europeans, there was no reason for them to assume that their fate would be similar; they were not necessarily allied with the beleaguered tribes, nor did they share a sense of racial kinship. Sharp cultural differences and even sharper linguistic differences separated the various Indian societies. While there was reason to fear and hate the Europeans as invaders who made indiscriminate war on all Indians, the fear was only that of being taken unawares and the hate could be modified if the tribes which had fallen victim thus far were strangers or even enemies. If the Indians of Virginia had any knowledge of Europeans, they must have been aware that the white men were fundamentally outnumbered, frequently unable to support themselves in an environment which the Indians found eminently satisfactory, and that European settlements were usually short lived. The appearance of the English was probably far less alarming than 350 years of hindsight indicate ought to have been the case.

This is demonstrated by the fact that the Virginia Indians under the leadership of Powhatan seem to have made their first adjustments to Europeans in terms of existing native conditions. Primary among these conditions were Powhatan's efforts to gain firmer control over his subject tribes and to fight tribes traditionally at enmity with his followers. It was expedient to help the settlers stay alive, for they could be useful allies in his established plans; but at the same time he could not allow them to gain ascendancy. The situation was complicated by factionalism in Powhatan's ranks and lack of accord among the settlers. However, recognition of the fundamental aboriginal situation makes the early events at Jamestown understandable on a rational basis. It offers a logical foundation for subsequent developments in Indian-white relationships and Indian adjustments to European civilization as the result of something more than barbaric cupidity and a thirst for the white man's blood.

Certainly a wary sensitivity to any sign of hostility or treachery characterized the behavior of both whites and Indians at the outset of settlement at Jamestown. The Europeans were still seriously concerned about the probable fate of Raleigh's colony and they had already been attacked by the Indians at Cape Henry. The Indians, in turn, may well have possessed information concerning the alarmingly retributive temperament of Europeans, at least in terms of the incident at nearby Aquascogoc, if not through generalized opinions derived from the long history of intermittent European contact along the east coast.

Nevertheless, the party of Europeans that set out on exploration of the country about Jamestown encountered a welcome at the various Indian villages different from the greetings offered at Cape Henry. Except for one cold but not overtly hostile reception in the Weanoc country, the white men were feted, fed, and flattered. At the same time a suggestion of the uncertainty of the next years occurred before the exploring party had even returned to their headquarters—at Jamestown the remaining colonists were attacked by a party of local Indians. Events of this nature as well as the general observations recorded during the first two years at Jamestown are particularly instructive in any attempt to understand Indian motivations and policy regarding the British.

The narratives are difficult to follow because of the variety of orthographies employed for Indian words. Certain features remain speculative because initial communication between whites and Indians was limited to the use of signs and the few native words that could be learned readily. However, it is possible to see native culture in terms of regularities and consistencies which were not obvious to the colonists. Likewise, the apparent inconsistencies on the part of the natives, recounted by the settlers as innate savage treachery, indicate that the aboriginal culture was in a process of growth, elaboration, and internal change. These phases of culture, which included both extensive tendencies of intertribal confederation and divisive reactions expressed by individual tribes, were interrupted and redirected but not initiated by the arrival of Europeans in 1607.

From the viewpoint of the twentieth century, it is difficult to realize that the material differences between the Indians and the European colonists, who lived before the full development of the industrial revolution, were equaled if not outweighed by the similarities of culture. This was especially true in Virginia, where a local florescence of culture and a demonstrated ability to prevail over other tribes gave the Indians a sense of strength which blinded them to the enormity of the threat posed by the presence of Europeans. There was actually little in the Europeans' imported bag of tricks which the Indians could not syncretize with their own experience. Metal was not unknown to them: they used native copper, brought in from the West, for decorative purposes. Metal weapons and domestic utensils were simply new and effective forms of familiar objects to accomplish familiar tasks. Even guns were readily mastered after the noise, which evoked astonishment at first, was understood

as necessary to their operation. Likewise, fabrics and articles of personal adornment were part of Indian technology. Many utilitarian objects such as nets, weirs, and gardening implements were very similar in both Indian and European culture. European ships were simply larger and different, as was fitting for a people interested in traveling greater distances by open water than the Indians had ever cared to do.

Expansive accounts of the size and permanence of the great European cities could easily have been likened by the natives to the impressive aboriginal developments in the lower Mississippi Valley; archeological evidence suggests that knowledge of this cultural complex was widespread. Even if these Indian models of nascent urbanization are discounted, the statements made by Europeans about their country and king may well have sounded like the exaggerations of outnumbered strangers endeavoring to buttress their weaknesses with talk of powerful but distant brothers. This explanation is admittedly conjectural, although we find ample documentation of the Indians' disinclination to admit any significant superiority in white culture at a somewhat later period. During the early nineteenth century, when the industrial revolution was underway and the eastern United States was heavily populated by whites, Indian visitors were brought from the West in the hope that they would be cowed by the white man's power and cease resistance to the forces of civilization. The Indians remained singularly unimpressed. Furthermore, at the time Jamestown was founded in the seventeenth century, the only knowledge Indians possessed concerning Europeans indicated that Indians were well able to oppose white settlement. Raleigh's ill-fated colony was a clear reminder of the European's mortality.

Although the early accounts tend to take a patronizing view of the Indians, the points on which the Europeans felt superior had little meaning for the aborigines: literacy, different sexual mores, ideas of modesty, good taste in dress and personal adornment, and Christian religious beliefs. The argument of technological superiority at that time was a weak one; despite guns and large ships the Europeans could not wrest a living from a terrain which, by Indian standards, supported an exceptionally large population. Scientific knowledge of generally predictable group reactions thus suggests that the degree of ethnocentrism was probably equal on both sides of the contact between Indians and Europeans in Virginia. Recognition of the Indians' self-appraisal is necessary for a clear understanding of their basis of motivation and consequent behavior in relation to Europeans.

Moreover, it was evident to the colonists that they were dealing with a fairly complex society, exhibiting many characteristics of leadership, social classes, occupational specialization, social control, and economic concepts that were eminently comprehensible in European terms. If the exploring parties overstated the case when they translated *weroance* as "king" and likened tribal territories to European kingdoms, they at least had a truer understanding of the nature of things than did the democratic Jefferson, who first designated the Virginia tribes as the "Powhatan Confederacy." Since the term "Confederacy" is so firmly entrenched in the literature, it will be retained here as a matter of convenience; but, in reality, Powhatan was in the process of building something that approximated an empire. By 1607 it was not an accomplished fact, but the outlines were apparent. . . .

. . . The Chesapeake Indians are included in the Confederacy, but this southernmost group was not fully under Powhatan's control at the time the settlers arrived. Their attack on the colonists at Cape Henry gave Powhatan the opportunity to gain favor with the English by swiftly avenging the hostile action. Although some historians have implied that Powhatan destroyed the entire tribe, it is far more likely that he simply killed the leaders and placed trusted kinsmen in these positions.

Powhatan's method of fighting and his policy of expanding political control combined a reasoned plan of action with quick ferocity and a minimum of bloodshed. Indian warfare was generally limited to surprise attacks and sniping from cover. Constant replacements of fighting men kept the enemy occupied and wore down their resistance, while actual casualties were relatively limited in number. Accounts of Powhatan's conquests and the occurrences observed after 1607 point to a carefully devised method of establishing his control over a wide territory. Entire communities might be killed if they proved exceptionally obstinate in rendering homage and paying tribute, but in most cases Powhatan simply defeated groups of questionable loyalty and upon their surrender moved them to areas where he could keep better watch over them. Trusted members of the Confederacy were then sent to occupy the vacated regions, while Powhatan's relatives were distributed throughout the tribes in positions of leadership. Mook's studies indicate that the degree of Powhatan's leadership decreased in almost direct proportion to the increase in geographical distance between the Pamunkey and the location of a given tribe. Throughout the entire region, however, the combination of ample sustenance, effective techniques of production, provident habits of food storage, and distribution of supplies through exchange offset shortcomings in the political framework connecting the tribes and helped to cement social ties and produce a commonality of culture. . . .

. . . At the outset of colonization in 1607 Powhatan's polices can best be understood in relation to circumstances antedating the arrival of the Jamestown settlers. Powhatan saw the whites in his territory as potential allies and as a source of new and deadly weapons to be used in furthering his own plans for maintaining control over his Confederacy and protecting the Confederacy as a whole against the threat posed by the alien tribes of the piedmont region. Likewise, existing concepts of intertribal trade in foodstuffs and other commodities were extended to include trade with the newly arrived whites. It is worth noting that European novelties, apart from weapons, were of far less interest to Powhatan than the fact that the British possessed copper, an object vested with traditional native values and heretofore obtained with great difficulty.

In the initial stages of contact between the Indians and the whites, therefore, it is hardly surprising that Powhatan and his people felt at least equal to the English. The chieftain could appreciate the foreigners as allies in the familiar business of warfare and trade, but in general there seemed little to emulate in European culture and much to dislike about the white men. However, even in the most difficult phases of their early relationship, Powhatan did not indulge in a full-scale attack against the settlers. At that time he was still engaged in strengthening his Confederacy and perhaps he could not risk extensive Indian defection to the side of the whites. But there is an equal likelihood that Powhatan's primary motivation was the desire to control and use the whites for his own purposes rather than to annihilate them.

At the time Jamestown was founded, native civilization was enjoying a period of expansion, and Powhatan had ample reason for sometimes considering the English as more an annoyance than a serious danger. The unusually rich natural environment and the security offered by the Confederacy stimulated the growth of social institutions and cultural refinements. In addition, the Virginia Indians were exceptionally powerful and, by aboriginal standards, their population was large: the entire Confederacy numbered some 8,500 to 9,000 people, or a density of approximately one person to every square mile. The Indians lived according to a well-ordered and impressively complex system of government. They dwelled in secure villages, had substantial houses and extensive gardens, and had a notable assemblage of artifacts for utilitarian, religious, and decorative purposes.

The Indians won the grudging respect of the colonists for their advanced technology, but the Europeans were contemptuous of their seemingly hopeless commitment to superstition, while their ceremonialism appeared to the whites a ridiculous presumption of dignity. A typical bias of communication between Europeans and Indians is seen in Smith's account of the Quiyounghcohannock chief who begged the settlers to pray to the Christian God for rain because their own deities had not fulfilled the Indians' requests. Smith asserted that the Indians appealed to the whites because they believed the Europeans' God superior to their own, just as the Europeans' guns were superior to bows and arrows. Yet Smith notes with some wonder that the Quiyoughcohannock chief, despite his cordiality and interest in the Christian deity, could not be prevailed upon to "forsake his false Gods." Actually this chief of one of the lesser tribes of the Confederacy illustrated the common logic of polytheistic people who often have no objection to adding foreign deities to their pantheon if it seems to assure more efficient control of the natural universe. The chief was not interested in changing his religious customs in emulation of the Europeans; he merely wished to improve his own culture by judicious borrowing—a gun at one time, a supernatural being at another.

Nor would the chief have dared respond to a new religion in its entirety, even if such an unlikely idea had occurred to him. The whole structure of tribal life relied upon controlling the mysterious aspects of the world by a traditional body of beliefs which required the use of religious functionaries, temples, idols, and rituals. These were awesome arrangements and not to be treated lightly, although improvement by minor innovations might be permitted.

The geopolitical sophistication of the Virginia tribes is reflected in the secular hierarchy of leadership which extended in orderly and expanding fashion from the villages, through the separate tribes, up to Powhatan as head of the entire Confederacy. A gauge of the complexity of government is the fact that the Confederacy shared with the Europeans such niceties of civilization as capital punishment. In small societies having a precarious economy, indemnities in goods or services are usually preferred to taking the life of a culprit even in crimes as serious as murder. However, where the life of the offender or one of his kinsmen is exacted for the life of the victim, punishment is the concern of the particular families involved; the rest of the group merely signifies approval of the process as a means of restoring social equilibrium after an offense is committed. Powhatan's government, however, was much closer to that of the English than it was to many of the tribes of North America. Punishment was meted out by a designated executioner for an offense against the society as the society was symbolized in the person of the leader.

Nevertheless, despite its elaborate civil structure, the Confederacy exhibited a universal rule of any society: a complex theory of government does not necessarily assure complete success in application. Powhatan not only had unruly subjects to deal with, but entire tribes in his domain could not be trusted. Relations between whites and Indians therefore were always uncertain, largely because of political developments within the Confederacy. When the colonists were supported by Powhatan, they were in mortal danger from those dissatisfied tribes of the Confederacy which had the foresight to realize that the English might one day assist Powhatan to enforce his authority. When Powhatan and his closest associates turned upon the settlers, the less dependable tribes became friendly to the whites.

In view of this morass of political allegiances, it is little wonder that early accounts of the settlers are replete with material which seems to prove the innate treachery of the Indians. Yet the militant phases of Indian activity, as illustrated by the initial attack on Jamestown and Powhatan's vengeance on the offending Chesapeake tribe, must be seen as part of a larger policy involving alternative methods of settling inter-group differences. Although the settlers knew that dissatisfaction among Powhatan's followers offered a means of preventing a coordinated

Indian attack, they also discovered that established mechanisms of diplomacy existed among the Indians that could be employed for their benefit. For example, the Jamestown settlement was located in the territory of the Paspehegh tribe, and relations with this tribe frequently became strained. The Powhatan forces represented by the leaders of the Pamunkey, Arrohattoc, Youghtanund, and Mattaponi offered to act as intermediaries in negotiating peace with the Paspehegh and other hostile tribes or, if necessary, to join forces with the settlers in an armed assault on mutual enemies.

If the Europeans found it difficult to live among the Indians, the Europeans seemed equally unpredictable to the Indians. Early in his relationship with the English, Powhatan was promised five hundred men and supplies for a march on the Monacan and Manahoac; but instead of finding wholehearted support among his allies for this campaign, Powhatan discovered that the whites were helpless to support themselves in the New World. As time wore on and they became increasingly desperate for food, the Europeans were less careful in the difficult business of trying to distinguish friends from enemies. They extorted supplies promiscuously, driving hard bargains by the expedient of burning villages and canoes.

It is problematical whether, as Smith implies, Powhatan was actually unable to destroy the handful of English because he could not organize his tribes for a full-scale offensive or whether he was biding his time in the hope of eventually establishing a clear-cut power structure in which the colonists would be allowed to survive but remain subservient to his designs in native warfare. At any rate, after two years of English occupation at Jamestown, Powhatan moved from his traditional home on the Pamunkey River some fifteen miles from the Europeans and settled in a more remote village upstream on the Chickahominy River. Violence flared periodically during these early years: colonists were frequently killed and often captured. Sometimes, being far from united in their allegiance, they fled to the Indian villages, where they were usually well treated. Captives and runaways were exchanged as hostages when one side or the other found it convenient. However, if Powhatan was willing to take advantage of dissident feeling among the whites, he was no fool and he finally put to death two colonists who seemed to be traitors to both sides at the same time. The execution was much to Smith's satisfaction, for it saved him from performing the task and assured a far more brutal punishment than he would have been able to inflict upon the renegades.

Throughout the period from 1607 to 1609, the chronicles include a complexity of half-told tales involving alliances and enmities and mutual suspicions, of Indians living among settlers and settlers living among Indians. Although this interaction was of an individual nature, the two groups learned something of each other; yet each side maintained its own values and traditions as a social entity. The Indians were primarily concerned with obtaining new material goods. By theft, trade, and the occupation of European artisans in their villages, they increased their supply of armaments and metal work. With the use of Indian guides and informants, the settlers became familiar with the geography of the region, and they also learned the secrets of exploiting their new environment through techniques of native gardening. For the most part, however, conscious efforts to bridge the cultural gap were unavailing. There was one amusing attempt to syncretize concepts of Indian and European monarchy and thereby bring about closer communication, when Powhatan was treated to an elaborate "coronation." The chief *weroance* was only made more vain by the ceremonies; he was by no means transformed into a loyal subject of the English sovereign, as the white settlers had intended.

An increasing number of settlers arrived in Virginia and, with the help of Indians who by this time had ample reason to let the whites perish, managed to weather the hazards of the "starving time." As the whites became more firmly established, competition between Europeans and Indians took on the familiar form of a struggle for land. Armed clashes occurred frequently, but there were no organized hostilities, and the Indians continued to trade with the English. A peace which was formally established in 1614 and lasted until 1622 is often attributed to a refinement of Powhatan's sensibilities because of the marriage of Pocahontas and John Rolfe. Although Pocahontas was indeed the favorite child of Powhatan, it is likely that the chieftain's interest in her marriage was not entirely paternal. This strengthening of the social bond between Indians and Europeans helped solidify Powhatan's power and prestige among the confederated tribes, as he was thus enduringly allied with the whites.

Continuation of harmony between Indians and whites for a period of eight years was doubtless rendered possible because enough land still remained in Virginia for both settlers and Indians to live according to their accustomed habits. The seriousness of the loss of Indian land along the James River was lessened by the existence of a strip of virtually unoccupied territory just east of the fall line which ran the length of the Confederacy's holdings. If properly armed and not disturbed by internal dissensions and skirmishes with the English, the Powhatan tribes could afford to settle at the doorstep of their piedmont neighbors and even hope to expand into enemy territory. Hostilities require weapons, and peaceful trade with the English meant easier access to arms which the Confederacy could turn against the Monacan and Manahoac. It is also possible that by this time Powhatan realized the vast strength of the English across the sea and was persuaded to keep the settlers as friends. Knowledge of Europe would have been available to the chieftain through such Indians as Machumps, described by William Strachey as having spent "somtym in England" as well as moving "to and fro amongst us as he dares and as Powhatan gives him leave."

Whatever were Powhatan's reasons for

accepting the peace, it appears that he utilized the lull in hostilities to unify the Confederacy and deal with his traditional enemies. We have no direct evidence of activities against the piedmont tribes, for there is little historical data regarding the western area at this time. However, by the time the fur trade became important in the West the Monacan and Manahoac had lost the power which had once inspired fear among the tribes of the Confederacy. In view of Powhatan's years of scheming and the probable closer proximity of the Confederacy to the piedmont region after 1614, it may be conjectured that the Virginia chieftain and his people took some part in the down fall of the Monacan and Manahoac.

When Powhatan died in 1618, his brother Opechancanough succeeded him as leader of the Confederacy. Opechancanough continued to observe Powhatan's policy of peace for four years, although relations between Indians and Europeans were again degenerating. The Indians' natural resources were threatened as the increasing tobacco crops encroached on land, where berries had grown in abundance and game had once been hunted. In the face of European advance, the Indians became restive and complained of the settlers' activities; but these signs went unnoticed by the colonists. Opechancanough was aware that the real danger to the Confederacy arose from neither internal dissensions nor traditional Indian enemies but from the inexorable growth of European society in Virginia. He was apparently able to convince all the member tribes of this fact, if they had not already drawn their own conclusions. The subsequent uprising of 1622 was a well-planned shock to the English; it was alarming not so much for the destruction wrought, since by that time the Europeans could sustain the loss of several hundred people, but for the fact that the Confederacy could now operate as a unified fighting organization. This was a solidarity which Powhatan either had been unable or was disinclined to achieve.

Doubtless Opechancanough expected re-

prisals, but he was totally unprepared for the unprecedented and utter devastation of his lands and the wholesale slaughter of his people. The tribes were scattered, some far beyond the traditional boundaries of their lands, and several of the smaller groups simply ceased to exist as definable entities. Gradually as the fury of revenge died down, the remnants of the Confederacy regrouped and began to return to their homelands. However, the settlers were no longer complacent about their Indian neighbors. In addition to campaigning against the natives, they erected a string of fortifications between Chesiac and Jamestown, and they tended to settle Virginia in the south rather than toward the north and west. In effect, therefore, Opechancanough accomplished a limited objective; a line was established between Indians and Europeans, but the line was only temporary and the Indians paid a terrible price.

Moreover, the cultural gap widened during the ensuing years. Following the period of reprisals the Indians were left to make a living and manage their affairs as best they could. Many old grievances seemed to be forgotten, and the natives gave the appearance of accepting their defeat for all time. Opechancanough, who had eluded capture immediately after the attack of 1622, remained at large, but the Europeans attempted to win tribes away from his influence rather than hunt him down at the risk of inflaming his followers. Finally, white settlement once more began to spread beyond the safety of concentrated colonial population. Tensions were re-created on the frontier, and there were minor skirmishes; the Indians complained to the English, but they also continued their trading activities. Thus matters continued for more than twenty years until large-scale hostilities again broke out.

The uprising of 1644 was surprisingly effective. It is generally known that in both the 1622 and the 1644 uprisings the percentage of Indians killed in relation to the total Indian population was far greater than the percentage of settlers killed in relation to the total white population. Yet with far fewer Indians to do the fighting, Opechancanough managed to kill at least as many Europeans in the second attack as he had in the first. The uprising is another proof that the Indians' method of adjusting to changes wrought by the Europeans continued to be an attempt to prevail over or remove the source of anxiety—the settlers—rather than to adapt themselves to the foreign culture. Certainly the Indians never felt that their difficulties would be resolved by assimilation among the whites, a solution which the colonists at times hoped to effect through the adoption of Indian children, intermarriage, and Indian servitude.

Hopeless though the uprising appears in retrospect, it was entirely logical within Opechancanough's own cultural frame of reasoning. It is impossible to determine whether the Indians were aware of the futility of their action, nor do we know enough about the psychology of these people to ascribe to them such a grim fatalism that they would prefer a quick and honorable death to the indignities of living in subjection to the whites. But there is something impressive about Opechancanough, an old and enfeebled man, being carried on a litter to the scene of battle. Whatever the outcome his days were numbered. His young warriors, however, knew of the horrible reprisals of 1622 and they understood the cost of being defeated by the white man. Yet they too were willing to risk an all-out attack.

There is little doubt that Opechancanough realized the danger inherent in rebellion. He was a shrewd strategist and a respected leader. It is entirely possible that he hoped for assistance from forces outside the Confederacy. Tension had existed between the whites of Virginia and Maryland for a number of years, and in one instance the Virginians had hoped to incite the Confederacy against their neighbors. Maryland had been settled only ten years before the second uprising, and although hostile incidents between whites and Indians had occurred, her Indian policy had been more just and humane than Virginia's. If Opechancanough did expect military assistance from whites for his uprising against whites, he had historical precedent to inspire him. Powhatan had exploited factionalism among the Jamestown settlers, and it may be that the tension between Virginia and Maryland suggested an extension of his policy to Opechancanough. Whatever the motivations behind Opechancanough's design for rebellion, the second uprising attested to the strength of the old Confederacy and indicated clearly the stubborn resistance of the Indians to cultural annihilation.

Although the usual revenge followed the attack of 1644, Virginia's Indian policy was beginning to change. The Powhatan tribes were too seriously reduced in numbers to benefit greatly by the progress, but their treatment at the hands of the colonists following the uprising marked a new development in Indian-white relations, one which eventually culminated in the modern reservation system. In 1646 a formal treaty was signed with the Powhatan Confederacy establishing a line between Indian and white lands and promising the Indians certain rights and protection in their holdings. While their movements were to be strictly regulated, the natives were guaranteed recognition for redress of wrongs before the law. There were two particularly important features of the treaty. First, the Indians were to act as scouts and allies against the possibility of outside tribes' invading the colony; this policy was in contrast to the earlier device of attempting to win the friendship of peripheral tribes to enforce order among the local Indians. Second, and consistent with the growing importance of the fur trade in colonial economics, the Indians were to pay a tribute each year in beaver skins. During the following years various legislative acts were adopted to protect the Indians in their rights and establish mutual responsibilities with the tribes.

Enslavement of Africans in America

WINTHROP D. JORDAN

A number of American historians have explored the origins of slavery in the British colonies and, not surprisingly, have failed to reach a unanimous verdict. Oscar and Mary Handlin, in their essay "Origins of the Southern Labor System" (William and Mary Quarterly, Third Series, VII, April, 1950, 199–222), concluded that there was essentially little difference between the treatment of black and white servants in the South between the time the first boatload of Africans landed at Jamestown in 1619 and the enactment of the Navigation Acts (which regulated trade between Great Britain and her colonies) in the 1660s. Only after tobacco cultivation had expanded, and unit costs of production had to be lowered for increased profitability, did slavery emerge as a clearly defined institution and then, primarily, because the blacks provided the "cheapest, most available, most exploitable labor supply." Carl Degler (Out of Our Past, New York: Harper & Row, 1959), on the other hand, argued that "discrimination preceded slavery and thereby conditioned it," by showing examples of differential treatment between black and white servants during the forty-year period, 1619 through 1660. He concluded that slavery was in vogue earlier than the Handlins suggested. In one of the most significant works on blacks in colonial America, White Over Black *(Chapel Hill: University of North Carolina Press, 1968),* Winthrop D. Jordan *takes a midway approach. He acknowledges the existence of slavery before 1660 but refuses to generalize about the conditions of the blacks in the colonies before that time. Jordan points out that too little is known about colonial policies between 1620 and 1640 to make any intelligent evaluation: that between 1640 and 1660 slavery existed but available evidence is too scanty to suggest its extent; and that only after 1660 did the institution crystallize. The chapter entitled "Unthinking Decision," from Jordan's* White Man's Burden *(an abridgement, published by Oxford University Press in 1974, of* White Over Black*) and reprinted below, summarizes his position on this controversy. In this selection Jordan also discusses the Elizabethan cultural and social predispositions and the New World conditions that produced, at first, a possibly ambiguous state between servitude and slavery and, by the 1660s, the emergence of a racially determined chattel system that was not fundamentally altered until the Civil War.*

At the start of English settlement in America, no one had in mind to establish the institution of Negro slavery. Yet in less than a century the foundations of a peculiar institution had been laid. The first Africans landed in Virginia in 1619, though very little is known about their precise status during the next twenty years. Between 1640 and 1660 there is evidence of enslavement, and after 1660 slavery crystallized on the statute books of Maryland, Virginia, and other colonies. By 1700, when Africans began flooding into English America, they were treated as somehow deserving a life and status radically different from English and other European settlers. Englishmen in America had created a new legal status which ran counter to English law.

Unfortunately the details of this process can never be completely reconstructed; there is simply not enough evidence to show precisely when and how and why Negroes came to be treated so differently from white men. Concerning the first years of contact especially we have very little information as to what impression Negroes made upon English settlers: accordingly, we are left knowing less about the formative years than about later periods of American slavery. That those early years were crucial is obvious, for it was then that the cycle of Negro debasement began; once the African became fully the slave it is not hard to see why Englishmen looked down upon him. Yet precisely because understanding the dynamics of these early years is so important to understanding the centuries which followed, it is necessary to bear with the less than satisfactory data and to attempt to reconstruct the course of debasement undergone by Africans in seventeenth-century America.

THE NECESSITIES OF A NEW WORLD

When Englishmen crossed the Atlantic to settle in America, they were immediately subject to novel strains. A large proportion of migrants were dead within a year. The survivors were isolated from the world as they had known it, cut off from friends and family and the familiar sights and sounds and smells which have always told men who and where they are. A similar sense of isolation and disorientation was inevitable even in the settlements that did not suffer through a starving time. English settlers had undergone the shock of detachment from home in order to set forth upon a dangerous voyage of from ten to thirteen weeks that ranged from unpleasant to fatal and that seared into every passenger's memory the ceaselessly tossing distance that separated him from his old way of life.

Life in America put great pressure upon the traditional social and economic controls that Englishmen assumed were to be exercised by civil and often ecclesiastical authority. Somehow the empty woods seemed to lead much more toward license than restraint. At the same time, by reaction, this unfettering resulted in an almost pathetic social conservatism, a yearning for the forms and symbols of the old familiar social order. When in 1618, for example, the Virginia Company wangled a knighthood for a newly appointed governor of the colony the objection from the settlers was not that this artificial elevation was inappropriate to wilderness conditions but that it did not go far enough to meet them. English social forms were transplanted to America not simply because they were nice to have around but because without them the new settlements would have fallen apart and English settlers' would have become men of the forest, savage men devoid of civilization.

For the same reason, the communal goals and values that animated the settlement of the colonies acquired great functional importance in the wilderness; they served as antidotes to social and individual disintegration. For Englishmen planting in America, it was of the utmost importance to know that they were Englishmen, which was to say that they were educated (to a degree suitable to their station), Christian (of an appropriate Protestant variety), civilized, and (again to an appropriate degree) free men.

It was with personal freedom, of course, that wilderness conditions most suddenly reshaped English laws, assumptions, and practices. In America land was plentiful, labor scarce, and, as in all new colonies, a cash crop desperately needed. These economic conditions were to remain crucial for many years; in general they tended to encourage greater geographical mobility, less specialization, higher rewards, and fewer restraints on the processes and products of labor. In general men who invested capital in agriculture in America came under fewer customary and legal restraints than in England concerning what they did with their land and with the people who worked on it. On the other hand their activities were restricted by the economic necessity of producing cash crops for export. Men without capital could obtain land relatively easily: hence the shortage of labor and the notably blurred line between men who had capital and men who did not.

Three major systems of labor emerged amid the interplay of these social and economic conditions in America. One, which was present from the beginning, was free wage labor. Another, which was the last to appear, was chattel slavery. The third, which virtually coincided with first settlement in America, was temporary servitude, in which contractual arrangements gave shape to the entire system. It was this third system, indentured servitude, which permitted so many English settlers to cross the Atlantic barrier. Indentured servitude was linked to the development of chattel slavery in America, and its operation deserves closer examination.

A very sizable proportion of settlers in the English colonies came as indentured servants bound by contract to serve a master for a specified number of years, usually from four to seven or until age twenty-one, as repayment for their ocean passage. The time of service to which the servant bound himself was negotiable property, and he might be sold or conveyed from one master to another at any time up to the expiration of his indenture, at which point he became a free man. (Actually it was his *labor* which was owned

and sold, not his *person,* though this distinction was neither important nor obvious at the time.) Custom and statute law regulated the relationship between servant and master. Obligation was reciprocal: the master undertook to feed and clothe and sometimes to educate his servant and to refrain from abusing him, while the servant was obliged to perform such work as his master set him and to obey his master in all things.

FREEDOM AND BONDAGE IN THE ENGLISH TRADITION

While in retrospect we can readily see these three distinct categories, thinking about freedom and bondage in Tudor England was in fact confused and self-contradictory. In a period of social dislocation there was considerable disagreement among contemporary observers as to what actually was going on and even as to what ought to be. *Ideas* about personal freedom tended to run both ahead of and behind actual social conditions. Both statute and common law were sometimes considerably more than a century out of phase with actual practice and with commonly held notions about servitude. Finally, both ideas and practices were changing rapidly. It is possible, however, to identify certain important tenets of social thought that served as anchor points amid this chaos.

Englishmen lacked accurate methods of ascertaining what actually was happening to their social institutions, but they were not wrong in supposing that villenage, or bondage" as they more often called it, had virtually disappeared in England. In the middle ages, being a villein had meant dependence upon the will of a feudal lord but by no means deprivation of all social and legal rights. By the fourteenth century villenage had decayed markedly, and it no longer existed as a viable social institution in the second half of the sixteenth century. Personal freedom had become the normal status of Englishmen. Most contemporaries welcomed this fact; indeed it was after about 1550 that there began to develop in England that preening consciousness of the peculiar glories of English liberties. This consciousness was to flower in America as well.

How had it all happened? Among those observers who tried to explain, there was agreement that Christianity was primarily responsible. They thought of villenage as a mitigation of ancient bond slavery and that the continuing trend to liberty was animated, as Sir Thomas Smith said in a famous passage, by the "perswasion . . . of Christians not to make nor keepe his brother in Christ, servile, bond and underling for ever unto him, as a beast rather than as a man." They agreed also that the trend had been forwarded by the common law, in which the disposition was always, as the phrase went, "in favor of liberty."

At the same time there were in English society people who seemed badly out of control. From at least the 1530's the countryside swarmed with vagrants, sturdy beggars, rogues, and vagabonds, with men who *could* (it was thought) but *would not* work. They committed all manner of crimes, the worst of which was remaining idle. It was an article of faith among Tudor commentators that idleness was the mother of all vice and the chief danger to a well-ordered state. Tudor statesmen valiantly attempted to suppress idleness by means of the famous vagrancy laws which provided for houses of correction and (finally) for whipping the vagrant from constable to constable until he reached his home parish. They assumed that everyone belonged in a specific niche and that anyone failing to labor in the niche assigned to him by Providence must be compelled to do so by authority.

In response, Tudor authorities gradually hammered out the legal framework of a labor system which permitted compulsion but which did *not* permit so total a loss of freedom as lifetime hereditary slavery. And as things turned out, it was indentured servitude which best met the requirements for settling in America. Of course there were other forms of bound labor which contributed to the process of settlement: many convicts

were sent and many children abducted. Yet among all the numerous varieties and degrees of non-freedom which existed in England, there was none which could have served as a well-formed model for the chattel slavery which developed in America. This is not to say, though, that slavery was an unheard-of novelty in Tudor England. On the contrary, "bond slavery" was a memory trace of long standing. Vague and confused as the concept of slavery was in the minds of Englishmen, it possessed certain fairly consistent connotations which were to help shape English perceptions of the way Europeans should properly treat the newly discovered peoples overseas.

THE CONCEPT OF SLAVERY

At first glance, one is likely to see merely a fog of inconsistency and vagueness enveloping the terms *servant* and *slave* as they were used both in England and in seventeenth-century America. When Hamlet declaims "O what a rogue and peasant slave am I," the term seems to have a certain elasticity. When Peter Heylyn defines it in 1627 as "that ignominious word, *Slave;* whereby we use to call ignoble fellowes, and the more base sort of people," the term seems useless as a key to a specific social status.

In one sense it was, since the concept embodied in the terms *servitude, service,* and *servant* was widely embracive. *Servant* was more a generic term than *slave.* Slaves could be "servants," but servants *should not* be "slaves." This principle, which was common in England, suggests a measure of precision in the concept of slavery. In fact there was a large measure which merits closer inspection.

First of all, the "slave's" loss of freedom was complete. "Of all men which be destitute of libertie or freedome," explained one commentator in 1590, "the slave is in greatest subjection, for a slave is that person which is in servitude or bondage to an other, even against nature." "Even his children," moreover, ". . . are infected with the Leprosie of his father's bondage.'' At law, much more closely than in literary usage, ''bond slavery'' implied utter deprivation of liberty.

Slavery was also thought of as a perpetual condition. While it had not yet come invariably to mean lifetime labor, it was frequently thought of in those terms. Except sometimes in instances of punishment for crime, slavery was open ended; in contrast to servitude, it did not involve a definite term of years. Slavery was perpetual also in the sense that it was often thought of as hereditary. It was these dual aspects of perpetuality which were to assume such importance in America.

So much was slavery a complete loss of liberty that it seemed to Englishmen somehow akin to loss of humanity. No theme was more persistent than the claim that to treat a man as a slave was to treat him as a beast. Almost half a century after Sir Thomas Smith had made this connection a Puritan divine was condemning masters who used ''their servants as slaves, or rather as beasts.'' No analogy could have better demonstrated how strongly Englishmen felt about total loss of personal freedom.

Certain prevalent assumptions about the origins of slavery paralleled this analogy at a different level of intellectual construction. Lawyers and divines alike assumed that slavery was impossible before the Fall, that it violated natural law, that it was instituted by positive human laws, and, more generally, that in various ways it was connected with sin. These ideas were as old as the church fathers and the Roman writers on natural law. Sir Edward Coke, the great jurist, spelled out what was perhaps the most important and widely acknowledged attribute to slavery: ''. . . it was ordained by Constitution of Nations . . . that he that was taken in Battle should remain Bond to his taker for ever, and he to do with him, all that should come of him, his Will and Pleasure, as with his Beast, or any other Cattle, to give, or to sell, or to kill.'' This final power, Coke noted, had since been taken away (owing to ''the

Cruelty of some Lords'') and placed in the hands only of kings. The animating rationale here was that captivity in war meant an end to a person's claim to life as a human being; by sparing the captive's life, the captor acquired virtually absolute power over the life of the man who had lost the power to control his own.

More than any other single quality, *captivity* differentiated slavery from servitude. Although there were other, subsidiary ways of becoming a slave, such as being born of slave parents, selling oneself into slavery, or being adjudged to slavery for crime, none of these was considered to explain the way slavery had originated. Slavery was a power relationship; servitude was a relationship of service. Men were ''slaves'' to the devil but ''servants'' of God. Men were ''galley-slaves,'' not galley servants.

This tendency to equate slavery with captivity had important ramifications. Warfare was usually waged against another people; captives were usually foreigners—''strangers'' as they were termed. Until the emergence of nation-states in Europe, by far the most important category of strangers was the non-Christian. International warfare seemed above all a ceaseless struggle between Christians and Muslims. In the sixteenth and seventeenth centuries Englishmen at home could read scores of accounts concerning the miserable fate of Englishmen and other Christians taken into ''captivity'' by Turks and Moors and oppressed by the ''verie worst manner of bondmanship and slaverie.'' Clearly slavery was tinged by the spirit of religious difference.

It is clear, therefore, that Englishmen did possess a *concept* of slavery, formed by the clustering of several rough but not illogical equations. The slave was treated like a beast. Slavery was inseparable from the evil in men; it was God's punishment upon Ham's prurient disobedience. Enslavement was captivity, the loser's lot in a contest of power. Slaves were infidels or heathens.

On every count, Negroes qualified.

THE PRACTICES OF PORTINGALS AND SPANYARDS

Which is not to say that Englishmen were casting about for a people to enslave. What happened was that they found thrust before them not only instances of Negroes' being taken into slavery but attractive opportunities for joining in that business. Englishmen actually were rather slow to seize these opportunities; on most of the sixteenth-century English voyages to West Africa there was no dealing in slaves. The notion that it was appropriate to do so seems to have been drawn chiefly from the example set by the Spanish and Portuguese.

Without inquiring into the reasons, it can be said that slavery had persisted since ancient times in Spain and Portugal, that prior to the discoveries it was primarily a function of the religious wars against the Moors, that Portuguese explorers pressing down the coast in the fifteenth century captured thousands of Negroes whom they carried back to Portugal as slaves, and that after 1500, Portuguese ships began supplying Spanish and Portuguese settlements in America with Negro slaves. By 1500 European enslavement of Negroes had become a fixture of the New World.

There is no need to inquire into the precise nature of this slavery except to point out that in actual practice it did fit the English concept of bond slavery. The question which needs answering pertains to contemporary English knowledge of what was going on. And the answer may be given concisely: Englishmen had easily at hand a great deal of not very precise information.

The news that Africans were being carried off to forced labor in America was broadcast across the pages of the widely read Hakluyt and Purchas collections. While only one account stated explicitly that Negroes "be their slaves during their life," it was clear that the Portuguese and Spaniards treated Negroes and frequently the Indians as "slaves." This was the term customarily used by English voyagers and by translators of foreign documents. William Towrson was told by an African in 1556 "that the Portingals were bad men, and that they made them slaves, if they could take them, and would put yrons upon their legges." There were "rich trades" on that coast in Negroes "which be caried continually to the West Indies." The Portuguese in the Congo "have divers rich Commodities from this Kingdome, but the most important is every yeere about five thousand Slaves, which they transport from thence, and sell them at good round prices in . . . the West Indies."

Some Englishmen decided that there might be profit in supplying the Spanish with Negroes, despite the somewhat theoretical prohibition of foreigners from the Spanish dominions in the New World. John Hawkins was first; in the 1560's he made three voyages to Africa, the Caribbean, and home. The first two were successful; the third met disaster when the Spanish attacked his ships, took most of them, and turned the captured English seamen over to the Inquisition. This famous incident helped discourage English slave trading in favor of other maritime activities. English vessels were not again active frequently in the slave trade until the seventeenth century. But Englishmen learned, from the accounts published by Richard Hakluyt, that Hawkins had taken Africans in Africa and sold them as "marchandise" in the West Indies.

By the end of the first quarter of the seventeenth century it had become abundantly evident in England that Negroes were being enslaved on an international scale. Clearly an equation had developed between Africans and slavery. Primarily, the associations were with the Portuguese and Spanish, with captivity, with buying and selling in Guinea and in America. Yet there is no reason to suppose Englishmen especially eager to enslave Negroes, nor even to regard the traveler Richard Jobson eccentric in his response to an African chief's offer to buy some "slaves": "I made answer, We were a people, who did not deale in any such commodities, neither did wee buy or sell one another, or any that had our owne shapes." By the seventeenth century, after all, English prejudices as well as English law were "in favor of liberty."

When they came to settle in America, Englishmen found that things happened to liberty, some favorable, some not. Negroes became slaves, partly because there were economic necessities in America which called for some sort of bound, controlled labor. The Portuguese and Spanish had set an example, which, however rough in outline, proved to be, at very least, suggestive to Englishmen. It would be surprising if there had been a clear-cut line of influence from Latin to English slavery. Elizabethans were not in the business of modeling themselves after Spaniards. Yet from about 1550, Englishmen were in such continual contact with the Spanish that they could hardly have failed to acquire the notion that Negroes could be enslaved. The terms *negro* and *mulatto* were incorporated into English from the Hispanic languages. This is the more striking because a perfectly adequate term, identical in meaning to *negro,* already existed in English; of course *black* was used also, though not so commonly in the sixteenth century as later.

By 1640 it was becoming apparent that in many of their new colonies overseas English settlers had bought Negroes and were holding them, frequently, as hereditary slaves for life. In considering this development, it is important to remember that the status of slave was at first distinguished from servitude more by duration than by onerousness; the key term in many early descriptions of the Negro's condition was *perpetual.* Negroes served "for ever" and so would their children. Englishmen did not do so. Servitude, no matter how long, brutal, and involuntary, was not the same thing as perpetual slavery. Servitude comprehended alike the young apprentice, the orphan, the indentured servant, the convicted debtor or criminal, the political prisoner, and, even, the Scottish and Irish captive of war who was

sold as a "slave" to New England or Barbados. None of these persons, no matter how miserably treated, served for life in the colonies, though of course many died before their term ended. Hereditary lifetime service was restricted to Indians and Africans. Among the various English colonies in the New World, this service known as "slavery" seems first to have developed in the international cockpit known as the Caribbean.

ENSLAVEMENT: THE WEST INDIES

The Englishmen who settled the Caribbean colonies were not very different from those who went to Virginia, Bermuda, Maryland, or even New England. Their experience in the islands, however, was very different indeed. By 1640 there were roughly as many English (and Irish and Scots) in the little islands as on the American continent. A half-century after the first settlements were established in the 1620's, many of the major islands—Barbados, and the Leeward Islands—were overcrowded. Thousands of whites who had been squeezed off the land by sugar plantations migrated to other English colonies, including much larger Jamaica which had been captured from the Spanish in 1655. Their places were taken by African slaves who had been shipped to the islands, particularly after 1640, to meet an insatiable demand for labor which was cheap to maintain, easy to dragoon, and simple to replace when worked to death. Negroes outnumbered whites in Barbados as early as 1660.

In that colony, at least, this helpful idea that Negroes served for life seems to have existed even before they were purchased in large numbers. Any doubt which may have existed as to the appropriate status of Africans was dispelled in 1636 when the Governor and Council resolved "that *Negroes* and *Indians,* that came here to be sold, should serve for life, unless a Contract was before made to the contrary." Europeans were not treated in this manner. In the 1650's several observers referred to the lifetime slavery of Negroes as if it were a matter of common knowledge. "It's the Custome for a Christian servant to serve foure yeares," one wrote at the beginning of the decade, "and then enjoy his freedome . . . the Negroes and Indians (of which latter there are but few here) they and the generation are Slaves to their owners to perpetuity." As another visitor described the people of the island in 1655:

The genterey heare doth live far better than ours doue in England: they have most of them 100 or 2 or 3 of slaves apes whou they command as they pleas. . . . This Island is inhabited with all sortes: with English, french, Duch, Scotes, Irish, Spaniards they being Jues: with Ingones and miserabell Negors borne to perpetuall slavery thay and thayer seed . . . some planters will have 30 more or les about 4 or 5 years ould: they sele them from one to the other as we doue shepe. This Illand is the Dunghill wharone England doth cast forth its rubidg: Rodgs and hors and such like peopel are those which are gennerally Broght heare.

Dunghill or no dunghill, Barbados was treating its Negroes as slaves for life.

ENSLAVEMENT: NEW ENGLAND

It was ironic that slavery in the West Indies should have influenced, of all places, New England. The question with slavery in New England is not why it was weakly rooted, but why it existed at all. No staple crop demanded regiments of raw labor. That there was no compelling economic demand for Negroes is evident in the numbers actually imported: there could have been no need for a distinct status for only 3 per cent of the labor force. Indentured servitude was completely adequate to New England's needs. Why, then, did New Englanders enslave Negroes, probably as early as 1638? Why was it that the Puritans rather mindlessly (which was not their way) accepted slavery for blacks and Indians but not for whites?

The early appearance of slavery in New England may in part be explained by the fact that the first Negroes were imported in the ship *Desire* in 1638 from an island colony where Negroes were already being held perpetually. After 1640 a brisk trade got under way between New England and the English Caribbean islands. These strange Negroes from the West Indies must surely have brought with them to New England prevailing notions about their usual status. Ship masters who purchased perpetual service in Barbados would not have been likely to sell service for term in Boston.

No amount of contact with the West Indies could have by itself created Negro slavery in New England; settlers there had to be willing to accept the proposition. Because they were Englishmen, they were so prepared—and at the same time they were not. Characteristically, as Puritans, they officially codified this ambivalence in 1641 as follows: ". . . there shall never be any bond-slavery, villenage or captivitie amongst us; unlesse it be lawfull captives taken in just warrs, and such strangers as willingly sell themselves, or are solde to us. . . ." Thus as early as 1641 the Puritan settlers were seeking to guarantee their own liberty without closing off the opportunity of taking it from others whom they identified with the Biblical term, "strangers."

It would be wrong to suppose, though, that all the Puritans' preconceived ideas about freedom and bondage worked in the same direction. While the concepts of difference in religion and the captivity worked against Indians and Negroes, certain Scriptural injunctions and English pride in liberty told in the opposite direction. In Massachusetts the magistrates demonstrated that they were not about to tolerate glaring breaches of "the Law of God established in Israel" even when the victims were Africans. In 1646 the authorities arrested two mariners who had carried two Negroes directly from Africa and sold them in Massachusetts. What distressed the General Court was that the Negroes had been obtained during a raid on an African village and that this "haynos and crying sinn of man stealing" had taken place on the

Lord's Day. The General Court decided to free the unfortunate victims and ship them back to Africa, though the death penalty for the crime (clearly mandatory in Scripture) was not imposed. More quietly than in this dramatic incident, Puritan authorities extended the same protections against maltreatment to Negroes and Indians as to white servants.

From the first, however, there were scattered signs in New England that Negroes were regarded as different from English people not merely in their status as slaves. In 1652, for example, the Massachusetts General Court ordered that Scotsmen, Indians, and Negroes should train with the English in the militia, but four years later abruptly excluded Negroes, as did Connecticut in 1660. Evidently Negroes, even free Negroes, were regarded as distinct from the English. They were, in New England where economic necessities were not sufficiently pressing to determine the decision, treated differently from other men.

ENSLAVEMENT: VIRGINIA AND MARYLAND

In Virginia and Maryland the development of Negro slavery followed a very different course, for several reasons. Most obviously, geographic conditions and the intentions of the settlers quickly combined to produce a successful agricultural staple. Ten years after settlers first landed at Jamestown they were on the way to proving, in the face of assertions to the contrary, that it was possible "to found an empire upon smoke." More than the miscellaneous productions of New England, tobacco required labor which was cheap but not temporary, mobile but not independent, and tireless rather than skilled. In the Chesapeake area more than anywhere to the northward, the shortage of labor and the abundance of land—the "frontier"—placed a premium on involuntary labor.

This need for labor played more directly upon these settlers' ideas about freedom and bondage than it did either in the West Indies

or in New England. Perhaps it would be more accurate to say that settlers in Virginia (and in Maryland after settlement in 1634) made their decisions concerning Negroes while relatively virginal, relatively free from external influences and from firm preconceptions. Of all the important early English settlements, Virginia had the least contact with the Spanish. Portuguese, Dutch, and other English colonies. At the same time, the settlers of Virginia did not possess either the legal or Scriptural learning of the New England Puritans whose conception of the just war had opened the way to the enslavement of Indians. Slavery in the tobacco colonies did not begin as an adjunct of captivity; in marked contrast to the Puritan response to the Pequot War, the settlers of Virginia did not react to the Indian massacre of 1622 with propositions for taking captives and selling them as "slaves."

In the absence, then, of these influences in other English colonies, slavery as it developed in Virginia and Maryland assumes a special interest and importance over and above the fact that Negro slavery was to become a vitally important institution there and, later, to the southwards. In the tobacco colonies it is possible to watch Negro slavery *develop,* not pop up full-grown overnight, and it is therefore possible to trace, very imperfectly, the development of the shadowy, unexamined rationale which supported it. The concept of Negro slavery there was neither borrowed from foreigners, nor extracted from books, nor invented out of whole cloth, nor extrapolated from servitude, nor generated by English reaction to Negroes as such, nor necessitated by the exigencies of the New World. Not any one of these made the Negro a slave, but all.

In rough outline, slavery's development in the tobacco colonies seems to have undergone three stages. Africans first arrived in 1619, an event Captain John Smith referred to with the utmost unconcern: "About the last of August came in a dutch man of warre that sold us twenty Negars." Africans trickled in slowly for the next half-century; one report in 1649 estimated that there were three hundred among Virginia's population of fifteen thousand—about 2 per cent. Long before there were more appreciable numbers, the development of slavery had, so far as we can tell, shifted gears. Prior to about 1640 there is very little evidence to show how Negroes were treated. After 1640 there is mounting evidence that some Negroes were in fact being treated as slaves. This is to say that the twin essences of slavery—lifetime service and inherited status—first became evident during the twenty years prior to the beginning of legal formulation. After 1660 slavery was written into statute law.

Concerning the first of these stages, there is only one major historical certainty. There simply is not enough evidence to indicate whether Negroes were treated like white servants or not. At least we can be confident, therefore, that the two most common assertions about the first Negroes—that they were slaves and that they were servants—are *unfounded,* though not necessarily incorrect. And what of the positive evidence?

Some of the first group bore Spanish names and presumably had been baptized, which would mean they were at least nominally Christian, though of the Papist sort. They had been ''sold'' to the English; so had other Englishmen but not by the Dutch. Probably these Negroes were not fully free, but many Englishmen were not. It can be said, though, that from the first in Virginia Negroes were set apart from white men by the word *Negroes*. The earliest Virginia census reports plainly distinguished Negroes from white men; often Negroes were listed as such with no personal names—a critical distinction. It seems logical to suppose that this perception of the Negro as being distinct from the Englishman must have operated to debase his status rather than to raise it, for in the absence of countervailing social factors the need for labor in the colonies usually told in the direction of non-freedom. There were few countervailing factors present, surely, in such instances as in 1629 when a group of Negroes were brought to Virginia freshly captured from a Portuguese ship which had snatched them from Angola a few weeks earlier. Given the context of English thought and experience sketched in this chapter, it seems probable that the Negro's status was not ever the same as that accorded the white servant. But we do not know for sure.

When the first fragmentary evidence appears about 1640 it becomes clear that *some* Negroes in both Virginia and Maryland were serving for life and some Negro children inheriting the same obligation. Not all blacks, certainly, for after the mid-1640's the court records show that some Negroes were incontestably free and were accumulating property of their own. At least one black freeman, Anthony Johnson, himself owned a slave. Some blacks served only terms of usual length, but others were held for terms far longer than custom and statute permitted with white servants. The first fairly clear indication that slavery was practiced in the tobacco colonies appears in 1639, when a Maryland statute declared that ''all the Inhabitants of this Province being Christians (Slaves excepted) Shall have and enjoy all such rights liberties immunities privileges and free customs within this Province as any naturall born subject of England.'' Another Maryland law passed the same year provided that ''all persons being Christians (Slaves excepted)'' over eighteen who were imported without indentures would serve for four years. These laws make very little sense unless the term *slaves* meant Negroes and perhaps Indians.

The next year, 1640, the first definite indication of outright enslavement appears in Virginia. The General Court pronounced sentence on three servants who had been retaken after absconding to Maryland. Two of them, both white, were ordered to serve their masters for one additional year and then the colony for three more, but ''the third being a negro named John Punch shall serve his said master or his assigns for the time of his natural life here or else where.'' No white servant in any English colony, so far as is known, ever received a like sentence.

After 1640, when surviving Virginia county court records began to mention Negroes, sales for life, often including any future progeny, were recorded in unmistakable language. In 1646 Francis Pott sold a Negro woman and boy to Stephen Charlton "to the use of him . . . forever." Similarly, six years later William Whittington sold to John Pott "one Negro girle named Jowan; aged about Ten yeares and with her Issue and produce duringe her (or either of them) for their Life tyme. And their Successors forever"; and a Maryland man in 1649 deeded two Negro men and a woman "and all their issue both male and Female." The executors of a York County estate in 1647 disposed of eight Negroes—four men, two women, and two children—to Captain John Chisman "to have hold occupy posesse and injoy and every one of the afforementioned Negroes forever."

Further evidence that some Negroes were serving for life in this period lies in the prices paid for them. In many instances the valuations placed on Negroes (in estate inventories and bills of sale) were far higher than for white servants, even those servants with full terms yet to serve. Higher prices must have meant that Negroes were more highly valued because of their greater length of service. The labor owned by James Stone in 1648, for example, was evaluated as follows:

	lb tobo
Thomas Groves, 4 yeares to serve	1300
Francis Bomley for 6 yeares	1500
John Thackstone for 3 yeares	1300
Susan Davis for 3 yeares	1000
Emaniell a Negro man	2000
Roger Stone 3 yeares	1300
Mingo a Negro man	2000

Besides setting a higher value on Negroes, these inventories failed to indicate a last name and the number of years they had still to serve, presumably because their service was for an unlimited time.

Where Negro women were involved, higher valuations probably reflected the facts that their issue were valuable and that they could be used for field work while white women generally were not. This latter discrimination between black and white women did not necessarily involve perpetual service, but it meant that blacks were set apart in a way clearly not to their advantage. This was not the only instance in which Negroes were subjected to degrading distinctions not immediately and necessarily attached to the concept of slavery. Blacks were singled out for special treatment in several ways which suggest a generalized debasement of blacks as a group. Significantly, the first indications of this debasement appeared at about the same time as the first indications of actual enslavement.

The distinction concerning field work is a case in point. A law of 1643 provided that *all* adult men were taxable and, in addition, *Negro* women. The same distinction was made twice again before 1660. Maryland adopted a similar policy beginning in 1654. This official discrimination between black women and other women was made by white men who were accustomed to thinking of field work as being ordinarily the work of men exclusively. The essentially racial character of this discrimination stood out clearly in a law passed in 1668 at the time slavery was taking shape in the statute books:

Whereas some doubts, have arisen whether negro women set free were still to be accompted tithable according to a former act, *It is declared by this grand assembly* that negro women, though permitted to enjoy their Freedome yet ought not in all respects to be admitted to a full fruition of the exemptions and impunities of the English, and are still lyable to payment of taxes.

Virginia law set blacks apart from all other groups in a second way by denying them the important right and obligation to bear arms. Few restraints could indicate more clearly the denial to Africans of membership in the English community. This first foreshadowing of the slave codes came in 1640, at just the time when other indications first appeared that blacks were subject to special treatment.

Finally, an even more compelling sense of

the separateness of Negroes was revealed in early reactions to sexual union between the races. Prior to 1660 the evidence concerning these reactions is equivocal, and it is not possible to tell whether repugnance for intermixture preceded legislative enactment of slavery. In the early 1660's, however, when slavery was gaining statutory recognition, the assemblies acted with full-throated indignation against miscegenation. These acts aimed at more than merely avoiding confusion of status. In 1662 Virginia declared that "if any christian shall committ Fornication with a negro man or woman, hee or shee soe offending" should pay double the usual fine. Two years later Maryland regulated interracial marriages: "forasmuch as divers freeborne English women forgettfull of their free Condicion and to the disgrace of our Nation doe intermarry with Negro Slaves by which alsoe divers suites may arise touching the issue of such woemen and a great damage doth befall the Masters of such Negros for prevention whereof for deterring such freeborne women from such shameful Matches," strong language indeed if "divers suites" had been the only problem. A Maryland act of 1681 described marriages of white women with Negroes as, among other things, "always to the Satisfaccion of theire Lascivious and Lustfull desires, and to the disgrace not only of the English butt allso of many other Christian Nations." When Virginia finally prohibited all interracial liaisons in 1691, the Assembly vigorously denounced miscegenation and its fruits as "that abominable mixture and spurious issue."

From the surviving evidence it appears that outright enslavement and these other forms of debasement appeared at about the same time in Maryland and Virginia. Indications of perpetual service, the very nub of slavery, coincided with indications that English settlers discriminated against Negro women, withheld arms from Negroes, and—though the timing is far less certain— reacted unfavorably to interracial sexual union. The coincidence suggests a mutual re-lationship between slavery and unfavorable assessment of blacks. Rather than slavery causing "prejudice," or vice versa, they seem rather to have generated each other. Both were, after all, twin aspects of a general debasement of the Negro. Slavery and "prejudice" may have been equally cause and effect, continuously reacting upon each other, dynamically joining hands to hustle the Negro down the road to complete degradation. Much more than with the other English colonies, where the enslavement of Africans was to some extent a borrowed practice, the available evidence for Maryland and Virginia points to less borrowing and to this kind of process: a mutually interactive growth of slavery and unfavorable assessment, with no cause for either which did not cause the other as well. If slavery caused prejudice, then invidious distinctions concerning working in the fields, bearing arms, and sexual union should have appeared *after* slavery's firm establishment. If prejudice caused slavery, then one would expect to find these lesser discriminations preceding the greater discrimination of outright enslavement. Taken as a whole, the evidence reveals a process of debasement of which hereditary lifetime service, while important, was not the only part.

Certainly it was the case in Maryland and Virginia that the legal enactment of Negro slavery followed social practice, rather than vice versa. In 1661 the Virginia Assembly indirectly provided statutory recognition that some Negroes served for life: "That in case any English servant shall run away in company with any negroes who are incapable of makeing satisfaction by addition of time," he must serve for the Negroes' lost time as well as his own. Maryland enacted a similar law in 1663, and in the following year came out with the categorical declaration that Negroes were to serve "Durante Vita"—for life. During the next twenty-odd years a succession of acts in both colonies defined with increasing precision what sorts of persons might be treated as slaves.

By about 1700 the slave ships began spilling forth their black cargoes in greater and greater numbers. By that time racial slavery and the necessary police powers had been written into law. By that time, too, slavery had lost all resemblance to a perpetual and hereditary version of English servitude, though service for life still seemed to contemporaries its most essential feature. In the last quarter of the seventeenth century the trend was to treat Negroes more like property and less like people, to send them to the fields at younger ages, to deny them automatic existence as inherent members of the community, to tighten the bonds on their personal and civil freedom, and correspondingly to loosen the traditional restraints on the master's freedom to deal with his human property as he saw fit. In 1705 Virginia gathered up the random statutes of a whole generation and baled them into a "slave code" which would not have been out of place in the nineteenth century.

THE UN-ENGLISH: SCOTS, IRISH, AND INDIANS

In the minds of overseas Englishmen, slavery, the new tyranny, did not apply to any Europeans. Something about Africans, and to lesser extent Indians, set them apart for drastic exploitation, oppression, and degradation. In order to discover why, it is useful to turn the problem inside out, to inquire why Englishmen in America did not treat any other peoples as they did Negroes. It is especially revealing to see how English settlers looked upon the Scotch (as they frequently called them) and the Irish, whom they often had opportunity and "reason" to enslave, and upon the Indians, whom they enslaved, though only, as it were, casually.

In the early years Englishmen treated the increasingly numerous settlers from other European countries, especially Scottish and Irish servants, with condescension and frequently with exploitive brutality. Englishmen seemed to regard their colonies as exclusively *English* preserves and to wish to protect English persons especially from the exploitation which inevitably accompanied settlement in the New World. In Barbados, for example, the assembly in 1661 denounced the kidnapping of youngsters for service in the colony in a law which applied only to "Children of the *English* Nation."

While Englishmen distinguished themselves from other peoples, they also distinguished *among* those different peoples who failed to be English. It seems almost as if Englishmen possessed a view of other peoples which placed the English nation at the center of widening concentric circles, each of which contained a people more alien than the one inside it. On occasion these social distances felt by Englishmen may be gauged with considerable precision, as in the sequence employed by the Committee for Trade and Foreign Plantations in a query to the governor of Connecticut in 1680: "What number of English, Scotch, Irish or Foreigners have... come yearly to... your Corporation. And also, what Blacks and Slaves have been brought in." Sometimes the English sense of distance seems to have been based upon a scale of values which would be thought of today in terms of nationality. At other times, though, the sense of foreignness seems to have been explicitly religious, as instanced by a letter from Barbados in 1667: "We have more than a good many Irish amongst us, therefore I am for the down right Scott, who I am certain will fight without a crucifix about his neck." It is scarcely surprising that hostility toward the numerous Irish servants should have been especially strong, for they were doubly damned as foreign and papist. Already, for Englishmen in the seventeenth century the Irish were a special case, and it required more than an ocean voyage to alter this perception.

As time went on Englishmen began to absorb the idea that their settlements in America were not going to remain exclusively English preserves. In 1671 Virginia began encouraging naturalization of legal aliens, so that they might enjoy "all such liberties, priviledges, immunities whatsoever, as a naturall borne Englishman is capable of,'' and Maryland accomplished the same end with private naturalization acts.

The necessity of peopling the colonies transformed the long-standing urge to diserated into military campaigns of exterminanecessity. Which of the non-English were sufficiently different and foreign to warrant treating as ''perpetual servants''? The need to answer this question did not mean, of course, that upon arrival in America the colonists immediately jettisoned their sense of distance from those persons they did not actually enslave. They discriminated against Welshmen and Scotsmen who, while admittedly ''the best servants,'' were typically the servants of Englishmen. There was a considerably stronger tendency to discriminate against papist Irishmen, those ''worst'' servants, but never to make slaves of them. And here lay the crucial difference. Even the Scottish prisoners taken by Cromwell during the English Civil Wars—captives in a just war!—were never treated as slaves in England or the colonies.

Indians too seemed radically different from Englishmen, far more so than any Europeans. They were enslaved, like Africans, and so fell on the losing side of a crucial dividing line. It is easy to see why: whether considered in terms of religion, nationality, savagery, or geographical location, Indians seemed more like Negroes than like Englishmen. Given this resemblance the essential problem becomes why Indian slavery never became an important institution in the colonies. Why did Indian slavery remain numerically insignificant and typically incidental in character? Why were Indian slaves valued at much lower prices than Negroes? Why were Indians, as a kind of people, treated like Negroes and yet at the same time very differently?

Certain obvious factors made for important differentiations in the minds of the English colonists. As was the case with first confrontations in America and Africa, the different contexts of confrontation made Englishmen more interested in converting and civilizing Indians than Negroes. That this campaign in America too frequently degenerated into military campaigns of extermination did nothing to eradicate the initial distinction. Entirely apart from English intentions, the culture of the eastern American Indians probably meant that they were less readily enslavable than Africans. By comparison, they were less used to settled agriculture, and their own variety of slavery was probably even less similar to the chattel slavery which Englishmen practiced in America than was the domestic and political slavery of the various West African cultures. But it was the transformation of English intentions in the wilderness which counted most heavily in the long run. The Bible and the treaty so often gave way to the clash of flintlock and tomahawk. The colonists' perceptions of the Indians came to be organized not only in pulpits and printshops but at the bloody cutting edge of the English thrust into the Indians' lands. Thus the most pressing and mundane circumstances worked to make Indians seem very different from Negroes. In the early years especially, Indians were in a position to mount murderous reprisals upon the English settlers, while the few scattered Africans were not. When English-Indian relations did not turn upon sheer power they rested on diplomacy. In many instances the colonists took careful precautions to prevent abuse of Indians belonging to friendly tribes. Most of the Indians enslaved by the English had their own tribal enemies to thank. It became common practice to ship Indian slaves to the West Indies where they could be exchanged for slaves who had no compatriots lurking on the outskirts of English settlements. In contrast, Negroes presented much less of a threat—at first.

Equally important, Negroes had to be dealt with as individuals—with supremely impartial anonymity, to be sure—rather than as nations. Englishmen wanted and had to live with ''their'' Negroes, as it were, side by side. Accordingly their impressions of blacks were forged in the heat of continual, inescapable personal contacts. There were few pressures urging Englishmen to treat Indians as integral constituents in their society, which Negroes were whether Englishmen liked or not. At a distance the Indian could be viewed with greater detachment and his characteristics acknowledged and approached more cooly and more rationally. At a distance too, Indians could retain the quality of nationality, a quality which Englishmen admired in themselves and expected in other peoples. Under contrasting circumstances in America, the Negro nations tended to become Negro people.

Here lay the rudiments of certain shadowy but persistent themes in what turned out to be a multi-racial nation. Americans came to impute to the braves of the Indian "nations" an ungovernable individuality and at the same time to impart to Africans all the qualities of an eminently governable sub-nation, in which African tribal distinctions were assumed to be of no consequence. More immediately, Indians and Africans rapidly came to serve as two fixed points from which English settlers could triangulate their own position in America; the separate meanings of *Indian* and *Negro* helped define the meaning of living in America. The Indian became for Americans a symbol of their American experience; it was no mere luck of the toss that placed the profile of an American Indian rather than an American Negro on the famous old five-cent piece. Confronting the Indian in America was a testing experience, common to all the colonies. Conquering the Indian symbolized and personified the conquest of the American difficulties, the surmounting of the wilderness. To push back the Indian was to prove the worth of one's own mission, to make straight in the desert a highway for civilization. With the Negro it was utterly different.

RACIAL SLAVERY: FROM REASONS TO RATIONALE

And *difference,* surely, was the indispensable key to the degradation of Africans in English America. In scanning the problem of *why* Negroes were enslaved in America, certain constant elements in a complex situation can be readily, if roughly, identified. *It may be taken as given* that there would have been no enslavement without economic need, that is, without persistent demand for labor in underpopulated colonies. Of crucial importance, too, was the fact that Africans in America were relatively powerless. In themselves, however, these two elements will not explain the enslavement of Indians and Negroes. The pressing need in America was labor, and Irish, Scottish, and English servants were available. Most of them would have been helpless to ward off outright enslavement if their masters had thought themselves privileged to enslave them. As a group, though, masters did not think themselves so empowered. Only with Indians and Africans did Englishmen attempt so radical a deprivation of liberty—which brings the matter abruptly to the most difficult and imponderable question of all: what was it about Indians and Negroes which set them apart from Englishmen, which rendered them *different,* which made them special candidates for degradation?

To ask such questions is to inquire into the *content* of English attitudes, and unfortunately there is little evidence with which to build an answer. It may be said, however, that the heathen condition of Negroes seemed of considerable importance to English settlers in America more so than to English voyagers upon the coasts of Africa—and that heathenism was associated in some settlers' minds with the condition of slavery. Clearly, though, this is not to say that English colonists enslaved Africans merely because of religious difference. In the early years, the English settlers most frequently contrasted themselves with Negroes by the term *Christian,* though they also sometimes described themselves as *English.* Yet the concept embodied by the term *Christian* embraced so much more meaning than was contained in specific doctrinal affirmations that it is scarcely possible to assume on this basis that Englishmen set Negroes apart because they were heathen. The historical experience of the English people in the sixteenth century had made for fusion of religion and nationality; the qualities of being English and Christian had become so inseparably blended that it seemed perfectly consistent to the Virginia Assembly in 1670 to declare that "noe negroe or Indian though baptised and enjoyned their owne Freedome shall be capable of any such purchase of christians, but yet not debarred from buying any of their owne nation."

From the first, then, the concept embedded in the term *Christian* seems to have conveyed much of the idea and feeling of *we* as against *they:* to be Christian was to be civilized rather than barbarous, English rather than African, white rather than black. The term *Christian* itself proved to have remarkable elasticity, for by the end of the seventeenth century it was being used to define a kind of slavery which had altogether lost any connection with explicit religious difference. In the Virginia code of 1705, for example, the term sounded much more like a definition of race than of religion: "And for a further christian care and usage of all christian servants, *Be it also enacted* . . . That no negroes, mulattos, or Indians, although christians, or Jews, Moors, Mahometans, or other infidels, shall, at any time, purchase any christian servant, nor any other, except of their own complexion, or such as are declared slaves by this act." By this time "Christianity" had somehow become intimately and explicitly linked with "complexion." The 1705 statute declared "That all servants imported and brought into this country, by sea or land, who were not christians in their native country . . . shall be accounted and be slaves, and as such be here bought and sold notwithstanding a conversion to christinaity afterwards." As late as 1753 the Virginia slave code anachronistically defined slavery in terms of religion when everyone knew that slavery had for generations been based on the racial and not the religious difference.

It is worth making still closer scrutiny of the terminology which Englishmen employed when referring both to themselves and to the two peoples they enslaved, for this terminology affords the best single means of probing the content of their sense of difference. The terms *Indian* and *Negro* were both borrowed from the Hispanic languages, the one originally deriving from (mistaken) geographical locality and the other from human complexion. When referring to the Indians the English colonists either used that proper name or called them *savages,* a term which reflected primarily their view of Indians as uncivilized. In significant contrast, the colonists referred to *negroes,* and by the eighteenth century to *blacks* and to *Africans,* but almost never to African *heathens* or *pagans* or *savages*. Most suggestive of all, there seems to have been something of a shift during the seventeenth century in the terminology which Englishmen in the colonies applied to themselves. From the initially most common term *Christian,* at mid-century there was a marked shift toward the terms *English* and *free*. After about 1680, taking the colonies as a whole, a new term of self-identification appeared—*white*.

So far as the weight of analysis may be imposed upon such terms, diminishing reliance upon *Christian* suggests a gradual muting of the specifically religious elements in the Christian-Negro distinction in favor of secular nationality: Negroes were, in 1667, "not in all respects to be admitted to a full fruition of the exemptions and impunities of the English." As time went on, as some Negroes became assimilated to the English colonial culture, as more "raw Africans" arrived, and as increasing numbers of non-English Europeans were attracted to the colonies, English colonists turned increasingly to what they saw as the striking physiognomic difference. In Maryland a revised law prohibiting miscegenation (1692) retained *white* and *English* but dropped the term *Christian*—a symptomatic modification. By the end of the seventeenth century dark complexion had become an independent rationale for enslavement: in 1709 Samuel Sewall noted in his diary that a "Spaniard" had petitioned the Massachusetts Council for freedom but that "Capt. Teat alledg'd that all of that Color were Slaves." Here was a barrier between "we" and "they" which was visible and permanent: the black man could not become a white man. Not, at least, as yet.

What had occurred was not a change in the justification of slavery from religion to race. No such justifications were made. There seems to have been, within the unarticulated concept of the Negro as a different sort of person, a subtle but highly significant shift in emphasis. A perception of Negro heathenism remained through the eighteenth and into the nineteenth and even the twentieth century, and an awareness, at very least, of the African's different appearance was present from the beginning. The shift was an alteration in emphasis within a single concept of difference rather than a development of a novel conceptualization. Throughout the colonies the terms *Christian, free, English,* and *white* were for many years employed indiscriminately as synonyms. A Maryland law of 1681 used all four terms in one short paragraph.

Whatever the limitations of terminology as an index to thought and feeling, it seems likely that the English colonists' initial sense of difference from Africans was founded not on a single characteristic but on a cluster of qualities which, taken as a whole, seemed to set the Negro apart. Virtually every quality in "the Negro" invited pejorative feelings. What may have been his two most striking characteristics, his heathenism and his appearance, were probably prerequisite to his complete debasement. His heathenism alone could not have led to permanent enslavement since conversion easily wiped out that failing. If his appearance, his racial characteristics, meant nothing to the English settler, it is difficult to see how slavery based on race ever emerged, how the concept of complexion as the mark of slavery ever entered the colonists' minds. Even if the English col-

onists were most unfavorably struck by the Negro's color, though, blackness itself did not urge the complete debasement of slavery. Other cultural qualities—the strangeness of his language, gestures, eating habits, and so on—certainly must have contributed to the English colonists' sense that he was very different, perhaps disturbingly so. In Africa these qualities had for Englishmen added up to *savagery;* they were major components in that sense of *difference* which provided the mental margin absolutely requisite for placing the European on the deck of the slave ship and the African in the hold.

The available evidence (what little there is) suggests that for Englishmen settling in America, the specific religious difference was initially of greater importance than color, certainly of much greater relative importance than for the Englishmen who confronted Negroes in their African homeland. Perhaps Englishmen in Virginia, tanning seasonally under a hot sun and in almost daily contact with tawny Indians, found the Negro's color less arresting than they might have in other circumstances. Perhaps, too, these first Virginians sensed how inadequately they had reconstructed the institutions and practices of Christian piety in the wilderness; they would perhaps appear less as failures to themselves in this respect if compared to persons who as Christians were *totally* defective. Perhaps, though, the Jamestown settlers were told in 1619 by the Dutch shipmaster that these "negars" were heathens and could be treated as such. We do not know. The available data will not bear all the weight that the really crucial questions impose.

Of course once the cycle of degradation was fully under way, once slavery and racial discrimination were completely linked together, once the engine of oppression was in full operation, then *there is no need to plead* lack of knowledge. By the end of the seventeenth century in all the colonies of the English empire there was chattel racial slavery of a kind which would have seemed familiar to men living in the nineteenth century. No

Elizabethan Englishman would have found it familiar, though certain strands of thought and feeling in Elizabethan England had intertwined with reports about the Spanish and Portuguese to engender a willingness on the part of English settlers in the New World to treat some men as suitable for private exploitation. During the seventeenth century New World conditions had enlarged this predisposition, so much so that English colonials of the eighteenth century were faced with full-blown slavery—something they thought of not as an institution but as a host of ever present problems, dangers, and opportunities.

The German Problem of Colonial Pennsylvania

DIETMAR ROTHERMUND

The Germans were the most important non-English-speaking immigrants in the colonial era. Originally attracted to Pennsylvania, where William Penn had promised them religious freedom, large numbers of Germans also settled in the South and in New York. They formed tightly knit enclaves wherever they went, preferring to live apart from the rest of the community. Pennsylvania remained their major center of settlement; in 1766 Germans accounted for one-third of the colony's population.

Once in Pennsylvania the Germans transformed the land west of Philadelphia (Pennsylvania Dutch country) into an area of prosperous, well-kept farms. The English, however, feared their presence. Germans opposed outside interference in their culture, refused to learn English, and resisted the assimilation of their children into the dominant Anglo-colonial culture. Benjamin Franklin, who became the spokesman for the English-speaking majority in Pennsylvania, castigated the Germans for clinging to their supposedly inferior, non-English, customs that many feared might dominate Pennsylvania and "Germanize us instead of our Anglifying them."

The following article, by German scholar Dietmar Rothermund, depicts the enormously complex relations within a nationality group and its interaction with the predominant Anglo-American element. Rothermund's study of German participation in Pennsylvania cultural and political affairs between the 1740s and 1760s disclosed the variety of religious faiths in this minority enclave, the ramifications that such sectarian diversity had for political alignments, educational and religious issues, and policies in the colony, and the ambivalent feelings between the native American elite and the German communities.

The situation of the Germans in colonial Pennsylvania presents an interesting political and cultural phenomenon which can be viewed in a fresh aspect from a number of hitherto unpublished manuscripts. These documents, selected for their revealing comments on contemporary attitudes, may serve as a useful supplement to the work of historians who have traced the growth of democracy in Pennsylvania, the relations of

From Dietmar Rothermund, "The German Problem of Colonial Pennsylvania," *Pennsylvania Magazine of History and Biography* (January 1960). Reprinted by permission of the author and publisher.

the Pennsylvania Germans with the government, and the impact of the French and Indian wars on the colony. Since most of the political alignments of these years followed the lines of religious affiliations, it is well to point out some of the interrelations between denominations and parties, and also to stress patterns of leadership and the interactions of groups.

In the short period between the Great Awakening and the days of the Stamp Act, colonial Pennsylvania experienced all the familiar American problems and reactions caused by mass immigration. This particular period, however, deserves special study because it saw the first major encounter between different European ethnic groups in the New World and because the percentage of immigrants was higher than at any later time. Most of these immigrants of the mid-eighteenth century came from Germany. Obstinate adherence to their language and culture set them apart from the main stream of Anglo-Saxon colonial society. Political rights granted to them seemed to endanger the predominant position of earlier English-speaking settlers. However, the encounter was not one of solid fronts. The social, religious, and political dynamics of an era of rapid transition caught older settlers and immigrants alike in a network of contending factions. Yielding to these pressures, the German immigrants soon began to vote on both sides of political issues. When this occurred, and they no longer constituted an alarmingly solid support for one party only, the Germans ceased to be a worrisome political problem in Pennsylvania.

By 1740 the involvements of the British Empire began to catch up with Pennsylvania's "Holy Experiment." The distant refuge of quietist sects had become a wealthy and expanding colony. Britain had to defend its empire against the envy and competition of European neighbors. Migration across the ocean was no longer restricted to persecuted religious minorities preferring a life in the wilderness to a loss of integrity; more and more settlers were attracted by the legend of a fabulous New World. Diversification of population, as well as imperial problems, disturbed the earlier placid group control and made political affairs a matter of mounting concern to the public. Groups that wanted to maintain political control had to find support among other bodies in the populace at large. All immigrants, therefore, became of immediate interest to the politician. Liberal legislation which provided for easy naturalization made it possible for the immigrant to become a citizen before he ever learned the language of his new country. In Pennsylvania, a powerful Assembly, whose privileges had been granted by the reluctant William Penn at the time of his visit in 1701, gave weight to the vote of many citizens. Since the Assembly had the power of the purse, met on its own adjournment, but was subject to annual elections, the scene was set for vigorous political campaigns. The "ticket" was introduced as a new device to marshal the vote of a diversified electorate.

The party system of colonial Pennsylvania came into its own in the 1740's. For a long time the differences between the Proprietary and Antiproprietary factions were insufficient to give rise to a real two-party system. The Antiproprietary Quakers who controlled the Assembly had found little competition from the small group of "governor's friends" who were partisan chiefly because they held Proprietary offices. However, when the threat of war in 1740 raised the question of the defense of the province, the Proprietary party found a cause which was popular among nonpacifist Pennsylvanians. There seemed to be a possibility at last of cornering the all-powerful Quakers by turning their own religious tenets against them.

After a number of years of quiescence in political affairs, the Great Awakening and the War of Jenkins' Ear created a rising tide of political campaigns and partisan strife. The Quakers called upon the German sectarians to defend pacifism at the polls. The Presbyterians, who formed the hard core of the Proprietary party, in trying to frighten away the Germans only increased the perseverance of their adversaries. Conrad Weiser, a prominent German in Proprietary employ, tried to bring the message of the Proprietary party to his countrymen, but to no avail. The Germantown publisher Christopher Sauer, a radical pietist, exercised a much greater influence among the Germans. Known for his integrity, independence, and frankness, but also for his bias against clergymen and government officers, he imbued his countrymen with a spirit of insistence on their rights as citizens and of resistance to government plans that might lead to an encroachment upon the privileges that they enjoyed in Pennsylvania. As long as Pennsylvania was not actually invaded by an enemy, the argument of Sauer and the Quakers remained without a flaw and the Proprietary party was hard pressed to adduce proof to the contrary. Even the German church people, the Reformed and Lutheran groups, although not bound by a belief in pacifism, were not sufficiently motivated to rally around the flag of the party which advocated measures for the defense of the province.

The unity and strength of the Quaker-German coalition was a source of deep frustration to the men of the Proprietary party. Since the language barrier prevented the English politicians from gaining more detailed knowledge of the structure of the German groups, the Germans appeared to them as one vast inarticulate mass of people, mysteriously manipulated by Quaker leaders. The rapid increase of German immigration in the 1740's and early 1750's seemed to turn this nuisance into a menace.

Paradoxically enough, this outward impression of unity was caused by upehavals within the German community itself. The Moravian revival among the German church people, which was at its peak from 1741 to 1747, was a matter of intense controversy and retarded the activities of the church leadership. For this reason, the German clergy and German vestrymen did not become a major factor in Pennsylvania politics until the 1760's. Experienced leaders like Henry Melchior Muhlenberg avoided jeopardizing

their efforts to organize their churches by making unpopular political commitments, while an inexperienced man like Michael Schlatter rushed toward his political defeat.

It was the self-imposed restraint of the church leaders and the clear-cut position of the sectarians that made the German community look like a stubborn phalanx seemingly at the beck and call of the Quakers. However, for the Quakers themselves the management of their German allies became increasingly difficult as the German community became more heterogeneous.

The spectacular career of John Kinsey, chief justice of Pennsylvania and speaker of the Assembly, was partly built on the fact that he posed as a patron of the Germans. Kinsey was the product of a particular period of transition. At a time when political control had switched from the Quaker meeting to a larger public he happened to be equally at home in the meeting and in the management of public affairs, and, being a good lawyer, he seized the control of the judiciary and legislative branches of the government. Furthermore, in a time of rapid economic expansion he ran the Loan Office of the province as if it were his own private bank. The province was at his mercy, and he evidently chose to be particularly merciful toward the Germans. By monopolizing power and popularity, Kinsey preserved Quaker control for another decade.

When the mighty man died in 1750 there was a considerable breakdown of control. Richard Peters, the secretary of the Proprietors, complained that there was nobody to whom he could talk in order to get things done. And the Quakers quarreled in the Assembly over what to do about a deficit in the Loan Office which Kinsey had left to them as an unfortunate heritage. The vacuum left by the death of Kinsey fostered the ambitions of other men. Since no single person was in a position to inherit all of Kinsey's functions, he was bound to have a number of political heirs. William Allen became chief justice, Isaac Norris speaker of the Assembly, and Benjamin Franklin, who had himself elected to the Assembly in 1751, shared with Israel Pemberton the role of political manipulator.

This transfer of power took place at a time of peace when no immediate crisis tested the new alignments. The greatest problem was German immigration and the rapid expansion of German settlements, which produced a strange concord. In order to maintain the status quo, the Proprietary and Quaker parties combined in a measure which was designed to gerrymander the Germans out of their voting rights. The old counties were so divided that new counties could be established which would comprise a major part of the German population, and which would have only one or two representatives in the Assembly. The Proprietary councilor Dr. Thomas Graeme described this measure very astutely in a letter to Thomas Penn: "The present clamour of a great many people here of all Ranks, Friends as much as others, is that the Dutch, by their numbers and Industry, will soon become Masters of the province, and also a Majority in the Legislature. . . . the late Instance of a tumultuous Election in the New County of York is aduced as an Instance of their disposition and manners. . . ." Graeme then reported a conversation with Governor Hamilton about the danger of the "Dutch" getting a majority in the legislature:

I replyed that there was an easie way to prevent it, and seemingly to please the Dutch too. . . . I told him he might observe that the Legislature in Erecting the two late Countys, allow'd them only Two Members each, and that upon the division of the Countys of Philada & Bucks, which was also much wanting, if they brought the division line 16 or 18 Miles to the Southward of Reading, and that of Bucks as far to the Southward of the Forks, and to each County Two Members, they would by this division comprehend to a triffle the whole Body of the Dutch and consequently forever exclude them from becoming a Majority in the assembly, for allow Lancaster, York and the Two not yet appointed Countys to send all Dutch it would make but Ten Members in 38, and to this if the assembly would be induc'd to add Two more to the City of Philada it would still strengthen this Scheme.

Mr. Hamilton said he had consider'd it long as a Subject of great importance, and had fallen on the very same thought, as the best expedient for preventing the Evil in Prospect; yes I told him it ought to be done in time and with privacy in regard to the Intention, for the Dutch might soon discover which way this would operate, he in this readily agreed.

The Quaker-dominated Assembly endorsed this measure despite the fact that it was introduced by the governor and his friends who hoped by it to deprive the Quakers of their German allies. However, Kinsey being dead, the Quakers themselves could no longer depend on a reliable management of their German allies and were, at least for some time, better off by playing it safe and restricting the bulk of the representation to the old rural settlements in the east where most of the Quakers lived.

Naturally, the German allies of the Quakers felt that they had been betrayed. In trying to defend their political rights they greatly increased their political awareness. The draft of a resolution written by the Schwenkfelder leader Christopher Schultze in 1752 vividly expresses this awareness:

The good and well-meaning inhabitants of Berks County who have been greatly pleased by the conduct and good manners of previous sessions of the Assembly in troublesome times are now highly displeased since they find themselves deprived of 7/8th of their former right to elect capable men as their representatives in the Assembly. They apprehend that in future dangerous times they may be easily overruled in this way as far as good elections, the welfare of the province, and the guarantee of the present laudable constitution are concerned, and that they, on the contrary, may be forced to accept such matters which are against their conscience and against their present valuable privileges. For this reason . . . they think that any propertied and capable Freeholder of this province should have equal participation and equal rights in the election of the members of the legislature of this province. This they deem to be not only natural but also extremely necessary for the preservation of our dearly beloved liberties. And since all good Patriots in Philadelphia and other Counties have to admit . . . that the said inhabitants have contributed to the best of their knowledge with great steadfastness, eagerness, and unanimity to the encouragement of good elections... which we have maintained by God's grace at times when it was rather difficult, [these Patriots] must necessarily be rather distressed (and this they really are) at the fact that their good neighbors and faithful supporters are weakened to such an extent and in such an important point. It remains to be hoped that a future Assembly will foresee such consequences and take care that such a breach may be healed and that our future constitution may be guaranteed, to the pleasure of all Patriots and of all those who have migrated to this country refuge to escape the suppression of their conscience. Many will testify to the truth of what is said here in case it should be demanded. God preserve us.

These protests were of no avail. The restriction of representation in the western counties had come to stay until the Revolution changed the whole pattern radically.

Even though the restriction of representation seemed to have solved the German problem politically, it was clearly no solution to the social and cultural aspects of increasing German immigration. Benjamin Franklin, who had given some thought to the "Peopling of Countries," was particularly aware of this fact. Franklin had had frustrating experiences with the Germans as a printer and as a politician. His early attempt to launch a German newspaper had been a failure. Although he never gave up his efforts to capture a part of the expanding German book market, his German competitors were far more successful. As a politician he had been disappointed by the lack of response among the Germans to his carefully planned Association for Defense. However, Franklin was not only a printer and local politician, he was also a statesman, striving for an enlightened and unified British Empire. A large and unassimilated group of aliens in one of the key provinces of this empire seemed to him to be a threat to the realization of this aim. In a reply to seven proposals of Peter Collinson he described his point of view most concisely:

With regard to the Germans, I think Methods of great tenderness should be used, and nothing that looks like a hardship be imposed. Their fondness for their own Language & Manners is natural; It is not a Crime. When people are induced to settle a new Country by a promise of Privileges, that Promise shou'd be bona fide performed, and the privileges never infringed: If they are, how shall we be believed another time, when we want to people another Colony? Your *first* proposal of establishing English Schools among them is an excellent one, provided them are free Schools, & can be supported. As your Poet Young says

. . . . .The Dutch Wou'd fain save all the Money that they touch.

If they can have English Schooling gratis, as much as they love their own language they will not pay for German Schooling.

The second proposal, of an Act of Parliament, disqualifying them to accept of any post of Trust, profit, or Honour, unless they can speak English intelligibly, will be justifyed by the reason of the thing, and will not seem an hardship; But it does not seem necessary to include the Children. If the Father takes pains to learn English, the same Sense of its usefulness will induce him to teach it to his Children.

The third proposal, to invalidate all Deeds, Bonds, or other legal Writings written in a foreign Language (Wills made on a Man's Death Bed excepted, as an English Scribe may not be always at hand) is not at all amiss. I think it absolutely necessary, and that it cannot be complain'd of.

The fourth proposal, to suppress all German printing houses, &c. will seem too harsh. As will be the fifth, to prohibit all Importation of German Books. If the other Methods are taken, the printing Houses will in time wear out, as they become unnecessary, & the Importation of Books will cease of itself.

The sixth proposal of Encouraging Intermarriages between the English & Germans, by Donations, &c. I think would either cost too much, or have no Effect. The German Women are generally so disagreeable to an English Eye, that it wou'd require great portions to induce Englishmen to marry them. Nor would the German Ideas of Beauty generally agree with our Women: *dick und starcke,* that is, *thick & strong,* always enter into their Description of a pretty Girl; for the value of a Wife with them consists much in the

Work she is able to do. So that it would require a round Sum with an English Wife to make up to a Dutch Man the difference in Labour & Frugality. This Matter therefore I think had better be left to itself.

The seventh proposal of discouraging the sending more Germans to Pennsylvania is a good one; those who are already here would approve of it. They complain of the late great Importations, & wish they could be prevented. They say the Germans that came formerly were a good sober industrious honest people; but now Germany is swept, scour'd & scumm'd by the Merchants, who, for the gain by the Freight, bring all the Refuse Wretches poor and helpless who are burthensome to the old Settlers, or Knaves & Rascals that live by Sharking & Cheating them. The Stream may therefore be well enough turned to the other Colonies you mention. And our Land Owners will have no Cause to complain, if English, Welsh, & Protestant Irish are encouraged to come hither instead of Germans, which will still continue the rising Value of Lands; and at the same time by mixing with our Germans restore by degrees the predominancy of our Language &c. Nor would the British Subjects be miss'd at home, if my Opinions in the paper I formerly sent on the peopling of Countries, are right, as I still think they really are.

The quintessence of Franklin's opinion was that an attempt should be made to divert the present stream of immigrants and to make an intensive and extensive attempt to educate the children of the German immigrants in free English schools. Young William Smith, who came to know about these proposals while traveling in England, combined this scheme with another one which had been advocated two years earlier by the Reverend Michael Schlatter, who had written to Thomas Penn:

I must assure you, Honoured Sir, that the Large body of Germans that inhabite your territorie are in danger of growing savage, if there are not some wise methods taken to reclaim them: the want of a regular ministry, and of the instructions, that are administred thereby, has such a desperate influence upon there morals, that they must in such a situation, by becoming bad men, become also very bad and troublesome subjects, of which we have seen fatal instances alredy. The Annals of the German History prove this truth, by a number of extraordinary revolutions, their uncultivated Tempers has often made Sovereigns tremble on their Thrones, because it was often attended with Rebellion and Revolt: Now by the introduction of an orderly discipline and ministry, which is the end of the fund in question, the Instructions of Religion being regularly administered, of Pastors not intirely dependent upon them—and the motives to virtue being properly inculcated, the fatal effects of Ignorance and vice may (thro' the blessing of God be happily) prevented: and many made good subjects, who at present can scarcely be called men.

When the plan finally came to pass, the money collected to support the catechetical services of German ministers and the funds raised to establish free or charity schools were placed at the disposal of one board of trustees which was controlled by the eager Reverend William Smith. Schlatter became inspector of the free schools, and unknowingly jeopardized his position among the Germans in a twofold way. Smith refused to turn over the money earmarked for the German Reformed ministers to the German Reformed Coetus because he did not want to lose direct control of these ministers. The ministers, in turn, were irritated by this measure and blamed Schlatter for the arrangement. On the other hand, the free school movement ran into bitter opposition among many German groups, whose attention also focused on Schlatter. He was rightly suspected of having depicted the Germans as a treacherous crowd in order to promote his own plans. As pressures mounted, Schlatter was dropped by his own colleagues; finally he resigned and joined the British army as a chaplain.

The opposition against the free schools was not, however, founded merely on objections to Schlatter's conduct. There were several cultural and social reasons which caused this reaction. Christopher Sauer, in an interesting letter of September 16, 1755, to Conrad Weiser, summarized the attitudes which stood against the free school plan:

I received your friendly letter and returned the answer by the messenger who brought your letter. In the meantime I had doubts whether it is really true that Gilbert Tennent, Schlatter, Peters, Hamilton, Allen, Turner, Shippen, Smith, Franklin, Muehlenberg, Brunholtz, Handschuh, etc., do care in the least for the real conversion of the ignorant Germans in Pennsylvania, or whether the institution of Free Schools is rather supposed to be the foundation for the subjection of this country, since everybody will pursue his own selfish ends by means of this scheme. As far as Hamilton, Peters, Allen, Turner, Shippen and Franklin are concerned, I know that they care very little either for religion or for the cultivation of the Germans; they rather want the Germans to stick out their necks by serving in the militia in order to protect the property of these gentlemen. These men do not know about faith or trust in God. Their wealth is their God, and it is their only mortification that they cannot compel the people to protect their Gods. Tennent may firmly believe that his religion is the best and if it can be achieved with Schlatter's help that the Germans get English preachers who are paid for, and if such preachers can be produced at Philadelphia or at New Jersey |College|, then Tennent will have honor and Schlatter food and the Germans will unfailingly elect Hamilton, Peters, Shippen, Allen, Turner, etc., to assemblymen in order to please their benefactors. These assemblymen then will make a law with R.H.M. to establish a militia, to build fortifications, drill soldiers, and to fix a stipendium or salary for preachers and schoolteachers, so that it will no longer be necessary to write letters to Halle pleading for funds of which they are ashamed and are looked upon as liars when these letters come back to the province in print. Fiat! Thus we all will achieve our ends and there is no better pretext than the *Poor Germans.* I live here, so to speak, at a corner and hear many things that people say. One says: I do not like the idea of having my children taught by means of alms because I do not need to depend on alms and can pay for their education myself. Others say: Where many children come together one child will always rather learn something bad rather than something good from the other children. I will teach my children myself in reading and writing and I do not like their getting together with other children. Others say: If the German children know how to speak English and get around with the others then they will also want to be dressed according to the English fashion, and it

will be hard to get this foolishness out of their heads. Others say: We poor people do not derive any benefit from the alms of the King and of the Society [for the free schools] because if there is not a schoolhouse or a schoolmaster every ten miles, the *Poor* cannot participate in the scheme, since a child cannot attend a school which is farther than five miles away; otherwise it will be much too great a distance to walk twice a day, and poor people cannot send their children to board with others nor can they afford clothes for their children fit enough to go among the stately people. Thus the scheme is only for the rich and for the English. The people are supposed to petition to their own temporal and eternal detriment. I have read an English booklet on the principles of the Freemasons, the 3rd Edition, printed in England. In these |principles| I saw the greatest contrast to the Kingdom of Jesus Christ, yes, indeed, the complete prevention of it, and the people who are the instigators of the free school scheme are Grand Masters, Wardens . . . among the Freemasons and the pillars of their society. Do you think they have anything else in mind but what they think best for themselves?

If they would invite Zuebly I will confess that I have been mistaken, since if they want to combat the foolishness of sectarian imagination and want to promote truth alone, then Zuebly would be one among a thousand [who would be able to do it]. But I fear they are afraid of him because there is a sentence in the pamphlet which runs as follows: "There is nothing they |the Quakers| more fear than to see the Germans pay any regard to regular ministers. Whenever they know any such minister in good Terms with his People, they immediately attack his character by means of this Printer and distress him by dividing his congregation *and encouraging Vagabonds and pretended Preachers whom they every now and then raise up.* This serves a double end."

When I consider the Freemasons as they are described in their booklet which a goldsmith among the Freemasons gave to Siron and which Siron gave to me, I do not know what I should think of Professor Smith's praise of the author and the booklet "The Life of God in the Soul of Men." Perhaps he praises it for political or some such reasons.

The free school plan failed largely because its English promoters did not put the execution of the plan into the hands of a popular and independent German leader. Zuebly, backed by Sauer, would have had much better chances of success. The fact that independent leadership could have made the free school plan work was demonstrated by Muhlenberg, who received money from the free school fund and with it supported the schools connected with the Lutheran churches in Pennsylvania. A stable organization of his own made it possible for him to accept the money more or less on his own terms without becoming dependent upon the promoters of the free school plan. When Smith finally decided that the free school enterprise should be supplemented by a German press subsidized by the school fund, it was Muhlenberg with whom he bargained for the establishment of the press, and the Reverend Johann Friedrich Handschuh, one of Muhlenberg's colleagues, became the editor of a newspaper printed on this press. Franklin sold the press to the free school society, but he lent his name for the enterprise, since it was hoped that his newly gained popularity with the Germans would be a boon to the venture. Franklin had achieved this popularity when he hired German teams and wagons for General Braddock's campaign and obtained good payment for them.

The critical years of the French and Indian wars, which gave new vigor to Pennsylvania's partisan strife, caused a number of political changes which influenced the relationship between the English and the German Pennsylvanians. For one, the team that had worked for the free school scheme disintegrated swiftly. Franklin, who had carefully built up his political stature, was now ready to cash in on his work. Since the Proprietary party did not seem to offer the right platform for his political plans, he joined the Quaker party, which was in need of up-to-date leadership. While he was sent to England as the trusted representative of the people, and of the Quaker party, his former colleague Smith was thrown into jail by an irate Assembly because he had attacked that august body and had also printed his attacks in German in the newspaper sponsored by the free school society. Schlatter left the scene of his frus-

trations as a chaplain. The free school movement had come to an end, although the free school society was kept alive until 1763.

Indian invasions jeopardized the position of the pacifist sects and provided the first serious issue of disagreement between the German sects and the German church people. The radical pacifist wing of the Quakers withdrew from the Assembly and concentrated their activities in the Friendly Association for Regaining and Preserving Peace with the Indians. The German sects contributed freely to this enterprise. The earlier practice of the 1740's of actively soliciting German support was revived to an unprecedented degree by these dissident Quakers, who made many field trips to the western counties in order to raise funds for the Friendly Association and to negotiate with the Indians. A more vivid interest among Quaker leaders in the religious views of some German sects seems to have been a by-product of these activities.

When the wars were over and Pennsylvania was calm again, the Quaker party could close its ranks once more. The pacifists made their peace with those leaders of the Quaker party who had preferred to stay in power. Good relations with the German sects which had been renewed by the dissenting Quakers by means of the Friendly Association were a valuable asset to the Quaker party in the 1760's.

In the meantime, the Proprietary party had gained the respect of the German church people by their insistence on the defense of the frontier. Presbyterian military leaders like Colonel John Armstrong and Colonel James Burd became advocates of the Proprietary party in the western counties. The astute Samuel Purviance, Jr., took care of party affairs in Philadelphia proper. In the crucial years of 1764 and 1765, these men made as much use as they could of the emerging leadership of the German church people. They considered them an important factor which should not be overlooked in making up "tickets." The correspondence of Purviance and Burd provides some good examples of these political calculations. On September 10, 1764, Purviance wrote to Burd in Lancaster:

The News which I brought from Lancaster of the Quakers & Menonists having made a powerful Party to thawrt |sic| the Measures your Friends have so vigorously pursued of late for thrusting out of the Assembly those men who have lately endanger'd our happy Constitution by their precipitate Measures, has given great Concern to all your friends here; & very much dampen'd our hopes w|hic|h were very sanguine that there could be no danger of carrying the Election in yr County to our Wishes: This unfavorable Prospect has induced several Gentlemen here, to think that in order to prevent our being defeated at so critical a Time when measures are taken to bring about a general Change thro the whole Province, It will be expedient to fall on some alteration of the Ticket lately proposed by a few leading Friends, & submitted to yr Consideration, for Alteration or Amendment against the Borough Election, Vizt. to put in Emanl. Carpenter Dr. Adam Choan |Kuhn| or Jacob Carpenter & Isaac Saunders & John Hayse or Andrew Worke: The design is by putting in two Germans to draw such a Party of them as will turn the scale in our Favour & tho by such a Measure we must reject Mr. Ross, yet I'm persuaded he has too much regard for the Public Good to be offended at such a measure when taken purely to defeat the Views of our Antagonists. . . .

A week later Burd informed Purviance that

We have on our side the Lutherin & Calvanists Dutch with many others of the Germains, we think ourselves strong Enough for the Task we have undertaken, and I can only assure you that no stone shall be left unturn'd on my part to accomplish the Laudable Design. But at the same time I think if our freinds in Philada. could prevail upon Mr. Henry Kiply |Heinrich Keppele| to write up Circular letters to his freinds for this County to join me in the Ticket & those letters warmly wrote it would greatly help our cause and if such thing should be approved off by our freinds with you & done I should be glad to have a list of the Peoples Names that Mr. Kiply writes to that I may talk to them upon the subject.

The election of Heinrich Keppele for assemblyman in Philadelphia in 1764 was sig-

nificant in many respects. It definitely marked the end of Pennsylvania's German problem which had caused so much apprehension ten years earlier. There could no longer be any doubt that German voters were on both sides of the issues of the day. And, as the campaigns proved, communication with the German populace was no longer a monopoly of any one group. Another fact demonstrated by this election was the coherence and political assertiveness of the German Lutherans. This coherence was largely the achievement of Henry Melchior Muhlenberg, who had moved to Philadelphia in 1761 and had succeeded in establishing a new church constitution providing for the annual free election of vestrymen, thus preventing a break between the older and richer vestrymen led by Keppele and the younger and poorer laymen who felt themselves excluded from church affairs. It may be suggested that Keppele's political success was largely based on his willing acceptance of this democratic church constitution.

It was a kind of special irony that Keppele's success was bound up with a defeat of Franklin. Ten years earlier Franklin had hoped that the Germans might express themselves independently, and not follow Quaker advice. When this finally came to pass, Franklin happened to be on the other side of the political fence. In addition to this, Franklin's political enemies had rediscovered the little pamphlet on the "Peopling of Countries," in the concluding part of which he had made some unguarded remarks about "Palatine Boors." Thus, Franklin was pitted against Franklin.

The political change among the Germans had been accompanied by a social and cultural change as well. Wealth had been accumulated by both the church people and the sectarians. The sects tried to preserve their original austerity and drifted toward isolation. The church people, on the other hand, became accustomed to finer buildings and more fashionable ceremonies. Even Muhlenberg himself thought at times that he might soon be considered no longer stylish enough for his urbane congregation. He had to preach more frequently in English in order to satisfy the young people who wanted to listen to English sermons. In order to obtain their political support the German churches had been given charters by the governor. Although this was an act of political expediency, it was nevertheless an outward sign of the coming of age and of the importance of these churches in Philadelphia.

The environment of the German sects was subject to changes too. The diversification of Pennsylvania's sects and denominations produced tolerance but, at times, indifference also. A letter of the Schwenkfelder leader Christopher Schultze to a Schwenkfelder who had remained in Silesia portrays this situation very well:

You can hardly imagine how many denominations you will find here when you are attending a big gathering like that of Abraham Heydrich's or Abram Jaeckel's funeral. . . .

We are all going to and fro like fish in water but always at peace with each other; anybody of whom it were known that he hates somebody else because of his religion would immediately be considered a fool. However, everybody speaks his mind freely. A Mennonite preacher is my nearest neighbor and I could not wish for a better one; on the other side I have a big Catholic church. The present Jesuit Father here comes from Vienna and his name is Johann Baptista Ritter. He confides in me more than in those who come to him for confession; when he has a problem he comes to me. These gentlemen have learned perfectly to adjust to the tempo.

Next to them the Lutherans and Reformed have their congregations here, the latter being the most numerous here. On Sunday we meet all these coming to and fro, but it does not mean anything. . . .

The Separatists live here like birds sitting in the midst of seeds. Whoever is punished for something or other by the members of his denomination . . . becomes a Separatist immediately, and if anybody starts talking about religion or salvation, it is their common confession to mock at preachers and denominations. Their children proceed one step further: they become Epicureans, Atheists, or pagans, or whatever you wish to call them. Dear Friend, think of the unlimited freedom, think of the unfathomable wickedness of Adam's offspring, consider the narrow path of life and the mortification of the flesh, and you will understand in what dangers we are concerning our children. As far as sects go, it is no longer especially dangerous here, but alas! the indifference toward religion increases like a cancerous growth and infiltrates among the old and the young. They say, I want to preserve my freedom, and then they add one link to the other until the end of the chain is firmly fixed in the rock of atheism. . . .

In such an atmosphere only withdrawal could preserve the integrity of the sects who had come to Pennsylvania in order to go out of the "world." As the centuries passed, those groups which succeeded in preserving their identity have become conspicuous because of their withdrawal. The other groups, primarily the church people, who achieved in a surprisingly short time an influential position in Pennsylvania politics and were thus assimilated by the main stream of events, have attracted less interest in later times.

The integration of a major part of the German groups into the political life of Pennsylvania and the relatively quick disappearance of a "German problem" remain important incidents in the Americanization of immigrants of diverse origins.

The Scotch-Irish

JAMES G. LEYBURN

In the following selection, adapted from his excellent book on the Scotch-Irish, sociologist James G. Leyburn traces the course of this ethnic minority from their roots in Northern Ireland to their impact upon colonial and early national America. Leyburn underscores their invaluable contributions to the frontier spirit of democracy, to religious liberty, and to the emerging sense of nationhood. The role of the Scotch-Irish in inspiring and reinforcing these impulses and in initiating educational efforts ranging from frontier log schools to institutions of higher learning, made this group an embodiment of the qualities that distinguished the new nation from any other country in the world, and a crucial source of vitality and cohesion for the young republic.

Scotch-Irish settlements concentrated on the western, frontier edge of the colonies. Hence their espousal of liberty, equality, and nationalism gives substance to the controversial and seminal frontier thesis of Frederick Jackson Turner. In 1893, Turner, one of the most imaginative historians the United States has ever produced, enunciated what was then considered a revolutionary interpretation of America's growth: "The existence of an area of free land, its continuous recession, and the advance of American settlement westward, explain American development." He credited the strength and well-being of the American people to this continually receding frontier where men had to build society out of wilderness, and individuals through persevering labor could earn their status. The desolate conditions of the frontier, according to Turner, fostered democracy, individualism, and cooperation. Where all men operated under the same conditions hereditary gradations in position or selfish aloofness could not survive.

The Scotch-Irish (known simply as the "Irish" in colonial parlance), one of the first immigrant groups to pass through the settled areas and make homes on the western borders of established communities in New England, Pennsylvania, and the southern colonies, emigrated from Ulster, Ireland, in the early part of the eighteenth century. About one hundred years earlier their ancestors had left Scotland in the hope of finding a better life in Northern Ireland. By the beginning of the 1700s, however, the British navigation acts and other restrictive policies had severely affected Ulster woolen and linen manufacturers, shipbuilders, and cattle grazers. Absentee landlords charged prohibitive rents, taxes had to be paid to support the Anglican Church regardless of religious affiliation (most of the Scotch-Irish were Presbyterian), and the Scotch-Irish could neither vote, hold office, nor maintain their own schools. These disabilities proving too burdensome, between 1717 and 1776 about 250,000 left Ulster for the New World. As described by Leyburn, the Scotch-Irish experiences in British North America conform almost exactly to the Turner thesis.

Millions of Americans have Scotch-Irish ancestors, for when this country gained its independence perhaps one out of every ten persons was Scotch-Irish. Few descendants among these millions, however, know much about their ancestors—about what the hyphenated name implies, where the original Scotch-Irishmen came from and why, or what part this vigorous folk played in early American history.

Because the thirteen original American colonies were English, with government in English hands and the population predominantly from England, the tendency of our history books has been to make us see colonial history as the product of transplanted Englishmen. Every American child learns about Jamestown, Pilgrims and Puritans, Tidewater planters, landed proprietors and gentry—all English; but few schoolbooks make a child aware of the non-English "first Americans." In quite recent years our attention has been insistently called to the blacks who made up one sixth of our first census in 1790; and the very names of German, Dutch, Portuguese Jewish, and French Huguenot elements tell us who these early Americans were. But who were the Scotch-Irish?

Next to the English they were the most numerous of all colonists, with settlements from Maine to Georgia. Some historians suggest that they were "archetypal" Americans, in the sense that their ideals and attitudes, limitations and prepossessions, virtues and vices, proved to be common national characteristics of nineteenth-century Americans. If such a claim has any validity, the people themselves deserve to be more than a vague name.

To English colonists who were their neighbors from 1717 to 1775 any idea that immigrants from northern Ireland might presage future American character would have been startling if not dismaying. Few of the settled colonists had kind words for the newcomers in those days. Pennsylvania received the largest numbers of them, and James Logan, secretary to the Penn family and an Irishman himself, lamented that "the settlement of five families of [Scotch-Irishmen] gives me more trouble than fifty of any other people." When they continued to pour into the colony, Logan, fearing that the decent Quaker element might be submerged, fumed: "It is strange that they thus crowd where they are not wanted." Cotton Mather in Massachusetts was more forthright; he fulminated against their presence as one of "the formidable attempts of Satan and his Sons to Unsettle us." On the eve of the Revolution a loyal English colonist declared the Scotch-Irish to be, with few exceptions, "the most God-provoking democrats on this side of Hell."

Such initial hostility toward a wave of foreigners was to become commonplace during the next century, when America received some thirty million immigrants from Europe. By comparison with these late-comers, however, the Scotch-Irish were fortunate, since they experienced active hostility for only a brief time. Practically all of them pushed as quickly as possible to the cheap lands of the back country, where, out of sight, they no longer offended the sensibilities of English colonists by their "oddities."

In many ways the Scotch-Irish pioneers were indeed an augury of Americans-to-be. They were probably the first settlers to identify themselves as Americans—not as Pennsylvanians or Virginians or citizens of some other colony, or as Englishmen or

Germans or any European nationality. Their daily experience of living on the outer fringe of settlement, of making small farms in the forests, of facing the danger of Indian attack and fighting back, called for qualities of self-reliance, ingenuity, and improvisation that Americans have ranked high as virtues. They were inaugurators of the heroic myth of the winning of the West that was to dominate our nineteenth-century history. Their Presbyterian Church, with its tradition of formality in worship and its insistence upon an educated ministry, was the first denomination to make tentative, if reluctant, adjustments to the realities of frontier life. Social mixing and intermarriage with their neighbors, irrespective of national background, made any such qualifier as Scotch-Irish (or northern Irish or Ulsterman) disappear within a generation.

When the Revolutionary War came, Scotch-Irishmen were the most wholehearted supporters of the American cause in each of the thirteen colonies. If before 1775 they were still regarded as aliens and immigrants, their zeal as patriots and soldiers changed all that. At home and abroad they were credited with playing a vital part in the struggle for independence. A Hessian captain wrote in 1778, "Call this war by whatever name you may, only call it not an American rebellion; it is nothing more or less than a Scotch Irish Presbyterian rebellion." King George was reported to have characterized the Revolution as "a Presbyterian war," and Horace Walpole told Parliament that "there is no use crying about it. Cousin America has run off with a Presbyterian parson, and that is the end of it." A representative of Lord Dartmouth wrote from New York in 1776 that "Presbyterianism is really at the Bottom of this whole Conspiracy, has supplied it with Vigour, and will never rest, till something is decided upon it." Such testimony to enthusiasm for the American cause was not given to any other group of immigrants.

Upon the conclusion of the war, when the great Ohio and Mississippi valleys were opened up and the rush westward began,

sons and daughters of the original Scotch-Irishmen led the way across the mountains to the new frontiers. Theodore Roosevelt is not the only historian who suggests that the institutions, attitudes, and characteristics of these trans-Allegheny pioneers constituted the practical middle ground into which the diversities of easterners and southerners might merge into something new—American culture.

The hyphenated term "Scotch-Irish" is an Americanism, generally unknown in Scotland and Ireland and rarely used by British historians. In American usage it refers to people of Scottish descent who, having lived for a time in the north of Ireland, migrated in considerable numbers to the American colonies during the half century before the Revolutionary War. Perhaps 250,000 of them actually crossed the sea to America, and they bred rapidly; their sons, like later arrivals from Ulster, constantly extended settlements westward to the Appalachians. The mountains then sent the flow of newcomers north and especially south from Pennsylvania until they constituted a dominant element in many colonies.

Only occasionally were these people then called Scotch-Irish; the usual designation was simply "Irish." "Scotch-Irish" is accurate, yet many Irish-American critics assert that it is an appellation born of snobbish pride and prejudice. They are not entirely wrong. During the years of immigration, from 1717 to 1775, none of the newcomers seem to have insisted upon the "Scotch" part of the name; this insistence developed only among their descendants, and for interesting reasons.

As is well known, after the potato famines of 1845 and 1846 the Irish began to pour into the United States. These people were desperately poor; they were Roman Catholics coming to a Protestant-dominated country; they were mostly illiterate, often uncouth by American standards, and they were very visible in their concentration in Eastern cities. Prejudice against the "shanty Irish" was rampant for decades. In these very decades, antiquarian interest was quickening among Americans; local historical societies burgeoned; people looked for distinguished ancestors among their colonial forefathers. Descendants of the people from Ulster, whose grandparents had not objected to being called Irish, now preferred the hyphenated name Scotch-Irish—all the more enthusiastically because Sir Walter Scott had beguiled the nation with his romantic picture of Scots and of Scotland. A Scotch-Irish Society was founded, and its annual meetings, like its publications, boasted of notable ancestors and important contributions to the United States.*

The ostentatious pride of these later Scotch-Irish, and their boasts of importance to America, aroused first the anger of many Irish-Americans and then their sarcastic wit. The newly invented hyphenated name was called a cant phrase, a shibboleth, a mongrel absurdity, a delusion; and the Scotch-Irish Society was proclaimed "an organized humbug." One Irish-American, in a waggish poem entitled "The Gathering of the Scotch-Irish Clans," lampooned the false pretenses of Irishmen who would not admit their true origins:

Are ye gangin' to the meetin', to the meetin' o' the clans,
With your tartans and your pibrochs and your bonnets and brogans?
There are Neeleys from New Hampshire and Mulligans from Maine,
McCarthys from Missouri and a Tennessee McShane.

There follows a succession of straight Irish names, and the satire ends:

*One typical list of distinguished Americans whose forebears were Scotch-Irish was published in 1920. It included the names (listed alphabetically) of Thomas Hart Benton, James G. Blaine, John C. Calhoun, John G. Carlisle, Andrew Carnegie, George Rogers Clark, Jefferson Davis, Ulysses S. Grant, Horace Greeley, Alexander Hamilton, Mark Hanna, Samuel Houston, Andrew Jackson, Thomas Jonathan "Stonewall" Jackson, John Paul Jones, George B. McClellan, William McKinley, Oliver Hazard Perry, John D. Rockefeller, Edward Rutledge, Winfield Scott, Zachary Taylor, Matthew Thornton, Anthony Wayne, and Woodrow Wilson.

We'll sit upon the pint-stoup and we'll talk of auld lang syne
As we quaff the flowing haggis to our lasses' bonnie eyne.
And we'll join the jubilation for the thing that we are not;
For we say we aren't Irish, and God knows we aren't Scot!

(The members of the Scotch-Irish Society might have informed the satirist that one does not "quaff" haggis, a formidable pudding made with a sheep's viscera.)

Yet for all the implicit snobbishness in the double name, it directs attention to geographical, historical, and cultural facts in the background of the Scotch-Irish people. The persistence of ancestral traits of character can be exaggerated and even given a mystical quality; but there is no doubt that tradition, ancient "sets" of mind, religious convictions, limitations of outlook, and abiding prejudices gave the Scotch-Irish qualities of personality and character that affected their life in America.

The people who began to come to America in 1717 were not Scots, and certainly they were not Irish: already they were Scotch-Irish, even though this name was rarely given them. The hyphen bespeaks two centuries of historical events, many of them tragic ("dark and drublie" was the Scottish phrase), some of them heroic. The ancestors of these people had come, in the century after 1610, from the Lowlands of Scotland across the twenty-mile channel to the northern province of Ireland (Ulster) as a result of a political experiment undertaken by England. It was called the Plantation of Ulster, and it was simply one of England's many attempts to solve "the Irish problem."

For five centuries, ever since the time of Henry II (1133–89), England had tried to rule Ireland, but the Irish refused to become docile subjects. Their resistance was intensified into bitterness when England became Protestant and tried to extirpate the Roman Catholic religion in Ireland. Finally, in Queen Elizabeth's closing years, Irish earls in the north, after a desperate struggle, were defeated and exiled, and the Crown confiscated all their lands. James I, who followed Elizabeth in 1603, proposed (at the suggestion of Edmund Spenser and others of his counsellors) to settle this region with loyal English and Scottish Protestants who, in return for cheap land, would keep the Irish under control. Since the king had been James VI of Scotland before succeeding to the English crown, he was successful in persuading thousands of his Scottish subjects to cross to Ulster and start a new life there under advantageous economic circumstances.

Only a vivid modern imagination can conceive the squalor, indeed the near savagery, of the northern Irish counties around 1600. Queen Elizabeth called the inhabitants "the wild Irish." She and her advisers looked upon them much as Victorians did African natives and other "lesser breeds without the law." These Irishmen had no cities, no education, no refinements; they lived from hand to mouth at a primitive level (maintained, of course, by centuries of guerrilla fighting against the English). Their Catholic religion, a patriotic rallying point and a blessed solace, had acquired many elements of magic and superstition. Almost utter demoralization had ensued upon the defeat and exile of their leaders in the 1590's.

The Scots who were invited (along with English Protestants) by King James to settle Ulster and subdue its natives were thus the first Scotch-Irishmen. They came from the Lowlands, that region nearest the English border and longest in contact with English ways, language, and ideas. They were not the romantic Highland figures of Scott's novels. They were not clansmen who wore kilts and who marched, complete with dirk, sporran, brooch, and bonnet, to the skirling of bagpipes in the glens. On the contrary, they were farmers who eked out a bare living on thin soil as tenants of a laird. Three words best characterize them: they were poor, Presbyterian, and pertinacious.

Their farming methods were primitive. Crops were not rotated, and the yield was meager; starvation was always imminent in the long winters, for both man and beast. King James's offer of a new start in Ireland on larger farms whose land had lain fallow was, therefore, very appealing, all the more because lairds in the Lowlands had recently demanded higher rents and contracts that made farmers feel a loss of traditional rights and dignity.

The first Scotsmen to pioneer in Ulster succeeded well enough to allure other thousands of Lowlanders, and when, in mid-century, troubles arose with the English king and his church, the exodus increased. The new Ulstermen ran the gamut of character, as pioneers do. Their motives for migration—desire for a better living, escape from problems and debts—indicate ambition and initiative. Some of the adventurers proved to be shiftless; others had qualities needing only opportunity to bring them to full flower. Most of the "planters" took their families with them, thus proclaiming their intention to stay and establish themselves. Socially, they were generally humble folk (aristocrats rarely migrate), but with tenacious qualities indispensable for pioneers.

They were Presbyterians to a man, and Scottish Presbyterianism was unique in its intensity, even in those religious days. The Reformation in Scotland, led by John Knox, had achieved immediate and almost universal success among Lowlanders. Their Calvinist "kirk" became the Church of Scotland, a nationalist symbol for the people, who supported it all the more loyally because of the initial struggle against "popery" and the subsequent resistance against royal efforts to make it Anglican. A notable aspect of the Reformation in Scotland was the enthusiastic commitment of the people to education, not only for ministers but also for laymen. It was as if a dormant ideal had suddenly and permanently come to flower. The highest aspiration of a Lowland family was that a son might attend a university and become a minister or dominie. The passion for education carried over to northern Ireland and to America, with far-reaching results in the colonies.

It is likely that the quality of the Lowlanders that made the king most hopeful of their success in the Ulster Plantation was their well-known stubbornness and dourness ("dour" and "durable" are linguistically related). He counted on these traits to hold them in Ulster even when things went badly, and to make them keep the "wild Irish" in tow, and his confidence proved justified. Had not an elder of the kirk besought the Lord that he might always be right, "for Thou knowest, Lord, that I am unco' hard to turn"?

In the century between 1610 and 1717 perhaps as many as one hundred thousand Lowlanders came across from Scotland, and by the latter date there were some five Scots to every three Irishmen and one Englishman in Ulster. The English planters represented the Establishment; high civil officials, Anglican churchmen, businessmen, and the Army; but the preponderant Scots set the tone of the new culture of northern Ireland. It is a culture that, as the recent troubles there have painfully shown, is still self-consciously different from that of the rest of the island.

The Ulster experience was a fitting preparation for pioneering in America. The farmers had constantly to be on guard against native Irish uprisings. Agricultural methods decidedly improved under English example. Feudalism, which still existed in Scotland, simply disappeared in Ulster, for farmers were no longer subject to an overlord or attached to one locality. The Presbyterian Church, with its members "straitly" watched over and disciplined by the session of each parish kirk, stiffened the moral fiber of the people, and with its own presbyteries, not subject to the Scottish Kirk, gave the members experience in self-government.

In one respect, however, the Scotch-Irish seemed to be deficient. The Renaissance did not reach Scotland until the eighteenth century, many years after the Lowlanders had left. From the moment of their arrival in northern Ireland comment was made by Englishmen on the apparently complete lack of aesthetic sensibility on the part of these Scots. As one observer remarked, if a Scotsman in Ulster "builds a cottage, it is a prison in miniature; if he has a lawn, it is only grass; the fence of his grounds is a stone wall, seldom a hedge. He has a sluggish imagination: it may be awakened by the gloomy or terrific, but seldom revels in the beautiful." The same limitations apparently characterized the Scotch-Irish in America.

In the very decades when at last the Ulster Plantation seemed to be achieving its purpose, with the Irish subdued, Protestantism dominant, English rule secured, and prosperity imminent, the great migration to America got under way. As usually happens when thousands of people undertake so hazardous an enterprise as crossing an ocean to find a new home, there was both a push from the old country and a pull from the new.

Paradoxically, Ulster's growing prosperity was one cause of the first wave of migration. A lucrative woolen and linen industry, developing since the 1690's, alarmed the English Parliament and led to the passage of a series of crippling protective acts whose results were resentment on the part of Ulstermen, economic depression, and recurrent unemployment. A second cause touched men personally and turned many thoughts to migration: this was the hated practice of rack-renting. The term referred to a landlord's raising rent when a long lease on his land expired—and in the decade after 1710 hundreds of leases came up for renewal. To us, such a practice seems normal; but Ulster farmers felt it to be a violation of tradition, a moral injury, because a tenant was treated impersonally. If the farmer could not or would not pay the higher rent, he had only two practical alternatives: a return to the poverty of Scotland, or migration to the New World.

Still other causes stimulated emigration. Six years in succession after 1714 brought dire drought, with depression in the flax industry and soaring costs of food. In 1716 sheep were afflicted with a destructive disease; severe frosts throughout the decade discouraged farmers; a smallpox epidemic scourged Ulster. In addition there was a goad from the Anglican religious establishment. Deserting the tolerant policy of William III, the High-Church party, ascendant during the reign of Queen Anne (1702–14), secured the passage of a Test Act, requiring all officeholders in Ireland to take the sacrament according to prescriptions of the Church of England. Although aimed at Irish Catholics, the weight of this requirement fell heavily upon substantial Presbyterians who held magistracies and other civil posts. By extension, Presbyterian ministers could no longer perform legal marriages or even bury the dead, nor could "dissenters" teach school. This unwise law, though not everywhere rigidly enforced, caused resentment among the stubborn Scots, intensified by the fact that they had been loyal to the Crown and had proved a bulwark of defense against the rampageous Irish.

For all these reasons some five thousand Ulster Scots went to America in 1717 and 1718. After that initial migration, the pull of America began to exert more effect than the push from northern Ireland. Reports coming from the colonies were highly favorable, especially from Pennsylvania. Land was cheap and plentiful, authorities were well disposed, the soil was fertile beyond all imagination, and opportunities were boundless. Only two drawbacks loomed: the perils of an ocean crossing, and the expense of the passage. The former was very real in those days; but optimism persuaded young people that the nightmare of several weeks on a tiny, overcrowded ship, with much illness, was rarely fatal and that grim memories would soon fade. As for passage money, the practice of indenture had long been a familiar device. Few who had made up their minds to go would be deterred by having to work for a master in America for a period of years to pay off their passage fee, for then came freedom and a new life in a country which, according to some, resembled paradise.

Five great waves brought a quarter million Ulster Scots to America, turned them into Scotch-Irish Americans, depressed the economy of Ulster, and depopulated parts of that

province. The tides ebbed and flowed partly with conditions in Ulster, partly with upsurges of what was called migration fever. The chief waves were those of 1717–18, 1725–29, 1740–41, 1754–55, and 1771–75; and each benefited particular colonies. The first two helped fill up the back country of Pennsylvania and soon began spilling over into the Shenandoah Valley of Virginia. The third further peopled the Shenandoah Valley and spread into the piedmont and upcountry of North Carolina. That colony and South Carolina drew most of the people in the fourth wave, while the final group, coming just before the Revolutionary War, spread out widely from New York to Georgia.

In each wave, other colonies also drew settlers. Because the Delaware River early proved the favorite entryway, the colonies of New Jersey, Delaware, and Maryland soon had many Ulstermen. Massachusetts reluctantly admitted a few but so disliked their uncongenial ways that later arrivals in Boston went on to New Hampshire or Maine.

Two facts about the migration are significant for American history. First, there was almost no further influx from northern Ireland after the Revolutionary War; thus, there was no addition to the Scotch-Irish element from abroad nor any inducement to maintain sentimental ties or a "national" identity with a country ruled by England. Second, the concentration of Scotch-Irishmen in the geographically central colonies of Pennsylvania and Virginia made a kind of reservoir from which the people spread north and south through all other colonies; moreover, their farms just east of the Alleghenies were nearest the Great West when that vast territory opened up after 1783. Scotch-Irishmen were thus the vanguard of the trans-Allegheny pioneers.

It has already been observed that no other immigrants were so patriotically unanimous in support of the American cause as the Scotch-Irish. One group of patriotic settlers in Mecklenburg County, North Carolina, drew up a set of resolutions on May 20, 1775, declaring the people of that county free and independent of the British Crown. This predominantly Scotch-Irish assemblage thus anticipated by more than a year the Declaration of Independence. The Revolutionary War might not have been won without Scotch-Irish fighting men.

With independence gained, the Scotch-Irish almost everywhere exerted a unifying, an *American,* influence, favoring a central government of truly united states. The very fact of their recent arrival in the country and their spread through all thirteen colonies had prevented the growth of strong ties to a particular colony and therefore of an insistent demand for states' rights. In Pennsylvania and Virginia support by the Scotch-Irish may have been decisive in shaping state constitutions that were extraordinarily liberal for the times. In Pennsylvania power was wrested from the Philadelphia Quakers and given to the majority of the people, thanks to the combined efforts of Scotch-Irish, Germans, and non-Quaker English settlers in the western regions. In Virginia also, the Scotch-Irish of the Shenandoah Valley strongly supported a constitution remarkable for its break with tradition—one that abolished quitrents, entails, primogeniture, and the slave trade, and guaranteed religious liberty. (It must be noted, however, that leadership for all these liberal measures came from Jefferson, Madison, and other English Virginians.)

Scotch-Irishmen struck a real blow for religious liberty in this country. In 1738 the royal governor of Virginia and the Tidewater planters actively sought to persuade newcomers to the Pennsylvania frontier to leave that crowded region and settle in the Shenandoah Valley. An ancestor of John C. Calhoun presented to Governor William Gooch a memorial drawn up by the Presbyterian Synod of Philadelphia requiring religious toleration as a prerequisite for settlement. Gooch acceded to the demand, to the benefit of Virginia and of later American freedom.

From the first, Scotch-Irishmen took an active part in politics. They were elected to office in their communities, became effective lawyers, and in significantly large numbers served in legislatures, on high courts, and as governors—though hardly because their ancestors had come from Scotland and northern Ireland. With the election of Andrew Jackson as President, the descendants of the Scotch-Irish had attained the highest office in the land, and most of them had by then ceased to emphasize their ancestry.

In education and religion it may be asserted that many American ideals and standards derive from the happy agreement of two self-assured colonial groups, the Scotch-Irish and the New England Yankees. Alone, neither people might have been weighty enough or (in the case of the Yankees) unprovincial enough to have prevailed; but their common Calvinism and earnestness gave America its first commitment to general education as well as its tendency to identify religion with upright moral character.

For both people, schools followed churches as the first institutions to be formed. The Word of God must be expounded by educated ministers, and colonists could not send their sons abroad for training. The connection between church and school, going back to the Reformation, was to remain close for descendants of both Presbyterians and Puritans until the present century. Ministers were schoolmasters as well as preachers. Curricula in Scotch-Irish log schools on the frontier resembled those of the town schools in earlier New England, with training in the three R's, the Bible, and the catechisms, while higher education was directed toward training for the ministry. The Puritans founded Harvard and Yale well before the Presbyterians established Princeton and Hampden-Sydney and Dickinson; but from these first colleges came a host of others, whose students were not wholly ministerial. Until the Civil War the great majority of colleges in the country were founded by religious denominations and still remained under their control. (The state's responsibility for higher education had not yet been widely claimed.) Of the 207 permanent colleges founded before 1861, well over half were established by Presbyterians and New

Englanders; and many of them were notable as "mothers" of still other colleges.

The distinctive religious influence of the Scotch-Irish and New Englanders was not in their common Calvinism, though certainly Calvinist theology has had its effect upon America: it was rather in persuading millions of Americans that religion and character are synonyms. In most other parts of the world religion is likely to mean ritual observance, adherence to a creed, customary pious acts, or some combination of these; but when an American says that a person is deeply religious he is likely to mean first of all that he is upright and highly moral. Both Puritans and Scotch-Irish insisted upon rectitude of life and behavior, stubborn adherence to principle, scorn of compromise, and a stern severity that could be as hard upon others as upon self. Neither people could accept the idea that a man's religious duty consisted only of acts performed on Sunday or of doctrinal orthodoxy. Since America quickly became pluralistic in religion, there could never have been agreement upon ritual, creed, or observances to unify us religiously; but all Americans could agree on admirable character and high moral rectitude. What the Puritans and Scotch-Irish made of religion was immensely reinforced when the Baptist and Methodist movements, rising to ascendancy in the nineteenth century, taught the same ideas.

In certain ways the Presbyterian Church of the Scotch-Irish was the first important denomination to become "Americanized" and broadly "American." In log churches on a frontier, with a congregation of pioneer farmers, many formal traditions of the dignified Presbyterian Church quietly vanished —the Geneva gown and stock, the separate pulpit, the attendance of the minister by a beadle, the set prayers. Many of the colonial Presbyterian ministers experimented with unconventional, direct methods of evangelism, in order to speak clearly to a people losing interest in dignity for the sake of tradition. (The approval of the presbyteries for this informality was not won, however; and because the dynamic Methodists and Baptists felt free to adopt resourceful methods of evangelism, they drew thousands of adherents among descendants of the Scotch-Irish.)

The Church of England was the established religion in six colonies and the Congregational faith in three others; both, then, were identified with the upper-class English Establishment; but the Presbyterian Church was nowhere official, elite, or English. Moreover, these other two dominant churches were regional, strong only in the Tidewater and in New England; but the Presbyterian Church, like the Scotch-Irish people, was present in every colony. Its ministers were supported not by legally exacted tithes but by free contributions of members; these ministers in their work moved freely from one region to another. The organization of the church was controlled by presbyteries that ranged from New York to the South. The "federal" structure of the church of the Scotch-Irish seemed congenial to American conditions and exerted a unifying influence in our early history.

If we of the twentieth century wish to admire the Scotch-Irish as representative prototypes of later Americans, we must ruefully note that their Ulster forefathers' neglect of things aesthetic was carried over to the new country. European visitors and critics in the nineteenth century, indeed, considered all Americans deficient in such matters; but we now know how wrong they were, for our museums are full of beautiful early American art and artifacts from New England, from the Tidewater, from German farmlands, and from many other regions and districts—but not from Scotch-Irish settlements. Nothing in the background of these people in either Scotland or northern Ireland had attracted them to painting, sculpture, architecture, music, and literature, and nothing in their way of life in the colonies apparently changed their attitude. They liked what was practical and seemed indifferent to whether it was beautiful. The lists of distinguished scions of the Scotch-Irish in nineteenth-century

America include no names of artists and poets.

By 1800 the young United States was growing strong and self-confident, with a continent to win. Already the authority of the thirteen original states was losing its hold over the rising generation. If a farsighted historian of the time had been inclined to identify representative types of inhabitants who would probably become the most characteristic Americans of the new century, he might well have named the restless frontiersman and the rising middle-class townsman. The former was rapidly winning the West, clearing the wilderness, exploiting America's fabulous wealth, adding romance to the American myth; the latter was establishing law and order, building industry, adding comfort to utility, and treasuring respectability and responsibility. If the same historian had sought to find the embodiment of each of his representative types, he could have pointed immediately to the descendants of the vigorous Scotch-Irish, now thoroughly American, with no further accretions from abroad. Most of them had even forgotten the adjective formerly applied to them. The daily life of being an American was too absorbing to permit adulation of one's ancestors, even though these had been the admirable Scotch-Irish.

2

THE YOUNG REPUBLIC

Between the end of the American Revolution and the start of the Civil War 5,250,000 immigrants came to the United States. The vast majority, approximately 5,000,000, arrived between 1815 and 1860, that is, after the defeat of Napoleon again opened the sea lanes across the Atlantic and before the Civil War temporarily halted the influx from abroad. After 1808, when the official closing of the slave trade led to the smuggling in of African blacks, recorded newcomers came almost exclusively from northern and western Europe. The tremendous increase of migration during the post-1815 period, and particularly after the 1820s, can be attributed chiefly to a population explosion in Europe beginning around 1750, which created a surplus of manpower on the farms and in the cities; to the development of the factory system, which dislocated many artisans; and to the emergence of large-scale, market-oriented, scientific agriculture, which displaced millions of peasant farmers and agricultural laborers. This last factor operated with the greatest severity during the enclosure movements, which consolidated estates in Britain, Ireland, Scandinavia, and southwestern Germany. Political frustrations played a less important role in stimulating emigration but brought over many defeated revolutionaries or counter-revolutionaries from France during the 1790s and refugees from the abortive republican and nationalist uprisings of the 1840s in Germany, Italy, Austria, Hungary, and Ireland. Religious persecutions of Norwegian Quakers and Prussian Lutherans, for example, accounted for a minor part of the great ethnic migrations in this era. The mass movement from the Old World to the New was further facilitated when England, Scandinavia, and Germany dropped their emigration restrictions during the years between 1820 and 1860, by the spread of information about America, and by the establishment of regular, faster, safer, and more inexpensive transportation across the Atlantic.

Relatively few newcomers entered before the 1820s despite the arrival of a few individuals who achieved enormous fame and success in America. These were most notably the Swiss aristocrat Albert Gallatin, Thomas Jefferson's Secretary of the Treasury; the English artisan Samuel Slater, who established the first American cotton factory in Pawtucket, Rhode Island; and John Jacob Astor, the German butcher's son, whose achievements in the fur trade and in New York real estate made him the richest American of his time.

Mass migrations of Europeans began in the 1830s when almost 600,000 people entered the United States. The major nationalities involved in this titanic movement—1,713,000 came in the 1840s and 2,600,000 in the 1850s—were the Irish, the Germans, and the English.

More than 2,000,000 Irish emigrants embarked for America in the thirty years preceding the start of the Civil War. In Europe they suffered the greatest population density and endured an iniquitous agricultural system of absentee landlords (mostly British), rural poverty, high rents, and insecure land tenure. Overpopulation in Ireland had led to intense competition for land that was subdivided because of the system of land inheritance into tiny plots barely sufficient to provide enough food for survival. The collapse of Irish grain exports after the Napoleonic Wars, the opening of the British market to Irish farm produce in 1826, the enclosure of small units into more efficient larger holdings, and the potato blight of 1845–49 drove millions of starving peasants from Ireland.

Similar but less harsh circumstances accounted for the German immigration. The exodus, chiefly from Wurtemburg, Baden, and Bavaria, peaked in the decade from 1846 to

1855 when revolution and crop failures combined with land consolidation by wealthy farmers or nobles to bring 1,500,000 Germans who settled in the United States between 1815 and 1860. The movement then diminished because the conversion of southwestern German agriculture into a modern process had been completed. German immigrants as a whole were better off than the Irish because they had been more prosperous in their home country, and because they numbered a greater proportion of middle-class revolutionaries, wealthy farmers who feared for the future, and artisans, merchants, and professionals.

The 790,000 Englishmen who arrived during these decades were chiefly artisans and skilled workers displaced by the introduction of machinery into the textile and mining industries and by unemployment during the depression of the 1840s, and agricultural laborers whom the enclosure movement rendered landless and who feared disastrous agricultural competition after repeal of the protective tariffs on grains after 1846. Since their ranks included skilled workers and some prosperous farmers, and since English agriculture was not as impoverished as Irish, they, too, brought more wealth with them than Ireland's peasants.

Out of the total American population of 31,500,000 in 1860 some 4,136,000 were foreign born. With the exception of 500,000 recorded in the slave states, most of the newcomers lived north of the Mason-Dixon line and east of the Mississippi. New York, Pennsylvania, Ohio, Illinois, Wisconsin, and Massachusetts, in descending order, contained the most numerous foreign born. Among these were the states with the highest levels of urbanization and industrialization and with the most accessible fertile land. By 1860 it was already apparent that the destinies of the city and the immigrant were intertwined. The heaviest concentration of the foreign born lay in urban centers. Nearly 50 percent of the populations of New York, Chicago, Milwaukee, Detroit, and San Francisco consisted of European immigrants; 60 percent of the residents of St. Louis and one-third of those in New Orleans, Baltimore, and Boston came from abroad.

Poverty, enduring bitterness over their agrarian experience at home, and need for immediate employment confined the Irish, more than any other ethnic minority, to the city. In 1860 two-thirds of the 1,611,000 Irish Americans lived in New York, Pennsylvania, New Jersey, and New England, the vast majority dwelling in the cities of these states. Germans, somewhat better off and more determined to resume farming, were more likely to leave the cities. About one-half of the 1,301,000 Germans who had come to this country by 1860 resided on fertile farms in the Upper Mississippi and Ohio valleys, particularly in Illinois, Wisconsin, and Missouri. Lacking capital and also skill with the axe and rifle, Germans and other immigrants, such as the Scandinavians, who settled mainly in Wisconsin, Minnesota, Iowa, and Illinois, avoided the frontier and sought land that had already been cleared. More than 50 percent of the nearly 600,000 Americans of British birth could be found immediately south of the Great Lakes, in New York, Michigan, Wisconsin, and Illinois, while most of the rest concentrated themselves in New England. As with other nationalities their place of settlement was determined by port of disembarkation, financial resources, occupational skills, and available jobs. Many of the British, along with great numbers of other immigrants, followed the course of ocean commerce from Liverpool to New York or Boston. Upon arrival, Welsh coal miners made their way to eastern Pennsylvania's coal fields, Cornish miners to the lead, copper, and iron mines in Wisconsin, Illinois, and Michigan, and textile workers to the cotton manufacturing centers in Massachusetts and New York. Smaller ethnic groups also gravitated toward certain localities and vocations: Dutch settled on farms in Michigan, New York, Wisconsin, and Iowa; and Jewish petty tradesmen or professionals appeared in cities and small towns or scoured the country as peddlers. Chinese, attracted by menial labor jobs in Gold Rush mining camps, immigrated to California in the 1840s and '50s.

No ethnic group in this period, except for the Indians and the blacks, endured greater deprivation than the Irish. In 1855 one-half of the Irish working population in New York City were laborers, carters, porters, waiters, or domestic servants; in Boston during the same years, two-thirds occupied menial positions. In contrast, during the 1850s New York City's Germans made up only 5 percent of its laborers, carters, and waiters. The immigrants, again particularly the Irish, were also overrepresented in proportion to their percentage of the population in crime and poverty statistics. Over one-half the paupers recorded in mid-nineteenth-century New York and Boston were foreign born; over half of those arrested for crime in Boston in 1859 came from abroad. In most cases drunkenness, petty thievery, and disorderly conduct rather than serious dereliction accounted for the arrests. Nonetheless the brushes with the law indicate friction between the newcomers and those who received them and reveal difficulties in adjustment to the new environment.

Flurries of resentment on the part of the native born added to the problems of the new arrivals. Typically, the Irish and the Chinese experienced the greatest difficulties. The mass migrations between 1830 and 1860 roughly coincided with the gradual disintegration of the Union and many uneasy native-born Americans discerned in the newcomers another threat to national unity. Some suspicions existed that German immigrants in the west were tainted with atheistic radicalism, but hostility was primarily directed against the Irish because of anxiety over so-called papal intrigue. America had always been a predominantly Protestant country and a large share of the new arrivals were Catholics. The first massive Catholic influx raised fears among those who associated freedom with Anglo-Saxon Protestantism that the country's liberty would be destroyed. Dramatic manifestations of negative feelings started in the 1830s with the burning of the Ursuline Convent in Charlestown, Massachusetts, and the publication of a false but sensational account of sex and sadism in a Catholic convent, *Maria Monk's Awful Disclosures of the Hotel Dieu Nunnery of Montreal*. In the 1840s the public school controversy over use of the King James Bible and anti-Catholic riots in Philadelphia and New York intensified the xenophobia. During the next decade the agitation reached its height, culminating in 1855 when the nativist Know-Nothing or American Party elected six governors, dominated several state legislatures, and sent many congressmen to Washington.

On the West Coast the Chinese suffered even more oppression than the Irish did in the East. Xenophobia in California kept Orientals in low-paying, backbreaking menial labor and denied the immigrants fundamental civil rights. They could not testify in state courts until 1870 and therefore were unable to defend property claims against Caucasian interlopers; they also were subject to discriminatory taxes and barred from public schools.

The trials of the nation's older ethnic minorities, the blacks and Indians, dwarfed the problems of the immigrants. The Indians continued in a dreary round of broken treaties, forced removals, and futile resistance. Fifty thousand Cherokees, Creeks, Choctaws, Chickasaws, and Seminoles found themselves gradually surrounded by the expansion of white settlements into the South and Southwest. In the North, the Sacs, Foxes, Kickappos,

Pottawatomies, and other tribes were forced ever westward by the oncoming settlers. Georgia refused to observe treaties contracted between the United States and the Cherokees and evicted the tribe in the 1830s. In the same decade the Choctaws migrated in midwinter from Mississippi to the Red River country, the Creeks resisting expulsion from Alabama left in chains, and the Seminoles were tricked and terrorized into leaving Florida. When the Indians resorted to battle in order to resist these encroachments, as in the cases of the Black Hawk War in Illinois in 1832 and the Seminole War of 1835, they were invariably defeated with heavy loss of life.

For the nation's largest ethnic minority, the blacks, the Revolutionary era had given promise of terminating bondage. Even southern slave owners apologized for the institution and there were hopes for eventual manumission. Optimistic views faded, however, by the 1830s. With the discovery of the cotton gin in 1793, the growing demand for raw cotton, and the spread of slavery into Texas, Alabama, Mississippi, and Louisiana, the position of the blacks, liberated or slave, significantly deteriorated. Abolitionist tirades combined with so-called slave revolts—notably Gabriel's Revolt (1800), Denmark Vesey's Plot (1822), which may only have been a figment of the slaveholders' imaginations, and Nat Turner's insurrection (1831)—led guilty and harried whites to pass more restrictive legislation resulting in the exclusion of free blacks from most southern states. The legislation made bondage more onerous by restricting movement, by making emancipation extremely rare and quite difficult, and by prohibiting the education of blacks and unsupervised religious activities on the plantation. After the 1820s the South, increasingly dependent on and isolated by the slave system, became more rigid in its desire to preserve the "peculiar institution."

Between 1830 and 1850 America experienced the first of a series of mass migrations from the Old World and the first significant influx of Orientals to the West Coast. Those most alien to the national culture, the Chinese and Irish, were the most poorly received. Conversely the Germans and English, considered contributors to America's cultural and commercial growth, were welcomed more eagerly. Massive waves of post-Civil War newcomers would experience similar treatment. Those, like the Irish, who came with minimal skills and capital and who aroused hostility from other Americans would suffer most under the burdens of poverty and bigotry. For the Indians and blacks the era between Independence and the Civil War resulted in tragic massacre, displacement, and heightened repression. Later immigrant groups would repeat the cycle of poverty and alienation but most managed to assimilate into the dominant majority. Generations of Indians and blacks, however, were doomed to genocide or suppression.

SELECTED BIBLIOGRAPHY

Reginald Horsman, *Expansion and American Indian Policy, 1783–1812* (East Lansing: Michigan State University Press, 1967), is a good summary, but for the Jacksonian era readers should probe Ronald N. Satz, *American Indian Policy in the Jacksonian Era* (Lincoln: University of Nebraska Press, 1975), and Michael P. Rogin, *Fathers and Children: Andrew Jackson and the Subjugation of the American Indian* (New York: Alfred A. Knopf, 1975).

On the blacks the literature is voluminous. Eugene D. Genovese, *Roll, Jordan, Roll: The World the Slaves Made* (New York: Pantheon, 1972), is a masterful analysis, while

Robert William Fogel and Stanley L. Engerman, *Time on the Cross: The Economics of American Negro Slavery* (Boston: Little, Brown, 1974), is perhaps the most controversial book ever written on the subject. Leon F. Litwack, *North of Slavery* (University of Chicago Press, 1961), details the story of the free blacks above the Mason-Dixon line before the Civil War; Irwin Unger and David M. Reimers, eds., *The Slave Experience in the United States* (New York: Holt, Rinehart and Winston, 1970), is a collection of readable essays.

Good studies of the immigrant experience include Robert Ernst, *Immigrant Life in New York City, 1825–1863* (New York: King's Crown Press, 1949); Oscar Handlin, *Boston's Immigrants* (revised and enlarged edition; New York: Atheneum, 1968), the classic study of the Irish in America; Andrew M. Greeley, *That Most Distressful Nation: The Taming of the American Irish* (Chicago: Quadrangle Books, 1972); John A. Hawgood, *The Tragedy of German-America* (New York: G. P. Putnam's Sons, 1940); and Stuart Creighton Miller, *The Unwelcome Immigrant: The American Image of the Chinese, 1785–1882* (Berkeley: University of California Press, 1969). A good comparative study is Jay P. Dolan, *The Immigrant Church: New York's Irish and German Catholics, 1815–1865* (Baltimore: Johns Hopkins University Press, 1975).

Indian Removal and Land Allotment:
The Civilized Tribes and Jacksonian Justice

MARY E. YOUNG

Colonial society attempted to find a place for the Indian in the white man's world. By the early national period, however, Americans had an apparently insatiable desire for land and an increasing obsession with the vision of continental empire. Indians forced into the interior during the seventeenth and eighteenth centuries had little desire to move again but most Americans believed that the red man had to be pushed still farther west. What territory could be purchased was purchased, what had to be fought for was fought for, and what could be obtained by mutual agreement was obtained by mutual agreement. Indians who moved willingly were lauded. Regardless of obstacles, and willing to adopt any means necessary to acquire land, Americans pressed ever westward. In the following essay Mary Young details the methods Americans used to obtain desired tracts from 60,000 Cherokees, Creeks, Choctaws, and Chickasaws in the southeastern United States.

By the year 1830, the vanguard of the southern frontier had crossed the Mississippi and was pressing through Louisiana, Arkansas, and Missouri. But the line of settlement was by no means as solid as frontier lines were classically supposed to be. East of the Mississippi, white occupancy was limited by Indian tenure of northeastern Georgia, enclaves in western North Carolina and southern Tennessee, eastern Alabama, and the northern two thirds of Mississippi. In this twenty-five-million-acre domain lived nearly 60,000 Cherokees, Creeks, Choctaws, and Chickasaws.

The Jackson administration sought to correct this anomaly by removing the tribes be-

yond the reach of white settlements, west of the Mississippi. As the President demanded of Congress in December, 1830: "What good man would prefer a country covered with forests and ranged by a few thousand savages to our extensive Republic, studded with cities, towns, and prosperous farms, embellished with all the improvements which art can devise or industry execute, occupied by more than 12,000,000 happy people, and filled with all the blessings of liberty, civilization, and religion?"

The President's justification of Indian removal was the one usually applied to the displacement of the Indians by newer Americans—the superiority of a farming to a hunt-

From *American Historical Review*, 64 (1958), 31–45. Reprinted by permission.

ing culture, and of Anglo-American "liberty, civilization, and religion" to the strange and barbarous way of the red man. The superior capacity of the farmer to exploit the gifts of nature and of nature's God was one of the principal warranties of the triumph of westward-moving "civilization."

Such a rationalization had one serious weakness as an instrument of policy. The farmer's right of eminent domain over the lands of the savage could be asserted consistently only so long as the tribes involved were "savage." The southeastern tribes, however, were agriculturists as well as hunters. For two or three generations prior to 1830, farmers among them fenced their plantations and "mixed their labor with the soil," making it their private property according to accepted definitions of natural law. White traders who settled among the Indians in the mid-eighteenth century gave original impetus to this imitation of Anglo-American agricultural methods. Later, agents of the United States encouraged the traders and mechanics, their half-breed descendants, and their full-blood imitators who settled out from the tribal villages, fenced their farms, used the plow, and cultivated cotton and corn for the market. In the decade following the War of 1812, missionaries of various Protestant denominations worked among the Cherokees, Choctaws, and Chickasaws, training hundreds of Indian children in the agricultural, mechanical, and household arts and introducing both children and parents to the further blessings of literacy and Christianity.

The "civilization" of a portion of these tribes embarrassed United States policy in more ways than one. Long-term contact between the southeastern tribes and white traders, missionaries, and government officials created and trained numerous half-breeds. The half-breed men acted as intermediaries between the less sophisticated Indians and the white Americans. Acquiring direct or indirect control of tribal politics, they often determined the outcome of treaty negotiations. Since they proved to be skillful bar-

gainers, it became common practice to win their assistance by thinly veiled bribery. The rise of the half-breeds to power, the rewards they received, and their efforts on behalf of tribal reform gave rise to bitter opposition. By the mid-1820's this opposition made it dangerous for them to sell tribal lands. Furthermore, many of the new leaders had valuable plantations, mills, and trading establishments on these lands. Particularly among the Cherokees and Choctaws, they took pride in their achievements and those of their people in assimilating the trappings of civilization. As "founding Fathers," they prized the political and territorial integrity of the newly organized Indian "nations." These interests and convictions gave birth to a fixed determination, embodied in tribal laws and intertribal agreements, that no more cessions of land should be made. The tribes must be permitted to develop their new way of life in what was left of their ancient domain.

Today it is a commonplace of studies in culture contact that the assimilation of alien habits affects different individuals and social strata in different ways and that their levels of acculturation vary considerably. Among the American Indian tribes, it is most often the families with white or half-breed models who most readily adopt the Anglo-American way of life. It is not surprising that half-breeds and whites living among the Indians should use their position as go-betweens to improve their status and power among the natives. Their access to influence and their efforts toward reform combine with pressures from outside to disturb old life ways, old securities, and established prerogatives. Resistance to their leadership and to the cultural alternatives they espouse is a fertile source of intratribal factions.

To Jacksonian officials, however, the tactics of the half-breeds and the struggles among tribal factions seemed to reflect a diabolical plot. Treaty negotiators saw the poverty and "depravity" of the common Indian, who suffered from the scarcity of game, the missionary attacks on his accustomed habits and ceremonies, and the ravages of "demon rum" and who failed to find solace in the values of Christian and commercial civilization. Not unreasonably, they concluded that it was to the interest of the tribesman to remove west of the Mississippi. There, sheltered from the intruder and the whisky merchant, he could lose his savagery while improving his nobility. Since this seemed so obviously to the Indian's interest, the negotiators conveniently concluded that it was also his desire. What, then, deterred emigration? Only the rapacity of the half-breeds, who were unwilling to give up their extensive properties and their exalted position.

These observers recognized that the government's difficulties were in part of its own making. The United States had pursued an essentially contradictory policy toward the Indians, encouraging both segregation and assimilation. Since Jefferson's administration, the government had tried periodically to secure the emigration of the eastern tribes across the Mississippi. At the same time, it had paid agents and subsidized missionaries who encouraged the Indian to follow the white man's way. Thus it had helped create the class of tribesmen skilled in agriculture, pecuniary accumulation, and political leadership. Furthermore, by encouraging the southeastern Indians to become cultivators and Christians, the government had undermined its own moral claim to eminent domain over tribal lands. The people it now hoped to displace could by no stretch of dialectic be classed as mere wandering savages.

By the time Jackson became President, then, the situation of the United States vis-à-vis the southeastern tribes was superficially that of irresistible force and immovable object. But the President, together with such close advisers as Secretary of War John H. Eaton and General John Coffee, viewed the problem in a more encouraging perspective. They believed that the government faced not the intent of whole tribes to remain near the bones of their ancestors but the selfish determination of a few quasi Indian leaders to

retain their riches and their ill-used power. Besides, the moral right of the civilized tribes to their lands was a claim not on their whole domain but rather on the part cultivated by individuals. Both the Indian's natural right to his land and his political capacity for keeping it were products of his imitation of white "civilization." Both might be eliminated by a rigorous application of the principle that to treat an Indian fairly was to treat him like a white man. Treaty negotiations by the tried methods of purchase and selective bribery had failed. The use of naked force without the form of voluntary agreement was forbidden by custom, by conscience, and by fear that the administration's opponents would exploit religious sentiment which cherished the rights of the red man. But within the confines of legality and the formulas of voluntarism it was still possible to acquire the much coveted domain of the civilized tribes.

The technique used to effect this object was simple: the entire population of the tribes was forced to deal with white men on terms familiar only to the most acculturated portion of them. If the Indian is civilized, he can behave like a white man. Then let him take for his own as much land as he can cultivate, become a citizen of the state where he lives, and accept the burdens which citizenship entails. If he is not capable of living like this, he should be liberated from the tyranny of his chiefs and allowed to follow his own best interest by emigrating beyond the farthest frontiers of white settlement. By the restriction of the civilized to the lands they cultivate and by the emigration of the savages millions of acres will be opened to white settlement.

The first step dictated by this line of reasoning was the extension of state laws over the Indian tribes. Beginning soon after Jackson's election, Georgia, Alabama, Mississippi, and Tennessee gradually brought the Indians inside their borders under their jurisdiction. Thus an Indian could be sued for trespass or debt, though only in Mississippi and Tennessee was his testimony invariably acceptable in a court of law. In Mississippi, the tribesmen were further harassed by subjection—or the threat of subjection—to such duties as mustering with the militia, working on roads, and paying taxes. State laws establishing county governments within the tribal domains and, in some cases, giving legal protection to purchasers of Indian improvements encouraged the intrusion of white settlers on Indian lands. The laws nullified the legal force of Indian customs, except those relating to marriage. They provided heavy penalties for anyone who might enact or enforce tribal law. Finally, they threatened punishment to any person who might attempt to deter another from signing a removal treaty or enrolling for emigration. The object of these laws was to destroy the tribal governments and to thrust upon individual Indians the uncongenial alternative of adjusting to the burdens of citizenship or removing beyond state jurisdiction.

The alternative was not offered on the unenlightened supposition that the Indians generally were capable of managing their affairs unaided in a white man's world. Governor Gayle of Alabama, addressing the "former chiefs and headmen of the Creek Indians" in June of 1834 urged them to remove from the state on the grounds that

you speak a different language from ours. You do not understand our laws and from your habits, cannot be brought to understand them. You are ignorant of the arts of civilized life. You have not like your white neighbors been raised in habits of industry and economy, the only means by which anyone can live, in settled countries, in even tolerable comfort. You know nothing of the skill of the white man in trading and making bargains, and cannot be guarded against the artful contrivances which dishonest men will resort to, to obtain your property under forms of contracts. In all these respects you are unequal to the white men, and if your people remain where they are, you will soon behold them in a miserable, degraded, and destitute condition.

The intentions of federal officials who favored the extension of state laws are revealed in a letter written to Jackson by General Coffee. Referring to the Cherokees, Coffee remarked:

Deprive the chiefs of the power they now possess, take from them their own code of laws, and reduce them to plain citizenship... and they will soon determine to move, and then there will be no difficulty in getting the poor Indians to give their consent. All this will be done by the State of Georgia if the U. States do not interfere with her law—... This will of course silence those in our country who constantly seek for causes to complain—It may indeed turn them loose upon Georgia, but that matters not, it is Georgia who clamors for the Indian lands, and she alone is entitled to the blame if any there be.

Even before the laws were extended, the threat of state jurisdiction was used in confidential "talks" to the chiefs. After the states had acted, the secretary of war instructed each Indian agent to explain to his charges the meaning of state jurisdiction and to inform them that the President could not protect them against the enforcement of the laws. Although the Supreme Court, in *Worcester* vs. *Georgia*, decided that the state had no right to extend its laws over the Cherokee nation, the Indian tribes being "domestic dependent nations" with limits defined by treaty, the President refused to enforce this decision. There was only one means by which the government might have made "John Marshall's decision" effective— directing federal troops to exclude state officials and other intruders from the Indian domain. In January, 1832, the President informed an Alabama congressman that the United States government no longer assumed the right to remove citizens of Alabama from the Indian country. By this time, the soldiers who had protected the territory of the southeastern tribes against intruders had been withdrawn. In their unwearying efforts to pressure the Indians into ceding their lands, federal negotiators emphasized the terrors of state jurisdiction.

Congress in May, 1830, complemented the efforts of the states by appropriating $500,000 and authorizing the President to negotiate removal treaties with all the tribes east of the Mississippi. The vote on this bill was close in both houses. By skillful use of pamphlets, petitions, and lobbyists, missionary organizations had enlisted leading congressmen in their campaign against the administration's attempt to force the tribes to emigrate. In the congressional debates, opponents of the bill agreed that savage tribes were duty-bound to relinquish their hunting grounds to the agriculturist, but they argued that the southeastern tribes were no longer savage. In any case, such relinquishment must be made in a freely contracted treaty. The extension of state laws over the Indian country was coercion; this made the negotiation of a free contract impossible. Both supporters and opponents of the bill agreed on one cardinal point—the Indian's moral right to keep his land depended on his actual cultivation of it.

A logical corollary of vesting rights in land in proportion to cultivation was the reservation to individuals of as much land as they had improved at the time a treaty was signed. In 1816, Secretary of War William H. Crawford had proposed such reservations, or allotments, as a means of accommodating the removal policy to the program of assimiliation. According to Crawford's plan, individual Indians who had demonstrated their capacity for civilization by establishing farms and who were willing to become citizens should be given the option of keeping their cultivated lands, by fee simple title, rather than emigrating. This offer was expected to reconcile the property-loving half-breeds to the policy of emigration. It also recognized their superior claim, as cultivators, on the regard and generosity of the government. The proposal was based on the assumption that few of the Indians were sufficiently civilized to want to become full-time farmers or state citizens.

The Crawford policy was applied in the Cherokee treaties of 1817 and 1819 and the Choctaw treaty of 1820. These agreements offered fee simple allotments to heads of Indian families having improved lands within the areas ceded to the government. Only 311 Cherokees and eight Choctaws took advantage of the offer. This seemed to bear out the assumption that only a minority of the tribesmen would care to take allotments. Actually, these experiments were not reliable. In both cases, the tribes ceded only a fraction of their holdings. Comparatively few took allotments; but on the other hand, few emigrated. The majority simply remained within the diminished tribal territories east of the Mississippi.

The offer of fee simple allotments was an important feature of the negotiations with the tribes in the 1820s. When the extension of state laws made removal of the tribes imperative, it was to be expected that allotments would comprise part of the consideration offered for the ceded lands. Both the ideology which rationalized the removal policy and the conclusions erroneously drawn from experience with the earlier allotment treaties led government negotiators to assume that a few hundred allotments at most would be required.

The Choctaws were the first to cede their eastern lands. The treaty of Dancing Rabbit Creek, signed in September, 1830, provided for several types of allotments. Special reservations were given to the chiefs and their numerous family connections; a possible 1,600 allotments of 80 to 480 acres, in proportion to the size of the beneficiary's farm, were offered others who intended to emigrate. These were intended for sale to private persons or to the government, so that the Indian might get the maximum price for his improvements. The fourteenth article of the treaty offered any head of an Indian family who did not plan to emigrate the right to take up a quantity of land proportional to the number of his dependents. At the end of five years' residence those who received these allotments were to have fee simple title to their lands and become citizens. It was expected that approximately two hundred persons would take land under this article.

The Creeks refused to sign any agreements promising to emigrate, but their chiefs were persuaded that the only way to put an end to intrusions on their lands was to sign an allotment treaty. In March, 1832, a Creek delegation in Washington signed a treaty calling for the allotment of 320 acres to each head of a family, the granting of certain supplementary lands to the chiefs and to orphans, and the cession of the remaining territory to the United States. If the Indian owners remained on their allotments for five years, they were to receive fee simple titles and become citizens. Returning to Alabama, the chiefs informed their people that they had not actually sold the tribal lands but "had only made each individual their own guardian, that they might take care of their own possessions, and act as agents for themselves.

Unlike the Creeks, the Chickasaws were willing to admit the inevitability of removal. But they needed land east of the Mississippi on which they might live until they acquired a home in the west. The Chickasaw treaty of May, 1832, therefore, provided generous allotments for heads of families, ranging from 640 to 3,200 acres, depending on the size of the family and the number of its slaves. These allotments were to be auctioned publicly when the tribe emigrated and the owners compensated for their improvements out of the proceeds. Although the fullblood Chickasaws apparently approved of the plan for a collective sale of the allotments, the half-breeds, abetted by white traders and planters, persuaded the government to allow those who held allotments to sell them individually. An amended treaty of 1834 complied with the half-breeds' proposals. It further stipulated that leading half-breeds and the old chiefs of the tribe comprise a committee to determine the competence of individual Chickasaws to manage their property. Since the committee itself disposed of the lands of the "incompetents," this gave both protection to the unsophisticated and additional advantage fo the half-breeds.

Widespread intrusion on Indian lands began with the extension of state laws over the tribal domains. In the treaties of cession, the government promised to remove intruders, but its policy in this respect was vacillating and ineffective. Indians whose allotments covered valuable plantations proved anxious to promote the sale of their property by allowing buyers to enter the ceded territory as soon as possible. Once this group of whites was admitted, it became difficult to discriminate against others. Thus a large number of intruders settled among the Indians with the passive connivance of the War Department and the tribal leaders. The task of removing them was so formidable that after making a few gestures the government generally evaded its obligation. The misery of the common Indians, surrounded by intruders and confused by the disruption of tribal authority, was so acute that any method for securing their removal seemed worth trying. Furthermore, their emigration would serve the interest of white settlers, land speculators, and their representatives in Washington. The government therefore chose to facilitate the sale of allotments even before the Indians received fee simple title to them.

The right to sell his allotment was useful to the sophisticated tribesman with a large plantation. Such men were accustomed to selling their crops and hiring labor. Through their experience in treaty negotiations, they had learned to bargain over the price of lands. Many of them received handsome payment for their allotments. Some kept part of their holdings and remained in Alabama and Mississippi as planters—like other planters, practicing as land speculators on the side. Nearly all the Indians had some experience in trade, but to most of them the conception of land as a salable commodity was foreign. They had little notion of the exact meaning of an "acre" or the probable value of their allotments. The government confused them still further by parceling out the lands according to Anglo-American, rather than aboriginal notions of family structure and land ownership. Officials insisted, for example, that the "father" rather than the "mother" must be defined as head of the

family and righteously refused to take cogni-
zance of the fact that many of the "fathers"
had "a plurality of wives."

Under these conditions, it is not surprising
that the common Indian's legal freedom of
contract in selling his allotment did not
necessarily lead him to make the best bargain
possible in terms of his pecuniary interests.
Nor did the proceeds of the sales transform
each seller into an emigrant of large independent means. A right of property and freedom to contract for its sale did not automati-
cally invest the Indian owner with the habits,
values, and skills of a sober land speculator.
His acquisition of property and freedom actually increased his dependence on those
who traditionally mediated for him in contractual relations with white Americans.

Prominent among these mediators were
white men with Indian wives who made their
living as planters and traders in the Indian
nations, men from nearby settlements who
traded with the leading Indians or performed
legal services for them, and interpreters. In
the past, such individuals had been appropriately compensated for using their influence in favor of land cessions. It is likely that
their speculative foresight was in part responsible for the allotment features in the
treaties of the 1830's. When the process of
allotting lands to individuals began, these
speculative gentlemen made loans of whisky, muslin, horses, slaves, and other useful
commodities to the new property-owner.
They received in return the Indian's written
promise to sell his allotment to them as soon
as its boundaries were defined. Generally
they were on hand to help him locate it on
"desirable" lands. They, in turn, sold their
"interest" in the lands to men of capital.
Government agents encouraged the enterprising investor, since it was in the Indian's
interest and the government's policy that the
lands be sold and the tribes emigrate. Unfortunately, the community of interest among
the government, the speculator, and the Indian proved largely fictitious. The
speculator's interest in Indian lands led to
frauds which impoverished the Indians,

soiled the reputation of the government, and
retarded the emigration of the tribes.

An important factor in this series of complications was the government's fallacious
assumption that most of the "real Indians"
were anxious to emigrate. Under the Choctaw treaty, for example, registration for fee
simple allotments was optional, the government expecting no more than two hundred
registrants. When several hundred full-
bloods applied for lands, the Choctaw agent
assumed that they were being led astray by
"designing men" and told them they must
emigrate. Attorneys took up the Choctaw
claims, located thousands of allotments in
hopes that Congress would confirm them,
and supported their clients in Mississippi for
twelve to fifteen years while the government
debated and acted on the validity of the
claims. There was good reason for this de-
lay. Settlers and rival speculators, opposing
confirmation of the claims, advanced numerous depositions asserting that the attorneys, in their enterprising search for clients,
had materially increased the number of
claimants. Among the Creeks, the Upper
Towns, traditionally the conservative faction
of the tribe, refused to sell their allotments.
Since the Lower Towns proved more com-
pliant, speculators hired willing Indians from
the Lower Towns to impersonate the unwilling owners. They then bought the land from
the impersonators. The government judi-
ciously conducted several investigations of
these frauds, but in the end the speculators
outmaneuvered the investigators. Meanwhile, the speculators kept the Indians from
emigrating until their contracts were approved. Only the outbreak of fighting between starving Creeks and their settler
neighbors enabled the government, under
pretext of a pacification, to remove the tribe.

Besides embarrassing the government, the
speculators contributed to the demoralization
of the Indians. Universal complaint held that
after paying the tribesman for his land they
often borrowed back the money without serious intent of repaying it, or recovered it in
return for overpriced goods, of which a

popular article was whisky. Apprised of this situation, Secretary of War Lewis Cass replied that once the Indian had been paid for his land, the War Department had no authority to circumscribe his freedom to do what he wished with the proceeds.

Nevertheless, within their conception of the proper role of government, officials who dealt with the tribes tried to be helpful. Although the Indian must be left free to contract for the sale of his lands, the United States sent agents to determine the validity of the contracts. These agents sometimes refused to approve a contract that did not specify a fair price for the land in question. They also refused official sanction when it could not be shown that the Indian owner had at some time been in possession of the sum stipulated. This protective action on the part of the government, together with its several investigations into frauds in the sale of Indian lands, apparently did secure the payment of more money than the tribesmen might otherwise have had. But the effort was seriously hampered by the near impossibility of obtaining disinterested testimony.

In the dealing with the Chickasaws, the government managed to avoid most of the vexing problems which had arisen in executing the allotment program among their southeastern neighbors. This was due in part to the improvement of administrative procedures, in part to the methods adopted by speculators in Chickasaw allotments, and probably most of all to the inflated value of cotton lands during the period in which the Chickasaw territory was sold. Both the government and the Chickasaws recognized that the lands granted individuals under the treaty were generally to be sold, not settled. They therefore concentrated on provisions for supervising sales and safeguarding the proceeds. Speculators in Chickasaw lands, having abundant resources, paid an average price of $1.70 per acre. The Chickasaws thereby received a better return than the government did at its own auctions. The buyers' generosity may be attributed to their belief that the Chickasaw lands represented the last

first-rate cotton country within what were then the boundaries of the public domain. In their pursuit of a secure title, untainted by fraud, the capitalists operating in the Chickasaw cession established a speculators' claim association which settled disputes among rival purchasers. Thus they avoided the plots, counterplots, and mutual recriminations which had hampered both speculators and government in their dealings with the Creeks and Choctaws.

A superficially ironic consequence of the allotment policy as a method of acquiring land for white settlers was the fact that it facilitated the engrossment of land by speculators. With their superior command of capital and the influence it would buy, speculators acquired 80 to 90 per cent of the lands alloted to the southeastern tribesmen.

For most of the Indian beneficiaries of the policy, its most important consequence was to leave them landless. After selling their allotment, or a claim to it, they might take to the swamp, live for a while on the bounty of a still hopeful speculator, or scavenge on their settler neighbors. But ultimately most of them faced the alternative of emigration or destitution, and chose to emigrate. The machinations of the speculators and the hopes they nurtured that the Indians might somehow be able to keep a part of their allotted lands made the timing of removals less predictable than it might otherwise have been. This unpredictability compounded the evils inherent in a mass migration managed by a government committed to economy and unversed in the arts of economic planning. The result was the "Trail of Tears."

The spectacular frauds committed among the Choctaws and Creeks, the administrative complications they created and the impression they gave that certain self-styled champions of the people were consorting with the avaricious speculator gave the allotment policy a bad reputation. The administration rejected it in dealing with the Cherokees, and the policy was not revived on any considerable scale until 1854, when it was applied, with similar consequences, to the Indians of

Kansas. In the 1880's, when allotment in severalty became a basic feature of American Indian policy, the "civilized tribes," then in Oklahoma, strenuously resisted its application to them. They cited their memories of the 1830's as an important reason for their intransigence.

The allotment treaties of the 1830's represent an attempt to apply Anglo-American notions of justice, which enshrined private property in land and freedom of contract as virtually absolute values, to Indian tribes whose tastes and traditions were otherwise. Their history illustrates the limitations of intercultural application of the Golden Rule. In a more practical sense, the treaties typified an effort to force on the Indians the alternative of complete assimilation or complete segregation by placing individuals of varying levels of sophistication in situations where they must use the skills of businessmen or lose their means of livelihood. This policy secured tribal lands while preserving the forms of respect for property rights and freedom of contract, but it proved costly to both the government and the Indians.

How lightly that cost was reckoned, and how enduring the motives and rationalizations that gave rise to it, may be gathered from the subsequent experience of the southeastern tribes in Oklahoma. There, early in the twentieth century, the allotment policy was again enforced, with safeguards hardly more helpful to the unsophisticated than those of the 1830's. Once more, tribal land changed owners for the greater glory of liberty, civilization, and profit.

Slave Songs and Slave Consciousness

LAWRENCE W. LEVINE

By 1860 the black population in the United States stood at 4,441,830. Unlike the white ethnic minorities, the blacks and Indians encountered diminishing prospects of political liberty, economic viability, and social equality. Whether living in the North or South, bonded or free, the privileges and rights of the Afro-Americans gradually disappeared. From the end of colonial times to the beginning of the Civil War, slaves endured increasing obstacles to emancipation, even by the wish of their owners, and mounting difficulties in voluntary assembly for religious or other purposes. Free Negroes were disenfranchised and lost jobs to the new immigrants, especially the Irish.

Religion and music provided the blacks with means of coping with deprivation and oppression. As Professor Lawrence Levine shows in "Slave Songs and Slave Consciousness," spirituals and other songs, and religious faith helped the blacks to create a sense of community. The cultural integrity, partly African in origin, reflected in their music and worship inhibited the imposition of stereotyped images projected upon them by their masters. The vitality of these cultural forms belied the assumptions of the Caucasian majority that slaves were either childlike or brutal, acquiescent, gleeful or irrationally indignant in their servitude, and incapable or unappreciative of freedom.

Negroes in the United States, both during and after slavery, were anything but inarticulate. They sang songs, told stories, played verbal games, listened and responded to sermons, and expressed their aspirations, fears, and values through the medium of an oral tradition that had characterized the West African cultures from which their ancestors had come. By largely ignoring this tradition, much of which has been preserved, historians have rendered an articulate people historically inarticulate, and have allowed the record of their consciousness to go unexplored.

Having worked my way carefully through thousands of Negro songs, folktales, jokes, and games, I am painfully aware of the problems inherent in the use of such materials. They are difficult, often impossible, to date with any precision. Their geographical dis-

From *Anonymous Americans: Explorations in Nineteenth-Century Social History,* Tamara K. Hareven, editor. Copyright © 1971 by Prentice-Hall, Inc. Reprinted by permission of Prentice-Hall, Englewood Cliffs, N.J.

tribution is usually unclear. They were collected belatedly, most frequently by men and women who had little understanding of the culture from which they sprang, and little scruple about altering or suppressing them. Such major collectors as John Lomax, Howard Odum, and Newman White all admitted openly that many of the songs they collected were "unprintable" by the moral standards which guided them and presumably their readers. But historians have overcome imperfect records before. They have learned how to deal with altered documents, with consciously or unconsciously biased firsthand accounts, with manuscript collections that were deposited in archives only after being filtered through the overprotective hands of fearful relatives, and with the comparative lack of contemporary sources and the need to use their materials retrospectively. The challenge presented by the materials of folk and popular culture is neither totally unique nor insurmountable.

In this essay I want to illustrate the possible use of materials of this kind by discussing the contribution that an understanding of Negro songs can make to the recent debate over slave personality. In the process I will discuss several aspects of the literature and problems related to the use of slave songs.

The subject of Negro music in slavery has produced a large and varied literature, little of which has been devoted to questions of meaning and function. The one major exception is Miles Mark Fisher's 1953 study, *Negro Slave Songs in the United States,* which attempts to get at the essence of slave life through an analysis of slave songs. Unfortunately, Fisher's rich insights are too often marred by his rather loose scholarly standards, and despite its continuing value his study is in many respects an example of how *not* to use Negro songs. Asserting, correctly, that the words of slave songs "show both accidental and intentional errors of transmission," Fisher changes the words almost at will to fit his own image of their pristine form. Arguing persuasively that "transplanted Negroes continued to promote

their own culture by music," Fisher makes their songs part of an "African cult" which he simply wills into existence. Maintaining (again, I think, correctly), that "slave songs preserved in joyful strains the adjustment which Negroes made to their living conditions within the United States," Fisher traces the major patterns of that adjustment by arbitrarily dating these songs, apparently unperturbed by the almost total lack of evidence pertaining to the origins and introduction of individual slave songs.

Fisher aside, most other major studies of slave music have focused almost entirely upon musical structure and origin. This latter question especially has given rise to a long and heated debate. The earliest collectors and students of slave music were impressed by how different that music was from anything familiar to them. Following a visit to the Sea Islands in 1862, Lucy McKim despaired of being able "to express the entire character of these negro ballads by mere musical notes and signs. The odd turns made in the throat; and that curious rhythmic effect produced by single voices chiming in at different irregular intervals, seem almost as impossible to place on score, as the singing of birds, or the tones of an Aeolian Harp." Although some of these early collectors maintained, as did W. F. Allen in 1865, that much of the slave's music "might no doubt be traced to tunes which they have heard from the whites, and transformed to their own use, . . . their music . . . is rather European than African in its character," they more often stressed the distinctiveness of the Negro's music and attributed it to racial characteristics, African origins, and indigenous developments resulting from the slave's unique experience in the New World.

This tradition, which has had many influential twentieth-century adherents, was increasingly challenged in the early decades of this century. Such scholars as Newman White, Guy Johnson, and George Pullen Jackson argued that the earlier school lacked a comparative grounding in Anglo-American folk song. Comparing Negro spirituals with

Methodist and Baptist evangelical religious music of the late eighteenth and early nineteenth centuries, White, Johnson, and Jackson found similarities in words, subject matter, tunes, and musical structure. Although they tended to exaggerate both qualitatively and quantitatively the degrees of similarity, their comparisons were often a persuasive and important corrective to the work of their predecessors. But their studies were inevitably weakened by their ethnocentric assumption that similarities alone settled the argument over origins. Never could they contemplate the possibility that the direction of cultural diffusion might have been from black to white as well as the other way. In fact, insofar as white evangelical music departed from traditional Protestant hymnology and embodied or approached the complex rhythmic structure, the percussive qualities, the polymeter, the syncopation, the emphasis on overlapping call and response patterns that characterized Negro music both in West Africa and the New World, the possibility that it was influenced by slaves who attended and joined in the singing at religious meetings is quite high.

These scholars tended to use the similarities between black and white religious music to deny the significance of slave songs in still another way. Newman White, for example, argued that since white evangelical hymns also used such expression as "freedom," the "Promised Land," and the "Egyptian Bondage," "without thought of other than spiritual meaning," these images when they occurred in Negro spirituals could not have been symbolic "of the Negro's longing for physical freedom." The familiar process by which different cultural groups can derive varied meanings from identical images is enough to cast doubt on the logic of White's argument. In the case of white and black religious music, however, the problem may be much less complex, since it is quite possible that the similar images in the songs of both groups in fact served similar purposes. Many of those whites who flocked to the camp meetings of the Methodists and

Baptists were themselves on the social and economic margins of their society, and had psychic and emotional needs which, qualitatively, may not have been vastly different from those of black slaves. Interestingly, George Pullen Jackson, in his attempt to prove the white origin of Negro spirituals, makes exactly this point: "I may mention in closing the chief remaining argument of the die-hards for the Negro source of the Negro spirituals. . . . How could any, the argument runs, but a natively musical and solely oppressed race create such beautiful things as 'Swing Low,' 'Steal Away,' and 'Deep River'? . . . But were not the whites of the mountains and the hard-scrabble hill country also 'musical and oppressed'? . . . Yes, these whites were musical, and oppressed too. If their condition was any more tolerable than that of the Negroes, one certainly does not get that impression from any of their songs of release and escape." If this is true, the presence of similar images in white music would merely heighten rather than detract from the significance of these images in Negro songs. Clearly, the function and meaning of white religious music during the late eighteenth and early nineteenth centuries demands far more attention than it has received. In the interim, we must be wary of allowing the mere fact of similarities to deter us from attempting to comprehend the cultural dynamics of slave music.

Contemporary scholars, tending to transcend the more simplistic lines of the old debate, have focused upon the process of syncretism to explain the development of Negro music in the United States. The rich West African musical tradition common to almost all of the specific cultures from which Negro slaves came, the comparative cultural isolation in which large numbers of slaves lived, the tolerance and even encouragement which their white masters accorded to their musical activities, and the fact that, for all its differences, nothing in the European musical tradition with which they came into contact in America was totally alien to their own traditions—all these were conducive to a situation which allowed the slaves to retain a good deal of the integrity of their own musical heritage while fusing to it compatible elements of Anglo-American music. Slaves often took over entire white hymns and folk songs, as White and Jackson maintained, but altered them significantly in terms of words, musical structure, and especially performance before making them their own. The result was a hybrid with a strong African base.

One of the more interesting aspects of this debate over origins is that no one engaged in it, not even advocates of the white derivation theory, denied that the slaves possessed their own distinctive music. Newman White took particular pains to point out again and again that the notion that Negro song is purely an imitation of the white man's music "is fully as unjust and inaccurate, in the final analysis, as the Negro's assumption that his folk-song is entirely original." He observed that in the slaves' separate religious meetings they were free to do as they would with the music they first learned from the whites, with the result that their spirituals became "the greatest single outlet for the expression of the Negro folk-mind." Similarly, George Pullen Jackson, after admitting that he could find no white parallels for over two-thirds of the existing Negro spirituals, reasoned that these were produced by Negro singers in true folk fashion "by endless singing of heard tunes and by endless, inevitable and concomitant singing differentiation." Going even further, Jackson asserted that the lack of deep roots in Anglo-American culture left the black man "even freer than the white man to make songs over unconsciously as he sang . . . the free play has resulted in the very large number of songs which, though formed primarily in the white man's moulds, have lost all recognizable relationship to known individual white-sung melodic entities." This debate over origins indicates clearly that a belief in the direct continuity of African musical traditions or in the process of syncretism is not a necessary prerequisite to the conclusion that the Negro slaves' music was their own, regardless of where they received

the components out of which it was fashioned; a conclusion which is crucial to any attempt to utilize these songs as an aid in reconstructing the slaves' consciousness.

Equally important is the process by which slave songs were created and transmitted. When James McKim asked a freedman on the Sea Islands during the Civil War where the slaves got their songs, the answer was eloquently simple: "Dey make em, sah." Precisely *how* they made them worried and fascinated Thomas Wentworth Higginson, who became familiar with slave music through the singing of the black Union soldiers in his Civil War regiment. Were their songs, he wondered, a "conscious and definite" product of "some leading mind," or did they grow "by gradual accretion, in an almost unconscious way"? A freedman rowing Higginson and some of his troops between the Sea Islands helped to resolve the problem when he described a spiritual which he had a hand in creating:

Once we boys went for some rice and de nigger-driver he keep a-callin' on us; and I say, "O de ole nigger-driver!" Den anudder said, "Fust ting my mammy tole me was, notin' so bad as nigger-driver." Den I made a sing, just puttin' a word, and den anudder word.

He then began to sing his song:

O, de ole nigger-driver!
  O, gwine away!
Fust ting my mammy tell me,
  O, gwine away!

Tell me 'bout de nigger-driver,
  O, gwine away!
Nigger-driver second devil
  O, gwine away!

Higginson's black soldiers, after a moment's hesitation, joined in the singing of a song they had never heard before as if they had long been familiar with it. "I saw," Higginson concluded, "how easily a new 'sing' took root among them."

This spontaneity, this sense of almost instantaneous community which so impressed Higginson, constitutes a central element in every account of slave singing. The English musician Henry Russell, who lived in the United States in the 1830's, was forcibly struck by the ease with which a slave congregation in Vicksburg, Mississippi, took a "fine old psalm tune" and, by suddenly and spontaneously accelerating the tempo, transformed it "into a kind of negro melody." "Us old heads," an ex-slave told Jeanette Robinson Murphy, "use ter make 'em up on de spurn of de moment. Notes is good enough for you people, but us likes a mixtery." Her account of the creation of a spiritual is typical and important:

We'd all be at the "prayer house" de Lord's day, and de white preacher he's splain de word and read whar Esekial done say—

Dry bones gwine ter lib ergin.

And, honey, de Lord would come a-shinin' thoo dem pages and revive dis ole nigger's heart, and I'd jump up dar and den and holler and shout and sing and pat, and dey would all cotch de words and I'd sing it to some ole shout song I'd heard 'em sing from Africa, and dey'd all take it up and keep at it, and keep a-addin' to it, and den it would be a spiritual.

This "internal" account has been verified again and again by the descriptions of observers, many of whom were witnessing not slave services but religious meetings of rural southern Negroes long after emancipation. The essential continuity of the Negro folk process in the more isolated sections of the rural South through the early decades of the twentieth century makes these accounts relevant for the slave period as well. Natalie Curtis Burlin, whose collection of spirituals is musically the most accurate one we have, and who had a long and close acquaintance with Negro music, never lost her sense of awe at the process by which these songs were molded. On a hot July Sunday in rural Virginia, she sat in a Negro meeting house listening to the preacher deliver his prayer, interrupted now and then by an "O Lord!" or "Amen, Amen" from the congregation.

Minutes passed, long minutes of strange intensity. The mutterings, the ejaculations, grew louder, more dramatic, till suddenly I felt the creative thrill dart through the people like an electric vibration, that same half-audible hum arose,—emotion was gathering atmospherically as clouds gather—and then, up from the depths of some "sinner's" remorse and imploring came a pitiful little plea, a real "moan," sobbed in musical cadence. From somewhere in that bowed gathering another voice improvised a response: the plea sounded again, louder this time and more impassioned; then other voices joined in the answer, shaping it into a musical phrase; and so, before our ears, as one might say, from this molten metal of music a new song was smithied out, composed then and there by no one in particular and by everyone in general.

Clifton Furness has given us an even more graphic description. During a visit to an isolated South Carolina plantation in 1926, he attended a prayer meeting held in the old slave cabins. The preacher began his reading of the Scriptures slowly, then increased his tempo and emotional fervor, assuring his flock that "Gawd's lightnin' gwine strike! Gawd's thunder swaller de ert!"

Gradually moaning became audible in the shadowy corners where the women sat. Some patted their bundled babies in time to the flow of the words, and began swaying backward and forward. Several men moved their feet alternately, in strange syncopation. A rhythm was born, almost without reference to the words that were being spoken by the preacher. It seemed to take shape almost visibly, and grow. I was gripped with the feeling of a mass-intelligence, a self-conscious entity, gradually informing the crowd and taking possession of every mind there, including my own.

In the midst of this increasing intensity, a black man sitting directly in front of Furness, his head bowed, his body swaying, his feet patting up and down, suddenly cried out: "Git right—sodger! Git right—sodger! Git right-wit Gawd!"

Instantly the crowd took it up, moulding a melody out of half-formed familiar phrases based upon a spiritual tune, hummed here and there among the crowd. A distinct melodic outline became more and more prominent, shaping itself around the central theme of the words, "Git right, sodger!"

Scraps of other words and tunes were flung into the medley of sound by individual singers from time to time, but the general trend was carried on by a deep undercurrent, which appeared to be stronger than the mind of any individual present, for it bore the mass of improvised harmony and rhythms into the most effective climax of incremental repetition that I have ever heard. I felt as if some conscious plan or purpose were carrying us along, call it mob-mind, communal composition, or what you will.

Shortly after the Civil War, Elizabeth Kilham witnessed a similar scene among the freedmen, and described it in terms almost identical to those used by observers many years later. "A fog seemed to fill the church," she wrote, ". . . an invisible power seemed to hold us in its iron grasp; . . . A few moments more, and I think we should have shrieked in unison with the crowd."

These accounts and others like them make it clear that spirituals both during and after slavery were the product of an improvisational communal consciousness. They were not, as some observers thought, totally new creations, but were forged out of many preexisting bits of old songs mixed together with snatches of new tunes and lyrics and fit into a fairly traditional but never wholly static metrical pattern. They were, to answer Higginson's question, *simultaneously* the result of individual and mass creativity. They were products of that folk process which has been called "communal re-creation," through which older songs are constantly recreated into essentially new entities. Anyone who has read through large numbers of Negro songs is familiar with this process. Identical or slightly varied stanzas appear in song after song; identical tunes are made to accommodate completely different sets of lyrics; the same song appears in different collections in widely varied forms. In 1845 a traveler observed that the only permanent elements in Negro song were the music and the chorus. "The blacks themselves leave out old stanzas, and introduce new ones at pleasure. Travelling through the South, you may, in passing from Virginia to Louisiana, hear the same tune a hundred times, but sel-

dom the same words accompanying it." Another observer noted in 1870 that during a single religious meeting the freedmen would often sing the words of one spiritual to several different tunes, and then take a tune that particularly pleased them and fit the words of several different songs to it. Slave songs, then, were never static; at no time did Negroes create a "final" version of any spiritual. Always the community felt free to alter and recreate them.

The two facts that I have attempted to establish thus far—that slave music, regardless of its origins, was a distinctive cultural form, and that it was created or constantly recreated through a communal process—are essential if one is to justify the use of these songs as keys to slave consciousness. But these facts in themselves say a good deal about the nature and quality of slave life and personality. That black slaves could create and continually recreate songs marked by the poetic beauty, the emotional intensity, the rich imagery which characterized the spirituals—songs which even one of the most devout proponents of the white man's origins school admits are "the most impressive religious folk songs in our language"—should be enough to make us seriously question recent theories which conceive of slavery as a closed system which destroyed the vitality of the Negro and left him a dependent child. For all of its horrors, slavery was never so complete a system of psychic assault that it prevented the slaves from carving out independent cultural forms. It never pervaded all of the interstices of their minds and their culture, and in those gaps they were able to create an independent art form and a distinctive voice. If North American slavery eroded the African's linguistic and institutional life, if it prevented him from preserving and developing his rich heritage of graphic and plastic art, it nevertheless allowed him to continue and to develop the patterns of verbal art which were so central to his past culture. Historians have not yet come to terms with what the continuance of the oral tradition meant to blacks in slavery.

In Africa, songs, tales, proverbs, and verbal games served the dual function of not only preserving communal values and solidarity, but also of providing occasions for the individual to transcend, at least symbolically, the inevitable restrictions of his environment and his society by permitting him to express deeply held feelings which he ordinarily was not allowed to verbalize. Among the Ashanti and the Dahomeans, for example, periods were set aside when the inhabitants were encouraged to gather together and, through the medium of song, dance, and tales, to openly express their feelings about each other. The psychological release this afforded seems to have been well understood. "You know that everyone has a *sunsum* (soul) that may get hurt or knocked about or become sick, and so make the body ill," an Ashanti high priest explained to the English anthropologist R. S. Rattray:

Very often . . . ill health is caused by the evil and the hate that another has in his head against you. Again, you too may have hatred in your head against another, because of something that person has done to you, and that, too, causes your *sunsum* to fret and become sick. Our forbears knew this to be the case, and so they ordained a time, once every year, when every man and woman, free man and slave, should have freedom to speak out just what was in their head, to tell their neighbours just what they thought of them, and of their actions, and not only their neighbours, but also the king or chief. When a man has spoken freely thus, he will feel his *sunsum* cool and quieted, and the *sunsum* of the other person against whom he has now openly spoken will be quieted also.

Utilization of verbal art for this purpose was widespread throughout Africa, and was not confined to those ceremonial occasions when one could directly state one's feelings. Through innuendo, metaphor, and circumlocution, Africans could utilize their songs as outlets for individual release without disturbing communal solidarity.

There is abundant internal evidence that the verbal art of the slaves in the United States served many of these traditional functions. Just as the process by which the spirituals were created allowed for simultaneous individual and communal creativity,

so their very structure provided simultaneous outlets for individual and communal expression. The overriding antiphonal structure of the spirituals—the call and response pattern which Negroes brought with them from Africa and which was reinforced by the relatively similar white practice of "lining out" hymns—placed the individual in continual dialogue with his community, allowing him at one and the same time to preserve his voice as a distinct entity and to blend it with those of his fellows. Here again slave music confronts us with evidence which indicates that however seriously the slave system may have diminished the strong sense of community that had bound Africans together, it never totally destroyed it or left the individual atomized and emotionally and psychically defenseless before his white masters. In fact, the form and structure of slave music presented the slave with a potential outlet for his individual feelings even while it continually drew him back into the communal presence and permitted him the comfort of basking in the warmth of the shared assumptions of those around him.

Those "shared assumptions" can be further examined by an analysis of the content of slave songs. Our preoccupation in recent years with the degree to which the slaves actually resembled the "Sambo" image held by their white masters has obscured the fact that the slaves developed images of their own which must be consulted and studied before any discussion of slave personality can be meaningful. The image of the trickster, who through cunning and unscrupulousness prevails over his more powerful antagonists, pervades slave tales. The trickster figure is rarely encountered in the slave's religious songs, though its presence is sometimes felt in the slave's many allusions to his narrow escapes from the devil.

The Devil's mad and I'm glad,
He lost the soul he thought he had.

Ole Satan toss a ball at me.
O me no weary yet . . .

Him tink de ball would hit my soul.
O me no weary yet . . .

De ball for hell and I for heaven.
O me no weary yet . . .

Ole Satan thought he had a mighty aim;
He missed my soul and caught my sins.
Cry Amen, cry Amen, cry Amen to God!

He took my sins upon his back;
Went muttering and grumbling down to hell.
Cry Amen, cry Amen, cry Amen to God!

The single most persistent image the slave songs contain, however, is that of the chosen people. The vast majority of the spirituals identify the singers as "de people dat is born of God," "We are the people of God," "we are de people of de Lord," "I really do believe I'm a child of God," "I'm a child ob God, wid my soul sot free," "I'm born of God, I know I am." Nor is there ever any doubt that "To the promised land I'm bound to go," "I walk de heavenly road," "Heav'n shall-a be my home," "I gwine to meet my Saviour," "I seek my Lord and I find Him," "I'll hear the trumpet sound/In that morning."

The force of this image cannot be diminished by the observation that similar images were present in the religious singing of the white evangelical churches during the first half of the nineteenth century. White Americans could be expected to sing of triumph and salvation, given their long-standing heritage of the idea of a chosen people which was reinforced in this era by the belief in inevitable progress and manifest destiny, the spread-eagle oratory, the bombastic folklore, and, paradoxically, the deep insecurities concomitant with the tasks of taming a continent and developing an identity. But for this same message to be expressed by Negro slaves who were told endlessly that they were members of the lowliest of races *is* significant. It offers an insight into the kinds of barriers the slaves had available to them against the internalization of the stereotyped images their masters held and attempted consciously and unconsciously to foist upon them.

The question of the chosen people image leads directly into the larger problem of what role religion played in the songs of the slave. Writing in 1862, James McKim noted that the songs of the Sea Island freedmen "are all religious, barcaroles and all. I speak without exception. So far as I heard or was told of their singing, it was all religious." Others who worked with recently emancipated slaves recorded the same experience, and Colonel Higginson reported that he rarely heard his troops sing a profane or vulgar song. With a few exceptions, "all had a religious motive." In spite of this testimony, there can be little doubt that the slaves sang nonreligious songs. In 1774, an English visitor to the United States, after his first encounter with slave music, wrote in his journal: "In their songs they generally relate the usage they have received from their Masters or Mistresses in a very satirical stile and manner." Songs fitting this description can be found in the nineteenth-century narratives of fugitive slaves. Harriet Jacobs recorded that during the Christmas season the slaves would ridicule stingy whites by singing:

Poor Massa, so dey say;
Down in de heel, so dey say;
Got no money, so dey say;
God A'mighty bress you, so dey say.

"Once in a while among a mass of nonsense and wild frolic," Frederick Douglass noted, "a sharp hit was given to the meanness of slaveholders."

We raise de wheat,
Dey gib us de corn;
We bake de bread,
Dey gib us de crust;
We sif de meal,
Dey gib us de huss;
We peal de meat,
Dey gib us de skin;
And dat's de way
Dey take us in;
We skim de pot,
Dey gib us de liquor,
And say dat's good enough for nigger.

Both of these songs are in the African tradition of utilizing song to bypass both internal and external censors and give vent to feelings which could be expressed in no other form. Nonreligious songs were not limited to the slave's relations with his masters, however, as these rowing songs, collected by contemporary white observers, indicate:

We are going down to Georgia, boys
    Aye, aye.
  To see the pretty girls, boys,
    Yoe, yoe.
We'll give 'em a pint of brandy, boys,
    Aye, aye.
  And a hearty kiss, besides, boys,
    Yoe, yoe.

Jenny shake her toe at me,
  Jenny gone away;
Jenny shake her toe at me,
  Jenny gone away.
Hurrah! Miss Susy, oh!
  Jenny gone away;
Hurrah! Miss Susy, oh!
  Jenny gone away

The variety of nonreligious songs in the slave's repertory was wide. There were songs of in-group and out-group satire, songs of nostalgia, nonsense songs, songs of play and work and love. Nevertheless, our total stock of these songs is very small. It is possible to add to these by incorporating such post-bellum secular songs which have an authentic slavery ring to them as "De Blue-Tail Fly," with its ill-concealed satisfaction at the death of a master, or the ubiquitous

My old Mistiss promise me,
W'en she died, she's set me free,
She lived so long dat 'er head got bal',
An' she give out'n de notion a dyin' at all.

The number can be further expanded by following Constance Rourke's suggestion that we attempt to disentangle elements of Negro origin from those of white creation in the "Ethiopian melodies" of the white minstrel shows, many of which were similar to the songs I have just quoted. Either of these possibilities, however, forces the historian to work with sources far more potentially spurious than those with which he normally is comfortable.

Spirituals, on the other hand, for all the problems associated with their being filtered through white hands before they were published, and despite the many errors in transcription that inevitably occurred, constitute a much more satisfactory source. They were collected by the hundreds directly from slaves and freedmen during the Civil War and the decades immediately following, and although they came from widely different geographical areas they share a common structure and content, which seems to have been characteristic of Negro music wherever slavery existed in the United States. It is possible that we have a greater number of religious than nonreligious songs because slaves were more willing to sing these ostensibly innocent songs to white collectors who in turn were more anxious to record them, since they fit easily with their positive and negative images of the Negro. But I would argue that the vast preponderance of spirituals over any other sort of slave music, rather than being merely the result of accident or error, is instead an accurate reflection of slave culture during the ante-bellum period. Whatever songs the slaves may have sung before their wholesale conversion to Christianity in the late eighteenth and early nineteenth centuries, by the latter century spirituals were quantitatively and qualitatively their most significant musical creation. In this form of expression slaves found a medium which resembled in many important ways the world view they had brought with them from Africa, and afforded them the possibility of both adapting to and transcending their situation.

It is significant that the most common form of slave music we know of is sacred song. I use the term "sacred" not in its present usage as something antithetical to the secular world; neither the slaves nor their African forebears ever drew modernity's clear line between the sacred and the secular. The uses to which spirituals were put are an unmistakable indication of this. They were not sung solely or even primarily in churches or praise houses, but were used as rowing songs, field songs, work songs, and social songs. On the Sea Islands during the Civil War, Lucy McKim heard the spiritual "Poor Rosy" sung in a wide variety of contexts and tempos.

On the water, the oars dip "Poor Rosy" to an even andante; a stout boy and girl at the hominy-mill will make the same "Poor Rosy" fly, to keep up with the whirling stone; and in the evening, after the day's work is done, "Heab'n shall-a be my home" [the final line of each stanza] peals up slowly and mournfully from the distant quarters.

For the slaves, then, songs of God and the mythic heroes of their religion were not confined to any specific time or place, but were appropriate to almost every situation. It is in this sense that I use the concept sacred—not to signify a rejection of the present world but to describe the process of incorporating within this world all the elements of the divine. The religious historian Mircea Eliade, whose definition of sacred has shaped my own, has maintained that for men in traditional societies religion is a means of extending the world spatially upward so that communication with the other world becomes ritually possible, and extending it temporally backward so that the paradigmatic acts of the gods and mythical ancestors can be continually re-enacted and indefinitely recoverable. By creating sacred time and space, man can perpetually live in the presence of his gods, can hold on to the certainty that within one's own lifetime "rebirth" is continually possible, and can impose order on the chaos of the universe. "Life," as Eliade puts it, "is lived on a twofold plane; it takes its course as human existence and, at the same time, shares in a trans-human life, that of the cosmos or the gods."

This notion of sacredness gets at the essence of the spirituals, and through them at the essence of the slave's world view. Denied the possibility of achieving an adjustment to the external world of the ante-bellum South which involved meaningful forms of personal integration, attainment of status, and feelings of individual worth that all human beings crave and need, the slaves created a new world by transcending the narrow confines of the one in which they were forced to live. They extended the boundaries of their restrictive universe backward until it fused with the world of the Old Testament, and upward until it became one with the world beyond. The spirituals are the record of a people who found the status, the harmony, the values, the order they needed to survive by internally creating an expanded universe, by literally willing themselves reborn. In this respect I agree with the anthropologist Paul Radin that

The ante-bellum Negro was not converted to God. He converted God to himself. In the Christian God he found a fixed point and he needed a fixed point, for both within and outside of himself, he could see only vacillation and endless shifting.... There was no other safety for people faced on all sides by doubt and the threat of personal disintegration, by the thwarting of instincts and the annihilation of values.

The confinement of much of the slave's new world to dream and fantasies does not free us from the historical obligation of examining its contours, weighing its implications for the development of the slave's psychic and emotional structure, and eschewing the kind of facile reasoning that leads Professor Elkins to imply that, since the slaves had no alternatives open to them, their fantasy life was "limited to catfish and watermelons." Their spirituals indicate clearly that there *were* alternatives open to them—alternatives which they themselves fashioned out of the fusion of their African heritage and their new religion—and that their fantasy life was so rich and so important to them that it demands understanding if we are even to begin to comprehend their inner world.

The God the slaves sang of was neither remote nor abstract, but as intimate, personal, and immediate as the gods of Africa had been. "O when I talk I talk wid God,"

"Mass Jesus is my bosom friend," "I'm goin' to walk with [talk with, live with, see] King Jesus by myself, by myself," were refrains that echoed through the spirituals.

In de mornin' when I rise
  Tell my Jesus huddy [howdy] oh,
I wash my hands in de mornin' glory,
  Tell my Jesus huddy oh.

Gwine to argue wid de Father and chatter wid
  de son,
The last trumpet shall sound, I'll be there.
Gwine talk 'bout de bright world dey des' come
  from,
The last trumpet shall sound, I'll be there.

Gwine to write to Massa Jesus,
To send some Valiant soldier
To turn back Pharaoh's army, Hallelu!

The heroes of the Scriptures—"Sister Mary," "Brudder Jonah," "Brudder Moses," "Brudder Daniel"—were greeted with similar intimacy and immediacy. In the world of the spirituals, it was not the masters and mistresses but God and Jesus and the entire pantheon of Old Testament figures who set the standards, established the precedents, and defined the values; who, in short, constituted the "significant others." The world described by the slave songs was a black world in which no reference was ever made to any white contemporaries. The slave's positive reference group was composed entirely of his own peers: his mother, father, sister, brother, uncles, aunts, preacher, fellow "sinners" and "mourners" of whom he sang endlessly, to whom he sent messages via the dying, and with whom he was reunited joyfully in the next world.

The same sense of sacred time and space which shaped the slave's portraits of his gods and heroes also made his visions of the past and future immediate and compelling. Descriptions of the Crucifixion communicate a sense of the actual presence of the singers: "Dey pierced Him in the side . . . Dey nail Him to de cross . . . Dey rivet His feet . . . Dey hanged him high . . . Dey stretch Him wide. . . ."

Oh sometimes it causes me to
  tremble,—tremble,
  —tremble,
Were you there when they crucified my Lord?

The Slave's "shout"—that counterclockwise, shuffling dance which frequently occurred after the religious service and lasted long into the night—often became a medium through which the ecstatic dancers were transformed into actual participants in historic actions: Joshua's army marching around the walls of Jericho, the children of Israel following Moses out of Egypt.

The thin line between time dimensions is nowhere better illustrated than in the slave's visions of the future, which were, of course, a direct negation of his present. Among the most striking spirituals are those which pile detail upon detail in describing the Day of Judgment: "You'll see de world on fire . . . see de element a meltin', . . . see the stars a fallin' . . . see the moon a bleedin' . . . see the forked lightning, . . . Hear the rumblin' thunder . . . see the righteous marching, . . . see my Jesus coming . . . ," and the world to come where "Dere's no sun to burn you . . . no hard trials . . . no whips a crackin' . . . no stormy weather . . . no tribulation . . . no evil-doers . . . All is gladness in de Kingdom." This vividness was matched by the slave's certainty that he would partake of the triumph of judgment and the joys of the new world:

Dere's room enough, room enough, room
  enough in de heaven, my Lord
Room enough, room enough, I can't stay
  behind.

Continually, the slaves sang of reaching out beyond the world that confined them, of seeing Jesus "in de wilderness," of praying "in de lonesome valley," of breathing in the freedom of the mountain peaks:

Did yo' ever
Stan' on mountun,
Wash yo' han's
In a cloud?

Continually, they held out the possibility of imminent rebirth; "I look at de worl' an' de worl' look new, . . . I look at my hands an' they look so too . . . I looked at my feet, my feet was too."

These possibilities, these certainties were not surprising. The religious revivals which swept large numbers of slaves into the Christian fold in the late eighteenth and early nineteenth centuries were based upon a *practical* (not necessarily theological) Arminianism: God would save all who believed in Him; Salvation was there for all to take hold of if they would. The effects of this message upon the slaves who were exposed to and converted by it have been passed over too easily by historians. Those effects are illustrated graphically in the spirituals which were the products of these revivals and which continued to spread the evangelical word long after the revivals had passed into history.

The religious music of the slaves is almost devoid of feelings of depravity or unworthiness, but is rather, as I have tried to show, pervaded by a sense of change, transcendence, ultimate justice, and personal worth. The spirituals have been referred to as "sorrow songs," and in some respects they were. The slaves sang of "rollin' thro' an unfriendly world," of being "a-trouble in de mind," of living in a world which was a "howling wilderness," "a hell to me," of feeling like a "motherless child," "a po' little orphan chile in de worl'," a "home-e-less child," of fearing that "Trouble will bury me down.'"

But these feelings were rarely pervasive or permanent; almost always they were overshadowed by a triumphant note of affirmation. Even so despairing a wail as "Nobody Knows the Trouble I've Had" could suddenly have its mood transformed by lines like: "One morning I was a-walking down, . . . Saw some berries a-hanging down, . . . I pick de berry and I suck de juice, . . . Just as sweet as de honey in de comb." Similarly, amid the deep sorrow of "Sometimes I feel like a Motherless chile,"

sudden release could come with the lines: "Sometimes I feel like A eagle in de air. . . . Spread my wings an'/Fly, fly, fly." Slaves spent little time singing of the horrors of hell or damnation. Their songs of the Devil, quoted earlier, pictured a harsh but almost semicomic figure (often, one suspects, a surrogate for the white man), over whom they triumphed with reassuring regularity. For all their inevitable sadness, slave songs were characterized more by a feeling of confidence than of despair. There was confidence that contemporary power relationships were not immutable: "Did not old Pharaoh get lost, get lost, get lost, . . . get lost in the Red Sea?"; confidence in the possibilities of instantaneous change: "Jesus make de dumb to speak. . . . Jesus make de cripple walk. . . . Jesus give de blind his sight. . . . Jesus do most anything"; confidence in the rewards of persistence: "Keep a' inching along like a poor inch-worm,/Jesus will come by'nd bye"; confidence that nothing could stand in the way of the justice they would receive: "You kin hender me here, but you can't do it dah," "O no man, no man, no man can hinder me"; confidence in the prospects of the future: "We'll walk de golden streets/Of de New Jerusalem." Religion, the slaves sang, "is good for anything, . . . Religion make you happy, . . . Religion gib me patience . . . O member, get Religion . . . Religion is so sweet."

The slaves often pursued the "sweetness" of their religion in the face of many obstacles. Becky Ilsey, who was 16 when she was emancipated, recalled many years later:

'Fo' de war when we'd have a meetin' at night, wuz mos' always 'way in de woods or de bushes some whar so de white folks couldn't hear, an' when dey'd sing a spiritual an' de spirit 'gin to shout some de elders would go 'mongst de folks an' put dey han' over day mouf an' some times put a clof in dey mouf an' say: "Spirit don talk so loud or de patterol break us up." You know dey had white patterols what went 'roun' at night to see de niggers didn't cut up no devilment, an' den de meetin' would break up an' some would go to one house an' some to er nudder an' dey would groan er w'ile, den go home.

Elizabeth Ross Hite testified that although she and her fellow slaves on a Louisiana plantation were Catholics, "lots didn't like that 'ligion."

We used to hide behind some bricks and hold church ourselves. You see, the Catholic preachers from France wouldn't let us shout, and the Lawd done said you gotta shout if you want to be saved. That's in the Bible.

Sometimes we held church all night long, 'til way in the mornin'. We burned some grease in a can for the preacher to see the Bible by. . . .

See, our master didn't like us to have much 'ligion, said it made us lag in our work. He jest wanted us to be Catholicses on Sundays and go to mass and not study 'bout nothin' like that on week days. He didn't want us shoutin' and moanin' all day'-long, but you gotta shout and you gotta moan if you wants to be saved.

The slaves clearly craved the affirmation and promise of their religion. It would be a mistake, however, to see this urge as exclusively otherworldly. When Thomas Wentworth Higginson observed that the spirituals exhibited "nothing but patience for this life,—nothing but triumph in the next," he, and later observers who elaborated upon this judgment, were indulging in hyperbole. Although Jesus was ubiquitous in the spirituals, it was not invariably the Jesus of the New Testament of whom the slaves sang, but frequently a Jesus transformed into an Old Testament warrior: "Mass' Jesus" who engaged in personal combat with the Devil; "King Jesus" seated on a milk-white horse with sword and shield in hand. "Ride on, King Jesus," "Ride on, conquering King," "The God I serve is a man of war," the slaves sang. This transformation of Jesus is symptomatic of the slaves' selectivity in choosing those parts of the Bible which were to serve as the basis of their religious consciousness. Howard Thurman, a Negro minister who as a boy had the duty of reading the Bible to his grandmother, was perplexed by her refusal to allow him to read from the Epistles of Paul.

When at length I asked the reason, she told me that during the days of slavery, the minister (white) on the plantation was always preaching from the Pauline letters—"Slaves, be obedient to your masters," etc. "I vowed to myself," she said, "that if freedom ever came and I learned to read, I would never read that part of the Bible!"

Nor, apparently, did this part of the Scriptures ever constitute a vital element in slave songs or sermons. The emphasis of the spirituals, as Higginson himself noted, was upon the Old Testament and the exploits of the Hebrew children. It is important that Daniel and David and Joshua and Jonah and Moses and Noah, all of whom fill the lines of the spirituals, were delivered in *this* world and delivered in ways which struck the imagination of the slaves. Over and over their songs dwelt upon the spectacle of the Red Sea opening to allow the Hebrew slaves past before inundating the mighty armies of the Pharaoh. They lingered delightedly upon the image of little David humbling the great Goliath with a stone—a pretechnological victory which post-bellum Negroes were to expand upon in their songs of John Henry. They retold in endless variation the stories of the blind and humbled Samson bringing down the mansions of his conquerors; of the ridiculed Noah patiently building the ark which would deliver him from the doom of a mocking world; of the timid Jonah attaining freedom from his confinement through faith. The similarity of these tales to the situation of the slave was too clear for him not to see it; too clear for us to believe that the songs had no worldly content for the black man in bondage. "O my Lord delivered Daniel," the slaves observed, and responded logically: "O why not deliver me, too?"

He delivered Daniel from de lion's den,
  Jonah from de belly ob de whale,
And de Hebrew children from de fiery furnace,
  And why not every man?

These lines state as clearly as anything can the manner in which the sacred world of the slaves was able to fuse the precedents of the past, the conditions of the present, and the promise of the future into one connected reality. In this respect there was always a latent and symbolic element of protest in the slave's religious songs which frequently became overt and explicit. Frederick Douglass asserted that for him and many of his fellow slaves the song, "O Canaan, sweet Canaan,/I am bound for the land of Canaan," symbolized "something more than a hope of reaching heaven. We meant to reach the *North,* and the North was our Canaan," and he wrote that the lines of another spiritual, "Run to Jesus, shun the danger,/I don't expect to stay much longer here," had a double meaning which first suggested to him the thought of escaping from slavery. Similarly, when the black troops in Higginson's regiment sang:

We'll soon be free, [three times]
When de Lord will call us home.

a young drummer boy explained to him, "Dey think *de Lord* mean for say *de Yankees.*" Nor is there any reason to doubt that slaves could have used their songs as a means of secret communication. An ex-slave told Lydia Parrish that when he and his fellow slaves "suspicioned" that one of their number was telling tales to the driver, they would sing lines like the following while working in the field:

O Judyas he wuz a 'ceitful man
He went an' betray a mos' innocen' man.
Fo' thirty pieces a silver dat it wuz done
He went in de woods an' e' self he hung.

And it is possible, as many writers have argued, that such spirituals as the commonly heard "Steal away, steal away, steal away to Jesus!" were used as explicit calls to secret meetings.

But it is not necessary to invest the spirituals with a secular function only at the price of divesting them of their religious content, as Miles Mark Fisher has done. While we may make such clear-cut distinctions, I have tried to show that the slaves did not. For them religion never constituted a simple escape from this world, because their conception of the world was more expansive than modern man's. Nowhere is this better illustrated than

during the Civil War itself. While the war gave rise to such new spirituals as "Before I'd be a slave/I'd be buried in my grave,/And go home to my Lord and be saved!" or the popular "Many thousand Go," with its jubilant rejection of all the facets of slave life— "No more peck o' corn for me, . . . No more driver's lash for me, . . . No more pint o' salt for me, . . . No more hundred lash for me, . . . No more mistress' call for me"—the important thing was not that large numbers of slaves now could create new songs which openly expressed their views of slavery; that was to be expected. More significant was the ease with which their old songs fit their new situation. With so much of their inspiration drawn from the events of the Old Testament and the Book of Revelation, the slaves had long sung of wars, of battles, of the Army of the Lord, of Soldiers of the Cross, of trumpets summoning the faithful, of vanquishing the hosts of evil. These songs especially were, as Higginson put it, "available for camp purposes with very little strain upon their symbolism." "We'll cross de mighty river," his troops sang while marching or rowing,

We'll cross de danger water, . . .
O Pharaoh's army drownded!
My army cross over.

"O blow your trumpet, Gabriel," they sang,

Blow your trumpet louder;
And I want dat trumpet to blow me home
To my new Jerusalem.

But they also found their less overtly militant songs quite as appropriate to warfare. Their most popular and effective marching song was:

Jesus call you, Go in de wilderness,
   Go in de wilderness, go in de wilderness,
Jesus call you. Go in de wilderness
   To wait upon de Lord.

Black Union soldiers found it no more incongruous to accompany their fight for freedom with the sacred songs of their bondage than they had found it inappropriate as slaves to sing their spirituals while picking cotton or shucking corn. Their religious songs, like their religion itself, was of this world as well as the next.

Slave songs by themselves, of course, do not present us with a definitive key to the life and mind of the slave. They have to be seen within the context of the slave's situation and examined alongside such other cultural materials as folk tales. But slave songs do indicate the need to rethink a number of assumptions that have shaped recent interpretations of slavery, such as the assumption that because slavery eroded the linguistic and institutional side of African life it wiped out almost all the more fundamental aspects of African culture. Culture, certainly, is more than merely the sum total of institutions and language. It is also expressed by something less tangible, which the anthropologist Robert Redfield has called "style of life." Peoples as different as the Lapp and the Bedouin, Redfield has argued, with diverse languages, religions, customs, and institutions, may still share an emphasis on certain virtues and ideals, certain manners of independence and hospitality, general ways of looking upon the world, which give them a similar life style. This argument applies to the West African cultures from which the slaves came. Though they varied widely in language, institutions, gods, and familial patterns, they shared a fundamental outlook toward the past, present, and future and common means of cultural expression which could well have constituted the basis of a sense of community and identity capable of surviving the impact of slavery.

Slave songs present us with abundant evidence that in the structure of their music and dance, in the uses to which music was put, in the survival of the oral tradition, in the retention of such practices as spirit possession which often accompanied the creation of spirituals, and in the ways in which the slaves expressed their new religion, important elements of their shared African heritage remained alive not just as quaint cultural vestiges but as vitally creative elements of slave

culture. This could never have happened if slavery was, as Professor Elkins maintains, a system which so completely closed in around the slave, so totally penetrated his personality structure as to infantilize him and reduce him to a kind of *tabula rasa* upon which the white man could write what he chose.

Slave songs provide us with the beginnings of a very different kind of hypothesis: that the preliterate, premodern Africans, with their sacred world view, were so imperfectly acculturated into the secular American society into which they were thrust, were so completely denied access to the ideology and dreams which formed the core of the consciousness of other Americans, that they were forced to fall back upon the only cultural frames of reference that made any sense to them and gave them any feeling of security. I use the word "forced" advisedly. Even if the slaves had had the opportunity to enter fully into the life of the larger society, they might still have chosen to retain and perpetuate certain elements of their African heritage. But the point is that they really had no choice. True acculturation was denied to most slaves. The alternatives were either to remain in a state of cultural limbo, divested of the old cultural patterns but not allowed to adopt those of their new homeland—which in the long run is no alternative at all—or to cling to as many as possible of the old ways of thinking and acting. The slaves' oral tradition, their music, and their religious outlook served this latter function and constituted a cultural refuge at least potentially capable of protecting their personalities from some of the worst ravages of the slave system.

The argument of Professors Tannenbaum and Elkins that the Protestant churches in the United States did not act as a buffer between the slave and his master is persuasive enough, but it betrays a modern preoccupation with purely institutional arrangements. Religion is more than an institution, and because Protestant churches failed to protect the slave's inner being from the incursions of the slave system, it does not follow that the spiritual message of Protestantism failed as well. Slave songs are a testament to the ways in which Christianity provided slaves with the precedents, heroes, and future promise that allowed them to transcend the purely temporal bonds of the Peculiar Institution.

Historians have frequently failed to perceive the full importance of this because they have not taken the slave's religiosity seriously enough. A people cannot create a music as forceful and striking as slave music out of a mere uninternalized anodyne. Those who have argued that Negroes did not oppose slavery in any meaningful way are writing from a modern, political context. What they really mean is that the slaves found no *political* means to oppose slavery. But slaves, to borrow Professor Hobsbawm's term, were prepolitical beings in a prepolitical situation. Within their frame of reference there were other—and from the point of view of personality development, not necessarily less effective—means of escape and opposition. If mid-twentieth-century historians have difficulty perceiving the sacred universe created by slaves as a serious alternative to the societal system created by southern slaveholders, the problem may be the historians' and not the slaves'.

Above all, the study of slave songs forces the historian to move out of his own culture, in which music plays a peripheral role, and offers him the opportunity to understand the ways in which black slaves were able to perpetuate much of the centrality and functional importance that music had for their African ancestors. In the concluding lines of his perceptive study of primitive song, C. M. Bowra has written:

Primitive song is indispensable to those who practice it. . . . they cannot do without song, which both formulates and answers their nagging questions, enables them to pursue action with zest and confidence, brings them into touch with gods and spirits, and makes them feel less strange in the natural world. . . . it gives to them a solid centre in what otherwise would be almost chaos, and a continuity in their being, which would too easily dissolve before the calls of the implacable present . . . through its words men, who might otherwise give in to the malice of circumstances, find their old powers revived or new powers stirring in them, and through these life itself is sustained and renewed and fulfilled.

This, I think, sums up concisely the function of song for the slave. Without a general understanding of that function, without a specific understanding of the content and meaning of slave song, there can be no full comprehension of the effects of slavery upon the slave or the meaning of the society from which slaves emerged at emancipation.

The Irish in Boston: Conflict of Ideas

The Irish have been the most long-suffering of the European immigrant groups in the United States. Most of them arrived in America between 1835 and 1865 too poor to travel inland; so they remained in the port cities of Boston and New York. Peasants and ill-educated, they were forced to accept low-paying, unskilled jobs with no prospects for advancement. In Boston Irishmen frequently labored fifteen hours a day, seven days a week. Servant girls rose at 5 a.m. and faced a workday of sixteen to eighteen hours in order to earn $1.50 a week. Massachusetts natives looked down upon the Irish. As Marcus L. Hansen, the late dean of American immigration historians, wrote about these New England newcomers:

Tradition has little that is pleasant to say regarding these Irish immigrants. They were stupid and dirty, superstitious and untrustworthy, diseased and in despair. They were beggars and thieves, the overflow of Irish poorhouses and outcasts from overpopulated estates.

The condition of their entry, their reception in the new land, and the fears and customs which the Irish brought over with them made it hard to adapt to American society and to form a community. Oscar Handlin's Boston's Immigrants, A Study in Acculturation, 1790–1860 *analyzes the struggles of the Boston Irish to establish themselves in their new surroundings. His study has become the model for all subsequent works on foreign-born groups. Before* Boston's Immigrants *appeared in 1941, with the exception of Marcus Hansen in* The Atlantic Migration *and* The Immigrant in American History, *historians had confined themselves chiefly to detailed descriptions of various phases of immigrant life. Handlin departed from convention by examining the development of Irish communities in Boston. Inevitably this type of investigation involved the merging of historical method with sociological and psychological techniques and concepts. By focusing on cultural adjustment and conflict, impulses toward assimilation or aloofness, and interaction between the Irish subculture and the larger Boston community,* Boston's Immigrants *broke radically with the traditional recounting of facts and anecdotes about movement and settlement. Handlin analyzed social change and the development and modification of institutions and attitudes over seventy years of group organization and interaction.*

"Conflict of Ideas," which is reproduced below, depicts the cultural isolation of the Irish from the Yankees and other immigrant groups in Boston. Pessimistic and fatalistic in outlook, the Irish clung to views, embodied in the Catholic Church, which contradicted the individualism, reform spirit, and secular rationality that permeated Boston in the 1840s and '50s. The diversion of these two sets of attitudes widened the gulf between the Irish and the rest of the urban community. With the Church as its center the Irish created group solidarity, but at a tremendous cost. Their own community set them against the larger society of Boston and became a defensive bastion, erected to withstand the attacks of an urban culture which they detested and which, in turn, despised them.

As long . . . as the traditions of one's national and local group remain unbroken, one remains so attached to its customary ways of thinking that the ways of thinking which are perceived in other groups are regarded as curiosities, errors, ambiguities, or heresies. At this stage one does not doubt either the correctness of one's own traditions of thought or the unity and uniformity of thought in general.

By 1845 Boston's cultural development had reached a point of close contact with the highest aspects of European civilization. Native Bostonians regarded England as the "mother country." They were proud of their British ancestry and remained "solidly and steadily English, settled down into an English mold and hardened into it." But they had also learned to "expect an importation of the opinions and manners of the old countries" and to "receive from Europe a considerable part of [their] intellectual persuasions and moral tastes. . . ." Newcomers, be they English, French or German, originating from similar backgrounds, and facing few problems of physical or economic adjustment, could participate in a cosmopolitan society on terms of direct and simple equality. For these came prepared to share the world of the Boston merchants—their music and literature, their ideas and politics, their rationalism and their all-pervading optimism. Whatever differences existed were in degree and pace, easily reconcilable.

The Irish who settled in Boston, however, were products of a milieu completely isolated from the intellectual influences of London, Paris, or even Dublin. And every phase of their experience in America heightened the disparity between their heritage and that of their neighbors. The physical barriers segregating them from the dominant cultural currents of the day disappeared in the New World; but the spiritual ones crossed the Atlantic in the hold of every immigrant ship. Reaffirmed and strengthened by the difficulties of the new environment, these restraints ruled Irish thoughts as vigorously in Boston as in Cork.

In Ireland, a circumscribed agrarian economy gave form to their ideas, to the "implicit . . . *assumptions,* or . . . *unconscious mental habits*" dominating their thoughts. In the bitter atmosphere of poverty and persecution, the Irish had found little in life that was not dark and nothing that was hopeful. Their utter helplessness before the most elemental forces fostered an immense sadness, a deep-rooted pessimism about the world and man's role in it, manifested even "on occasions of great joy and merriment . . . in grief and melancholy. . . ."

Nor was this feeling modified in the transit to the New World. Irishmen fled with no hope in their hearts—degraded, humiliated, mourning reluctantly-abandoned and dearly-loved homes. From the rotting immigrant hulks, they nostalgically joined the local poet in plaintive farewell:

Farewell to thee, Erin mavourneen,
    Thy valleys I'll tread never more;
This heart that now bleeds for thy sorrows,

Will waste on a far distant shore.
Thy green sods lie cold on my parents,
    A cross marks the place of their rest,—
The wind that moans sadly above them,
    Will waft their poor child to the West.

The old homeland grew lush in their
memories when compared with the miseries
of constricted tenement districts and the
hopelessness of the arbitrary factory economy. They found good cause to complain:

I am tired, fatigued, weary,
    Of this never ending strife—
Of the journey, lone and dreary,
    On the darksome path of life.

Filthy homes, wretched working conditions,
and constant hunger mocked the merchants'
optimisim, and bred, instead, the identical
pessimism in Boston as in Ireland. On both
sides of the Atlantic, Irish experience generated a brooding recognition that human relationships were transient, subject to the ever-
threatening intervention of impersonal evils.
The essential pessimism of these immigrants
was reflected in the prominent role of the
devil in their literature and even in the belief
in retributive justice at the hands of a *deus ex
machina* as compensation in a basically evil
world. Both as peasants, whose anxious
livelihood derived from the capricious soil,
and as cogs in an unpredictable industrial
machine, they were victims of incalculable
influences beyond their control. For those
who met it so frequently in their own experience, untimely disaster, even death, was
normal, a part of life accepted without complaint, indeed, without even the need for explanation.

Buffeted about in a hostile universe by
malevolent forces more powerful than themselves, Irish peasants could turn only to religion for consolation. The drama of salvation
unfolded at every mass became a living reality from which emerged dogmas held with a
tenacity beyond secular reason. Man's fall
through original sin and his deliverance by
grace were not theological abstractions but
insistent realities reflected in all the features
of their everyday existence.

When we luck at him there, we see our blissed
Saviour, stripped a'most naked lake ourselves;
whin we luck at the crown i'thorns on the head,
we see the Jews mockin' him, jist the same as—
some people mock ourselves for our religion;
whin we luck at his eyes, we see they wor niver
dry, like our own; whin we luck at the wound in
his side, why we think less of our own wounds an'
bruises, we get 'ithin and 'ithout, every day av
our lives.

To those who bore more than their share of
hardships, religion's most valued assurance
was its promise that "the world did not explain itself" and that man met his true destiny not in this constantly frustrating universe, but in the loftier sphere it preceded. At
the death of a child in a popular novel, the
priest inwardly "rejoiced that another soul
was about being housed from life's tem-
pests"; for all earthly affairs, life itself, were
insignificant and death was but a release for
the tremendous process of redemption. Preparation for that rebirth thoroughly eclipsed
the affairs of the immediate present, engen-
dering an attitude of complete acceptance
toward mundane problems so long as salvation was unthreatened.

Against the immense forces facing men,
reason and science counted for nothing. The
Irish scorned the independent rationalism
basic to the religious feelings of other Bostonians, and discouraged "reading the bible
and putting one's own construction upon it"
or allowing "every tinker and ploughboy to
interpret scripture as he thought proper."
The approval of the hierarchy reinforced this
attitude. The pastoral letter of the American
bishops in 1843 pointed out that "without
faith it is impossible to please God" and
warned against "preferring in the least point
the dictates of your erring reason."

The true guardian of the faith essential to
salvation was the Catholic Church. Two centuries of violent attack in Ireland had
strengthened and confirmed its position; for
national and economic issues had fused with
the religious in opposition to landlords who
were at once masters, aliens, and representatives of a hostile faith. Beliefs maintained at

great personal sacrifice were not lightly held, and among those who came to America the Church gained particular prestige, for it was one of the few familiar institutions that followed them across the Atlantic.

In the New World as in the Old, Catholicism assumed a distinctive cast from the background of its adherents. Universal rather than national in organization, and catholic in essential dogma, it nevertheless partook of the quality of the men who professed it; for the nature of the milieu modified even religious doctrines, particularly in their application to the problems of secular life. Irish priests and theologians rose from the ranks of the people, surrounded by popular influences which inevitably affected their later work. The continuous process of clerical adjustment to the ideas of those they served intensified Irish devoutness in America, because the conclusions Catholicism derived from its theology coincided with the ideas emanating from the inner circumstances of the peasant-laborer's life.

The confidence of the Irish confirmed the Church's paramount position in their own affairs; church doctrine extended this ascendancy over all man-made institutions, including the state, and urged that

Religious liberty means, not religious slavery, not simply the liberty of infidelity, the liberty to deny and blaspheme, but ... that religion herself is free ... to be herself, and to discharge her functions in her own way, without let or hindrance from the State. ... Who asserts the freedom of religion asserts the subjection of the State. Religion represents the Divine Sovereignty ... in the affairs of men; the State ... merely ... human sovereignty. Is the Divine Sovereignty higher than the human ... ? Then is religion ... higher than the State. ... Religion overrides all other sovereigns, and has the supreme authority over all the affairs of the world. . . .. This is a terrible doctrine to atheistical politicians, infidels, and anarchists; and hence ... they are the enemies ... of religious liberty. ...

Since the "freedom of religion" was "its sovereignty" and since "to assert its independence of the State" was "to assert its

supremacy over the State," secular government had merely to choose between particular measures within the limits of religious precepts, to which it must conform, and in conforming, compel its subjects to conform.

In defense of this position Catholics argued that

Christianity is "part and parcel of the law of the land." ... We are professedly a *Christian* State, and acknowledge ourselves bound by the law of nature as interpreted and re-enacted by Christianity.

There could be no true tolerance, for, no matter what their professed beliefs, all citizens must ultimately comply with the basic tenets of the "true religion" through its temporal agency, the state. This opinion forced a denial of

the liberty of each man to be of what religion he pleases, or of none ... a low and an altogether inadequate view ... merely a political ... not a religious right at all; for no religion that has any self-respect can acknowledge that one has the right to be of any religion he chooses. No man has or can have a *religious* or a *moral* right to be of any religion but the true religion. ... Every religion by its very nature is intolerant of every other, and condemns itself, if it is not.

Any deviation from this concept of "religious freedom" earned bitter condemnation as "latitudinarianism of the very worst sort."

The belief that non-Christians were "free to profess no portion of their religion which contravenes Christian morality" certainly contrasted with the native conviction, as set forth by Channing, that formal sectarian boundaries had little significance. While most Bostonians felt, with John Adams, that "every honest, well-disposed, moral man, even if he were an atheist, should be accounted a Christian," Brownson insisted that "a *Christian* Protestant, is to the Catholic mind simply a contradiction in terms." That disparity reflected a broad difference between the basic attitudes and unconscious presumptions of the rational, progressive optimist and of the religious, conservative pessimist.

This dichotomy was most marked when expressed in terms of concrete attitudes toward the pressing social problems of the period. The mental set of tenement or seminary scarcely harmonized with the rational Bostonian's concept of reform as an infallible guide along the straight path of progress to ultimate perfectibility. Indeed the Irish were completely alien to the idea of progress and necessarily antagonistic "to the spirit of the age." Reform was a delusion inflating men's sense of importance, distorting the relative significance of earthly values, and obscuring the true goals of their endeavor—salvation of the eternal soul. Such movements were suspect because they exaggerated the province of reason, exalting it above faith, futile because they relied upon temporal rather than spiritual agencies, and dangerous because they undermined respect for established institutions.

The failure of the Irish to comprehend fully the democratic feeling basic to reform intensified their hostility. Generations of enforced obedience bred a deep respect for class distinctions. Irishmen could scarcely have a firm appreciation of the equality of man when their very school books taught them

Q. If the poor will not try to be good, what will follow?
A. That the rich will not help them.

At best, this acquiescence developed into the feudal loyalty of retainer for master, but more frequently it became the complete servility described by Arthur Young:

A landlord . . . can scarcely invest an order which a servant, laborer or cottar dares to refuse to execute. Nothing satisfies him but unlimited submission. . . . A poor man would have his bones broken, if he offered to lift his hand in his own defense.

In America, too, the Irish agreed that everyone should "mate with their equals, high as well as low," and the *Pilot* pointed out that the poor Irish family was "much more happy and contented in its place in life" than the American. But Judith O'Rourke expressed this acceptance of class most clearly when, scoffing at the possibility of educating her children, she hoped that her sons would "grow up honest good men, like them that's gone afore them, not ashamed of their station, or honest toil," while her daughter "'ll be the same lady her mother is . . . an' that's good enough. . . . She'd look purty I'm thinkin' wid her music in one corner an' I wid my wash tub in another."

Thus, the whole galaxy of reforms that absorbed New England in the thirty years after 1835 met the determined opposition of the Irish Catholic population in Boston. Fundamental patterns of thought combined with group interests to turn them against their neighbors who "devoutly believe in any Woolly horse, any Kossuth, any Montes that may chance to come," and among whom "Freesoilerism, Millerism, Spiritual rappings, Mainea all are current." To follow such doctrines which had already "infected our whole society and turned a large portion of our citizens into madmen" was to become "a philanthropist . . . a person who loves everybody generally and hates everybody particularly."

"Leading in majesty and peerless fidelity, the beautiful constellation of reforms," was abolition. Against slavery the finest spirits in Boston united in a movement which, after 1830, gained steadily in adherents until it dominated the city. Yet the Irish concertedly opposed the spread of "Nigerology." They sometimes recognized that slavery was abstractly bad, and sometimes denied it; but in any case, humanitarianism was as powerless to eradicate the institution as to deal with the other evils in which the world abounded. A number of practical objections reinforced the theory that only the influence of the Church could counteract social maladies. The disruption of the Repeal Movement by O'Connell's anti-slavery speech revealed the danger of the issue; Catholic leaders hesitated to antagonize their powerful and influential communicants in Maryland, Louisiana, and throughout the south, dreading a controversy that might divide the Church as it had other religious groups. And beyond immediate interests and ideology lay a deep horror of endangering the social fabric, or disturbing the Union as it existed.

Even more concrete reasons tied the mass of unskilled Irish laborers to the Church in the belief that

... when the negroes shall be free
To cut the throats of all they see,
Then this dear land will come to be
The den of foul rascality.

They feared the competition of the hordes of freed slaves who might invade the North; and valued the security that came from the existence in the country of at least one social class below them. Rivalry for the same jobs as Negroes, elsewhere bondsmen, but in Boston economically and socially more secure than the Irish, strengthened this feeling and led the latter to object to Negro suffrage which aimed at "setting the Niggers high," to complain that colored people did not know their place, and to resent their "impertinence."

Irish Catholics also turned against the other humanitarian reforms; for these used the state as an instrument for strengthening secular as against religious forces. On these grounds the immigrants fought the current temperance movement, although drunkenness was particularly prominent among them. Inspired by Father Mathew's efforts, the Church itself had attempted to cope with the problem. But it actively challenged the right of the state to legislate on the matter; and therein enjoyed the support of laborers who jealously guarded their only form of relaxation.

Even the preponderance of Irish among the city's lawbreakers did not weaken the conviction that society was powerless to effect reforms attainable only through grace. Because Catholics felt that criminals were born evil, they objected to treating them "with maternal kindness," "merely as

afflicted patients." "A superabundance of humanity in the public sentiment" and particularly in the Prisoners' Friend Society pampered wrongdoers by permitting them to work, to receive occasional visitors and to hear church services on Sunday. These "sickly sentimentalists," "worse ... than the prisoners they whine over," were doomed to failure because most prisoners were

deliberate wrongdoers, intentionally at war with society; men who prefer to obtain a precarious livelihood by robbing ... to the comforts resulting from the unexciting routine of honest industry ... *men* who have thus become perverted. ...

Two current crusades seemed to strike at the roots of family life, and thus at Christian society. To those reared within the grooves of a patriarchal society the "domestic reformers" appeared to "have revived pagan orgies in the pitiful farce of "Women's Rights,' and Bloomerism." But more menacing to public morality were the common schools and the laws for compulsory education:

The general principle upon which these laws are based is radically unsound, untrue, Atheistical. ... It is, that the education of children is *not* the work of the Church, or of the Family, but that it is the work of the State. ... Two consequences flow from this principle. ... In the matter of education, the State is supreme over the Church and the Family. *Hence,* the State can and does exclude from the schools religious instruction. ... The inevitable consequence is, that ... the greater number of scholars must turn out to be Atheists, and accordingly the majority of non-Catholics are people of no religion. ... The other consequence ... leads the State to *adopt* the child, to weaken the ties which bind it to the parent. So laws are made compelling children to attend the state schools, and forbidding the parents, if they be poor, to withdraw their little ones from the school. ... The consequence of this policy is ... universal disobedience on the part of children. ... Our little boys scoff at their parents, call their fathers by the name of Old Man, Boss, or Governor. The mother is the Old Woman. The little boys smoke, drink, blaspheme, talk about fornication, and so far as they are physically able, commit it. Our little girls read novels . . . quarrel about their beaux, uphold Woman's Rights, and—. . . . We were a Boston school boy, and we speak of what we know.

When "second rate or tenth rate school masters . . . like Horace Mann . . ." were allowed "by the patient people to tinker over the schools until they . . . nearly ruined them," Irish parents hesitated to entrust their children to the common schools, and fought the laws that required them to do so. Persistent and unequivocal hostility to the "kidnapping" system generated sharp conflicts with other Bostonians who regarded Massachusetts public education as the keystone of its liberty and culture.

In the conflict of ideas the Irish found all other foreign groups in the city ranged with the native Bostonians against them. The Germans could be as optimistic, rational and romantic as the natives, for their emigration rested on hope rather than on bare necessity. Unlike the Irish, they went off singing,

Leb' wohl geliebtes Mädchen,
Jetzt reis' ich aus den städtchen
    Muss nun, Feinsliebchen, fort
    An einem fremden Ort.

And in America their economic and physical adjustment was relatively simple, so that within a short time they shared the ideas of the natives. Although divisions existed within the German groups, the predominant sentiment held the spirit of free enquiry and intellectual radicalism essential to human progress, measurable in terms of the development of the individual's personality as "a free man." Consequently, they took the same position as the natives on all social questions save temperance, and were far more extreme on the specific issue of slavery. Being few in number, the French did not always assume a position as a group. When they did, they were moderately liberal in politics and on the question of slavery, as were the English, Negroes, Italians, and smaller groups.

About one point only—the revolutions of 1848—was adjustment in the conflicting position of the Irish and other Bostonians at all possible. Coming when the immigrants had scarcely settled in their new homes, while the instruments of social control were still weak from the effects of transition, the exciting news from the Fatherland sent a tremendous wave of emotion among the Irish. Mobilized in the Repeal Movement, Irish national sentiment in America had grown steadily for several years. It had captured the *Boston Pilot,* originally a clerical paper founded by Bishop Fenwick, and turned it to support the revolutions against the conservative powers of Europe led by Austria. Through the *Boston Catholic Observer,* the clergy at first resisted this metamorphosis. But they capitulated in 1848 when the Young Irelanders, impatient with O'Connellite conservatism, raised the banners of rebellion from Cork to Belfast, enlisting the loyalty of the great majority of Irish Americans. Enthusiasm was so great the hierarchy dared not stand in the way. By August Archibishop Hughes of New York gave his approval, proclaiming that the rush to arms had transformed the revolution from "plot" to "fact," and sanctioned a Directory collecting funds in New York. Bishop Fitzpatrick did not weaken to the extent of backing the insurrection, but did not openly oppose it. His organ, the *Boston Catholic Observer,* edited by Brownson, cautiously reprinted the Archbishop's statement without comment.

The Bishop hesitated because of the uncertainty of Vatican policy. Pius IX had been regarded as a progressive from his accession. His early liberal efforts promised so much that the future editor of the *Boston Pilot,* Father John T. Roddan, a brilliant young American priest educated at the Propaganda, had returned to Boston "almost a Mazzinian . . . quite enamored of the European revolutionary movements." While the Pope was undecided, Catholic conservatives vacillated on the subject of revolution and permitted the radicals to dominate Irish opinion.

A common stake in revolutionary success drew the Irish closer to other groups. Young Ireland, influenced by continental ideas, was not far different from Young Italy. Though it lacked the broad humanitarianism of the Boston reformers and was openly sympathetic toward slavery, nationalism nevertheless provided a point of contact with other Bostonians. Collaboration with abolitionists like Quincy and Phillips was a potential wedge that might have split the Irish from their conservatism and opened their minds to the liberal position. Even the collapse of the insurrection did not discredit it, for many of its leaders eventually found their way to the United States. They were still popular; their opinions still carried weight; and for a time they exerted a positive liberalizing influence over their countrymen through lectures and through their newspapers, the *Irish-American* and the *Citizen*.

The rapproachement did not last long, however; it finally gave way before the revived and unified opposition of the clergy. The insurgency of the Roman republic alienated the papacy from the cause of revolution; and the victory of Radetsky's Austrian legions facilitated the adoption of a clear-cut, conservative policy. As a result, Archbishop Hughes and the *Freeman's Journal* disowned Young Ireland, and Catholic policy in Boston as elsewhere resolutely opposed the policies of red republicanism which, in retrospect, it linked with an atheistic plot of Protestants to undermine Catholic civilization. These, it charged:

saw the Church gathering America to her bosom.... They saw themselves losing ground everywhere and, as they gnashed their teeth with rage and pined away, the ministers in white choackers formed in England and in America an Alliance, and, resolved to carry the war into Italy,—to revolutionize that country. It would be a great triumph to them, and to their father, the devil, if they could match Catholic progress in Protestant countries with Protestant progress in Catholic countries.... They fermented the revolutions of 1848

by forming

a grand conspiracy, with its central government ... in London, and its ramifications ex-

tending even to this country ... armed not merely against monarchy, but against all legitimate authority, against all religion except an idolatrous worship of ... the GOD-PEOPLE ..., against all morality,... law,... order, and ... society itself.

The Church conducted a persistent campaign against the "spirit of radical Protestantism" which had "crept into every class of society, into every ... political order" and which "nought can destroy ... but the *true Catholic spirit*." Time after time it inveighed against the "political atheism" growing out of the belief that "the State, if not the sovereign, is at least not the subject of Religion," a belief that gave rise to "the revolutions, crimes, civil wars which have recently been and are coming again...." Led by Brownson, the Catholic press attacked the uprisings in Europe and their supporters in Boston, urging upon a restless people "the necessity of subordination and obedience to lawful rulers." "Good Catholics," they argued, "must accept ... the constitution of the State, when once established, whatever its form, yet ... have no right to conspire to change the constitution, or to effect a revolution in the State. Consequently ... our sympathies can never be with those who conspire against the law, or with the mad revolutionists and radicals, on the Continent of Europe, who are unsettling every thing."

In the face of this overwhelming propaganda, the influence of the Young Irelanders waned steadily. The success of the revolution might have furnished a concrete rallying point for progressive influences against the conservative tendencies in Irish life. As it was, the movement dissolved in endless talk. The conservatives easily recaptured the *Boston Pilot* when its owner, Patrick Donohoe, ignominiously capitulated to the Bishop and allowed his paper to be edited by an American priest, John T. Roddan, by now a disciple of Brownson. Continual quarrels divided the ranks of the radicals and desertion further depleted them. T. D. McGee withdrew first to the clerical party and then to the hated English from whom he accepted a cabinet post in Canada. Mitchel, disgusted, retired to the rusticity of Tennessee, and Meagher to a law practice in New York and the career of a Democratic politician. Although Fenianism revived Irish nationalism in 1859, it had none of the liberal ideas of 1848. By then the opposition to conservatism had disappeared, lingering only in the minds of a few diehards.

Flirtation with revolution was a passing interlude with no effect upon the normal Irish respect for authority. Always, conservatism segregated them from other Bostonians, who believed that all revolutions signified the dawn of a new era that would spread the light of American liberty over a renaissant Europe. Natives, and for that matter, non-Irish foreigners, had taken an active interest in the Polish struggle for liberty, and had hailed the French revolution of 1830 with delight, though Catholics dubbed it the work of "an irreligious and profligate minority." Americans approved of the uprisings of 1848 set off by the abdication of "that great swindle," Louis Philippe, as unanimously as the Irish eventually disapproved. Henry Adams was an ardent admirer of Garibaldi, and Margaret Fuller, among many, adored Mazzini whom the Irish hated. Almost all Bostonians liked the Hungarians and welcomed Kossuth, but Catholics branded him a disappointed manufacturer of humbugs. The Irish attacked the Swiss for sheltering rebels, and condemned the Fenian Brotherhoods in America; while in the Crimean War, which they called a struggle of "Civilized Society against red republican barbarism," they supported Russia against Protestant England and against Turkey, which had protected Kossuth.

Fighting radicalism everywhere, they consistently maintained the principles of conservatism by defending the Catholic powers of Europe—Spain, Austria, and Italy—the nations considered most backward, ignorant, and intolerant by Boston public opinion. Every unfavorable comment on these countries by an American provoked a bitter defense in the Irish press. In the Mediai matter, they upheld religious intolerance in Italy, and left themselves open to charges of having "a different set of principles to suit the market of every country." In the *Black Warrior* affair they championed Spain and in the Koszta case, Austria against the United States. They went to great lengths in vindicating Napoleon III although most Americans condemned the treachery of the coup d'état of 1851. The Irish were equally firm in shielding Catholic Latin America against filibustering Yankees whose "manifest destiny" led to repeated aggressions. They assailed alike the Texan "brigands" who threatened Mexico and those who attacked Cuba, while they supported the established church in Brazil, in a long series of unfortunate disputations which created bitterness by their very heat and which transferred, in the minds of many Bostonians, the qualities defended in these conservative countries to the Irish themselves.

These political differences testified to the strength of the barrier reared between Irish and non-Irish by diametrically opposed ideas, whose literary and cultural expressions reflected and perpetuated the distinction. Resting on basically different premises, developed in entirely different environments, two distinct cultures flourished in Boston with no more contact than if 3,000 miles of ocean rather than a wall of ideas stood between them.

Irish intellectual life had few contacts with that of their neighbors. Education, rare indeed in Ireland, was scarcely more widespread among the Irish in Boston. The ability to read was by no means commonplace, and repeated warnings against secular works narrowed the nature of what little the Irish did read. The few Irishmen conscious of Boston's contemporary literature were shocked and antagonized by its rational romanticism, regarding it as exclusively Protestant, overwhelmingly English, and suspect on both grounds. Completely alien to the city's literary tradition, they branded Shakespeare a barbaric poet whose "monstrous faces" "befoul the stage with every abomination." Milton became a heretic minion of the Drogheda monster Cromwell, and English literature—"the most pernicious" that ever existed—merely a degraded and degenerate justification of the reformation, typified by "that liar and infidel, Hume" and "that hideous atheist, Hobbs." Because this literature was basic to their thinking, the work of men like Emerson was necessarily rejected. C. M. O'Keefe spoke for many in gratitude that "We Irishmen are not yet reduced to that moral nakedness which startles and appals us in Mr. Emerson," whose "historical . . . is only . . . equalled by his philosophical ignorance."

In place of Emerson's "puerilities" the most popular Irish writing of the day was that which glorified Ireland, its historic tradition, and its Catholic past. The dateless conflict with England, in all its phases, furnished an endless source of romantic themes, at once reflecting and stimulating an Anglophobia out of place amidst the Boston veneration of things English. Stories of the Reformation—the root of all Irish misery—were always popular. A life of Mary, Queen of Scots, sold a thousand copies the day it was published in Boston, and the *Pilot* frequently printed romances and articles based upon the struggles of that period justifying the Catholic position. That conflict continued in a long series of literary arguments, forgetting the injunction of a great German controversialist that disputes should be treated "with the utmost charity, conciliation and mildness." On the contrary these theological battles, waged *fortiter in modo* as well as *in re,* wounded susceptibilities and stored up rancorous bitterness on all sides. Whatever the ultimate justice of the matter, defense of the inquisition and Saint Bartholomew's massacre, and continued attacks upon Luther, Calvin, and Henry VIII, the "infernal triumvirate" of Protestantism, and upon other propagators of "monstrous doctrines," scarcely drew the Irish closer to their neighbors who held completely different views.

The sporadic clashes that marked the early years of Irish settlement in Boston stimulated this antagonism. Fitted into a familiar pattern, these conflicts became mere extensions of the old battle against English Protestantism. The Charlestown Convent fire left a heritage of bitterness, never eradicated. Years later Irishmen resented it and declaimed

Foul midnight deed! I mark with pain
Yon ruins tapering o'er the plain;
Contrast them with your Bunker's height,
And shame will sicken at the sight!

Already thou hast learnt the rule,
Of Cromwell's bloody English school;
And far and wide the fame has flown,
Of crimes which thou must ever own.

Nor did the novels in which the Irish delighted most—tales of ancient Irish grandeur, glorifying Celtic culture at the expense of Saxon England—improve relations with other Bostonians. The common core of all was the inevitable contrast between Gael and Sassenach, decidedly to the disadvantage of the latter. A series of violent articles by Dr. John McElheran furnished a philosophical and pseudo-ethnological basis for this contrast. "The divine spark of genius radiates from the Celtic centre of the world. . . . The Egyptians . . . the pure Pelasgi of Athens . . . the Romans by themselves—and the ancient Irish . . . show us . . . the natural tendency of the pure Celtic race, uncontaminated by Gothic bestiality, or eastern sensuality." The Gothic race, including the Germans, Scandinavians, Russians, Turks and Anglo-Saxons, were completely different, "essentially stupid . . . false, cruel, treacherous, base and bloody . . ." with "little or no faculty for poetry, music, or abstract science." By every criterion of civilization, the latter were far inferior to the former. And the lowest of all were the Saxons, "the very dregs and offal of the white population in America. . . . These flaxen-haired German men and women . . . are lower than the race with black wool. . . . Even when they are well to do they send their children out to beg.'' Immensely popular, the publication of these articles elicited a steady stream of letters from readers asking for more of the same from the ''Saxon-hating Dr.''

As opposed to these discordant tendencies only one strain—pride in their contributions to the making of America—drew the Irish nearer their neighbors. Although ''the great current of American history'' was ''overwhelmingly heretic,'' and Catholic students could ''receive no support'' for their ''faith from reading it,'' they cherished its Irish episodes. The early Catholic explorers from St. Brandan to Marquette, and Charles Carroll, the Catholic signer, were important figures whose biographies appeared frequently in their reading. Though they distrusted live Orangemen, the Irish made the dead Scotch-Irish their own; they were fond of tales of John Barry and other Celtic military heroes. But even this was pushed to a dangerous extreme when McElheran claimed all great Americans were ''Celtic Normans, and French, and Spaniards, and Celtic Britons . . . and Gaels from Wales and Ireland and the north and west of Scotland. Look to the pedigree of your heroes . . . look at their physique, and say, Is it the type of Gothic nations? . . . Is it fat, lumpish, gross Anglo-Saxon?''

While the chasm between Irish and native ideas deepened, cultural contacts furthered the assimilation of other immigrants. The Irish alone diverged from the Boston norm. All others participated readily in the intellectual life of the community. Englishmen were obviously at home there; and Germans were soon familiar in many phases of the city's activities. Admiring its school system and respecting Harvard, they sent their children to common schools as a matter of course. Germans were widely acquainted with western European literature. Their magazines contained sections on ''Anglo-Amerikanischer,'' English, and French as well as German and German-American literature, while their own writing frequently used American themes and expressed the American spirit. The thought and culture of

Frenchmen was also broadly cosmopolitan; English and German works found a secure place in their reading. Meanwhile these groups enriched the natives with a new heritage accepted gratefully. Follen and Beck, together with the Americans, Bancroft, Longfellow, and Ticknor, popularized the German language until more than seventy Harvard men were studying it in the fifties. At the same time, the French press helped make the works of Balzac, Lamartine, and other authors and painters accessible to Bostonians.

Ease of adjustment did not reflect a flat uniformity in the non-Irish group. Each brought with it an intellectual tradition of which it was proud, and which it was anxious to preserve. But though different in detail, all had the same roots, and eventually coalesced without serious conflict. Thus the clash of two vigorous musical cultures that grew out of German immigration actually enriched both. At the beginning of the nineteenth century, Boston enjoyed a living, fruitful, musical tradition based upon the Anglo-Italianate musical life of eighteenth-century London. It first took concrete form in the Philo-harmonic Society (1810), an amateur group predominantly American in nativity, but including some Englishmen and a Russian, and led by an Anglo-German, Gottlieb Graupner, once oboist in Haydn's London Orchestra. From this nucleus grew the Handel and Haydn Society, an organization of some hundred amateurs formed in 1815 to interpret the oratorios of these composers. Later critics belittled its achievements, but its influence upon the mechanics and artisans who formed its rank and file was deep, and was perpetuated for many years in the rural ''singing skewls'' of all New England. Throughout at least the first thirty years of its existence, it vigorously sustained the music of those after whom it was named.

Nourished by the fruit of Beethoven's revolt, and steeped in romanticism, German music by 1840 had evolved a tradition that was quite different. At first contact native Bostonians rejected it. Centered in a group of music masters who gave periodic concerts, but whose chief income derived from teaching culturally ambitious Bostonians, their normal musical life had little room for strangers. Traveling professionals might stop for an occasional concert; but isolated performances left little impression and there was no incentive for teachers without pupils to remain in the city. Heinrich, for instance, preferred to live there, but was forced by the financial failure of his concerts to go to New York, and Charles Zeuner, who did remain, felt he was misunderstood. With no one to play the new music, Bostonians could not become familiar with or like it. Englishmen and a few Italians closely related to them remained the most popular foreign musicians. Such unfamiliar soil doomed the most valiant attempts at playing Beethoven to failure. Even Woodbridge and Mason confessed defeat after an unsuccessful series of concerts in the Boston Academy of Music, a product of their travels in Germany.

The coming of the Germans who wanted German music teachers for their children made room for the new music. As soon as there was a resident basis of such musicians, Bostonians found opportunities to hear and to like it. Very quickly they learned it was not really strange for it synchronized with the romantic tendencies already woven into their culture. In the spread of the new music, Germans like Dresel, Kreissmann, Leonhard, and Heinrich, the Germania Society which came to Boston in 1849, the Mendelssohn Quintet Club, and the itinerant foreign opera companies were influential, but hardly more so than native teachers like Lowell Mason, or *Dwight's Journal of Music*, which voiced the cause of German romanticism consistently after 1852. Once the two cultures met, they found a common basis, fused, and under the vigorous leadership of Carl Zerrahn produced an ever more fruitful growth thereafter. Germans and Americans, they were the same kind of people, their ideas and feelings were rooted in the same social background; there was no occasion for serious conflict.

The common store of ideas that made this adjustment possible was lacking in the intellectual relations of the Irish and non-Irish. The development of the fundamental aspects of their ideas left them so far apart there was no room for compromise. Contact bred conflict rather than conciliation. Irish Catholics could not think like their neighbors without a complete change in way of life. And natives could adopt no aspect of Catholic ideas without passing through a radical intellectual revolution.

One outstanding personality attempted to adapt Irish Catholicism to American thought and failed signally in the attempt. By 1842 Orestes A. Brownson's intellectual development had itself carried him to the acceptance of many Catholic concepts. In philosophy he felt the need for tradition and revelation; in theology, for grace to counteract original sin and man's innate corruptness. In politics he was a conservative Democrat, opposed to abolition and reform, trying to temper the rule of the people by placing "Justice" above the popular will. But the eminently Irish Bishop Fitzpatrick—"the hierarchical exponent of all that was traditional... in Catholic public life"— distrusted Brownson's philosophic background though it had brought him to the Church, and insisted upon complete renunciation before conversion. Brownson yielded, and for ten years loyally submitted to the dictates of his Irish religious superiors, handing over every line he wrote to the censorship of the Bishop. Until 1854 Brownson and the *Review* thoroughly expressed the ideas of Irish Catholicism.

In that year, stimulated by the criticisms of the Know-Nothing movement, Brownson reluctantly concluded that the Church in America must be American rather than Irish and thereby provoked a galling conflict with the Irish clergy that painfully grieved him and eventually drove him to New York where he hoped to profit from the less rigorous supervision of Archbishop Hughes. Thereafter, Brownson evolved a new social philosophy based on Gioberti's theology, which enabled him to attack slavery, support the Republican party, and attempt to reconcile the Church with American ideas by liberalizing it.

This endeavor met vigorous, relentless Irish disapproval. The *Pilot,* hitherto his cordial friend and follower, became his bitter foe, attacking his new position in a long series of sharp articles. His influence among the Irish vanished. Too late he recognized what Father Hecker had always known, that "The R. C. Church is not national with us, hence it does not meet our wants, nor does it fully understand and sympathize with the experience and dispositions of our people. It is principally made up of adopted and foreign individuals." Without a common basis of ideas there could be no conciliation.

The compromise too difficult for the acute mind of an intellectual aristocrat was never even attempted by the great mass of laboring Irishmen, completely preoccupied with the far more pressing problems of earning a bare livelihood. Hedged about by economic and physical as well as cultural barriers, they were strangers to the other society beside them. The development of Irish ideas created a further range of differences between themselves and all others in the city that stimulated and developed consciousness of group identity.

Ohio's Germans, 1840–1875

CARL WITTKE

During the colonial era Germans settled primarily in Pennsylvania and the interior regions to the south. After the American Revolution German immigration subsided, but between 1830 and 1890 more than three million Germans came to the United States, attracted by cheap lands, low taxes, and an absence of government conscription. They settled mainly in the Middle Atlantic and midwestern states, the largest numbers in New York, Pennsylvania, Illinois, Wisconsin, and Ohio. Some ventured farther west and south into Texas and Missouri, but Germans generally shunned the Old South because they opposed slavery. Many of the newcomers hoped to form enclaves where German customs and language could survive; except for a few scattered settlements their efforts failed.

In the hierarchy of national minority enclaves transplanted to the United States the Germans were regarded, next to the English born, by native Americans as the country's most desirable immigrant group. Sometimes praised for their competence, hard work, thrift, and success these nineteenth-century arrivals nonetheless often aroused the anger of puritanical Americans who resented their pleasure-loving ways and careless observance of the sabbath. In the 1850s American nativists castigated the "Godless Germans" and assaulted Rhinelanders in Cincinnati, Ohio, Covington, Kentucky, and Baltimore, Maryland. After a brawl between Germans and other Americans in Columbus, Ohio, on July 4, 1854, police, spurred on by mobs shouting epithets like "Hang the damned Hessians," arbitrarily arrested American citizens of German descent.

A comparison of noted immigrant historian Carl Wittke's "Ohio's Germans, 1840–1875," reprinted below, with the selection from Oscar Handlin's Boston's Immigrants *highlights the advantage of the former group in wealth, education, and occupation. Unlike the fatalistic, pessimistic, conservative, anti-black, and passionately Catholic "Celts," the "Teutons" tended toward cheerful activism, abolitionism, anti-clericalism, and backed the liberal European revolutionaries of 1848. German-Americans also differed from Irish-Americans in their greater commitment to intellectual life and in the richer variety and greater magnitude of their ethnic voluntary associations. These qualities and organizations succeeded in making life in America more agreeable and assimilation much easier and faster for Germans than for other newcomers. After two or three generations German-Americans entered the mainstream of life*

From Ohio Historical Quarterly, LXVI (1957), 339–54. Reprinted by permission of the publisher.

in the United States and, except for isolated groups like the Amish in Pennsylvania and the Hutterites in the Dakotas and Montana, a distinguishable German minority no longer exists.

The great period of German immigration is long since past, and the Germans have been diluted and absorbed, along with other nationality groups, into a composite Americanism. A century ago German immigrants, in number and quality, constituted one of the most important elements in the American population. Most of them were plain people, peasants, laborers, or craftsmen, motivated primarily by the desire to get ahead in a new, free land of opportunity. But among them also were men of education, culture, and social status, political refugees of the abortive German revolutions of 1830 and 1848, romantic idealists, and champions of a political and economic radicalism that often ran counter to prevailing American standards of a century ago.

Ohio attracted a large share of the German immigration to its rural areas and into the towns and cities. Pennsylvania Germans moved westward to settle in a broad belt of counties south of New England's Western Reserve. A much larger part of the German immigration, however, came directly from Germany, and its impact can be studied best by focusing attention upon several of the largest Ohio cities.

The city directory of Cincinnati for 1825 listed only sixty-four persons born in Germany. By 1850 there were 30,628, and twenty years later just under 50,000, in a total population of 216,239. Into the Cincinnati of Daniel Drake, Frances M. Trollope and Moncure D. Conway, with its New England and Virginia elements, flowed a Teutonic tide which mingled with and helped reshape the Anglo-American character of the Queen City of the West. In 1835 there were fifteen German families in Cleveland; the census of 1870 reported a German population of nearly 16,000. In 1843 Columbus already had three German schools, two German military companies, and two German charitable organizations. Its south side was known as a "Little Germany," inhabited by thrifty, hard-working craftsmen and storekeepers, who built more homes than were being constructed in any other section of the city. In 1850 Ohio had 111,257 Germans, more than double the number of Irish, their closest competitor. Twenty years later the German element constituted nearly half of the state's foreign born.

Before the end of the Civil War a certain German stereotype became fixed in the minds of many native Americans. It became customary to represent the Germans with heavy beards and mustaches, and wearing soft felt hats rather than the high stiff hats popular in America at the time. The native population quickly recognized that German bakers, tanners, tailors, and other craftsmen, trained in the rigid apprentice system of Europe, made dependable workmen and were making a substantial contribution to the economic development of the United States. German drug stores were a guarantee of reliability, for only German pharmacists had been trained in the fundamentals of chemistry. In Akron, Ferdinand Schumacher, as early as 1854, peddled oatmeal in glass jars, and developed a company which was one of the forerunners of the present-day Quaker Oats Company. In Cleveland, Koch and Loeb, in the 1840's, were making suits, linen dusters, and Alpaca coats, and laying the foundations for the Joseph and Feiss Company, one of the largest clothing manufacturers in the country.

Dozens of such examples of competence, thrift, and success can be cited, but these characteristics were sometimes submerged in the popular stereotype which represented the German as a *gemütlich* burgher, sitting in a beer garden with a stein of foaming lager beer before him, and a long pipe between his teeth, and listening to the music of a German band. Cincinnati's German community lay north of the canal and was known as "Over the Rhine,'' an area of beer gardens and concert halls and flourishing breweries. As late as 1890 a visitor reported that here the air had "a savory odor of Limburger, the aroma arising from a wienerwurst can [and] the vapors... from ... sidewalk drains,'' and here one heard the "tortured strains of murdered Strauss, Offenbach, or other composers'' of the fatherland. "Over the Rhine,'' in Cincinnati, and in the German sections of other cities, German craftsmen and storekeepers built little frame and brick houses flush with the sidewalks, and planted their backyards, fenced in with lattice-work, with flowers and vegetables.

In the German household the hardworking Hausfrau lived in relative contentment within the four walls of her home, where she cleaned and scrubbed and brought up children, and prepared such foreign dishes as pigs feet, smoked sausage, sauerbraten, and sauerkraut, or delicacies like cinnamon kuchen, apple dumplings, and cheese cake, which long since have found an honored place in America's culinary literature.

The men sought recreation in taverns, where they played pinochle, skat, and euchre. On Sundays they brought their families to the beer gardens, to listen to strains of familiar music, and to sip their foaming brew, "ever and again shaking it round their glasses with the peculiar circular motion which none but the German can impart to the beverage he loves.'' Rutherford B. Hayes found it politically advantageous to stop in regularly for his *Schoppen* of beer in one of Cincinnati's leading beer gardens, and George B. Cox, notorious Republican boss, was a regular patron of Wielert's Garden, which was equally renowned for good music and good beer. In Columbus, Volwinkel's beer hall offered its patrons band music, beer, pretzels, and "perfect *gesellschaft* under gas lights that rivalled the moon.''

By 1850 Cincinnati was one of the nation's great brewing and distilling centers, and ten years later it had over two thousand places where drinks were sold. Highly trained brewmasters from Germany practiced

their art in other cities, like Cleveland, Columbus, Sandusky, and Toledo, and brewing and wine-making were for decades a monopoly of the Germans.

Beer, *Gemütlichkeit,* and the wide-open Sunday are still associated in the minds of many Americans with the German stereotype. Yet there always were Germans who resented studying the character of Cincinnati solely through the bottom of a beer glass. Christina Esselen, a university-trained young idealist who published his periodical, the *Atlantis,* for a brief period in Cleveland, referred to the inhabitants "over the Rhine'' as devoid of all interests except freedom to drink beer, and believed that the Germans had sunk to a lower social scale in the United States than in their homeland. Many years later Professor Hugo Münsterberg, Germany's gift to Harvard's psychology and philosophy departments, in an article in the *Atlantic Monthly,* described the bulk of his fellow countrymen as shabbily dressed, rude sauerkraut eaters whose life revolved almost wholly around beer, pipes, and skat playing.

Most Germans have always combated what they called Puritan Sabbatarianism. As they contrasted the pleasures of the Continental Sunday with the American Sabbath, they concluded that in the United States "the rest of Sunday'' is "the rest of the tomb.'' They resisted every white-ribboned temperance crusader, and denounced them as "narrow-minded Puritans'' and "fanatical Methodists.'' "Teetotalism,'' they insisted, was utterly incompatible with "personal liberty.''

In the decade before the Civil War a city like Cincinnati simply ignored local ordinances which provided for Sunday closing. Its large German element insisted that "blue bellied Presbyterians'' could not degrade Americans into "a race of psalm singers.'' In Cleveland the moral forces of Yankeedom were locked in battle with the German voters in several municipal elections, and in 1872, when the city administration tried to close the saloons on Sunday, the Germans paraded through the town with beer kegs. At Lied's

Garden the flag was hauled down to half-mast and wrapped in mourning, and a German saloonkeeper loaded a table, which he put up before his place of business, with pitchers of ice water, milk, and lemonade and a Bible.

Interesting and amusing and generally truthful as such representations of the German group may be, they deal with only one side of the story, and to confine the account of life in Ohio's German communities to this phase of German-Americanism would be to overlook completely the many intellectual and cultural contributions which the German immigration made to America a century ago. The vast majority of the newcomers, although plain people who were attracted to the United States by cheap homesteads and good wages in "the common man's Utopia," nevertheless had imbibed much of the culture of the fatherland. Along with them came enough intellectuals sufficiently interested in the things of the mind and spirit to provide the leadership necessary to weld their fellow immigrants into an influential social group.

The Germans were a social people and seized upon every opportunity to arrange outings or picnics. For a time German communities made more of the Fourth of July than native Americans, for to them Independence Day was more than an occasion to satisfy their gregarious instincts—it was a day to commemorate because it marked the establishment of the liberty and equality which had brought them to America. In 1844 the Germans of Columbus celebrated the Fourth with a cannonade, a parade of military companies and bands, games for young and old at the picnic ground, and a huge banquet, at which a large picture of Washington looked down upon the assembled guests. Ten years later an effort to get the native Americans of Columbus to join with the Germans in a Fourth of July celebration proved unsuccessful, although the Germans provided the food and the Americans the fireworks. The next year's celebration ended in a bloody street riot.

Two or three dances a week were regularly advertised by German societies in the local press, and on one occasion the Columbus *Westbote* carried announcements for six in one week. In 1859 the Germans celebrated the Schiller centennial all over America. Columbus marked the event with a two-day festival, which began with exercises in Thalia Hall, the first German theater in the capital city, decorated for the occasion with evergreens and portraits of Schiller and Goethe. There were children's pageants, speeches by local celebrities, and songs by the Columbus *Männerchor,* and the festivities closed with the Wilhelm Tell overture, a play, and an elaborate banquet.

Like other immigrant groups the Germans loved military companies, which enabled them to parade in gaudy uniforms and meet regularly on drill days devoted as much to conviviality as to martial exercises. Several such German companies from Columbus and Cincinnati volunteered for the Mexican War. When Louis Kossuth, the hero of the Hungarian revolution of 1848, visited Cincinnati, he was greeted by a military parade, led by German cavalry, riflemen, sharpshooters, and the Steuben Guard, and their bands. In Columbus the Hungarian liberator was welcomed by German grenadiers and a company of artillery, which fired an artillery salvo at the break of day, and the day's demonstrations ended with a midnight serenade by a German singing society. Lincoln passed through Cincinnati in 1861 on his way to Washington and was welcomed by the Steuben Artillery and a German jäger company. When war came, German military companies from many Ohio communities volunteered *in corpore* to defend the Union.

One of Ohio's best-known Civil War outfits was the Ninth Ohio Volunteers, recruited almost entirely among the Germans of Cincinnati, and commanded by R. L. McCook, with August Willich, a German refugee of 1848 who had published a socialist labor paper in Cincinnati, the seond in command. The men reported in the white linen jackets of the German turner societies, and their commander drilled them while still dressed in civilian clothes, wearing a stove-pipe hat and with only a sword to distinguish him from his men. Of the nine thousand men who entered the army from Cuyahoga County, the Germans contributed over twenty-five percent. In a number of Ohio companies and in several regiments, all commands were originally given in German. The patriotic record of the Germans in the Civil War need not be retold here. It greatly modified the attitude of many native Americans toward their adopted fellow citizens.

The German theater owed much to the intellectuals of the German immigration of the 1850's who eagerly tried to lift the level of theatrical performances from the low comedy and farces of earlier years to productions of the great German masters. In Cincinnati Frederick Hassaurek, youthful veteran of the Vienna revolution, and Karl Obermann founded a German theater which gave four performances a week. On the eve of the Civil War the *Cincinnati Enquirer* commented that the monopoly enjoyed by German drama in the Queen City was challenged only by the minstrel shows. The *Enquirer* was especially flattering in its comments about the attention and interest of the audiences from "over the Rhine." The German theater in Cincinnati did not recover from the effects of the Civil War until 1879. In their later years the financial resources of German theater companies were often disastrously affected by sporadic enforcement of Sunday closing ordinances. In Columbus and Cleveland the arrival of the "Forty-Eighters," political refugees of the German revolution, raised the standards and improved the repertoire of the German theater by insisting on better stage settings, putting an end to smoking during the performances, and abolishing the dances which had followed the show as an inducement to get people to attend.

An unfriendly critic writing from Göttingen once remarked that wherever three Germans congregated in the United States, one opened a saloon so that the other two might have a place for their quarrels. How-

ever exaggerated and slanderous that characterization may be, there can be no doubt that wherever Germans settled they organized singing societies to sing the folk songs and practice the art songs of their nation. The first German singing society of Cincinnati rehearsed as early as 1838 in the dance hall of the Rising Sun Tavern, "over the Rhine." In 1846 a German workmen's organization of Cincinnati took the bold step of incorporating female voices in its singing society, and thereupon was able to present Haydn's *Creation* in full. In 1856 the German-American Cecilia Society of Cincinnati sang Mozart, Mendelssohn, and Haydn under the direction of F. L. Ritter.

The first German singing society of Cleveland dates from 1848 and was directed by a political refugee who soon left to join the gold rush to California. In 1850 the singers had to disband their organization and the majority joined the singing section of the local German Freethinkers' Society. The *Männerchor* of Columbus was founded in 1848 and is still in existence. The Columbus *Liederkranz* was organized in 1866. Akron had its *Liedertafel,* and there were other German singing societies in the more important cities of the state. Today the German singing societies of Cincinnati and Columbus are among the oldest in the country.

Before long the number of choral organizations was sufficient to support the annual *Sängerfeste* for which the Germans became famous in the United States. At these gatherings German singers gathered from a wide area to compete for prizes, and to enjoy the convivialities of the occasion. The first *Sängerfest* in America was held in Cincinnati in 1849. Twelve years later the city had to provide a special building for the two thousand singers who attended. Musical events of this kind were partly responsible for Cincinnati's famous May Festival, which Theodore Thomas brought to a high level of artistry in the 1870's.

In 1852 Columbus was host to a *Sängerfest* which was ushered in by artillery fire and a parade and which, in addition to its musical activities, included a picnic, an athletic spectacle, and drills by German militia companies. Seven years later in Cleveland twenty-four singing societies presented *Alessandro Stradella,* an operatic favorite of the Germans, and the program featured a mass chorus of four hundred voices. At the close of the musical activities the singers paraded to a picnic ground, escorted by the turner society, German light dragoons, and an artillery company. On another occasion a Cleveland audience of over five thousand attended a concert directed by Hans Balatka, a guest conductor from Milwaukee. The mass chorus presented parts of Mozart's *Magic Flute* and the orchestra played the overtures from *Wilhelm Tell* and *Martha.* It is not without significance to point out that German Jews participated in these musical events, as they did in all the cultural activities of the German immigration, and the German-Jewish press usually carried detailed accounts of the *Sängerfeste.*

German singing societies had to be largely rebuilt after the Civil War. By 1874, however, the *Sängerfest* was in full bloom again. Cleveland had erected a special "Temple" for the occasion. The sessions continued for an entire week; high-priced soloists and the New York Philharmonic Orchestra were engaged; the governor came to open the music festival; and the city's streets were decorated with German and American flags. Newspaper critics admitted that the programs were excellent, but criticized the visitors for manifesting a greater interest in social activities than in the more serious objectives of the convention. A bar had been installed under the orchestra pit of the concert hall and after the conclusion of each concert, many hours were spent there under the mellow patronage of Bacchus and King Gambrinus.

The German *Turnfeste* and *Schützenfeste* provided another outlet for the gregarious instincts of the German population. The turner movement, founded in 1811 in Berlin, when Prussia was under the heel of Napoleon, became an effective instrument for the development of German patriotism and nationalism. Its original purpose, to build sound bodies through systematic physical exercises, was soon expanded to include the building of a genuine political liberalism. The turner movement was one of the most important causes of the German revolution of 1848, and many turners fought under Sigel and Hecker in Baden, on the barricades of Dresden, and in the streets of Frankfurt.

Political refugees of 1848 revived the turner movement in the United States, and put such stress upon its liberal and radical traditions that the turner societies became centers of German radicalism in America. The first *Turngemeinde* in the United States was organized in Cincinnati in Ocotber 1848, when Friedrich Hecker, the incurable romantic of the German revolution, happened to be visiting friends in that city. Fourteen Cincinnati Germans responded to his call and began setting-up exercises in a vacant lot. Two years later they dedicated their first little turner hall; by 1851 the society was able to support a small library, a male chorus, and a monthly publication.

In Columbus the first *Turnverein* was established in 1851; the still prosperous Cleveland *Socialer Turn Verein* dates from 1867. Membership in turner societies was open to all, and included a conglomeration of ardent nationalists, sober, middle-of-the-road German-American burghers, socialists, avowed infidels, and many who joined solely for social reasons. But the original goal of the organization was to develop a more "refined humanity," and to insist upon complete freedom to reform the political, economic, and religious patterns of America. Thousands of turners became radical abolitionists and volunteered in such numbers for service in the Union army that in many areas their societies had to be virtually rebuilt after the Civil War.

The *Turnfeste,* which began in the 1850's, developed into gigantic festivals, attended by turners who came from considerable distances to demonstrate their physical prowess. These spectacles usually began with parades in which the marchers wore the white jackets and red ties characteristic of the turner clubs. There were torchlight processions, lusty renditions of turner and student songs, gymnastic competitions that generally ended with great tableaux, banquets, with endless toasts, and on the last day, the presentation of an opera and a grand ball. Prizes were awarded not only for physical feats but also for original essays, poems, and musical compositions. The turner organizations of Ohio figured prominently in the national *Turnfeste*. Moreover, in Cincinnati, Cleveland, Columbus, and elsewhere, the turner, after the Civil War, became interested in getting physical education courses and instruction in the German language into the curricula of the public schools. They were so successful in several Ohio cities that, in German neighborhoods, instruction in the first grade was in German and children of native Americans unfamiliar with the language were expected to acquire it.

Closely akin to the militia companies and turner societies were the organizations of German sharpshooters (*Schützenvereine*), whose members competed in shooting galleries for prizes. The *Schützenverein* was a direct importation from Germany, and grew rapidly after 1848. The competition in marksmanship sometimes continued for as much as a week, and ended, as in Germany, with a parade, a banquet, oratory, and an elaborate ceremony to crown a King of the Sharpshooters. Annual local competitions were held in Columbus as early as 1853, and six years later the Columbus *Schützenverein* started its own building, with ceremonies that began with the breaking of a bottle of beer over the cornerstone.

The political refugees of the revolutions of 1830 and 1848–49 boldly announced that they would not become mere "culture fertilizer" in a raw, new land, where, as in the Western Reserve of Ohio, even a Christmas tree erected in a German church was regarded as a "heathenish custom," "a plain case of idolatry," and a "groveling before the shrubs." Many "Forty-Eighters" stubbornly refused to discard "the intellectual achievements of a thousand years . . . for the culture of the primeval forest." In the New Germany across the sea they hoped to introduce and preserve German art, music, literature, philosophy, and science to combat the gloom of Puritans, "square-headed sectarians, and temperance fanatics." Above all, they were committed to disseminating a spirit of rationalism and enlightenment in a land suffering from what they regarded as the clerical tyranny of the American churches. The extremists opposed Sunday laws, the opening of public gatherings with prayer, the exemption of church property from taxation, and Bible reading in the schools. For the more radical among them, separation of church and state meant the annihilation of the church as a state within a state.

The vast majority of German immigrants belonged to the Catholic, Lutheran, or Reformed churches, and even the Methodists made many converts among them. Although the anti-clerical radicalism of an able and noisy minority never fastened its grip upon the masses of the German immigration, who wanted no truck with the "beer-fogged skepticism" of these "pioneers of heathenism," the German element remained badly divided because of the activities of a vociferous minority, and suffered for years from the hostility and prejudices which the radicals aroused among native Americans.

The foci of freethinking radicalism were to be found in German "Free Congregations," or freethinkers' societies. These organizations rejected every form of ritual, clericalism, dogmatism, and supernaturalism, and upheld the right of men to be atheists, agnostics, pantheists, or anything else they wished—so long as they observed the basic moralities. In this new *Kulturkampf* in America the leaders fought hard, and often unwisely and intolerantly, to substitute an enlightened humanism for the "dogmas of priestcraft" and superstition. They were indiscriminately labeled as infidels by their American critics.

In their meetings the freethinkers' clubs developed something of a ritual of their own, which stressed lectures and discussions of morality, science, literature, and other disciplines calculated to enrich and liberate the human spirit. They established private schools in Cleveland, Cincinnati, and other cities to make freethinkers of their children. The group in Cincinnati owned a hall, supported singing and dramatic sections, a mutual insurance society, and a woman's auxiliary, and met regularly on Sunday for lectures and debate. The Cleveland organization in the early 1850's had two hundred members, who sponsored dramatics, gymnastics, a German-English school, and debates, and annually celebrated the birthday of Tom Paine and the martyrdom of Robert Blum, the hero of 1848. In 1854 ten Ohio cities sent delegates to a convention in Cincinnati to draw up a "Platform of the Free Germans of Ohio." Besides the usual anticlerical pronouncements, the document advocated the abolition of slavery and the repeal of the fugitive slave law, a ten-hour day, free homesteads, public education, inheritance taxes, a mechanics lien law, and an end of capital punishment. A year earlier Cincinnati Germans had advocated a primary democracy for the United States, and in 1859 German radicals joined with Negroes in Cincinnati to honor John Brown.

The extreme radicalism and intolerant anti-clericalism of the German minority explain in part the nativist reaction against the heavy European immigration of the 1850's. Political nativism was a mixture of unadulterated bigotry and some sound reasons for objecting to the abuses connected with completely unrestricted immigration. The spearhead of its attack was directed against the Catholic Irish, but the Germans by no means escaped unscathed.

In Cincinnati in 1853 the anti-clericalism of the freethinkers' society was fanned into violence by unrelenting attacks in Hassaurek's *Hochwächter* upon Archbishop Gaetano Bedini, a visitor in the city, whom German radicals described as the "Bloodhound of Bologna,' because of his alleged responsibility for the execution of Italian revolutionary patriots in 1849. On Christmas Day hundreds of German freethinkers and radicals marched upon the residence of the archbishop of Cincinnati, where Bedini was a guest, carrying an effigy of the noted Italian clergyman swinging from a gallows. In the riot that ensued, which the Germans blamed on the Irish police and a mayor whom they described as a "tool of the priests," one man was killed and several were injured. Conservative papers, like the Columbus *Westbote,* blamed the Germans for the incident, and the Cleveland *Germania* denounced the "patent reformers" whose activities were bringing the entire German immigration into disrepute. Incidents of this kind served only to feed the fires of nativism against all the foreign-born.

In 1855 members of a Columbus singing society, returning from a *Sängerfest,* were attacked by nativist rowdies, and several weeks later, when the Germans were returning from a Fourth of July picnic, they were showered with stones, marchers and bystanders began to fire revolvers, and a number of casualties resulted. The local police searched the German neighborhood without proper warrants, and a howling mob shouted "kill the damn Dutch." In the same "bloody year" Cincinnati nativists drove a little band of German musicians from a tenement house and then marched, with fife and drum, to attack the Germans "over the Rhine." The latter met their assailants with gunfire from the windows of their homes, and threw up barricades in the streets, behind which the Saarsfield Guards and other militia companies, joined by a number of Irish, rallied to repel the nativist invasion. Election day riots were common in Ohio during these unhappy years, and on several occasions German saloons were raided and ballot boxes destroyed. But nativism soon had its day and was largely dissolved in the patriotic response of the foreign-born in defense of the Union in 1861.

The German vote was too important in Ohio to be long ignored by either major party. As early as 1834 the Jacksonians distributed campaign literature among the Pennsylvania Germans in Ohio, and in 1832 Jackson's bank veto was widely circulated in German translation. There were special German meetings during the famous log-cabin campaign of 1840. In 1844 the Democrats put out a campaign biography of James K. Polk in the German lanaguage. In the election of 1860 the German vote may well have been decisive in the northwestern states. Hassaurek of Cincinnati spoke for two and a half hours to the Cleveland Germans on behalf of Lincoln, and August Thieme, perhaps Cleveland's leading German intellectual, stumped Ohio for the Republicans. Carl Schurz, whom Lincoln described as "the foremost among the Republican orators," and whom the Democratic *Plain Dealer* of Cleveland denounced as "a red republican," with a black heart, came into the state in 1860 to try to garner the German vote for the Republican party.

The leaders of the German element were quick to demand political plums for services rendered at the polls, and Lincoln appointed a number of Ohio Germans to public office. After the war German veterans had the same claim as other soldiers on the gratitude of the country. By 1871 both parties in Ohio were nominating Germans for the office of lieutenant governor. In 1872 leading Ohio Germans figured prominently in the proceedings of the Liberal Republicans, who met in Cincinnati to plan a revolt against "Grantism," although many Germans had difficulty swallowing Horace Greeley, a "teetotaller," as the party's candidate. Subsequently, in the long drawn out controversy over greenbacks, free silver, and sound money, which reached a crisis in Ohio in the gubernatorial contest of 1875 between Rutherford B. Hayes and "Fog Horn Bill" Allen, the German vote again appeared decisive. Advocates of sound money, such as Charles Francis Adams, Charles Nordhoff, Murat Halstead, and Whitelaw Reid, thought it necessary to bring Schurz into Ohio, following his flattering reception in Germany, to make nine speeches to the Ohio Germans

on the money question. His address in the turner hall in Cincinnati in 1875 was a notable exposition of the intricacies of the currency problem, and the Republicans carried the state by about five thousand votes. In 1877 Hayes made Schurz his secretary of the interior.

The German-language press was the spokesman and the mirror for all phases of life in America's German communities and the most effective instrument for maintaining the necessary contact between the old country and the new in the critical years of readjustment. Ohio's German-language press once ranked among the most numerous and the most influential in the nation, and dozens of Ohio communities were able to support at least a German weekly. The first German-language paper was started in Lancaster in 1807, to serve the Pennsylvania-German population of central Ohio. The Columbus *Westbote* was founded in 1843; by 1860 Ohio had twenty-two German-language papers. Cincinnati in 1849 had four, edited in the next two decades by a galaxy of brilliant editors, including such outstanding "Forty-Eighters" as Frederick Hassaurek, August Willich, Johann Rittig, Gustav Tafel, and others. The *Cincinnati Volksblatt*, established in 1836 and published until World War I, for a time was the only German daily in the United States. The *Germania* was Cleveland's first German paper, but was soon overshadowed by the *Wächter am Erie*, founded in 1852, and launched by a group of German liberals who called themselves the "friends of progress." It was originally printed on the press of the *Cleveland Plain Dealer*. August Thieme, a distinguished revolutionary of 1848 with a doctor's degree from a German university, an intellectual aristocrat of independent mind and deep convictions, served as editor until his death in 1879.

Various other papers, like the *Columbia*, the *Deutsche Presse* and the *Biene* were published in Cleveland, but only the *Wächter* survived. Toledo's first German paper was the weekly *Ohio Staatszeitung*. Other papers appeared in Dayton, Akron, Mansfield, Bucyrus, and other cities, and while many were weeklies, some were dailies with considerable influence in their areas.

In 1848 Germans in the United States had welcomed the revolutionary upheavals in the German states with considerable confidence that they would result in a fatherland unified under a republican form of government. Their high hopes were trampled under foot by the heavy tread of Prussian grenadiers speedily mobilized to defend monarchy and reaction. The liberal movement ended in failure. The events of 1870–71, in contrast with the disappointments of 1848, brought unadulterated satisfaction to the great majority of the German element in the United States. The Franco-German War had a tremendous impact upon America's German population.

The war with France was marked by a series of brilliant military victories for the German armies as they swept on to capture Paris, and after centuries of struggle for German unification, the German Empire was established in 1871. Earlier dreams of a unified Germany along more liberal lines were quickly forgotten in the adulation poured on Bismarck and the Hohenzollern Kaiser. During the thrilling period of the Franco-German War the German element in the United States probably achieved its greatest unity. Old differences were forgotten in huge victory parades and peace celebrations in Cleveland, Cincinnati, and other Ohio cities, and throughout the land. Through all of them sounded a note of joy and satisfaction that the unification of Germany had at last united the Germans of America also. German-Americans were convinced that the establishment of the new national state in Europe would help dissipate whatever sense of inferiority they still felt as adopted citizens, and eradicate the remaining prejudices of the nativist period. German-Americans seized upon the events of 1870–71 to demonstrate to native Americans "what Germans could do when they are united." "Before long," concluded the editor of the Columbus *Westbote,* "the name 'Dutchman' may be changed into German."

While Ohio cities were being gradually transformed by the immigrant tide, Teutons were spreading over the whole northern and western map, and creating places as definitely German as Milwaukee, St. Louis, or Grand Island, Nebraska, and gaining recognition through the triumphs of a Theodore Thomas and a Hermann Raster of Chicago, a George Bunsen and a Friedrich Hecker of Belleville, the Engelmanns of Milwaukee, Hermann Kiefer of Detroit, Konrad Krez of Sheboygan, and dozens of others who made their mark upon the intellectual and cultural life of the emerging America. Three hundred and sixty-one men and women born in Germany proper appear in the *Dictionary of American Biography.*

The blend of Anglo-American and German cultures proceeded harmoniously until World War I suddenly brought immeasurable tragedy to millions of Americans of German blood who had never dreamed of the possibility of a war between their adopted fatherland and the country of their origin. In the hysteria against all things German which seized the United States in 1917 and 1918, many of their cherished institutions and cultural monuments suffered crushing attacks from which they have found it almost impossible to recover.

Cathay Comes to El Dorado

DAVID LINDSEY

Between the California Gold Rush of 1848 and the Chinese Exclusion Act of 1882 which barred the entry of Chinese workers into the United States, 290,610 immigrants made the passage from Cathay to America, the vast majority settling in California. Initially attracted by the Gold Rush, Chinese immigration was spurred by poverty in the old country and the hope of prosperity in the new land. At first Oriental newcomers received a more positive welcome here than did the Irish. They were not considered a papist threat to American religion and democracy and they were admired for their industry and cleanliness. In the 1850s, however, their color, customs, dress, and contention with native American and European workers for manual laboring jobs in mining and in railroad construction provoked significant opposition. As early as 1852 California legislators were presenting bills to bar "coolie labor" in the mines. The need for cheap casual labor, which led merchants and other capitalists to support Chinese immigration, and the desire to exclude Chinese, which came from workers and their unions who feared job competition, counterbalanced each other. In the midst of hard times and high unemployment on the Pacific Coast, the California state legislature, with the approval of the governor, passed a law in 1855 setting a head tax of $50 on the importation of persons who could not become citizens. But the state commissioner of immigrants refused to enforce this restriction aimed especially against Orientals, and the California Supreme Court declared it unconstitutional. Frustrated in their efforts at legal restriction, the anti-Chinese forces employed informal coercion, chiefly vigilante action, to discourage Oriental settlement. The Chinese were rendered virtually defenseless against these attacks by an 1854 state Supreme Court edict making inadmissible in state courts the testimony of "Mongolians" against Caucasians. In the 1880s, when American attitudes toward immigration were becoming less favorable, the Chinese achieved the dubious distinction of being the first ethnic minority barred from coming to the United States. The growing resistance to foreign entry, reinforced by traditional American prejudices against nonwhites, made the Chinese the first immigrant group sacrificed to xenophobia.

"Cathay Comes to El Dorado" depicts the experiences of the Chinese immigrants who came to California between 1850 and 1880. This article discloses that their motives for coming

From *American History Illustrated.* Reprinted by permission of The National Historical Society, publishers of *American History Illustrated*, 206 Hanover Street, Gettysburg, Pa. 17325. Published 10 times a year.

here, the type of work that they undertook, their social and economic status, and the bigotry that they encountered were similar to that of other recently arrived ethnic minorities.

Having cleared the Golden Gate, the ship from China tied up at the wharf on San Francisco's *embarcadero*. As one newsman saw it, "Her main deck is packed with Chinamen . . . who are gazing in silent wonder at the new land." Soon "a living stream of blue-coated men from Asia, bearing long bamboo poles across their shoulders," loaded with bedding and packages "pours down the [gang] plank. . . . [They have an] average age of 25 years, [are] healthy, active, able-bodied, they are all dressed in coarse but clean and new cotton blouses and baggy breeches, blue cotton cloth stockings . . . slippers or shoes with heavy wooden soles [and] broad-brimmed hats of split bamboo."

Beginning in 1848 this scene was repeated time and again during the ensuing thirty years. The flow of Chinese into California continued at a steady pace through the mid-19th century. By 1852 over 25,000 (43,800 in 1854) Chinese had reached San Francisco. For the next few years annual entries ranged from 2,240 to 8,430. In 1860 Chinese formed 10 percent of California's population. During the 1870's 123,000 new Chinese arrived in the state.

Although records are hazy and hard to come by, we know that a few Chinese were in the United States considerably before midcentury. Sailors and cabinboys stayed in American ports at various times, and it is clear that five Chinese students attended the Cornwall, Connecticut, foreign mission school from 1818–1825. In 1847 an American missionary returning from China brought with him three young men who began studies at Monson Academy in Massachusetts. One went on to Hamilton College, while another, Yung Wing, graduated from Yale, returned to China, and later served as adviser to the Manchu government and sponsored other students attending American colleges.

But the main stream of Chinese across the Pacific to America resulted from those age-old factors that sent millions of Europeans across the Atlantic—depressed conditions at home and promise of wealth in the United States. The chief difference was that most Chinese did not intend to stay.

Virtually all Chinese migrants to America between 1850 and 1880 came from Kwangtung Province in southern China, where conditions were in upheaval after 1840. China's defeat in the Opium War opened new ports (Amoy, Shanghai, Foochow) to foreign trade, transferred Hong Kong to Britain, and brought economic depression and unemployment to Canton, formerly China's open port to the world outside. To this were added in the countryside surrounding Canton severe crop failures from 1847 to 1850, with resulting dislocations and insurrections. Economic pressures made it increasingly difficult for farmers to make a living on small plots.

When news of the California gold discovery in 1848 reached China, America seemed the answer to troubles at home. If only one son of a Chinese farm family could get to America and strike it rich, he could then return and save the family from distress. The Chinese word for California, "Gum San," translates as "Land of the Golden Mountains." The lure was irresistible.

During 1849–1850 shipmasters and agents distributed broadsides and flyers advertising the "Land of the Golden Mountains" and offering passage from China for $40 to $50. The rush to California was on. By the end of 1849 some 500 Chinese had made the crossing. The next year forty-five ships left Hong Kong for California, jamming up to 500 men in the available space below decks. The long crossing lasted at least forty-five days and often up to sixty days and more. Food rations were meager, sanitary facilities primitive, access to open air infrequent. Fortunately, youth and health were on the side of the migrant, or death rates would have run high.

Only a few Chinese had gone to California

before the gold rush. One, Chum Ming, an enterprising seller of tea and other Chinese goods, was reportedly in San Francisco in 1847. On February 2, 1848 (nine days after the gold strike at Sutter's Mill) merchant Charles V. Gillespie returned from China to San Francisco with two Chinese men, who soon left for the gold mines, and one woman, who stayed on as a domestic servant.

The 1849 trickle of Chinese shortly grew to a steady stream in the 1850's. Young Chinese men (practically no women) regularly emerged from Kwangtung Province at Hong Kong. There the immigrant contacted a passage broker who advanced him funds for passage to America. Under this credit-ticket system, as it was called, the indebted immigrant hoped to pay off his debt from his earnings in America and then, by living frugally and saving his money, return home to his family as a rich man. Indeed, the family in Kwangtung was counting on receiving support from him while he was in America.

On arrival in San Francisco migrants were herded down the gangplank, where they waited eagerly on the wharf, looking at curious new sights, sniffing strange new smells. Amid great confusion, as one migrant later recalled, "out of the general babel some one called out in our local dialect, and like sheep . . . we blindly followed . . . into one of the waiting wagons." Then it was off to the Chinese quarter of the city.

What originally was haphazard soon became a regularized system for handling the rising flow of migrants. Among the 1849 newcomers were at least a few Chinese men of means who became merchants in San Francisco. The term merchant covered traders, shopowners, agents, contractors, proprietors, and money lenders, who combined the prestige of mandarins with the authority of a family head and the power of a creditor. "These self-constituted mandarins," observed a traveler in 1851, "exercised so much influence over the Chinese population . . . as to subject them to fines and bastinado [beatings]."

Norman As-sing, an 1849 arrival, became a merchant and proprietor of the Macao and Woosung Restaurant on Kearney Street and a chief over immigrants. "A sallow, dried, cadaverous, but active and keen old fellow," he wore "a singular mixture" of Chinese and American clothes crowned by "a queue and stovepipe hat at the same time." Merchants like As-sing quickly recognized the tremendous power their economic strength gave them over Chinese newcomers.

Meanwhile, on the evening of December 10, 1849 some 300 Chinese gathered at the Canton Restaurant on Jackson Street and resolved that as "strangers in a strange land" they needed "a counselor . . . in the event of unforeseen difficulties." The next day a committee of four, Ahe, Jon Ling, Atton, and Atung, called on and persuaded a local merchant, Selim E. Woodworth, to serve as an adviser to the Chinese community, members of which were called "China Boys."

At the start they were welcomed in San Francisco. In August 1850 Mayor John W. Geary included a contingent of "China Boys" in the parade mourning President Zachary Taylor's recent death. In their colorful costumes and hats they were a unique attraction then as well as in later celebrations of California's admission as a state, on Washington's Birthday, and on Independence Day. Merchant As-sing formally thanked the mayor on these occasions and later invited the mayor, other officials, "and many ladies" to celebrate "a grand feast in his private home."

As-sing and others in a similar position could well afford such entertainment since the credit-ticket system of importing Chinese workers was run almost exclusively by San Francisco's Chinese merchants. These men soon organized district companies which were not business companies as such but were a combination Chinese protective-benevolent society and control agency for managing Chinese laborers. A company was organized on a geographical basis reflecting the districts of the Pearl River Delta of Kwangtung Province from which the newcomers came. The earliest company, formed in 1851 and called Sam Yap, dealt with migrants from the three districts of Canton. By 1855 there were five companies (later six), which had by then handled numerous arrivals—Sam Yap some 8,400, Sze Yap 13,200, Yeong Wong 16,900, Yan Wo 2,100, and Ning Yeong 8,349. Each company maintained elaborate headquarters in San Francisco with branch offices in Sacramento and Stockton. Included in each complex were a Buddhist temple and a joss house, the center for ceremonies and celebrations.

Each company made all arrangements for newcomers from its districts in China, providing temporary housing and food and locating jobs. To find employment, a member had to register with his company, which recorded the amount of his credit-ticket debt, collected interest, and enforced payment of his debts. Usually the company also looked after its members' well-being, regulated their lives, mediated disputes, and sent his bones back to China when he died. Anyone wishing to return to China had to clear all debts with his company before booking passage. A few found that the "Land of the Golden Mountains" lived up to its reputation—notably the pair who found a $30,000 gold nugget at Moore's Flat and another pair who turned up a 40-pound chunk of gold on the Feather River. By 1855 they had some 8,900 other Chinese sojourners had earned enough to sail back to Kwangtung.

Most that remained worked in the mines. The San Francisco *Alta California* reported "a large party of Celestials [Chinese] . . . on their way to the Southern mines . . . each one carrying a pole . . . rolls of matting, mining tools and provisions." A little later the same paper noted, "our streets have swarmed with Chinese on their way to the mines . . . [with] dray-loads of shovels, picks, pans, matting, rockers and provisions."

The usual pattern for a new sojourner after a few days in San Francisco was to go "by the steamers to Sacramento, Stockton . . . and other points on the Sacramento and San Joaquin Rivers," from which a Chinese agent directed him to a mining camp. At Stockton the "portly Chinese agent," 35-year-old Si-Mong, was described as "one of our merchant princes," who was "quite wealthy and dressed in . . . American fashion" having disposed of "his tail appendage . . . and has taken unto himself a Mexican lady for a wife."

The typical Chinese miner wore his blue cotton blouse down to his knees, broad blue pants, wooden shoes, a broad-brimmed hat, and carried American-made boots. His hair was "close cropped before with a long jet black queue hanging down behind."

In the gold regions Chinese worked along the Feather, Yuba, and American Rivers, but their largest concentrations were in the southern mines of the Merced, Tuolumne, Stanislaus, and Calaveras rivers and tributaries. Indeed, as many as 20,000 Chinese were reported in camp at one time on the Stanislaus River. J. D. Borthwick, an observant traveler in the fifties, recorded "a whole bevy of Chinese" near Placerville in "a dozen or so small tents and brush houses." Again at Mississippi Bar on the Yuba he saw "a company of 150 of them living in a perfect village of small tents, all clustered together on the rocks. . . . Their camp was wonderfully clean."

Since other miners forcefully expelled them from lucrative mining areas, the Chinese generally operated in worked-over areas or unpromising sites. For their own protection against such hostility they normally worked together in gangs of a dozen or more, traveling lightly because of possible expulsion. For extracting gold they used only the most primitive placer mining methods—the usual pan plus the wooden rocker into which two men would shovel while another rocked the box to get the heavier gold particles to settle to the bottom. Such simple equipment could be picked up quickly and carried readily to a new location.

Because they worked in groups Chinese

miners were able to lay bare large sections of stream bed by building wing dams. One visitor marveled at "a Chinamen's dam . . . two or three hundred yards in length . . . built of large pine trees." "In handling such immense logs," wrote the observer, "they are exceedingly ingenious in applying mechanical power, particularly . . . the force of a large number of men upon one point."

At first the Chinese were admired for "the quietness and order, cheerfulness and temperance which is observable in their habits. . . . You will not find an idle Chinaman, and their cleanliness exceeds any other people." Governor John McDougal called them "one of the most worthy classes of our newly adopted citizens."

But the initial admiration wore off before long. Soon they were being called "long-tailed inhabitants from the infernal regions" and worse. In some mining areas their tents were burned, their equipment destroyed, themselves driven out, and signs posted warning other Chinese to stay out. Other harassments grew. In 1853 the state imposed a foreign miners tax of $3 a month (later raised to $4). One contemporary called it "semi-legalized robbery perpetrated upon the Chinese." Other forms of harassment and repression would follow.

Despite obstacles and harsh mistreatment Chinese miners continued to extract gold. How much they recovered is not known, since most of the gold passed into the hands of Chinese merchants and likely a good part of it went on to China. But that mining was sufficiently rewarding is suggested by the census figures showing that as late as 1860 Chinese population in the mining counties of El Dorado and Calaveras exceeded San Francisco's. Indeed, the proportion of Chinese miners grew from 500 out of 57,000 miners in 1850 to 26,000 out of 82,000 in 1860 and to 17,000 out of 33,000 in 1870. Among the Chinese themselves over 20,000 of the 36,500 in California in 1855 were miners, 30,000 of 48,000 in 1862, and ten years later the proportion was still high.

Since theirs were the leftovers, Chinese miners had to scratch twice as hard for what they got. But in 1856 in Auburn Ravine boss Ah-Sam, in charge of a thirty-five-man gang, acquired for $25 a large cabin that six American miners were leaving. Under his direction the gang scraped from the dirt floor $3,000 worth of gold dust that had been spilled there and left by the Americans.

Since the Chinese found American food distasteful, in every mining village of sufficient size they established a Chinese store featuring dried fish, rice, and tea as staples, with pork and chicken as occasional luxuries. The store became a gathering place and social center for Chinese miners of the area. Periodically the proprietor sent for new supplies from Stockton, Sacramento, or Marysville. If business flourished, he might add a wing for a Chinese herbalist and an itinerant barber. In time he would hire a cook, and perhaps build a restaurant with a side room for gambling, furnished with couches for opium smokers. If business warranted, he might even acquire a slave girl as a prostitute—bringing him even more business from the sex-starved miners.

The store and its accouterments provided a few hours' respite from a miner's drab existence and heavy toil. There he could enjoy fleeting moments of the pleasures of the flesh. It was an escape, a safety valve for a lonely man cut off from his homeland, sweating his life away in an alien, hostile environment. Around the store, as the mining town's population grew, there would spring up a small Chinatown.

But none could touch the matchless Chinatown of San Francisco. The earliest Chinese settled mainly on Sacramento Street. By 1853 they had spread to Dupont Street (now Grant Avenue); Chinatown was rapidly taking shape. Wealthy merchants imported carpenters, masons, and building materials to erect Chinese houses. Stores sprang up offering hams, dried fish, pork, tea, and rice along with copper pots, fans, shawls, incense sticks, and chess games.

Over their doors "were suspended brilliantly colored headboards... covered with Chinese characters and yards of red ribbon streaming from them."

In 1852 the first Cantonese opera was performed. A Chinese language semi-weekly paper began publishing in 1854, followed by a tri-weekly in 1855. By that time a Chinatown was a bustling community boasting 23 general stores, 15 apothecaries, 5 butchers, 5 bakers, 5 barbers, 5 herbalists, 3 lumber yards, a candle maker, a curio carver, and 5 restaurants. Visitors found the restaurants especially appealing for "they serve everything promptly, cleanly, hot and well cooked. They give dishes peculiar to every nation over and above their own particular soups, curries, ragouts, which cannot even be imitated elsewhere; and such are their quickness and civil attention that they anticipate your wants."

Although very few Chinese women migrated in the early years, a brothel was already functioning in 1852 under "the charming Miss Atoy, who each day parades our streets dressed in the most flashing European or American style," as the *Alta* reported. "Blooming with youth, beauty and rouge" and nicknamed the "Chinese Aspasia," she fought back when Chinese merchants tried to extort tribute. She also shattered merchant As-sing's efforts to have her deported and obtained a court order compelling him to post a bond not to harass her girls. "She cannot be easily humbugged," noted the *Alta,* this "strangely alluring" woman with her "laughing eyes." But in time prostitution fell under the Six Companies' control. The big Chinatown of San Francisco with its joss houses, gambling halls, and opium dens served as an escape from humdrum living for hardworking Chinese. Here a sojourner could relax and revive the elusive dream that had brought him to America years before.

Most Chinese sojourners toiled hard for a pittance ($2 a day in mining). Those few who did get rich were usually merchants. One of them, Ah Shang, was reported to have returned with a fortune to China, where he served the Manchu emperor as official expert on "barbarians" (meaning foreigners) in negotiations that ended the second Anglo-Chinese war in 1858. As men of wealth, heads of the Six Companies sought to cultivate good relations with the world outside Chinatown. In August 1865 in San Francisco's Chinatown they spread a lavish "Grand Complimentary Dinner" for national politician Schuyler Colfax. When Chu Pak, rich head of Sze Yap Company, became ensnared in a legal tangle, other company chiefs rallied to his support and had him acquitted in an American court. Years later, however, secret societies like the Hung Shun Tong and I Hing Tong emerged to challenge the Six Companies' control of gambling, opium, and prostitution through the use of hatchet men, in the process giving Chinatown a bad name.

As the accessible gold supply in California began to dwindle, the Chinese drifted off to other mining regions in Oregon, Idaho, Montana, Wyoming, Nevada, Utah, and as far east as Colorado. Or they took other jobs.

When railroads came to California, construction work boomed. In 1858 some fifty Chinese were taken on experimentally to grade and lay track for the Sacramento-Vallejo Railroad. A Sacramento newspaper pronounced them "very good working hands... [who] keep at it from sunrise to sunset. The experiment proved that "Chinese laborers can be profitably employed in grading railroads."

When construction of the Central Pacific Railroad began in 1863 with Leland Stanford's turning of the first spadeful of ground in Sacramento, however, some skeptics, notably J. H. Strobridge, construction superintendent for Charles Crocker & Co., the road's prime contractor, still viewed the Chinese as too slight of build for such heavy work. Two years later, with the rails laid only fifty miles eastward, Strobridge took on a few Chinese hands to fill dump carts and found them so effective that within seven months he engaged 3,000 more. A San Francisco mercantile firm, Sisson, Wallace & Co., handled overseas recruiting of additional men. There prospective Chinese workers were advanced $75 for passage to America, signing a note to be paid out of wages in the first seven months of employment.

Altogether 8,000—some estimate as many as 14,000—Chinese worked on building the Central Pacific. In 1868 Chinese newcomers tripled those of the previous year. Organized into thirty- to forty-man gangs under a Chinese boss, they lived in work camps, complete with a cook and common mess, stretching from Dutch Flat eastward to the Nevada line. Pay was $30 a month, but was later boosted to $35. Once a month on pay day "Chollee Clockah" rode into camp with funds for the gang boss who then parcelled out the pay to the men after deducting the cost of food.

Soon the work feats of the Chinese became legendary. In the upper American River canyon hundreds of them chiseled away at the rock while a long human chain hauled away the debris. Then came the graders, tampers, track layers, and hammer men. At the most challenging point, Cape Horn in the High Sierras, a sheer perpendicular cliff offered no foothold in its 1,400-foot face. Here Chinese workers were lowered from the top in baskets to drill holes and place explosives in the rock. Once they lit the fuses they were hauled swiftly up the rock face to escape the explosion. The road inched forward through the solid granite; more than a year passed, but the summit had not yet been reached.

Finally at Donner Summit, in the face of zero weather and heavy snows, the Chinese built their own community forty feet below the snow's surface (with tunnels and passages to bring in air, tools, and powder) and blasted their tunnel through the solid rock, sometimes gaining only inches in a twelve-hour work shift. At length, having passed the Sierras in 1868, they moved rapidly across Nevada to Utah.

The Chinese formed the celebrated crew that on April 28, 1869, set a record of laying ten miles of track in one day. Little wonder Charlie Crocker boasted to a congressional committee that in "hard work, stead pounding on the rock," the "Chinese are skilled in using the hammer and drill"; "they are very trusty, very intelligent and live up to their contracts." With the Central Pacific completed in May 1869, retained Chinese workers built 1,500 miles of the Southern Pacific in the 1870's.

Besides railroad work, Chinese found opportunities elsewhere. When they learned that $8 was the going rate for a basket of laundry in San Francisco, they did it for $5 and were swamped with business. Soon scores of laundries opened, often one group working daytime, another at night. Even in smaller towns the Chinese laundry became an institution—the lone laundryman wielding his iron long hours in an isolated existence, unable to communicate with Americans, dreaming only of his hoped-for return to China.

Farming, too, attracted Chinese workers. In the 1860's Agoston Haraszthy, "Father of California's Wine Industry," took on 100 Chinese in his vineyards and winery at $1 a day. Engaged also for seasonal hand work on wheat farms, they "did the work faithfully and well," according to one grower's testimony. By the 1870's one contemporary observed that "dairy men are largely employing Chinese" and on hops plantations "pickers in the garb of east Asiatics" were "working steadily and noiselessly from morning till night, gathering, curing and sacking the crop." In "fields of strawberries," in "vineyards and orchards . . . these fruits are gathered and boxed for market by this same people. They are expert pickers and packers of fruit. . . ."

In reclamation work the Chinese did most of the labor of draining the swamps of the great delta of the Sacramento and San Joaquin rivers and other parts of the Central Valley. In vegetable and flower growing they were soon running small, efficient farms, especially near San Francisco. Specializing in asters and chrysanthemums, they inaugurated the flower industry.

As early as 1854 the *Alta* reported numerous Chinese fishing villages on San Francisco Bay. "One settlement of 150 Chinese" had twenty-five boats; its "houses placed in a line on each side of the main street look neat and comfortable." Groups of people were "making fish lines and stacking quantities of fish," which were dried and "packed in barrels, boxes and sacks" and sent for sale in town, in the mines, or overseas. By 1880 Chinese fishermen were concentrating on shrimp and abalone, sending out in one year some $38,800 worth of abalone meat and $88,800 worth of shells to China for use as inlay in lacquer work.

Beginning in the 1860's Chinese houseboys were commonly engaged in well-to-do California households. There were many advantages to such a position—a home, food, clothes, wages, a chance to learn English in return for doing the cooking and household chores.

As noted earlier, Chinese cooks and restaurants were justly famous for the high quality and flavor of their food. Most towns in California and elsewhere in the West boasted at least one Chinese restaurant, often well patronized, as Americans savored the pleasures of Chinese cuisine. A formal Chinese dinner could consist of three parts, interspersed with half hour recesses "to smoke and talk and listen to music." Each part might include up to fifteen different dishes, including "shark's fin, stewed pigeon . . . fish sinews with ham, stewed chicken, water cress, seaweed, stewed duck, bamboo soups, birdnest soup, tea and cookies." Chop suey's origin is claimed by many Chinese restaurants, but traditionally it appeared to satisfy the taste of Chinese ambassador Li Hung Chang, "who preferred assorted vegetables with bits of chopped meat." Chow mein began by mistake when a Chinese cook accidentally dropped some noodles in a pan of deep fat.

Many other economic activities employed the Chinese. They dominated the cigar industry on the West Coast, and the same was true in woolen and clothing manufacturing. Makers of shoes, boots, and slippers in the West could not have operated without Chinese workers.

Despite the heavy contribution of Chinese to the West's economy, they became the target of hostile regulations and laws designed to drive them out. In the 1850's their testimony was ruled inadmissable in court, as they were ineligible to become citizens. In 1859 separate schools were authorized for the few Chinese children in California.

As immigration increased, restriction grew. In San Francisco a cubic air ordinance (1870) increased the required living space in sleeping rooms; a basket ordinance (1870) prohibited carrying bundles on bamboo poles; a queue ordinance (1870) required shaving heads of prisoners in county jails; a laundry tax of $15 every quarter was adopted. Most of these were later ruled unconstitutional. A Los Angeles riot in 1871 killed at least eighteen Chinese residents. Chinatowns in other, smaller towns suffered repeated physical assaults. The Workingmen's party, established in 1877 in San Francisco, repeated agitator Denis Kearney's chant "The Chinese Must Go." A new California constitution in 1870 prohibited government or corporation employment of Chinese workers. Outside California, in the late '70's and early '80's, attacks on the Chinese multiplied as armed mobs looted Chinese quarters and killed inhabitants at Tacoma and Seattle, Washington; Rock Springs, Wyoming; and Denver, Colorado.

A congressional bill to block all Chinese immigration in 1880 fell before a presidential veto since it violated the 1868 Burlingame Treaty with China. But in 1882 after the treaty was revised, Congress passed the Chinese Exclusion Act, which barred

Chinese workers' entrance into the United States for the next ten years. (Certain other classes—students, merchants—were still permitted.) The exclusion provision was renewed every ten years and was extended until it became an absolute bar. By the early 20th century few Americans recalled the enormous labors performed by Chinese newcomers in developing the mineral wealth, the agricultural resources, the fisheries, and the transcontinental transportation system of the country. Not until 1943, when the United States and China were partners in the war against Japan, would the immigration restrictions on a highly energetic, industrious, and extremely able and productive people be finally lifted.

3

THE INDUSTRIAL
TRANSFORMATION

Between the end of the Civil War and the beginning of the Second World War approximately 33,000,000 immigrants entered the United States. Over 27,000,000 of these people came from Europe. Nearly 2,900,000 hailed from Canada and Newfoundland and about another 600,000 were of Chinese or Japanese origin. Emigrants from southern and eastern Europe began to arrive in large numbers in the 1880s. The Chinese started moving to California in the late 1840s and, after Congress excluded them in 1882, an influx of Japanese people came to the West Coast. The southern and eastern Europeans predominated among those foreigners who arrived in the late nineteenth and early twentieth centuries but the Germans, Scandinavians, Irish, and English were still coming to the United States during these years. On the West Coast the Japanese made the greatest impact and in the Southwest the Mexicans, primarily a twentieth-century minority, were quite visible. Together with the Indians and blacks, these groups constituted the largest ethnic minorities of this period. The European, Canadian, and Oriental immigrants repeated, to a considerable extent, the experience of earlier newcomers. They toiled in unremunerative, blue-collar occupations for one, two, and sometimes three generations before moving into the mainstream of middle-class America. The Orientals and Mexicans also worked in factories and railroads but their contribution to the development of the West lay primarily in agricultural work. The Indians during this era became wards of the American government, confined to a barren existence on isolated reservations. For the blacks, the Civil War meant the end of slavery, but after a few false starts and weak efforts during Reconstruction the federal government abandoned them and the erstwhile slaves found themselves with little or no hope for future progress.

For several decades after the Civil War the bulk of immigrants continued to come from northern and western Europe. From 1881 to 1890 the influx from Germany, Ireland, the British Isles, and Scandinavia totaled 3,571,361, while those who moved from Italy, the Austro-Hungarian Empire, and Russia and the Baltic States amounted to 883,310. But the industrial and agricultural revolution in Europe, which earlier had dislocated millions of Germans, Irish, and English, moved eastward and southward in the second half of the nineteenth century. East Germany, Italy, the Balkans, and the Austro-Hungarian and Russian empires began to feel the impact of competition from American grain and British manufacturing as advances in rail and sea transport opened markets to the east. Improved transit also enabled dispossessed peasants, victims of agricultural modernization and consolidation, and displaced laborers and artisans, rendered superfluous by industrialization, to seek new lives elsewhere. As a result of these developments the major source of immigration shifted to southern and eastern Europe. From 1901 to 1910 there were 1,711,183 migrants who originated in Germany, Ireland, the British Isles, and Scandinavia, while 5,788,451 hailed from Italy, the Austro-Hungarian Empire, and Russia and the Baltic States. The only exception to this change in geographical concentration was the enormous increase of Scandinavian immigrants. Up to 1860 approximately 40,000 Danes, Swedes, Norwegians, and Finns had entered America; between 1861 and 1940 as many as 2,319,961 natives of these countries came here. Conflicts between Pietists and the established church in Norway influenced some to leave, but the fundamental cause, agricultural displacement as a consequence of modern farming technique and organization, was similar to the situation which spurred earlier emigration from England and Germany and contemporary mass movements from other parts of Europe. Despite the Scandinavian influx, newcomers from the southern and eastern regions of Europe continued to outnumber those from northern and western parts of that continent until the decade of the 1920s, when restrictive legislation curbed the inflow of Italians, Slavs, and Jews.

Most of the immigrants, old (those from northern and western Europe) and new (those from southern and eastern Europe), consisted of males who came over without their families. The Irish, where the females predominated, were the exception to this general trend, but 78 percent of the Italians were men. Many men married here or sent for their wives and children after they had established themselves in America, but others hoped to take their earnings back to their homeland. Having made money here, or out of loneliness or other forms of dissatisfaction with American life, millions went back. Between 1908 and 1914 immigration officials registered 6,709,357 arrivals and 2,063,767 departures. Perhaps as much as one-third of the total number of migrants returned; however, the specific proportions of returnees varied widely among the different national minorities. A high of almost 90 percent of the Balkan peoples and a low of only 5 percent of the Jews made the return voyage, as did more than half of the Hungarians, Italians, Croatians, and Slovenes.

The immigrants, with the exception of the Orientals and Scandinavians, tended to go to the same areas of the country that had attracted previous generations of foreign-born settlers. Eighty percent of the newcomers located in an area bounded roughly by Washington, D.C., in the southeast, St. Louis in the southwest, the Mississippi River, Canada, and the Atlantic Ocean. Two-thirds of all the immigrants dwelled in New York, New England, Pennsylvania, and New Jersey, while sizable numbers appeared in Illinois and Ohio. The Chinese and Japanese, who also left their homelands because of depressed agricultural conditions, for obvious geographical reasons settled on the West Coast. Before 1890 Scandinavians went mostly to the wheat-growing states of Illinois, Wisconsin, Iowa, Minnesota, the Dakotas, Kansas, and Nebraska. But the bitter winter of 1886-87 and the successive years of failing wheat crops motivated them to respond to industrial opportunities in the Northeast and Middle Atlantic states and to move to the lumber camps, ranching areas, and mining centers of Montana and the Pacific Northwest.

The major cities, especially New York and Chicago, still proved particularly attractive because of available employment, because of their location as disembarkation centers, because the immigrants often had no money to go farther inland, and because they were inhabited by compatriots who could help the immigrants adjust to their new environment. The 1910 census records showed that approximately 75 percent of the populations of New York, Chicago, Detroit, Cleveland, and Boston consisted of immigrants and their children. Foreign-born residents and their offspring also constituted majorities in New Orleans, San Francisco, Milwaukee, St. Louis, Cincinnati, Buffalo, Baltimore, Pittsburgh, and Providence. Most of the immigrant groups—the Irish, the Germans, the Italians, and the Jews—initially settled in urban centers. Even those, like the Scandinavians, who originally located on farms eventually gravitated toward the city. Every census after 1910 shows more than 60 percent of the Swedish-born and their children living in urban areas. In 1917 Chicago had the largest number of Swedes and Norwegians in the world next to Stockholm and Oslo, respectively.

The appearance of the new immigrants in the 1880s and '90s coincided with the growth of social unrest in the United States. Strikes, urban crime and poverty, and the emergence of socialist and anarchist movements alarmed America's white middle class, who attributed these trials of industrialism to the newcomers. The Haymarket Affair in 1886, in which the explosion of a bomb at a Chicago labor rally led to a riot and the killing of three policemen, gave rise to a stereotype of the immigrant as a lawless creature. Labor unions also opposed further entry of foreigners because numerous employers used colonies of Italians and Slavs as scabs. Finally, respectable reformers associated urban squalor with the new southern and eastern European immigrants and municipal politics with Irish-Catholic bosses.

The anxieties which the foreign born aroused spawned a variety of anti-immigration pressure groups. The Order of American Mechanics, the American Protective Association, the Immigration Restriction League, and some ministers and academicians coalesced to agitate against further infiltration of foreigners. In 1882 Congress barred Chinese, contract laborers, imbeciles, epileptics, and anarchists from American shores. Restrictionists gathered momentum in the 1890s and the Progressive era and their efforts culminated in the passage of a literacy test in 1917 and Quota Acts of 1921 and 1924. The Quota Acts, unlike most of the barriers erected earlier, were intended not to exclude general categories of undesirables but to establish quotas favoring newcomers from England, Germany, and Scandinavia. Because the Irish had also come to American shores in the earlier part of the nineteenth century the formula favored them as well.

Nativistic outbursts during World War I and the 1920s alarmed many members of the minority groups. The compulsive, ungenerous Americanism manifested itself in Henry Ford's anti-Semitic Dearborn *Independent* (Henry Ford was himself the grandson of an Irish immigrant who left in the famine), in the resurgence of the Ku Klux Klan, and in the bitter anti-Catholicism of the presidential campaign of 1928 when Herbert Hoover defeated Al Smith. On the West Coast white Americans persecuted those of Japanese descent. Segregated into ghettos, precluded by racial heritage from even second- or third-generation integration, and barred from numerous occupations because of prejudice, the Japanese-Americans shouldered enormous burdens. Restrictive legislation in California prohibited them from owning land and in the state of Washington they could not obtain even a fishing permit. The high point of hostility toward Japanese-Americans occurred during the Second World War when people of Japanese descent on the West Coast—both native and foreign born—were removed from their homes and placed behind barbed-wire detention camps in inland states like Utah and Arkansas.

Despite indications of vast hostility most of the white minority groups made significant political, social, and economic progress. The public schools opened a wide variety of opportunities for enterprising individuals and the mass amusement industries provided another avenue of escape from poverty and the ghetto. Intellectuals, journalists, public relations men, actors, and athletes embarked on professional careers in foreign language newspapers, the immigrant theater, or local sporting clubs. Some of the better known people who advanced themselves in this fashion include Walter Winchell, Ed Sullivan, Fanny Brice, Al Jolson, John McCormack, George M. Cohan, Frank Sinatra, Honus Wagner, Benny Leonard, and Rocky Graziano. Neighborhood ethnic groups vicariously shared the recognition received by exploits in the theater or the stadium.

As the minorities grew more experienced in American ways they realized that vital interests concerning employment, protection, and government benefits could be secured only by political power. Politics also offered a route to respectability, as well as a source of individual power, to sharp young first- or second-generation Americans. The Irish, the earliest minority group to settle in American cities, first cracked the Anglo-Saxon political monopoly. By the Civil War they controlled Tammany Hall in New York and were politically influential in Boston and Chicago. In antebellum Milwaukee and Cincinnati the Germans infiltrated urban machines. After the war the new immigrants, Slavs and Jews, sought careers in urban politics. Italians were relative latecomers to political power, but once started they achieved notable triumphs in the 1930s and '40s in Rhode Island, and in the 1940s they seized Tammany from the Irish.

Minority groups also organized voluntary associations to secure mutual benefits. At first the chief function of these organizations was to guarantee a decent burial for their members but soon they acquired other functions. As these organizations solidified their structures and established financial stability, they extended payment of benefits for injuries, illnesses, and insurance for survivors. A few of these groups flourished so splendidly that large surpluses accumulated and they assisted improvident compatriots who were not members. Orphanages, homes for the aged, and other charitable institutions were erected by the wealthy associations to care for the unfortunate with whom they had once shared tribulations. As the organizations grew in magnitude and wealth, informal arrangements gave way to constitutions, bylaws, elected officials, and incorporated bodies. The essential purpose of these groups, however, was not charity but sociability. Members could relax in warm conviviality with those who came from the old culture and, more often than not, from the same hometown. Typically those ethnic groups, Germans and Jews, for example, with the greatest resources, the highest rate of mobility, and the most efficient organizations formed the most useful societies.

The leaders of the voluntary associations were also the leaders of the various ethnic groups of which migrant society consisted. Prominence among the more accepted ethnic minorities came to those who had made good in their new environment, such as wealthy businessmen, who could contribute handsomely and who knew how to deal with the outside world. Ethnic elites were also recruited from those who had matured or had been born here. They knew both worlds and could interpret one for the other. Governor Alfred E. Smith of New York and Mayors Anton Cermack (Chicago), James Michael Curley (Boston), Abe Ruef (San Francisco), and Fiorello H. La Guardia (New York) are the best-known leaders of this type.

Substantial access to American society came through upward mobility and growing prosperity. Immigrants and their offspring gradually improved their status, but not all ethnic groups moved up at the same rate. Factors such as type and level of skills, amount of capital and nature of cultural values brought from abroad, region of ultimate settlement, era when migration occurred, reception given the incoming group, and the degree of preparation made by those already here determined how quickly each group would move in American society. The Germans, one of the most welcomed newcomers, possessing artisan and agricultural skills, aided by strong immigrant assistance societies, carrying over greater wealth than most other immigrant groups, found relatively free access to middle-class America. Jews, although considered less desirable, came with urban skills and characteristics. Their vocational and material accomplishments in industrial America were also due to a tightly knit, ambitious family structure, and a plenitude of effective benevolent agencies that enabled them to achieve great business and professional success in spite of anti-Semitism in the United States. The Irish and Italians, poorer than many other contemporary immigrant groups, and less educated and having fewer relevant skills than the Jews and Germans, progressed much more painfully and slowly in America. In general only a minority of the first generation were able to take that crucial small step from worker to individual proprietor of a neighborhood retail store. Many slipped back into blue-collar employment, but enough had risen to lend a semblance of reality to immigrant dreams that they or their children would not always be on the outside looking in. Especially for the second generation improved education and the growing need for experts and professionals in an increasingly technological society enabled thousands to move up into more desirable social statuses and functions. Many filled places in the burgeoning corporate and civil service bureaucracies. Even those whose mobility was limited by chance, poverty, skill, prejudice, personality, or lack of education frequently improved their situation. Growing national wealth and expansion of unions resulted in better working conditions and larger paychecks. Increased prosperity enabled them to imitate the lifestyles of middle-class America and provided better opportunities for their children, thus giving them a greater share in the American dream.

The American dream turned into a nightmare for those ethnic minorities barred by bigotry from sharing in the prestige and prosperity that came to other groups. Indians suffered most from the restrictions and prejudices of the dominant culture. For the last time in the 1880s and 1890s the Indians turned to fight for their remaining land. Forced into the Plains, the Rockies, and the Southwest by advancing settlement, the Apaches and the Dakota Sioux violently, but unsuccessfully, resisted imprisonment in reservations. With their defeat went the last shred of independent territory held by the red men. The 250,000 Indians remaining, a fraction of their earlier population, finally became wards of the government. Laws enacted in Washington and politics pursued by the Department of Interior's Indian Bureau destroyed the tribal structure and stripped future generations of their cultural heritage. Within twenty years of the Dawes Act (1887) the government had disposed of 60 percent of Indian land, three-quarters to white buyers. The money obtained from the sale was held in a trust fund to be used for "civilizing" the Indians. The federal government also set up boarding schools for Indian children outside the reservations. Children from the age of six and up were taken from their parents—willingly or unwillingly—and sent thousands of miles away where they were superficially trained for obsolete manual vocations. Unless the parents could pay their children's fare back to the reservations during vacations the boys and girls remained away from home for as long as ten years. Deprived of land, equipped neither for white society nor permitted to live in peace in their tribal community, robbed of their children, the Indians' lot was even more tragic after the white men's efforts to "help" the "Noble Savages" than it had been in an earlier day when red men had simply been forced to move westward.

In 1924 the American government, still committed to a policy of Americanization, sought to redress long-standing grievances by granting citizenship to all Indians. A decade later President Franklin D. Roosevelt appointed John Collier, the nation's most ardent champion of Indian rights, Commissioner of Indian Affairs. Collier drew attention to the dire results of white paternalism and attempted to encourage community revival through tribal ownership of land and rejuvenation of the Indians' cultural heritage. However, his efforts could not reverse decades of demoralization caused by acute poverty and cultural disintegration.

Unlike the Indians, the blacks had hopes for a better life after the Civil War. The Republican Congresses during Reconstruction emancipated the bondsmen, guaranteed them civil and political rights, and financed the Freedman's Bureau, which provided welfare and education for the ex-slaves. Reconstruction governments in the southern states, frequently containing black judges and legislators, also embarked upon improvement projects. Federal troops protected the black man's rights, and sympathetic northerners contributed money for relief and education. But land ownership was the major vehicle for independence in the agrarian South, and the failure of the state and federal governments to provide freedmen with forty acres and a mule doomed them to generations of agricultural peonage.

The North started removing its troops and withdrawing protection from southern blacks in the early 1870s. By 1900, spurred by conflicts over agricultural reform, the process of eliminating supposedly guaranteed constitutional rights was virtually complete. Poll taxes, literacy tests, and all-white primaries deprived blacks of political rights; terror, debt, segregation, violence, poor education, and the arbitrary use of the law oppressed them almost as severely as had slavery.

In the late nineteenth century sizable migrations to the North began. Even before the first massive influx during World War I, New York, Philadelphia, and Chicago had significant black enclaves. The desire to escape southern bigotry played a role in these evacuations, but economic factors, such as rural poverty, the ravages of the boll weevil on the cotton crop, and broader occupational opportunities, had a greater influence. Movement to the city accelerated during World War I when northern industry needed vast quantities of labor. This resettlement, combined with normal wartime tensions and anxieties, resulted in race riots and an expanding pattern of residential and social segregation. The fears of working-class whites led to bloody riots in East St. Louis in 1917 and thereafter in Philadelphia, Chicago, and other cities.

In the 1920s the black community made some strides in material self-improvement, cultural achievement, and ethnic pride. Blacks also made more vigorous demands for equal rights. The prosperity of the decade and the growing urbanization of the race enabled a few thousand to emerge from poverty into an expanding middle class. Black literary magazines, jazz spots, and coffee houses provided opportunities to exchange ideas and to publish or perform the work of black musicians, poets, and novelists. And for the first time in America, they were appreciated as serious performers by white audiences. The singer Paul Robeson was one of the most famous examples.

Improvements also occurred for those who remained in the working class. Long-standing exclusion from labor unions had made blacks readily available strikebreakers. While the pattern of exclusion and scab labor did not disappear, A. Philip Randolph succeeded in organizing railroad employees into the Brotherhood of Sleeping Car Porters, the first black labor union.

The New Deal and World War II also improved the status and the material condition of many American blacks. For the first time since Reconstruction the federal government gave them the feeling that their interests were of concern to Washington. Prominent New Dealers, particularly Eleanor Roosevelt and Harold Ickes, the Secretary of the Interior, voiced support for equal treatment, and an unprecedented number of blacks received federal patronage appointments. The real benefit of the New Deal, however, came not from humanitarian utterances or the official recognition of a few middle-class spokesmen but through the impact of relief programs. Segregation was the dominant practice in federal agencies, and the blacks received the smallest benefits, but for the first time since the Freedmen's Bureau, they shared in government bounties. Similar gains were made in the labor movement. The formation of the CIO, with its integrationist policy, was a tremendous spur toward organizing black workers and consequently to ending the use of black strikebreakers. Appreciative of the party responsible for this policy, large numbers of them switched their allegiance to the Democrats in the 1936 elections.

During World War II the pull of high wages in defense industries drew many blacks out of the rural South into northern, midwestern, and West Coast cities. War created prosperity, and scarcity of labor benefited black workers, businessmen, and professionals. But occupational progress and higher incomes were accompanied by race riots in New York and Detroit.

The militancy of black leaders also grew more pronounced during World War II. In the 1940s, with even greater vigor and better results than in the 1930s, the NAACP steadily undermined the legal defense of segregation and white political supremacy. A. Philip Randolph's threat to lead a march on Washington moved President Roosevelt to create the Fair Employment Practices Committee. In 1942 activists established the Congress of Racial Equality (CORE), an organization committed to nonviolent demonstrations for civil rights. At the same time the Reverend Adam Clayton Powell, Jr., led successful boycotts against Harlem chain stores lacking black employees.

Between the 1860s and the end of the Second World War ethnic minorities, except for the Indians and the Mexican-Americans, significantly improved their material conditions and occupational status. Irish teachers and public officials, Italian shopkeepers, Jewish businessmen and professionals, and the black urban bourgeoisie made vast leaps in American society. Some members of white minorities even achieved a social status equal to, or almost equal to, Americans with a longer lineage in the United States. Rarely, however, were blacks accepted in white residential areas; most white-collar jobs were still barred to them; and many hotels, restaurants, and recreation centers in every part of the country still refused their patronage. Economic advancement resulted in much greater social progress for whites than blacks during the major part of the industrial transformation. During the post-World War II period, however, the blacks would begin to make significant progress.

SELECTED BIBLIOGRAPHY

For the late nineteenth and early twentieth centuries the literature on minorities is voluminous. On the Indians one might start with Dee Brown, *Bury My Heart at Wounded Knee* (New York: Holt, Rinehart & Winston, 1971), and on the blacks, George M. Frederickson, *The Black Image in the White Mind: The Debate on Afro-American Character and Destiny, 1817–1914* (New York: Harper & Row, 1971). For the other groups the following books provide introductions and, in some cases, bibliographies as well: Jacques Ducharmes, *The Shadows of the Trees: The Story of French-Canadians in*

New England (New York: Harper & Bros., 1943); Theodore C. Blegen, *Norwegian Migration to America, 1825–1860* (Northfield, Minn.: The Norwegian-American Historical Association, 1931), and Blegen, ed., *Land of Their Choice* (Minneapolis: University of Minnesota Press, 1955); Richard Gambino, *Blood of My Blood* (New York: Doubleday, 1974), on the Italians; Henry L. Feingold, *Zion in America: The Jewish Experience from Colonial Times to the Present* (New York: Hippocrene Books, 1974); Emily Green Balch, *Our Slavic Fellow Citizens* (New York: Charities Publication Committee, 1910); Irving Howe, *World of Our Fathers* (New York and London: Harcourt Brace Jovanovich, 1976); Theodore Saloutos, *The Greeks in the United States* (Cambridge, Mass.: Harvard University Press, 1964); Henry S. Lucas, *Netherlanders in America* (Ann Arbor: The University of Michigan Press, 1955); Emil Lengyel, *Americans from Hungary* (Philadelphia: J. B. Lippincott, 1948); and Roger Daniels, *The Politics of Prejudice* (New York: Atheneum, 1968), on the Japanese. Joseph J. Barton, *Peasants and Strangers: Italians, Rumanians, and Slovaks in an American City, 1890–1950* (Cambridge: Harvard University Press, 1975), is a more specialized study from a sociological perspective.

An Indian's View of Indian Affairs

YOUNG JOSEPH

White Americans took whatever lands that they wanted from the Indians. Sometimes the taking was made legal in the white man's eyes because treaties were signed. On other occasions treaties were ignored because land-hungry frontiersmen and capitalists bent on expansion found them too constricting. Eventually Americans possessed virtually all the land that had belonged to Indians. The few red men who had not been killed were confined to reservations, usually the most arid and infertile lands where no white man saw immediate value.

One episode in the encroachment of white settlements into Indian land evoked the following selection, the lament of Chief Joseph. Joseph was chief of the Nez Percé Indians, a friendly tribe that inhabited the Snake Valley in western Idaho. In 1877, when settlers began to move into land reserved for his people, Chief Joseph led the Nez Percés out of their reservation across Idaho and Montana in a seventy-five-day flight. The fugitives did no damage and even paid farmers for supplies on the way. The army finally trapped the Nez Percés, and the federal government assigned them to barren lands in Indian territory in Oklahoma, where the tribe quickly succumbed to malaria and other diseases.

I wish that I had words at command in which to express adequately the interest with which I have read the extraordinary narrative which follows, and which I have the privilege of introducing to the readers of this "Review." I feel, however, that this *apologia* is so boldly marked by the charming *naïveté* and tender pathos which characterize the red-man, that it needs no introduction, much less any authentication; while in its smothered fire, in its deep sense of eternal righteousness and of present evil, and in its hopeful longings for the coming of a better time, this Indian chief's appeal reminds us of one of the old Hebrew prophets of the days of the captivity.

I have no special knowledge of the history of the Nez Percés, the Indians whose tale of sorrow Chief Joseph so pathetically tells— my Indian missions lying in a part at the West quite distant from their old home—and am not competent to judge their case upon its merits. The chief's narrative is, of course, *ex parte*, and many of his statements would no doubt be ardently disputed. General Howard, for instance, can hardly receive justice at his

From *North American Review*, 128 (1879), 412–33.

hands, so well known is he for his friendship to the Indian and for his distinguished success in pacifying some of the most desperate.

It should be remembered, too, in justice to the army, that it is rarely called upon to interfere in Indian affairs until the relations between the Indians and the whites have reached a desperate condition, and when the situation of affairs has become so involved and feeling on both sides runs so high that perhaps only more than human forbearance would attempt to solve the difficulty by disentangling the knot and not by cutting it.

Nevertheless, the chief's narrative is marked by so much candor, and so careful is he to qualify his statements, when qualification seems necessary, that every reader will give him credit for speaking his honest, even should they be thought by some to be mistaken, convictions. The chief, in his treatment of his defense, reminds one of those lawyers of whom we have heard that their splendid success was gained, not by disputation, but simply by their lucid and straightforward statement of their case. That he is something of a strategist as well as an advocate appears from this description of an event which occurred shortly after the breaking out of hostilities: "We crossed over Salmon River, hoping General Howard would follow. We were not disappointed. He did follow us, and we got between him and his supplies, and cut him off for three days." Occasionally the reader comes upon touches of those sentiments and feelings which at once establish a sense of kinship between all who possess them. Witness his description of his desperate attempt to rejoin his wife and children when a sudden dash of General Miles's soldiers had cut the Indian camp in two: "About seventy men, myself among them, were cut off. . . . I thought of my wife and children, who were now surrounded by soldiers, and I resolved to go to them. With a prayer in my mouth to the Great Spirit Chief who rules above, I dashed unarmed through the line of soldiers. . . . My clothes were cut to pieces, my horse was wounded, but I was not hurt." And again, when he speaks of his

father's death: "I saw he was dying. I took his hand in mine. He said: 'My son, my body is returning to my mother Earth, and my spirit is going very soon to see the Great Spirit Chief. . . . A few more years and the white men will be all around you. They have their eyes on this land. My son, never forget my dying words. This country holds your father's body—never sell the bones of your father and your mother.' I pressed my father's hand, and told him I would protect his grave with my life. My father smiled, and passed away to the spiritland. I buried him in that beautiful valley of Winding Waters. I love that land more than all the rest of the world. A man who would not love his father's grave is worse than a wild animal."

His appeals to the natural rights of man are surprisingly fine, and, however some may despise them as the utterances of an Indian, they are just those which, in our Declaration of Independence, have been most admired. "We are all sprung from a woman," he says, "although we are unlike in many things. You are as you were made, and, as you were made, you can remain. We are just as we were made by the Great Spirit, and you can not change us: then, why should children of one mother quarrel? Why should one try to cheat another? I do not believe that the Great Spirit Chief gave one kind of men the right to tell another kind of men what they must do."

But I will not detain the readers of the "Review" from the pleasure of perusing for themselves Chief Joseph's statement longer than is necessary to express the hope that those who have time for no more will at least read its closing paragraph, and to remark that the narrative brings clearly out these facts which ought to be regarded as well-recognized principles in dealing with the red-man:

1. The folly of any mode of treatment of the Indian which is not based upon a cordial and operative acknowledgment of his rights as our *fellow man*.

2. The danger of riding rough-shod over a people who are capable of high enthusiasm,

who know and value their national rights, and are brave enough to defend them.

3. The liability to want of harmony between different departments and different officials of our complex Government, from which it results that, while many promises are made to the Indians, few of them are kept. It is a home-thrust when Chief Joseph says: "The white people have too many chiefs. They do not understand each other.... I can not understand how the Government sends a man out to fight us, as it did General Miles, and then break his word. Such a Government has something wrong about it."

4. The unwisdom, in most cases in dealing with Indians, of what may be termed *military short-cuts,* instead of patient discussion, explanations, persuasion, and reasonable concessions.

5. The absence in an Indian tribe of any truly representative body competent to make a treaty which shall be binding upon all the bands. The failure to recognize this fact has been the source of endless difficulties. Chief Joseph, in this case, did not consider a treaty binding which his band had not agreed to, no matter how many other bands had signed it; and so it has been in many other cases.

6. Indian chiefs, however able and influential, are really without power, and for this reason, as well as others, the Indians, when by the march of events they are brought into intimate relations with the whites, should at the earliest practicable moment be given the support and protection of our Government and of our law; not *local* law, however, which is apt to be the result of *special* legislation, adopted solely in the interest of the stronger race.

WILLIAM H. HARE,
Missionary Bishop of Niobrara.

My friends, I have been asked to show you my heart. I am glad to have a chance to do so. I want the white people to understand my people. Some of you think an Indian is like a wild animal. This is a great mistake. I will tell you all about our people, and then you can judge whether an Indian is a man or not. I believe much trouble and blood would be saved if we opened our hearts more. I will tell you in my way how the Indian sees things. The white man has more words to tell you how they look to him, but it does not require many words to speak the truth. What I have to say will come from my heart, and I will speak with a straight tongue. Ah-cum-kin-i-ma-me-hut (the Great Spirit) is looking at me, and will hear me.

My name is In-mut-too-yah-lat-lat (Thunder traveling over the Mountains). I am chief of the Wal-lam-wat-kin band of Chute-pa-lu, or Nez Percés (nose-pierced Indians). I was born in eastern Oregon, thirty-eight winters ago. My father was chief before me. When a young man, he was called Joseph by Mr. Spaulding, a missionary. He died a few years ago. There was no stain on his hands of the blood of a white man. He left a good name on the earth. He advised me well for my people.

Our fathers gave us many laws, which they had learned from their fathers. These laws were good. They told us to treat all men as they treated us; that we should never be the first to break a bargain; that it was a disgrace to tell a lie; that we should speak only the truth; that it was a shame for one man to take from another his wife, or his property without paying for it. We were taught to believe that the Great Spirit sees and hears everything, and that he never forgets; that hereafter he will give every man a spirit-home according to his deserts: if he has been a good man, he will have a good home; if he has been a bad man, he will have a bad home. This I believe, and all my people believe the same.

We did not know there were other people besides the Indian until about one hundred winters ago, when some men with white faces came to our country. They brought many things with them to trade for furs and skins. They brought tobacco, which was new to us. They brought guns with flint stones on them, which frightened our women and children. Our people could not talk with these white-faced men, but they used signs which all people understand. These men were Frenchmen, and they called our people "Nez Percés," because they wore rings in their noses for ornaments. Although very few of our people wear them now, we are still called by the same name. These French trappers said a great many things to our fathers, which have been planted in our hearts. Some were good for us, but some were bad. Our people were divided in opinion about these men. Some thought they taught more bad than good. An Indian respects a brave man, but he despises a coward. He loves a straight tongue, but he hates a forked tongue. The French trappers told us some truths and some lies.

The first white men of your people who came to our country were named Lewis and Clarke. They also brought many things that our people had never seen. They talked straight, and our people gave them a great feast, as a proof that their hearts were friendly. These men were very kind. They made presents to our chiefs and our people made presents to them. We had a great many horses, of which we gave them what they needed, and they gave us guns and tobacco in return. All the Nez Percés made friends with Lewis and Clarke, and agreed to let them pass through their country, and never to make war on white men. This promise the Nez Percés have never broken. No white man can accuse them of bad faith, and speak with a straight tongue. It has always been the pride of the Nez Percés that they were the friends of the white men. When my father was a young man there came to our country a white man (Rev. Mr. Spaulding) who talked spirit law. He won the affections of our people because he spoke good things to them. At first he did not say anything about white men wanting to settle on our lands. Nothing was said about that until about twenty winters ago, when a number of white people came into our country and built houses and made farms. At first our people made no complaint. They thought there was room enough for all to live in peace, and they

were learning many things from the white men that seemed to be good. But we soon found that the white men were growing rich very fast, and were greedy to possess everything the Indian had. My father was the first to see through the schemes of the white men, and he warned his tribe to be careful about trading with them. He had suspicion of men who seemed so anxious to make money. I was a boy then, but I remember well my father's caution. He had sharper eyes than the rest of our people.

Next there came a white officer (Governor Stevens), who invited all the Nez Percés to a treaty council. After the council was opened he made known his heart. He said there were a great many white people in the country, and many more would come; that he wanted the land marked out so that the Indians and white men could be separated. If they were to live in peace it was necessary, he said, that the Indians should have a country set apart for them, and in that country they must stay. My father, who represented his band, refused to have anything to do with the council, because he wished to be a free man. He claimed that no man owned any part of the earth, and a man could not sell what he did not own.

Mr. Spaulding took hold of my father's arm and said, "Come and sign the treaty." My father pushed him away, and said: "Why do you ask me to sign away my country? It is your business to talk to us about spirit matters, and not to talk to us about parting with our land." Governor Stevens urged my father to sign his treaty, but he refused. "I will not sign your paper," he said; "you go where you please, so do I; you are not a child, I am no child; I can think for myself. No man can think for me. I have no other home than this. I will not give it up to any man. My people would have no home. Take away your paper. I will not touch it with my hand."

My father left the council. Some of the chiefs of the other bands of the Nez Percés signed the treaty, and then Governor Stevens gave them presents of blankets. My father cautioned his people to take no presents, for "after a while," he said, "they will claim that you have accepted pay for your country." Since that time four bands of the Nez Percés have received annuities from the United States. My father was invited to many councils, and they tried hard to make him sign the treaty, but he was firm as the rock, and would not sign away his home. His refusal caused a difference among the Nez Percés.

Eight years later (1863) was the next treaty council. A chief called Lawyer, because he was a great talker, took the lead in this council, and sold nearly all the Nez Percés country. My father was not there. He said to me: "When you go into council with the white man, always remember your country. Do not give it away. The white man will cheat you out of your home. I have taken no pay from the United States. I have never sold our land." In this treaty Lawyer acted without authority from our band. He had no right to sell the Wallowa (winding water) country. That had always belongs to my father's own people, and the other bands had never disputed our right to it. No other Indians ever claimed Wallowa.

In order to have all people understand how much land we owned, my father planted poles around it and said:

"Inside is the home of my people—the white man may take the land outside. Inside this boundary all our people were born. It circles around the graves of our fathers, and we will never give up these graves to any man."

The United States claimed they had bought all the Nez Percés country outside of Lapwai Reservation, from Lawyer and other chiefs, but we continued to live on this land in peace until eight years ago, when white men began to come inside the bounds my father had set. We warned them against this great wrong, but they would not leave our land, and some bad blood was raised. The white men represented that we were going upon the war-path. They reported many things that were false.

The United States Government again asked for a treaty council. My father had become blind and feeble. He could no longer speak for his people. It was then that I took my father's place as chief. In this council I made my first speech to white men. I said to the agent who held the council:

"I did not want to come to this council, but I came hoping that we could save blood. The white man has no right to come here and take our country. We have never accepted any presents from the Government. Neither Lawyer nor any other chief had authority to sell this land. It has always belonged to my people. It came unclouded to them from our fathers, and we will defend this land as long as a drop of Indian blood warms the hearts of our men."

The agent said he had orders, from the Great White Chief in Washington, for us to go upon the Lapwai Reservation, and that if we obeyed he would help us in many ways. "You *must* move to the agency," he said. I answered him: "I will not. I do not need your help; we have plenty, and we are contented and happy if the white man will let us alone. The reservation is too small for so many people with all their stock. You can keep your presents; we can go to your towns and pay for all we need; we have plenty of horses and cattle to sell, and we won't have any help from you; we are free now; we can go where we please. Our fathers were born here. Here they lived, here they died, here are their graves. We will never leave them." The agent went away, and we had peace for a little while.

Soon after this my father sent for me. I saw he was dying. I took his hand in mine. He said: "My son, my body is returning to my mother earth, and my spirit is going very soon to see the Great Spirit Chief. When I am gone, think of your country. You are the chief of these people. They look to you to guide them. Always remember that your father never sold his country. You must stop your ears whenever you are asked to sign a treaty selling your home. A few years more, and white men will be all around you. They have their eyes on this land. My son, never forget my dying words. This country holds your father's body. Never sell the bones of your father and your mother.'' I pressed my father's hand and told him I would protect his grave with my life. My father smiled and passed away to the spirit-land.

I buried him in that beautiful valley of winding waters. I love that land more than all the rest of the world. A man who would not love his father's grave is worse than a wild animal.

For a short time we lived quietly. But this could not last. White men had found gold in the mountains around the land of winding water. They stole a great many horses from us, and we could not get them back because we were Indians. The white men told lies for each other. They drove off a great many of our cattle. Some white men branded our young cattle so they could claim them. We had no friend who would plead our cause before the law councils. It seemed to me that some of the white men in Wallowa were doing these things on purpose to get up a war. They knew that we were not strong enough to fight them. I labored hard to avoid trouble and bloodshed. We gave up some of our country to the white men, thinking that then we could have peace. We were mistaken. The white man would not let us alone. We could have avenged our wrongs many times, but we did not. Whenever the Government has asked us to help them against other Indians, we have never refused. When the white men were few and we were strong we could have killed them all off, but the Nez Percés wished to live at peace.

If we have not done so, we have not been to blame. I believe that the old treaty has never been correctly reported. If we ever owned the land we own it still, for we never sold it. In the treaty councils the commissioners have claimed that our country had been sold to the Government. Suppose a white man should come to me and say, ''Joseph, I like your horses, and I want to buy them.'' I say to him, ''No, my horses suit me, I will not sell them.'' Then he goes to my neighbor, and says to him: ''Joseph has some good horses. I want to buy them, but he refuses to sell.'' My neighbor answers, ''Pay me the money, and I will sell you Joseph's horses.'' The white man returns to me, and says, ''Joseph, I have bought your horses, and you must let me have them.'' If we sold our lands to the Government, this is the way they were bought.

On account of the treaty made by the other bands of the Nez Percés, the white men claimed my lands. We were troubled greatly by white men crowding over the line. Some of these were good men, and we lived on peaceful terms with them, but they were not all good.

Nearly every year the agent came over from Lapwai and ordered us on to the reservation. We always replied that we were satisfied to live in Wallowa. We were careful to refuse the presents or annuities which he offered.

Through all the years since the white men came to Wallowa we have been threatened and taunted by them and the treaty Nez Percés. They have given us no rest. We have had a few good friends among white men, and they have always advised my people to bear these taunts without fighting. Our young men were quick-tempered, and I have had great trouble in keeping them from doing rash things. I have carried a heavy load on my back ever since I was a boy. I learned then that we were but few, while the white men were many, and that we could not hold our own with them. We were like deer. They were like grizzly bears. We had a small country. Their country was large. We were contented to let things remain as the Great Spirit Chief made them. They were not; and would change the rivers and mountains if they did not suit them.

Year after year we have been threatened, but no war was made upon my people until General Howard came to our country two years ago and told us that he was the white war-chief of all that country. He said: ''I have a great many soldiers at my back. I am going to bring them up here, and then I will talk to you again. I will not let white men laugh at me the next time I come. The country belongs to the Government, and I intend to make you go upon the reservation.''

I remonstrated with him against bringing more soldiers to the Nez Percés country. He had one house full of troops all the time at Fort Lapwai.

The next spring the agent at Umatilla agency sent an Indian runner to tell me to meet General Howard at Walla Walla. I could not go myself, but I sent my brother and five other head men to meet him, and they had a long talk.

General Howard said: "You have talked straight, and it is all right. You can stay in Wallowa.'' He insisted that my brother and his company should go with him to Fort Lapwai. When the party arrived there General Howard sent out runners and called all the Indians in to a grand council. I was in that council. I said to General Howard, "We are ready to listen.'' He answered that he would not talk then, but would hold a council next day, when he would talk plainly. I said to General Howard: "I am ready to talk to-day. I have been in a great many councils, but I am no wiser. We are all sprung from a woman, although we are unlike in many things. We can not be made over again. You are as you were made, and as you were made you can remain. We are just as we were made by the Great Spirit, and you can not change us; then why should children of one mother and one father quarrel—why should one try to cheat the other? I do not believe that the Great Spirit Chief gave one kind of men the right to tell another kind of men what they must do.''

General Howard replied: "You deny my authority, do you? You want to dictate to me, do you?''

Then one of my chiefs—Too-hool-hool-suit—rose in the council and said to General Howard: "The Great Spirit Chief made the world as it is, and as he wanted it, and he made a part of it for us to live upon. I do not see where you get authority to say that we shall not live where he placed us.''

General Howard lost his temper and said: "Shut up! I don't want to hear any more of such talk. The law says you shall go upon the reservation to live, and I want you to do so, but you persist in disobeying the law'' (meaning the treaty). "If you do not move, I will take the matter into my own hand, and make you suffer for your disobedience.''

Too-hool-hool-suit answered: "Who are you, that you ask us to talk, and then tell me I sha'n't talk? Are you the Great Spirit? Did you make the world? Did you make the sun? Did you make the rivers to run for us to drink? Did you make the grass to grow? Did you make all these things, that you talk to us as though we were boys? If you did, then you have the right to talk as you do.''

General Howard replied, "You are an impudent fellow, and I will put you in the guard-house,'' and then ordered a soldier to arrest him.

Too-hool-hool-suit made no resistance. He asked General Howard: "Is that your order? I don't care. I have expressed my heart to you. I have nothing to take back. I have spoken for my country. You can arrest me, but you can not change me or make me take back what I have said.''

The soldiers came forward and seized my friend and took him to the guard-house. My men whispered among themselves whether they should let this thing be done. I counseled them to submit. I knew if we resisted that all the white men present, including General Howard, would be killed in a moment, and we would be blamed. If I had said nothing, General Howard would never have given another unjust order against my men. I saw the danger, and, while they dragged Too-hool-hool-suit to prison, I arose and said: "*I am going to talk now.* I don't care whether you arrest me or not." I turned to my people and said: "The arrest of Too-hool-hool-suit was wrong, but we will not resent the insult. We were invited to this council to express our hearts, and we have done so." Too-hool-hool-suit was prisoner for five days before he was released.

The council broke up for that day. On the

next morning General Howard came to my lodge, and invited me to go with him and White-Bird and Looking-Glass, to look for land for my people. As we rode along we came to some good land that was already occupied by Indians and white people. General Howard, pointing to this land, said: "If you will come on to the reservation, I will give you these lands and move these people off."

I replied: "No. It would be wrong to disturb these people. I have no right to take their homes. I have never taken what did not belong to me. I will not now."

We rode all day upon the reservation, and found no good land unoccupied. I have been informed by men who do not lie that General Howard sent a letter that night, telling the soldiers at Walla Walla to go to Wallowa Valley, and drive us out upon our return home.

In the council, next day, General Howard informed me, in a haughty spirit, that he would give my people *thirty days* to go back home, collect all their stock, and move on to the reservation, saying, "If you are not here in that time, I shall consider that you want to fight, and will send my soldiers to drive you on."

I said: "War can be avoided, and it ought to be avoided. I want no war. My people have always been the friends of the white man. Why are you in such a hurry? I can not get ready to move in thirty days. Our stock is scattered, and Snake River is very high. Let us wait until fall, then the river will be low. We want time to hunt up our stock and gather supplies for winter."

General Howard replied, "If you let the time run over one day, the soldiers will be there to drive you on to the reservation, and all your cattle and horses outside of the reservation at that time will fall into the hands of the white men."

I knew I had never sold my country, and that I had no land in Lapwai; but I did not want bloodshed. I did not want my people killed. I did not want anybody killed. Some of my people had been murdered by white

men, and the white murderers were never punished for it. I told General Howard about this, and again said I wanted no war. I wanted the people who lived upon the lands I was to occupy at Lapwai to have time to gather their harvest.

I said in my heart that, rather than have war, I would give up my country. I would give up my father's grave. I would give up everything rather than have the blood of white men upon the hands of my people.

General Howard refused to allow me more than thirty days to move my people and their stock. I am sure that he began to prepare for war at once.

When I returned to Wallowa I found my people very much excited upon discovering that the soldiers were already in the Wallowa Valley. We held a council, and decided to move immediately, to avoid bloodshed.

Too-hool-hool-suit, who felt outraged by his imprisonment, talked for war, and made many of my young men willing to fight rather than be driven like dogs from the land where they were born. He declared that blood alone would wash out the disgrace General Howard had put upon him. It required a strong heart to stand up against such talk, but I urged my people to be quiet, and not to begin a war.

We gathered all the stock we could find, and made an attempt to move. We left many of our horses and cattle in Wallowa, and we lost several hundred in crossing the river. All of my people succeeded in getting across in safety. Many of the Nez Percés came together in Rocky Cañon to hold a grand council. I went with all my people. This council lasted ten days. There was a great deal of war-talk, and a great deal of excitement. There was one young brave present whose father had been killed by a white man five years before. This man's blood was bad against white men, and he left the council calling for revenge.

Again I counseled peace, and I thought the danger was past. We had not complied with General Howard's order because we could not, but we intended to do so as soon as possible. I was leaving the council to kill beef for my family, when news came that the young man whose father had been killed had gone out with several other hot-blooded young braves and killed four white men. He rode up to the council and shouted: "Why do you sit here like women? The war has begun already." I was deeply grieved. All the lodges were moved except my brother's and my own. I saw clearly that the war was upon us when I learned that my young men had been secretly buying ammunition. I heard then that Too-hool-hool-suit, who had been imprisoned by General Howard, had succeeded in organizing a war-party. I knew that their acts would involve all my people. I saw that the war could not then be prevented. The time had passed. I counseled peace from the beginning. I knew that we were too weak to fight the United States. We had many grievances, but I knew that war would bring more. We had good white friends, who advised us against taking the war-path. My friend and brother, Mr. Chapman, who has been with us since the surrender, told us just how the war would end. Mr. Chapman took sides against us, and helped General Howard. I do not blame him for doing so. He tried hard to prevent bloodshed. We hoped the white settlers would not join the soldiers. Before the war commenced we had discussed this matter all over, and many of my people were in favor of warning them that if they took no part against us they should not be molested in the event of war being begun by General Howard. This plan was voted down in the war-council.

There were bad men among my people who had quarreled with white men, and they talked of their wrongs until they roused all the bad hearts in the council. Still I could not believe that they would begin the war. I know that my young men did a great wrong, but I ask, Who was first to blame? They had been insulted a thousand times; their fathers and brothers had been killed; their mothers and wives had been disgraced; they had been driven to madness by whisky sold to them by white men; they had been told by General

Howard that all their horses and cattle which they had been unable to drive out of Wallowa were to fall into the hands of white men; and, added to all this, they were homeless and desperate.

I would have given my own life if I could have undone the killing of white men by my people. I blame my young men and I blame the white men. I blame General Howard for not giving my people time to get their stock away from Wallowa. I do not acknowledge that he had the right to order me to leave Wallowa at any time. I deny that either my father or myself ever sold that land. It is still our land. It may never again be our home, but my father sleeps there, and I love it as I love my mother. I left there, hoping to avoid bloodshed.

If General Howard had given me plenty of time to gather up my stock, and treated Too-hool-hool-suit as a man should be treated, there *would have been no war.*

My friends among white men have blamed me for the war. I am not to blame. When my young men began the killing, my heart was hurt. Although I did not justify them, I remember all the insults I had endured, and my blood was on fire. Still I would have taken my people to the buffalo country without fighting, if possible.

I could see no other way to avoid a war. We moved over to White Bird Creek, sixteen miles away, and there encamped, intending to collect our stock before leaving; but the soldiers attacked us, and the first battle was fought. We numbered in that battle sixty men, and the soldiers a hundred. The fight lasted but a few minutes, when the soldiers retreated before us for twelve miles. They lost thirty-three killed, and had seven wounded. When an Indian fights, he only shoots to kill; but soldiers shoot at random. None of the soldiers were scalped. We do not believe in scalping, nor in killing wounded men. Soldiers do not kill many Indians unless they are wounded and left upon the battle-field. Then they kill Indians.

Seven days after the first battle, General Howard arrived in the Nez Percés country, bringing seven hundred more soldiers. It was now war in earnest. We crossed over Salmon River, hoping General Howard would follow. We were not disappointed. He did follow us, and we got back between him and his supplies, and cut him off for three days. He sent out two companies to open the way. We attacked them, killing one officer, two guides, and ten men.

We withdrew, hoping the soldiers would follow, but they had got fighting enough for that day. They intrenched themselves, and next day we attacked them again. The battle lasted all day, and was renewed next morning. We killed four and wounded seven or eight.

About this time General Howard found out that we were in his rear. Five days later he attacked us with three hundred and fifty soldiers and settlers. We had two hundred and fifty warriors. The fight lasted twenty-seven hours. We lost four killed and several wounded. General Howard's loss was twenty-nine men killed and sixty wounded.

The following day the soldiers charged upon us, and we retreated with our families and stock a few miles, leaving eighty lodges to fall into General Howard's hands.

Finding that we were outnumbered, we retreated to Bitter Root Valley. Here another body of soldiers came upon us and demanded our surrender. We refused. They said, "You can not get by us." We answered, "We are going by you without fighting if you will let us, but we are going by you anyhow." We then made a treaty with these soldiers. We agreed not to molest any one, and they agreed that we might pass through the Bitter Root country in peace. We bought provisions and traded stock with white men there.

We understood that there was to be no more war. We intended to go peaceably to the buffalo country, and leave the question of returning to our country to be settled afterward.

With this understanding we traveled on for four days, and, thinking that the trouble was all over, we stopped and prepared tent-poles to take with us. We started again, and at the end of two days we saw three white men passing our camp. Thinking that peace had been made, we did not molest them. We could have killed or taken them prisoners, but we did not suspect them of being spies, which they were.

That night the soldiers surrounded our camp. About daybreak one of my men went out to look after his horses. The soldiers saw him and shot him down like a coyote. I have since learned that these soldiers were not those we had left behind. They had come upon us from another direction. The new white war-chief's name was Gibbon. He charged upon us while some of my people were still asleep. We had a hard fight. Some of my men crept around and attacked the soldiers from the rear. In this battle we lost nearly all our lodges, but we finally drove General Gibbon back.

Finding that he was not able to capture us, he sent to his camp a few miles away for his big guns (cannons), but my men had captured them and all the ammunition. We damaged the big guns all we could, and carried away the powder and lead. In the fight with General Gibbon we lost fifty women and children and thirty fighting men. We remained long enough to bury our dead. The Nez Percés never make war on women and children; we could have killed a great many women and children while the war lasted, but we would feel ashamed to do so cowardly an act.

We never scalp our enemies, but when General Howard came up and joined General Gibbon, their Indian scouts dug up our dead and scalped them. I have been told that General Howard did not order this great shame to be done.

We retreated as rapidly as we could toward the buffalo country. After six days General Howard came close to us, and we went out and attacked him, and captured nearly all his horses and mules (about two hundred and fifty head). We then marched on to the Yellowstone Basin.

On the way we captured one white man and two white women. We released them at the end of three days. They were treated kindly. The women were not insulted. Can the white soldiers tell me of one time when Indian women were taken prisoners, and held three days and then released without being insulted? Were the Nez Percés women who fell into the hands of General Howard's soldiers treated with as much respect? I deny that a Nez Percé was ever guilty of such a crime.

A few days later we captured two more white men. One of them stole a horse and escaped. We gave the other a poor horse and told him he was free.

Nine days' march brought us to the mouth of Clarke's Fork of the Yellowstone. We did not know what had become of General Howard, but we supposed that he had sent for more horses and mules. He did not come up, but another new war-chief (General Sturgis) attacked us. We held him in check while we moved all our women and children and stock out of danger, leaving a few men to cover our retreat.

Several days passed, and we heard nothing of General Howard, or Gibbon, or Sturgis. We had repulsed each in turn, and began to feel secure, when another army, under General Miles, struck us. This was the fourth army, each of which outnumbered our fighting force, that we had encountered within sixty days.

We had no knowledge of General Miles's army until a short time before he made a charge upon us, cutting our camp in two, and capturing nearly all of our horses. About seventy men, myself among them, were cut off. My little daughter, twelve years of age, was with me. I gave her a rope, and told her to catch a horse and join the others who were cut off from the camp. I have not seen her since, but I have learned that she is alive and well.

I thought of my wife and children, who were now surrounded by soldiers, and I resolved to go to them or die. With a prayer in my mouth to the Great Spirit Chief who rules above, I dashed unarmed through the line of soldiers. It seemed to me that there were many guns on every side, before and behind me. My clothes were cut to pieces and my horse was wounded, but I was not hurt. As I reached the door of my lodge, my wife handed me my rifle, saying: "Here's your gun. Fight!"

The soldiers kept up a continuous fire. Six of my men were killed in one spot near me. Ten or twelve soldiers charged into our camp and got possession of two lodges, killing three Nez Percés and losing three of their men, who fell inside our lines. I called my men to drive them back. We fought at close range, not more than twenty steps apart, and drove the soldiers back upon their main line, leaving their dead in our hands. We secured their arms and ammunition. We lost, the first day and night, eighteen men and three women. General Miles lost twenty-six killed and forty wounded. The following day General Miles sent a messenger into my camp under protection of a white flag. I sent my friend Yellow Bull to meet him.

Yellow Bull understood the messenger to say that General Miles wished me to consider the situation; that he did not want to kill my people unnecessarily. Yellow Bull understood this to be a demand for me to surrender and save blood. Upon reporting this message to me, Yellow Bull said he wondered whether General Miles was in earnest. I sent him back with my answer, that I had not made up my mind, but would think about it and send word soon. A little later he sent some Cheyenne scouts with another message. I went out to meet them. They said they believed that General Miles was sincere and really wanted peace. I walked on to General Miles's tent. He met me and we shook hands. He said, "Come, let us sit down by the fire and talk this matter over." I remained with him all night; next morning Yellow Bull came over to see if I was alive, and why I did not return.

General Miles would not let me leave the tent to see my friend alone.

Yellow Bull said to me: "They have got you in their power, and I am afraid they will never let you go again. I have an officer in our camp, and I will hold him until they let you go free.''

I said: ''I do not know what they mean to do with me, but if they kill me you must not kill the officer. It will do no good to avenge my death by killing him.''

Yellow Bull returned to my camp. I did not make any agreement that day with General Miles. The battle was renewed while I was with him. I was very anxious about my people. I knew that we were near Sitting Bull's camp in King George's land, and I thought maybe the Nez Percés who had escaped would return with assistance. No great damage was done to either party during the night.

On the following morning I returned to my camp by agreement, meeting the officer who had been held a prisoner in my camp at the flag of truce. My people were divided about surrendering. We could have escaped from Bear Paw Mountain if we had left our wounded, old women, and children behind. We were unwilling to do this. We had never heard of a wounded Indian recovering while in the hands of white men.

On the evening of the fourth day General Howard came in with a small escort, together with my friend Chapman. We could now talk understandingly. General Miles said to me in plain words, ''If you will come out and give up your arms, I will spare your lives and send you to your reservation.'' I do not know what passed between General Miles and General Howard.

I could not bear to see my wounded men and women suffer any longer; we had lost enough already. General Miles had promised that we might return to our own country with what stock we had left. I thought we could start again. I believed General Miles, or *I never would have surrendered*. I have heard that he has been censured for making the promise to return us to Lapwai. He could not have made any other terms with me at that time. I would have held him in check until my friends came to my assistance, and then neither of the generals nor their soldiers would have ever left Bear Paw Mountain alive.

On the fifth day I went to General Miles and gave up my gun, and said, ''From where the sun now stands I will fight no more.'' My people needed rest—we wanted peace.

I was told we could go with General Miles to Tongue River and stay there until spring, when we would be sent back to our country. Finally it was decided that we were to be taken to Tongue River. We had nothing to say about it. After our arrival at Tongue River, General Miles received orders to take us to Bismarck. The reason given was, that subsistence would be cheaper there.

General Miles was opposed to this order. He said: ''You must not blame me. I have endeavored to keep my word, but the chief who is over me has given the order, and I must obey it or resign. That would do you no good. Some other officer would carry out the order.''

I believe General Miles would have kept his word if he could have done so. I do not blame him for what we have suffered since the surrender. I do not know who is to blame. We gave up all our horses—over eleven hundred—and all our saddles—over one hundred—and we have not heard from them since. Somebody has got our horses.

General Miles turned my people over to another soldier, and we were taken to Bismarck. Captain Johnson, who now had charge of us, received an order to take us to Fort Leavenworth. At Leavenworth we were placed on a low river bottom, with no water except river-water to drink and cook with. We had always lived in a healthy country, where the mountains were high and the water was cold and clear. Many of my people sickened and died, and we buried them in this strange land. I can not tell how much my heart suffered for my people while at Leavenworth. The Great Spirit Chief who rules above seemed to be looking some other way, and did not see what was being done to my people.

During the hot days (July, 1878) we received notice that we were to be moved farther away from our own country. We were not asked if we were willing to go. We were ordered to get into the railroad-cars. Three of my people died on the way to Baxter Springs. It was worse to die there than to die fighting in the mountains.

We were moved from Baxter Springs (Kansas) to the Indian Territory, and set down without our lodges. We had but little medicine, and we were nearly all sick. Seventy of my people have died since we moved there.

We have had a great many visitors who have talked many ways. Some of the chiefs (General Fish and Colonel Stickney) from Washington came to see us, and selected land for us to live upon. We have not moved to that land, for it is not a good place to live.

The Commissioner Chief (E. A. Hayt) came to see us. I told him, as I told every one, that I expected General Miles's word would be carried out. He said it "could not be done; that white men now lived in my country and all the land was taken up; that, if I returned to Wallowa, I could not live in peace; that law-papers were out against my young men who began the war, and that the Government could not protect my people." This talk fell like a heavy stone upon my heart. I saw that I could not gain anything by talking to him. Other law chiefs (Congressional Committee) came to see me and said they would help me to get a healthy country. I did not know who to believe. The white people have too many chiefs. They do not understand each other. They do not all talk alike.

The Commissioner Chief (Mr. Hayt) invited me to go with him and hunt for a better home than we have now. I like the land we found (west of the Osage reservation) better than any place I have seen in that country; but it is not a healthy land. There are no mountains and rivers. The water is warm. It is not a good country for stock. I do not believe my people can live there. I am afraid they will all die. The Indians who occupy that country are dying off. I promised Chief Hayt to go there, and do the best I could until the Government got ready to make good General Miles's word. I was not satisfied, but I could not help myself.

Then the Inspector Chief (General McNiel) came to my camp and we had a long talk. He said I ought to have a home in the mountain country north, and that he would write a letter to the Great Chief at Washington. Again the hope of seeing the mountains of Idaho and Oregon grew up in my heart.

At last I was granted permission to come to Washington and bring my friend Yellow Bull and our interpreter with me. I am glad we came. I have shaken hands with a great many friends, but there are some things I want to know which no one seems able to explain. I can not understand how the Government sends a man out to fight us, as it did General Miles, and then breaks his word. Such a Government has something wrong about it. I can not understand why so many chiefs are allowed to talk so many different ways, and promise so many different things. I have seen the Great Father Chief (the President), the next Great Chief (Secretary of the Interior), the Commissioner Chief (Hayt), the Law Chief (General Butler), and many other law chiefs (Congressmen), and they all say they are my friends, and that I shall have justice, but while their mouths all talk right I do not understand why nothing is done for my people. I have heard talk and talk, but nothing is done. Good words do not last long unless they amount to something. Words do not pay for my dead people. They do not pay for my country, now overrun by white men. They do not protect my father's grave. They do not pay for all my horses and cattle. Good words will not give me back my children. Good words will not make good the promise of your War Chief General Miles. Good words will not give my people good health and stop them from dying. Good words will not get my people a home where they can live in peace and take care of themselves. I am tired of talk that comes to nothing. It makes my heart sick when I remember all the good words and all the broken promises. There has been too much talking by men who had no right to talk. Too many misrepresentations have been made, too many misunderstandings have come up between the white men about the Indians. If the white man wants to live in peace with the Indian he can live in peace. There need be no trouble. Treat all men alike. Give them all the same law. Give them all an even chance to live and grow. All men were made by the same Great Spirit Chief. They are all brothers. The earth is the mother of all people, and all people should have equal rights upon it. You might as well expect the rivers to run backward as that any man who was born a free man should be contented when penned up and denied liberty to go where he pleases. If you tie a horse to a stake, do you expect he will grow fat? If you pen an Indian up on a small spot of earth, and compel him to stay there, he will not be contented, nor will he grow and prosper. I have asked some of the great white chiefs where they get their authority to say to the Indian that he shall stay in one place, while he sees white men going where they please. They can not tell me.

I only ask of the Government to be treated as all other men are treated. If I can not go to my own home, let me have a home in some country where my people will not die so fast. I would like to go to Bitter Root Valley. There my people would be healthy; where they are now they are dying. Three have died

since I left my camp to come to Washington.

When I think of our condition my heart is heavy. I see men of my race treated as outlaws and driven from country to country, or shot down like animals.

I know that my race must change. We can not hold our own with the white men as we are. We only ask an even chance to live as other men live. We ask to be recognized as men. We ask that the same law shall work alike on all men. If the Indian breaks the law, punish him by the law. If the white man breaks the law, punish him also.

Let me be a free man—free to travel, free to stop, free to work, free to trade where I choose, free to choose my own teachers, free to follow the religion of my fathers, free to think and talk and act for myself—and I will obey every law, or submit to the penalty.

Whenever the white man treats the Indian as they treat each other, then we will have no more wars. We shall all be alike—brothers of one father and one mother, with one sky above us and one country around us, and one government for all. Then the Great Spirit Chief who rules above will smile upon this land, and send rain to wash out the bloody spots made by brothers' hands from the face of the earth. For this time the Indian race are waiting and praying. I hope that no more groans of wounded men and women will ever go to the ear of the Great Spirit Chief above, and that all people my be one people.

In-mut-too-yah-lat-lat has spoken for his people.

The Black Family in Boston

ELIZABETH PLECK

Until recent years the large number of female-headed, one-parent black families was considered a legacy of slavery. Bondage, it was argued by eminent sociologist Franklin Frazier in the 1930s and by Daniel P. Moynihan in the 1960s, created the matriarchal and unstable Afro-American household. Lack of a male model, and an unsettled family relationship, in turn, were blamed for much of the poverty, crime, and other forms of social dislocation that occurred in the black ghettos. Conclusions about the structure of the black family were made without any supporting data and have recently been challenged by historians who have examined census reports, especially the 1880 census. The Autumn 1975 issue of The Journal of Interdisciplinary History *(Vol. VI) contained three article showing that mid- and late-nineteenth-century blacks in several rural counties and cities in the South and in Philadelphia, Troy, New York, and Buffalo, New York, had rates of two-parent-headed families similar to those of whites living in these places. The relatively slight differences between families of different races resulted from unfavorable economic conditions and higher mortality rates in the black communities. In short, these studies show that cultural factors, for example, slavery, played an insignificant role in shaping this aspect of the Afro-American family. In the essay reprinted below, Elizabeth Pleck, analyzing data from the 1880 census, comes to similar conclusions regarding the black family in Boston.*

Once the most rural of American ethnic groups, Afro-Americans are now the most urban. Slavery, migration to the city and the adaptation to urban culture have had major effects on black life, yet we know little about the ways in which the most basic unit of black life, the family, was affected by these changes. Through research in the manuscript census schedules of the federal census for 1880 and other largely quantitative materials, I looked for answers to the following questions. What was the effect of migration on the black family? What was the occupational situation of black heads of household? How did urban and rural families differ in their adaptation to life in the city? How did literate and illiterate families differ? What family forms predominated? How frequent

From the *Journal of Social History*, Vol. VIII, No. 4, pp. 333–56. Copyright 1974, by Peter N. Stearns. Reprinted by permission of the editor.

was "family disorganization," as reflected in an imbalanced sex ratio, frequent desertions by the head of household and large numbers of female-headed households?

We can learn a great deal about black family life from an examination of Boston in the late nineteenth century. The Hub was a major northern metropolis, with a large and diversified economy, which should have offered opportunities for unskilled but willing black workers. As a result of the long efforts of blacks and whites in the abolitionist movement, the city had no segregated institutions and a widely respected system of free public schools. Boston had acquired a reputation among blacks as "the paradise of the Negro," a city of unparalleled freedom and opportunity. Since the black population was so small a percentage of the inhabitants of the city, the racial fears and animosities of the white population appeared, surfaced, but did not explode into major race riots like those in New York and Philadelphia during the Civil War. The large Irish and small black populations lived in an uneasy truce, with the two groups dwelling in close proximity in the west and south ends of the city. Unique in some ways, representative of major northern cities in others, Boston is an interesting city in which to study many facets of black family life.

The most typical black household in late nineteenth-century Boston included the husband and wife, or husband, wife, and children. This predominant household form prevailed among all occupational levels and among families of both urban and rural origins. By enlarging the household to include boarders, families from all occupational strata augmented the family income and provided homes for the large numbers of migrants in the population. This evidence from the manuscript census contradicts the commonly held association between "the tangle of pathology," "family disorganization" and the black family.

Before examining the composition of the black household, I will indicate how inferences were made about the origins and literacy of heads of household and I will discuss three aspects of social life in Boston—the transiency of the population, the depressing occupational position of black heads of household and the physical circumstances of life—which severely constrained family survival.

COMPARISON OF RURAL AND URBAN, LITERATE AND ILLITERATE HEADS OF HOUSEHOLD

In the analysis of one- and two-parent households which follows, the foreign-born heads of household were excluded since they offer too few cases for valid comparisons. Comparing the northern- and southern-born heads of household, I looked for possible differences in urban and rural family adaptation to life in Boston. Since the manuscript census schedules indicate the state of birth of an individual, but not the city or area where the individual was born or raised, the comparison is imperfect. Although a majority of northern-born blacks lived most of their lives in urban areas, the northern-born category also included farmers from New England, townspeople from western Massachusetts, and settlers from the free black communities of Ohio. By further separating those born in Massachusetts (mostly natives of Boston) from the rest of the northern-born, I was able to discern differences between that part of the population which was born in Boston and that portion of the population which migrated into the city.

While most southern-born blacks were rural folk, that category also includes city-dwellers from Richmond, Baltimore, or Washington, D.C. Even more difficult to distinguish are those southern-born blacks who were urban in experience, if not in place of birth. But despite these qualifications, it seems useful to perceive the northern-born as essentially an urban group, and the southern-born as a rural group.

The distinction between literacy and illiteracy may have been as important as the difference between urban and rural families.

Seven out of ten black adults could read a few words and sign their names, the nineteenth-century standard of literacy. Even this minimal knowledge reflected a variety of skills which facilitated successful adaptation to urban life. Those without such skills—the illiterates—were more at a disadvantage than they were on the farm and more noticeable for their deficiency as well. Whole families headed by illiterates faced far greater difficulties in cities than those headed by literate parents.

In the South, illiterates tended to be ex-slaves. (The equation of illiteracy and slave status would have been unnecessary had the Boston census takers directly enumerated the number of freedmen in the black population.) Under slavery, most blacks were not taught to read or write or were prevented from even learning. While there were exceptions, self-educated slaves (Frederick Douglass is the most well-known example), the opportunities for literacy were much greater for free blacks than for slaves. But before equating southern-born illiterates with ex-slaves, two important qualifications must be added. First, even the majority of free blacks, like the slaves, were untutored. Second, the number of illiterates was very low, far below any estimate we might make of the number of ex-slaves in the population. Thus, while illiteracy appeared in both northern- and southern-born families, its presence among the southern-born, in addition, reflects the existence of ex-slaves in the population.

GEOGRAPHIC MOBILITY

From the 3,496 blacks living in Boston in 1870, the population grew ten years later to include 5,873 persons. By 1910, the population had expanded three times to 13,654. In the same forty-year period, the white population grew over two and one-half times, and the foreign-born white population tripled. The metropolis was growing rapidly, and within the city the black population, although small in absolute number and size

relative to the white population—never more than 2% of the total population throughout the period—was growing at a rate faster than that of the foreign-born immigrants.

In the late nineteenth century the black population absorbed a large number of migrants. While a minority, 42%, of Boston's blacks in 1880 had been born in the North, a majority were strangers to northern life; 49% of the population was born in the South, while another 9% were born in foreign countries. Of the northern-born population, especially those born in Massachusetts, the majority probably were natives of Boston. Other northern-born blacks came from neighboring cities in the Northeast and a few were from rural areas in New England. For the foreign-born, their life in Boston was the culmination of the long journey from Nova Scotia, New Brunswick, or other parts of Canada, or the end of a long sea voyage from the West Indies. The largest group in the population, the southern-born, included migrants from the Upper South, especially Virginia.

These southern newcomers seem to contradict prevailing theories of migration to cities. Rather than traveling short distances and settling at the first stop along the way, these migrants moved as much as five hundred miles from home, often passing through other urban centers. Why did these men and women make the long journey? The usual explanation of black migration to the North refers to Jim Crow segregation, racism, and declining economic opportunities in the South, combined with the expanding economy and the promise of a freer life in the North. Pushed out by southern conditions, pulled to the North, the land of golden streets and busy factories, the combination of push and pull factors explains the Great Migration, the period during and after World War I. The earlier movement, described by Carter Woodson as the migration of the Talented Tenth, represented a period when blacks were more "pulled" to the North than "pushed" from the South. The absence of two factors—widespread agricultural depression and active recruitment of blacks by northern employment agents—further distinguished the earlier migration from the Great Migration of World War I. Despite the propaganda of some of their brethren and the appeals of some southern whites, the black emigrant was above all looking for a better life in the northern city. One migrant was Ella Beam, a young woman who left the South Carolina Sea Islands for Boston.

She stated that she did not leave home on account of hard times. When she left, her father was doing well on the farm. There were several boys in the family, so she was rarely called upon to go into the fields. She felt, however, that she was not especially needed at home. The fact that she manifested sufficient initiative to take the course at the training school [domestic science] is perhaps indicative of the courage and energy of a young woman who wanted to better her condition. She had been in Boston only one year when she received a simple job caring for children in the home of a Melrose family.

For the most part, the migrants included young adults above the age of twenty, very few of whom came with their families. In households headed by a southern-born parent, 72.1% of the oldest children in the family were born in the North. Among the oldest children of a Canadian parent, 60.7% had been born in the North. Six out of seven of

the oldest children in West Indian families had been born in the North. Thus the migration from the South and from foreign countries included single individuals or couples, but in very few cases did the whole family make the move.

The story of migration does not end with the arrival of the newcomer in Boston. Instead of settling down, the transient frequently packed up and left. Evidence from several nineteenth-century cities in the Northeast indicates a high rate of black migration, generally higher than that of other groups. But in the South and West the rate of black out-migration was about the same as or a little lower than among other groups. Assuming this pattern is substantiated in further research, it indicates the absence of job opportunities for black workers in nearby southern areas, as well as the proximity of many cities in the urban Northeast where the transient could find employment.

An examination of Boston city directories reveals that only 25% of adult black males listed in the 1880 census were enumerated in the 1890 city directory, while 64% of a respective sample of adult white males in 1880 remained in the city ten years later. The rate of persistence for blacks was very similar among all occupational levels, as Table 1 suggests, while the rate of persistence among

Table 1. Proportion of Adult Male Residents of Boston in 1880 Persisting There to 1890, by Racial Group, Household Status, and Occupational Level[a]

	(%) Overall Persistence Rate	(%) White Collar	(%) Skilled	(%) Unskilled and Service	N
White Residents[b]	64	72	63	56	1809
All Blacks	25	26	25	25	1992
Heads of household	31	35	28	32	1066
Sons	21	25	33	15	63

[a]The white-collar category includes professionals, clerical workers, and petty proprietors. Heads of household include black males in single-member households, as well as the more prevalent one- and two-parent households. Adult males were defined as those 21 and over. Sons include adult males residing at home. Persistence rates for women were extremely difficult to estimate because of name changes due to marriage and the incomplete city directory coverage given to women who were not heading households. There was no statistically significant relationship between occupational level and persistence for all blacks, nor was there a significant relationship for heads of households or sons.
[b]Data for white residents is from Stephan Thernstrom and Elizabeth H. Pleck, "The Last of the Immigrants? A Comparative Analysis of Immigrant and Black Social Mobility in Late Nineteenth-Century Boston," unpublished paper delivered at the annual meeting of the Organization of American Historians (April, 1970), p. 12.

white males decreased for lower-status workers. Among blacks heading households, the rate of persistence was 31%, compared with the 25% overall figure. Adult sons residing at home, although few in number, were more transient than their fathers, since only 21% of them remained in the city for the decade 1880–1890.

High rates of turnover were common in other northeastern cities. In the depression years of the 1870's black out-migration occurred frequently among Poughkeepsie and Buffalo residents. Only one-third of the black workers in Poughkeepsie in 1870 remained in the city ten years later. In a twenty-year trace of black adult males in Buffalo from 1855 to 1875, only 12% could be found.

The northern pattern of high black out-migration and much lower out-migration for other groups is reversed in the South and West. In Atlanta, for example, blacks were much more likely to remain in the city than either foreign-born whites or native whites. Even more remarkable, within all occupational categories, the black departure rate was lower than that of native white and foreign-born immigrants. For Birmingham, Alabama, the much higher rate of black persistence was the result of fewer opportunities elsewhere for black workers. During the depression decade 1870–1880, in San Antonio, blacks, European immigrants and native whites had very similar rates of persistence—36% for blacks, 36% for European immigrants, and 35% for native whites—while the Chicano population was the most transient, with only 25% of the male population remaining there ten years later. The question remains whether this pattern of southern black geographic stability was also reflected in long-lasting marriages and continuity of parental care for black children.

OCCUPATIONAL STRUCTURE

The occupational position of black heads of household placed a great strain on the black family. While the children of white immigrants moved up the occupational ladder, the black child, like his parent, remained fixed in a world of menial and temporary jobs. Eight occupations—waiter, servant, cook, barber, laborer, porter, laundress, and seamstress—accounted for 74% of all blacks at work in Boston in 1880. The largest group by far were the 858 servants who worked in white homes, hotels, and institutions. Two occupations, laundress and seamstress, were largely the preserve of single women and women heading households. The last hired and the first fired, blacks in late nineteenth-century Boston formed a surplus labor force at the bottom of society.

The concentration of blacks in unskilled and service occupations is demonstrated in Table 2. Overall, 86.7% of the total black work force consisted of unskilled and service workers, 7.2% of black workers held skilled positions, 2.9% performed clerical jobs or owned small shops, and 3.2% were professionals. Table 2 also includes the percentage of Irish workers in 1880 in each of these occupational status groups. An immigrant group of peasant origins, the Boston Irish were the white ethnic group which ranked lowest in the Boston social order. Except at the top of the occupational structure, where there was a slightly higher percentage of professionals among the black work force than among the Irish, Irish workers had much larger percentages of white-collar and skilled workers and much smaller percentages of unskilled and service workers than the black labor force. While 68.9% of the Irish were laborers, teamsters, hostlers, and other unskilled and service workers, 86.7% of blacks performed this low-status work. The classification of menial labor, moreover, tends to obscure the wage differences between the two groups. The black waiter and the Irish cotton mill operative both worked long hours at low pay, but the rewards were somewhat greater for the Irish worker than for his black counterpart.

Seven point two percent of all blacks earning wages and 19.8% of the Irish were skilled workers. Such work, particularly in the building trades, required apprenticeship

Table 2. Occupational Level of Black Male and Female Heads of Household, Black Non-Heads of Household, and Irish, 1880

	Black Heads of Household[a]		Black Non-Heads of Household		All Blacks at Work	All Irish at Work[b]
	Male	Female	Male	Female		
Professional	(36)	(1)	(25)	(25)	(87)	(562)
	3.4%[c]	.6%	2.3%	2.9%	3.2%	1.6%
White Collar	(33)	(2)	(52)	(6)	(93)	(3333)
	3.1%	1.3%	4.8%	.7%	2.9%	9.6%
Skilled	(72)	(31)	(54)	(84)	(241)	(6880)
	6.8%	19.4%	5.0%	9.7%	7.2%	19.8%
Unskilled and Service	(925)	(126)	(950)	(751)	(2752)	(23,970)
	86.8%	78.8%	87.9%	86.7%	86.7%	68.9%
	(1066)	(160)	(1081)	(866)	(3173)	(34,745)

[a]Heads of household with no occupation were omitted from the head of household group.
[b]Derived from data in Carroll Wright, *Social, Commercial, and Manufacturing Statistics of the City of Boston* (Boston: Rockwell and Churchill, 1882).
[c]Column percentages sometimes do not add up to 100 due to rounding. The relationship between occupational level and household status (head of household vs. non-head of household) is significant at .030 with three degrees of freedom for males, significant at .002 with three degrees of freedom for females.

training which was generally closed to blacks; even buying tools could be an expensive proposition for a black worker. The white-collar group, over three times as large among the Irish as among blacks, owed their jobs to the expansion of record-keeping, paper work, and sales in an industrial society. The new jobs in the Boston labor market—office personnel, sales clerk, even telephone and telegraph operator—employed some of the children of Irish parents, while job discrimination and lack of the proper educational qualifications closed this employment to the aspiring black worker. The figures for the white-collar group also reflected the larger proportion of petty proprietors among the Irish than among blacks.

For black professionals, Boston deserved its reputation as the city of the "Talented Tenth." The relatively large number of black lawyers, doctors, and other professionals, compared with the somewhat smaller Irish percentage, was the result of the attractiveness of the city to educated blacks from the South and other parts of the North, as well as the educational opportunities for the black elite in the New England area.

Thus the black child and the black parent faced more limited job opportunities than even the proletarian Boston Irish. How did the occupational situation of heads of household compare with that of the black worker with no family responsibilities? Although the head of household, in order to support dependents, needed to earn more money than the unattached black worker, Table 2 indicates that there were virtually no differences in occupational situation between blacks heading households and those not heading households. Among unskilled and service workers, one finds 86.8% of black heads of household and 87.9% of the unattached black workers.

Providing for a family was even more difficult for the widowed or deserted wife. Female-headed households included 22 women with no occupations and 105 women at work, most of them in unskilled and service jobs. The skilled category in Table 2, which includes 18% of female workers, is the result of the large number of black seamstresses among females heading households.

Black workers, including male heads of household, female heads of household, and workers with no family responsibilities, were concentrated in the lowest ranks of the occupational structure. While there were slight differences in occupational level for heads of household as compared with all other workers, heads of household, in general, were no more occupationally diverse than other black workers.

CONDITIONS OF LIFE

In vast new areas of Boston, large frame houses with plenty of rooms, indoor plumbing, and spacious backyards were being built for the middle class. But the streetcar suburbs of late nineteenth-century Boston were restricted to whites. In 1880, about 42% of the black population lived in the West End (sometimes referred to as "Nigger Hill"), a conglomeration of tiny alleyways and side-streets on the seamy side of Beacon Hill. Tenement commissioners visiting the area described filthy streets, polluted air, overcrowded housing, dirty cellars, unsanitary water closets, poor drainage, and unsafe buildings.

At No. — Anderson Street is a little court. Here a single water closet in a small shed, the bowl filled and in abominable condition, was the only accommodation in this line for eight or ten families of colored people, besides the hands in a stable and a couple of little shops.

Since the tenement rooms were crowded, poorly heated and ventilated, children played in the street. Playing stickball in the summer and using Anderson and Phillips streets as ski slopes in the winter, black children made the most of their urban environment. But street play also resulted in children's being crushed under the wheels of fast-moving teams of horses.

The poor physical conditions and the inability of parents to provide an adequate family income resulted in sickness and sometimes death for black children. Mission workers from a settlement in the West End found "a young girl, whose only bed was two broken chairs placed between the cooking stove and the door. She was dying with consumption and was left all day with the care of a two-year-old child, tied into a chair beside her, while its mother was at work." In the same neighborhood, they found a poor black child "who shared the floor with the rats and mice on a cold winter's night." These cases were probably the most dramatic, not the typical circumstances of black poverty in the West End. The mission workers, no doubt, chose examples which would underline the importance of their work and the need for hospital care for their clients.

Individual human tragedies like the deaths of these two children are hidden in the high death rates in the Boston black community. Although the birth rate for blacks was higher than for whites, the number of deaths was so great that deaths generally exceeded births. In fact, 1905–1910 was the first five-year period since the Civil War when the black birth rate was higher than the death rate. Year after year, the city registrar reported more black deaths than births. In 1884, the registrar speculated that "there can be no question that, so far as the limited field furnished by this city affords the means of judging, were accessions from without to cease, the colored population would, in time, disappear from our community." Arguing that the "colored" race was unsuited to northern climates, he concluded: "In short, it would not be too much to say, that were all opposing obstacles of every kind, and in every direction, to the entire liberty of the colored race removed, and they were allowed to seek and occupy any position they were qualified to fill, they would instinctively and inevitably gravitate to southern and congenial latitudes as naturally as water seeks its own level."

As a result of poor diet, extremely high rates of infant mortality and deaths for mothers in childbirth, and the frequent incidence of tuberculosis and contagious diseases, the mortality rate for the black population in 1886 was 41 per 1000, almost twice the white rate. A black person who grew up in the West End recalled that on Sundays after church his family discussed the number of deaths in the neighborhood and which of the neighbors were dying of consumption. Diseases connected with childbirth accounted for the slightly higher death rate among black females than among black males. In 1890 the death rate per 1000 for white males in Boston was 15.86, for black males, 32. Among white females the mortality rate was 24 out of 1000, while black females died at the rate of 35 for every 1000.

The death rate was highest among children under one year of age, and higher still among male children. But significant reductions in infant mortality for both whites and blacks led to a sharp decline in the death rate in the first decade of the twentieth century. From 1900 to 1910, the death rate for white children under one year of age fell from 189 per 1000 to 185, while the black death rate dropped from 322 to 294. These figures were comparable to the mortality rates in other northern and western cities.

The high death rate among adults created a large number of widowed persons. About one-third of women aged 41–50 and a little less than half of women aged 51–60 lost their husbands. Either as a result of migration or in consequence of a higher rate of remarriage, the census takers found only about one-third as many widowers as widows. Some of the widows remarried, others went to live with relatives, and the remaining women made up the bulk of one-parent households in the black community.

The death of both parents left about 17% of black children homeless in Boston in 1880. These orphans were a much larger part of the population in late nineteenth-century cities than were the black youngsters in 1968 (one out of ten) who were not living with one or both parents. Homeless black children, in most cases, lived with relatives or friends, for few such children found their way into asylums and homes for foundling children. Discrimination by public institutions combined with the desire of black families to adopt black children meant that few black children without parents became wards of the state.

FAMILY STRUCTURE

The high death rate and overcrowded, unsanitary tenements, the transiency of the population, and the low occupational position constitute the kinds of pressures often cited as the causes of family disorganization. But several quantitative indicators—the sex ratio, the small number of one-parent households, the infrequency of desertion, and the adaptation of the household to include large numbers of migrants—suggest that the black family structure maintained its organization despite the many depressing aspects of life in Boston.

Several statistics are useful gauges of the nature of family life. One such statistic is the sex ratio, the number of males per one hundred females in the population. A frontier area, with a ratio of males to females of ten to one, or even higher, would have little family life. For everyone who chooses to marry, a stable ratio of males to females would theoretically insure the selection of a mate. Another arrangement of sex ratio, a small male population and a large female population, is said to produce a society with few stable marriages and high rates of illegitimacy, desertion, delinquency and female-headed households. These theoretical possibilities, reasonable in the abstract, have less meaning in concrete historical situations. Even in societies with quite similar sex ratios, great deviations can occur in patterns of sexuality, marriage, and family life. Still, for a population on the move, such as the black population over the last one hundred years, the possibility of imbalanced sex ratios due to large numbers of migrants is an important consideration in assessing the framework of family life.

In fact, among blacks in late nineteenth-century Boston, parity of the sexes existed, as the third column of Table 3 discloses. The overall sex ratio in 1880 was 102.9, though much higher—121—for the marriageable age group (25 to 44). In two other age groups, the very young and the very old, there were more females than males, reflect-

Table 3. Sex Ratios for Native Whites, Foreign-Born Whites, and Blacks, 1880[a]

	Native White	Foreign-Born White	Black
All Ages	95.7	79.4	102.9
25–44	95.9	83.8	121.0

[a]Derived from data in Carroll Wright, *Social, Commercial, and Manufacturing Statistics*, pp. 94–95.

ing the differential mortality of the sexes. The preponderance of males in the 25 to 44 age group stems from the relatively greater economic opportunities drawing adult migrants to the city. Many of these males were "beachhead" migrants, husbands who sent for their wives after they had established themselves in Boston.

When the black sex ratio is contrasted with the sex ratio of the foreign-born and native white populations, we find greater imbalances in the two white groups. For all native whites in 1880 the sex ratio was 95.7, while it was much lower—79.4—for foreign-born whites. Among young adults, Table 3 indicates that there were 96 native white males for every one hundred females, and 83.8 foreign-born white males for every one hundred females. The larger number of adult females in the foreign-born white group reflects the presence of adult working women, usually employed as domestic servants and factory workers, some of whom were earning enough money to finance their dowries.

Throughout the last decades of the nineteenth century, there were slightly more males than females in the black population of Boston. Only in 1910 did the census takers find the reverse. Many young adult females, migrants to Boston, created this surplus of females in the population.

The second important statistic for assessing the possibilities of family life is the number of married persons deserted by their spouses. Even though parity in the sex ratio suggests the necessary environment for stable family life, it is still quite possible that a high number of desertions would modify this conclusion. The number of desertions

was determined by tabulating all those married persons in the census record who were not living with their spouse. Of those deserted by their spouses, there were 157 females, about 11% of all married women, and 167 males, about 13% of all married men in this category. The figures for males, as we noted earlier, were probably increased by the large number of men awaiting the arrival of their wives. In a middle-class district of late nineteenth-century Chicago, where few of the desertions could be explained as the result of large numbers of migrants, about 11% of households included a deserted wife or husband.

What seems impressive in these figures for blacks in Boston is the low rate of desertion and separation, given the extremely high rate of out-migration, even among heads of household, and the dismal occupational prospect that blacks faced. W. E. B. DuBois discussed some of the causes of desertion and separation among blacks in Philadelphia.

The economic difficulties arise continually among young waiters and servant girls; away from home and oppressed by the peculiar lonesomeness of a great city, they form chance acquaintances here and there, thoughtlessly marry and soon find that the husband's income cannot alone support a family, then comes a struggle which generally results in desertion or voluntary separation.

As a result of death, desertion, or voluntary separation, 18% of black households came to be headed by one parent. In nine out of ten instances the one parent was a female. In assessing one- and two-parent households, I included households in which there were no children present as well as those with children. If childless couples were excluded, we would be unable to examine households of young couples, that is, future parents, as well as those households where grown offspring had moved away.

How did one- and two-parent households differ? Without substantial historical evidence, it would be foolhardy to apply present-day, widely questioned theories about the "tangle of pathology" associated with one-parent households. Regrettably, I have found no qualitative evidence which bears on the issue of how members of the black community viewed the one-parent household.

Nevertheless, there was an important economic difference between the one- and two-parent households. Although precise income figures are not available for black households, black males enjoyed higher wages than black females. In consequence, a family dependent on a woman's wages almost always lived in poverty. The yearly wage among female domestic servants, for example, was half the wage of male domestic servants. Moreover, given the concentration of female heads of household in the most poorly remunerated occupations, overall income levels between male- and female-headed households were even more disparate. In many two-parent households, the husband's wage was supplemented by both the wife's earnings from domestic service or laundry work and rent money from the boarder. Without these several income sources, the one-parent household was at an even greater disadvantage. Lacking the wages or unpaid labor of a wife, even the one-parent household headed by a male suffered economically.

From an analysis of the manuscript census schedules, three important distinctions emerged among two-parent households in the black community. First, there were pro-portionately more two-parent households among migrants to Boston than among native Bostonians. Second, the proportion of two-parent households among rural blacks was greater than among urban blacks. Finally, literate blacks headed two-parent households more often than illiterate blacks.

As we observed above, the early movement of blacks to Boston brought persons especially attracted to the advantages of the northern city. Both those heads of household from the rural South and those northern heads of household from outside Massachusetts revealed large and almost identical proportions of two-parent households, 83.3% and 83.4% respectively, while native Bostonians contributed fewer two-parent households. Given the many theories about the disruptive nature of migration, we might expect a higher percentage of one-parent households among the newcomers to the city than among the long-established urban blacks. But Table 4 reveals that the percentage of two-parent households among the two migrant streams of the population was significantly greater than among black Bostonians. Thus, the stereotype of disruptive migration does not fit the situation of blacks in late nineteenth-century Boston.

The combined effects of rural origins and long-distance movement away from family and friends made southern-born, rural migrants to Boston a distinctive group. We can compare the effect of rural origins on the

Table 4. One and Two-Parent Households, by Place of Birth of the Head of Household[a]

	Born in Mass.	Born in North[b]	Total born in North	Born in South	N
One-Parent	(36)	(27)	(63)	(136)	(199)
	27.1%	16.6%	21.3%	16.7%	18.0%
Two-Parent	(97)	(136)	(233)	(676)	(909)
	72.9%	83.4%	78.7%	83.3%	82.0%
	(133)	(163)	(296)	(812)	(1108)

[a]This table omits foreign-born heads of household, heads of household with no place of birth, and single-member households. The relationship between place of birth and household status is significant at .02, with two degrees of freedom.
[b]Does not include Massachusetts.

household by contrasting rural heads of household (the southern-born) with urban heads of household (the northern-born). As we note in Table 4, slightly more two-parent households occurred among rural than among urban heads of household, 83.3% as opposed to 78.7%. If we assume that a majority of the southern-born blacks were freedmen, the large number of two-parent households among them is even more remarkable. The common argument, that the abrupt transition from rural to urban life created indelible strains on the black family, does not hold for late nineteenth-century Boston. If anything, we find the reverse of this common proposition. It is clear from column four of Table 4 that households in which both parents were present were more frequent among rural than among urban black heads of household.

Even greater than variations between urban and rural households were variations within these two types of households. Table 5 bears on this issue, differentiating urban and rural blacks according to the literacy of the head of household. For both urban and rural heads of household, a literate black was more likely to head a two-parent household than an illiterate. The percentage of two-

parent households dropped from 86.5% of southern-born literates to 75.7% among illiterates from the same region, and from 80.1% among northern-born literates to only 68.6% among illiterates born in the North. Although these northern-born illiterate heads of household were a very small group, only eleven persons, nevertheless it is striking that a larger percentage of one-parent households was found among them than among any other group in the population.

If slavery permanently weakened family ties among blacks one would expect to find greater numbers of one-parent households among the ex-slaves. To be sure, there were fewer two-parent households among ex-slaves (southern-born illiterates) than among southern-born literates, but the freedmen had two-parent households more often than northern-born heads of household who were also illiterate. Thus, among both northern- and southern-born heads of household, illiteracy was associated with higher proportions of one-parent households.

It is possible that the relationship between illiteracy and one-parent, generally female-headed households is only a statistical artifact, the consequence of a higher rate of illiteracy among females than males. In order to test whether Table 5 described a spurious relationship, I compared the number of illiterates among two groups of women, female heads of household and those females living with their husbands in two-parent households. If higher rates of illiteracy among one-parent households in both the North and the South were merely the result of the fact that one-parent households were mostly female, we would expect to find roughly similar proportions of illiterates among married women living with their spouses and among females heading households. Instead, female heads of household were much more commonly illiterate than women living with their husbands. Significantly, more female heads of household than married females were illiterate; about one-fourth of married women were illiterate, while more than a third of females heading households could

Table 5. One and Two-Parent Households, by Place of Birth and Literacy of the Head of Household, 1880[a]

	Literate	Illiterate	Total
Northern-Born	(52)	(11)	(63)
One-Parent	19.9%	31.4%	21.3%
Northern-Born	(209)	(24)	(233)
Two-Parent	80.1%	68.6%	78.7%
Southern-Born	(77)	(59)	(136)
One-Parent	13.5%	24.3%	16.7%
Southern-Born	(492)	(184)	(676)
Two-Parent	86.5%	75.7%	83.3%
	(830)	(278)	(1108)

[a]Table omits foreign-born heads of household, heads of household with no place of birth, and single-member households. The relationship between literacy and household status was significant at .180 with one degree of freedom for the northern-born, significant at .001 with one degree of freedom for the southern-born.

not read or write. Among the southern-born women, most of whom were born into slavery, the rate of illiteracy was much higher. However, the general pattern remained the same; while about one-third of married women were illiterate, almost half of females heading households were illiterate.

Whether or not illiterates thought less of themselves than blacks who learned to read or write the numbers will never tell us. What is clear, however, is that for both urban and rural heads of household there were significantly more one-parent households among the illiterates. Speculation might lead us to conclude that illiteracy was both a real handicap in an urban society and, in addition, a characteristic found among the most disadvantaged adults in the black community.

Migrants and native Bostonians, rural and urban adults, illiterate and literate persons differed significantly in the number of two-parent households they formed. Did differences appear as well in the composition of the household? A single individual or that person and boarders lived in one out of seven black households in Boston. These solitary adults were excluded from the analysis of household composition. The great majority of black households, as Table 6 indicates, consisted of nuclear families—usually husband and wife, or a husband, wife, and children, but occasionally a single parent and child. Families which added other relatives

to the nuclear family, in what is termed an extended household, were 9.7% of all black households. Finally, about one out of three black households included boarders, and in a few cases boarders and relatives, in addition to parents and children. DuBois discovered roughly the same number of augmented households—that is, households with boarders—in late nineteenth-century Philadelphia.

Virtually the same patterns of family composition existed among rural and urban blacks, as columns three and four of Table 6 disclose. In both cases the majority of households was nuclear, although a significant minority—about one-third—included boarders. Only when native Bostonians are separated from the rest of the northern-born do differences appear in the composition of the household. The household headed by a black person born in Boston was somewhat more likely to mix relatives or boarders in the home than a household headed by a migrant. However, the differences in household composition between blacks born in Massachusetts, other northern states, and the South are not striking. What is important, in fact, is the uniformity of household composition among migrant and stable, urban and rural heads of household.

It might be thought relatives were more frequent among the poorest families, huddling together because they could not afford to live by themselves. The figures in Table 7

Table 6. Nuclear, Extended, and Augmented Households, by Place of Birth of the Head of Household, 1880[a]

	Born in Mass.	Born in North[b]	Total born in North	Born in South	N
Nuclear	(68)	(93)	(161)	(462)	(623)
	51.2%	57.1%	54.5%	56.1%	56.2%
Extended	(16)	(15)	(31)	(80)	(111)
	12.0%	9.2%	10.5%	10.6%	10.0%
Augmented	(49)	(55)	(104)	(270)	(374)
	36.8%	33.7%	35.1%	33.3%	33.8%
	(133)	(163)	(296)	(812)	(1108)

[a]This table omits foreign-born heads of household, heads of household with no place of birth, and single-member households. The relationship between place of birth and family structure shown in this table is not statistically significant.
[b]Does not include Massachusetts.

Table 7. Nuclear, Extended, and Augmented Households, by Occupational Level of the Head of Household, 1880[a]

	Professional	White-Collar	Skilled	Unskilled	N
Nuclear	(19)	(16)	(49)	(558)	(642)
	52.8%	50.0%	57.6%	58.8%	
Extended	(7)	(6)	(8)	(84)	(105)
	19.4%	18.8%	9.4%	8.9%	
Augmented	(10)	(10)	(28)	(307)	(355)
	27.8%	31.3%	32.9%	32.3%	
	(36)	(32)	(85)	(949)	(1102)

[a]This table omits persons with no occupation and single-member heads of household. Heads of household from all places of birth are included. The relationship between occupation and family structure is not statistically significant.

demonstrate that this was not the case. Controlling for the occupational level of the head of household, the proportion of relatives increased among higher-status heads of household, while the proportion decreased among lower-status households. Relatives may have been more welcome to join the family in higher-status households which could afford to sustain additional members. The George Ruffins (he was a lawyer and a judge, she a prominent clubwoman and suffragist) absorbed into their home Mrs. Ruffin's niece, Daisy Nahar. In other cases, the presence of additional adult family members may have financed the education or supported the family business, which, in turn, resulted in the higher status of the head of household.

Relatives were more common in higher-status households, but lodgers appeared more often in lower-status households. The number of augmented households, as summarized in line three of Table 7, shows that about one-third of blue-collar households included a boarder, while slightly fewer boarders resided in professional and white-collar homes. Among households headed by unskilled and skilled workers, just as in the female-headed household, the lodger's rent money was often an essential part of the family budget. In response to the influx of southern migrants, the black family accommodated these lodgers, generally single women and men who worked as servants and waiters. The augmented household was a product

of necessity, but it met the housing needs of the lodgers as well as provided additional income requirements of black families.

Nineteenth-century observers often described the "demoralizing" influence of lodgers on the household. DuBois exemplified this attitude, fearing that "the privacy and intimacy of home life is destroyed, and elements of danger and demoralization admitted" when the lodger entered the black home. Given the desperate economic circumstances of black families, the boarder's rent money may have insured family survival rather than destroyed it. Moreover, boarders were common additions to higher-status households. The boarder in many cases became a "relative" of the family, in function if not in kinship. Richard Wright recalled that as a boarder he easily became a part of a Memphis home—more so than he liked, since a match-making mother was eager for the boarder to marry her daughter.

CONCLUSION

This study of the black family in late nineteenth-century Boston views the black family structure at one point in time. Subsequent studies must trace the family over the years in order to fully comprehend changes in the household. If we want to learn about the acculturation of children in the black family, it is particularly important to employ a dynamic perspective. For example, while we know that about seven out of ten black children in Boston in 1880 lived in two-parent households, we do not know how many of these children spent their early years in such a household. Nor, for that matter, among the minority of children in 1880 who were missing both parents do we know whether their family situation affected their future, for better or worse. This kind of analysis can only be pursued through the tracing of individuals, a method extremely arduous to undertake given the mobility of the population.

Any study of black family life largely employing quantitative information represents only a point of departure for further analysis of black families. While the high number of two-parent households, 82% of all black households in Boston, indicates the existence of much greater family organization than has been generally assumed, we need evidence about the cultural context in which the urban black family operated. How were one- and two-parent households viewed? Were different values placed on marriage, the family, even desertion in the black community than in other groups? Did the addition of boarders and relatives endanger the intimacy of the home or create additional adult models for black children? Except in the few instances of family diaries and personal accounts, these questions may prove difficult, if not impossible, to answer through literary materials.

While there are limitations to numerical analysis, it does allow for comparisons across time and space. How then did Boston compare with other cities? Perhaps one could argue that, despite the poverty-stricken condition of blacks in Boston, there was still some way in which Boston was, indeed, "the paradise of the Negro," if only because the situation of blacks in the South was so much worse. Although more studies need to be undertaken, overall figures from southern urban, southern rural, and northern urban centers in the late nineteenth century demonstrate a striking similarity in the percentages of two-parent households. Theodore Hershberg reports that in both 1880 and 1896 the two-parent household comprised 76% of all households among blacks in Philadelphia. He found roughly similar proportions of two-parent households in ante-bellum Philadelphia, where 77% of all black households were two-parent. Among a special group of about 87 slaves who had bought their freedom 91% formed two-parent households. From the major work of Herbert Gutman on the black family, the two-parent household in 1880 appeared among 81% of Adams County, Mississippi, black households and 77% of Mobile, Alabama, black households. In three urban areas in 1896, Atlanta, Nashville, and Cambridge, Massachusetts, Gutman found 77%, 85%, and 90%, respectively, of two-parent households. It would be tempting here to contrast the relative effects on the black household of southern urban, southern rural and northern urban environments. But what we find in the few areas studied is greater variation within than between locales. All in all, the two-parent household was the prevailing family form in southern rural, southern urban, and northern urban areas.

The figures cited above, except in the case of antebellum Philadelphia, do not distinguish between native-born city dwellers and rural migrants to the city. Such an analytic strategy is vital to the study of the effects of city and country origins and the migration from one area to another on the black household.

How did migration to the city affect the black family? The standard texts on black history scarcely mention the migration of blacks to northern cities before the Great Migration of World War I. On the whole, the northward migration was a movement of single individuals or couples; in few cases did the whole family move north. After the migrants from the South or other parts of the North reached Boston, an incredible number of single individuals and families left the city. This movement out of Boston in some cases left behind deserted wives and husbands, but the rate of desertion was rather low given the lack of occupational opportunity for blacks in Boston and the general rootlessness of the black population.

In the work of DuBois and E. Franklin Frazier, migration to the city is viewed as a disruptive factor which weakened the family and produced large numbers of one-parent households. DuBois wrote that "as a whole, it is true that the average of culture and wealth is far lower among immigrants than natives, and that this gives rise to the gravest of the Negro problems." What these writers generally meant by migration was the *transition* from rural to urban culture among southern migrants to the city. This disruptive transition was said to have been the source of desertion, delinquency, and female-headed households. Frazier, in his discussion of the "city of destruction," noted: "Family desertion among Negroes in cities, appears, then, to be one of the inevitable consequences of the impact of urban life on the simple family organization and folk culture which the Negro has evolved in the rural South."

At least for late nineteenth-century Boston, quantitative evidence calls Frazier's thesis into question. Two-parent households were more frequent among both migrant *and* rural black heads of household. Such evidence can be interpreted in two ways. One explanation would reverse the Frazier argument: instead of migration and the transition from rural to urban culture weakening the black family, these influences strengthened it. Persons who had invested so much effort to leave family, friends, and familiar ways had a greater stake in establishing households once they were settled in the city. Also, the limited expectations of rural blacks may have meant that city life in the North was, indeed, a significant improvement over life in the rural South. Finally, the special character of this early migration might have distinguished the early newcomers to the city (both in ante-bellum Philadelphia and in Boston about fifty years later) from more recent city-bound blacks.

A second explanation of the differences in the number of two-parent households, offered by Theodore Hershberg, is that neither slavery nor migration but the urban environment produced greater numbers of one-parent households. Tremendous differences in wealth, poor health conditions for blacks in cities, the destructiveness of urban culture—all these are cited as the causes of "family disorganization" among blacks. Without more knowledge of the internal workings of black culture, of the values blacks placed on different family forms, it is impossible to know whether the one-parent, female-headed household was viewed by blacks as "family disorganization." The use of this value-loaded term generally presupposes a hierarchy of family types, with the male-present, nuclear, and patriarchal household representing the most-valued family form.

Another danger in substituting one grand interpretation of "family disorganization" in place of another is that it may tend to obscure other important differences in family type and composition which do not appear between rural and urban, ex-slave and free-born blacks. Important differences between city dwellers and rural blacks must be noted. But in late nineteenth-century Boston the composition of the black household was similar for both rural and urban black heads of household. Moreover, significantly more one-parent households occurred among illiterate blacks from both rural and urban origins. The social meaning of illiteracy for blacks in the city remains enigmatic, but the discovery that the illiteracy of the head of household significantly altered the proportion of two-parent households hints at the existence of other fundamental social characteristics differentiating black households.

While variations in household composition and percentage of two-parent households which are associated with place of birth, illiteracy, and migration should be noted and considered, the similarities in two-parent households among diverse groups in the black population are even more striking. The evidence suggests a family pattern of nuclear, two-parent households which prevailed among migrant and rural black heads of household as well as among stable and urban black heads of household. Despite the existence of blacks at the lowest rung of the occupational ladder, most black children lived in homes where both parents were present, and black families generally included husband, wife, and children.

The presentation of these raw statistics forces us to challenge and revise previous conceptions about the black family. More lies hidden behind a high death rate, a transient population, and a poverty-stricken black community than the phrases "culture of poverty" or "family disorganization"

convey. Our vision of the family as an institution which reacts to and reflects changes is oversimplified, while there seems little understanding of the family as an institution which itself produces changes in individuals and institutions. If the black family were merely the image of the social conditions of urban blacks, we would find a rootless, disorganized mosaic of families. Notions of "black matriarchy" and "the tangle of pathology" of the black family have captivated sociologists and historians alike, but now the task before us is to tell the rather different story of the complex organization and continuity of the black household.

Quebec to "Little Canada": The Coming of the French Canadians to New England in the Nineteenth Century

IRIS SAUNDERS PODEA

Most American minorities came to the United States from the east, the south, or the west. Only the French-Canadians migrated from the north. They emigrated from Quebec in the 1840s because of depressed conditions in the shipbuilding and lumber industries and because of difficulty in obtaining land, most of which was in the hands of the speculators. Like most other minorities the French-Canadians sought greater economic opportunities. They settled mainly in New England, although some moved to Illinois, Wisconsin, Michigan, and New York and found employment as agricultural laborers, lumbermen, textile operators, and brickyard workers. New England Yankees dubbed them "the Chinese of the Eastern states," an indication, as Marcus Hansen has written, that New Englanders considered the Canadians ignorant, poor, and degraded; an unwelcome influx that would lower wages and raise the proportion of criminals; and an element that showed no disposition to become "American." Many natives also thought that the newcomers really were loyal to another country, or, since they were Catholic, ruled by the priesthood. For these worried New Englanders the French-Canadians constituted a dangerous class in the community.

By 1900 New England had about 275,000 French-Canadians; thereafter immigration declined as economic conditions in Canada improved. Diminished entry and the influx of southern and eastern Europeans at the end of the nineteenth century changed the older image of "the Chinese of the Eastern states." In the 1880s and '90s New Englanders started to describe French-Canadians as industrious, frugal, and quick to learn; the Italians, Greeks, and Syrians had replaced them on the lower rungs of society. Despite partial assimilation and acceptance, the French-Canadians clung to their own language and customs. The refusal to drop their own ways prevented the group from achieving social equality with Yankee New Englanders.

In the following selection Iris Saunders Podea describes the early experiences of French-Canadians in New England.

New Englanders have long been accustomed to hearing the French language spoken in the streets and shops of Lewiston, Manchester, Woonsocket, and other manufacturing

From the *New England Quarterly*, 23 (1950), 365–80. Reprinted by permission.

towns. This phenomenon may have led to a conjecture whether the "struggle for a continent" still continues, and the presence of the French Canadians in New England is but a phase of Quebec's expansion in North America. The Canadian French invaders who poured into new England in the last three or four decades of the nineteenth century, however, did not come as warriors. They were simply seeking their daily bread, and their peaceful penetration has proved far more successful than the earlier French efforts at military conquest. Leaving Quebec's impoverished farms, they entered the expanding American industrial life at an opportune moment and were quickly transformed into an urban people. A few, of course, remained farmers, especially in Vermont and New Hampshire, but they constitute a rural minority. This essay will be concerned with the ancestors of today's Franco-Americans, the French Canadians who migrated to New England mill towns prior to 1900.

This migration southward from their native province of Quebec was induced by a variety of reasons: geographical proximity, colonial struggles, and seasonal opportunities. Lumber camps and farms, canals and railroads, quarries and brickyards, river and lake steamers: all were clamoring for manpower in the growing Republic and Quebec had more than an ample supply. Political unrest in Canada before Confederation also contributed to the migration, but those who came as refugees after the 1837 Rebellion or as malcontents following the union of Upper and Lower Canada in 1840 were relatively few. Higher wages in the United States were always a magnet, but more important than occupational attractions across the frontier or political forces at home was the economic distress which became increasingly intense in rural Quebec throughout a large part of the nineteenth century.

No real understanding of the French-Canadian migration into New England can be gained without some idea of what the French Canadian left behind. Quebec agriculture presented a dismal outlook, and industry was undeveloped. In his journey through the province in 1819, Benjamin Silliman had commented on the wasteful farming techniques then employed, and this criticism was still valid half a century later. It was the prevailing prejudice that land improvement did not pay. The special committees appointed by the Legislative Assembly in 1849 and 1857 to investigate the extent and causes of emigration from Quebec confirmed the backward state of agricultural affairs. Many French-Canadian youths were landless, while crown lands remained too dear and requirements for settlement too difficult. Little land was available for colonization, and even when it was available, inadequate roads and bridges made it difficult of access and deprived it of markets for its produce. The committees' pleas for better roads, bridges, and other reforms such as homesteads and the guarantee of wood rights went almost unheeded, except by colonization societies, many of which were ineffective.

Quebec agriculture continued to decline. While the Dominion Government was making every effort to induce European immigrants to settle in the Canadian West, French Canadians continued to leave their farms for the United States, for the West, or for the cities. The *habitants* who remained behind still pursued their old methods of soil depletion and, in addition, the old inheritance system still prevailed. Farms, already small, were repeatedly subdivided among the many children of French Canada's large families, reducing them to strips too narrow to produce an adequate living. It is no wonder that the Seventh Census of Canada stated that it "was not in quest of a higher standard of living but to avoid a lower" that the French Canadian was impelled to migrate. The people of Quebec, rather than risk the shrinking of an already precarious existence, preferred to leave behind the land of their ancestors. It is hard to believe that a people so gregarious and loyal to their province as the French Canadians would have chosen to venture into a formerly hostile New England for the sake of uncertain financial gain, had it not been for these disheartening prospects at home.

In view of the predicament in which French-Canadian youth found itself, the Civil War in the United States was a welcome opportunity to many young men. The inducement of bounties for army recruits was irresistible, and it is estimated that approximately 40,000 French Canadians served in the Union armies, a number of whom undoubtedly were already resident in the United States. The war also coincided with and accelerated an unprecedented industrial development in New England. Labor was at a premium, and improved technology made it possible to employ unskilled workers to an increasing extent, a fact which vastly broadened the opportunities for women, children, and immigrants. With this crying need, it was not surprising that wide-awake mill owners in New England should tap Quebec's overflowing supply, especially when it lay so much nearer than Europe.

New England manufacturers gave French-Canadian workers a ready welcome. Even before the war they had discovered the advantages of importing French-Canadian labor—quick accessibility, low wages, industrious and uncomplaining employes. Factories adopted the practice of sending recruiting agents to Quebec and entire families and parishes were transported to New England. Many are the accounts of desolation in Quebec's deserted villages. Railroads were also instrumental in promoting the migration, first, by facilitating means of travel, and secondly, by stimulating this French-speaking traffic through agents and interpreters. The most effective recruiting agent of all, however, was the *émigré* himself. His letters home spread the *fièvre des Etats-Unis* among relatives and friends, and when he visited his native village dressed in city clothes, wearing the inevitable gold watch and chain, he personified success in the United States.

No more than mere mention can be made here of the growing alarm felt in Canada at increasing emigration from the province, but it was widespread. It became a subject of legislative investigation, ecclesiastical concern, and propagandistic literature. Discrediting motives were imputed to the departing inhabitants in an effort to stay the tide—misconduct, extravagance, love of luxury, adventure, and so on—but emigration continued to gain in volume until about 1896, a date which marked several significant trends. A period of prosperity in Canada followed close on the heels of its return in the United States, and the advent of the first French-Canadian Prime Minister enhanced Quebec's prestige. In this last decade of the century the Canadian-born French in the United States increased by over 90,000 but in the succeeding ten years they decreased by more than 9,000. French Canadians were apparently beginning to find a more adequate outlet for their talents at home.

In the meantime, what of the thousands of French-speaking workers absorbed in the gigantic maw of the New England mills? By no means the first immigrants to invade the northeastern states, they followed the Irish who had long since achieved the "second colonization" of New England. In many New England towns they were the first sizable group of non-English speaking people and by 1900 they numbered more than half a million in New England alone. Americans looked down upon *habitants* arriving on New England station platforms in rustic garb, followed by broods of children. These large families without financial reserves were obliged to seek work at once, and usually friends from their native village guided them to both jobs and shelter. Mostly farmers, they had no experience in the industrial world. The few who were skilled in various trades were handicapped by language and temporarily had to join the rank and file in the mills.

The cotton textile industry offered the greatest opportunity for unskilled labor and absorbed a large portion of these French Canadians, whose descendants have become "a permanent factor in the labor supply of the cotton mills" of New England. The

French Canadians made themselves felt in this industry in the 1870's, when there were over seven thousand Canadian-born engaged in it in New England. Within thirty years this number soared to nearly 60,000. French-Canadian operatives in cotton rose from 20% to nearly 37% of the total number in Massachusetts between 1890 and 1900, and in Maine and New Hampshire they exceeded 60%. In 1888 over 3,000 French-speaking women were employed in the cotton mills of Lewiston, Biddeford, Saco, and Waterville, out of a total of approximately five and a half thousand female employees. Although fewer French-Canadian women workers than those of any other nationality had ever been employed for wages before coming to the United States, over 40% of those in Massachusetts over ten years of age were employed in 1885.

In 1888 the Maine Bureau of Industrial and Labor Statistics appointed Flora Haines as special agent to survey conditions for women textile workers in that state. After more sordid accounts of textile mills, it is refreshing to come upon her description of a clean and cheerful spinning room with open windows, of the mill girls with neat white linen collars and whisk brooms to brush lint from their frocks. She reported defective eyes as a common ailment among the French and the use of tobacco by French-Canadian children. Women took snuff and signs were posted in French and English requesting those using tobacco not to "spit on the floor." Most French-Canadian girls lived at home in very crowded quarters, but those who lived in boarding houses enjoyed a good reputation in the community. In view of the French-Canadian retention of their language in the United States, it is worthy of note that Miss Haines recommended the use of textbooks such as those employed in New Brunswick where both English and French instruction was given. She felt that American children in the public schools could profit by learning a little French.

The charge has often been made that French Canadians, with their large families,

had more child operatives in the mills than any other group of workers. Child labor, nevertheless, was prevalent in the textile mills long before the coming of the French Canadians. They simply followed a long-established custom when they sent their children to work, one further reinforced by necessity. Actually a study of cotton mill workers made in 1905 indicated that the French-Canadian children contributed only one-third of the income of the families covered, while Irish children in the same survey contributed 45% of the family income.

More justifiable was the accusation that the French Canadians evaded the school laws, sometimes falsifying the ages of their children. The Massachusetts Bureau of Labor Statistics went so far as to state in its report of 1881 that when the French-Canadian parents were finally "cornered" by the school officers and "there is no other escape, often they scrabble together what few things they have, and move away to some other place where they are unknown, and where they hope by a repetition of the same deceits to escape the schools entirely, and keep the children at work right on in the mills." Although much evidence to the contrary was presented by indignant French Canadians in Massachusetts at a special hearing before the Bureau in 1881 in an effort to disprove this and other equally derogatory statements of the Report, there can be little doubt that very young French-Canadian children were commonly employed and that existing child labor laws were violated. At this time Commissioner Wright, head of the Massachusetts Bureau of Statistics of Labor, while admitting that the remarks were not true for Massachusetts, indicated that they were applicable to French Canadians in Connecticut and New York. This was confirmed by the Connecticut Bureau of Labor Statistics in its annual report for the year 1885:

Another element which affects child labor is that of race. The native American almost always wants to educate his children. The Irishman feels this want even more strongly, and will make great sacrifices for the sake of his family. On the other hand, the French Canadian in a great many instances regards his children as a means of adding to the earning capacity of the family, and, in making arrangements for work, he urges, and even insists upon the employment of the family as a whole, down to the very youngest children who can be of any possible service.

It is in places like Baltic, with a large French-Canadian population, that these evils have been felt in their severest form. There was a time when the Baltic Mills employed a large number of children under ten years of age. The worst of these abuses seem to have been done away with in that place; but there are many mills, especially among the less important ones, where it has been impossible to stop or even to detect them.

An overseer in Southbridge reported in 1872 that he used to tell the French Canadians that the law did not permit employment of children under ten years, "and the next day they were all ten." Reports of factory accidents of the 1860's and '70's included French-Canadian children under ten. Felix Gatineau, in his history of the Franco-Americans of Southbridge, observed the tendency of these first French Canadians to send children from seven to eight years old to work instead of to school.

It is certain that the school laws were poorly enforced in New England. Not only were parents and manufacturers hostile; the school authorities themselves did not want the schools flooded with the undisciplined children of the working class. Sometimes at the beginning of a semester, children were all turned out of the mills, but within a few weeks most of them were back. Although Massachusetts led in child labor legislation, statistics for 1891 showed a higher proportion of French-Canadian children at work in the cotton industry in that state than elsewhere in New England. Rhode Island likewise found fault with the French Canadians on the score of illiteracy and child labor. Evidence from a number of sources, therefore, obliges one to conclude that the French Canadians were conspicuous offenders, even where violations of school and minimum-age laws were common.

As newcomers, they had little choice but to accept the lowest wages. With their large families they were able to get along on less than the native American workers used to a higher standard of living. This and the fact that they were frequently introduced into New England industry as strike-breakers did not endear them to their co-workers. At West Rutland, Vermont, when they were imported into the marble quarries during a turn-out of Irish quarrymen in 1868, bloodshed resulted. In Fall River during a strike in 1879, employers had to build special houses in the mill-yards for French-Canadian "knobstick" spinners, for fear strikers would persuade them to leave town. Many similar instances of strike-breaking occurred. Thanks to this unfortunate role, which immigrants in the United States have often been called upon to play, they won the enmity of organized labor. Nor did they wish to join in strikes and unions. Experience had taught them, they claimed, that when they did participate in strikes they lost their jobs while others went back to work without telling them. The Knights of Labor (condemned in Quebec by Cardinal Taschereau) were not very successful in recruiting French-Canadian members and tried to influence state legislation against them. French-Canadian influence was held partly responsible for the failure of New England cotton mill operatives to build a stronger organization, but rather than do without wages during strikes they preferred a low income regularly.

On the other hand, there were evidences of a dawning labor consciousness among them before the end of the century. A few joined the Knights of St. Crispin and even the Knights of Labor. At the time Chinese were introduced into the Sampson shoe factory at North Adams in 1870, several French Canadians participated in the protest against the Chinese. In 1879 sixty French Canadians at the Douglas Axe Company in Massachusetts struck for a 10% wage increase. Unions, which at first had been indifferent toward immigrants, began to print notices in French. In Worcester, French-Canadian carpenters formed their own union. After being in the United States long enough to understand labor aims and methods, their attitude began to change. In general, however, the language barrier and the influence of their leaders discouraged the early French-Canadian *émigrés* from association with strikes and labor organizations. They prided themselves on refusing to take part and on being law-abiding citizens.

Although general wages and working conditions slowly improved, wages in the textile and paper industries lagged behind, a fact especially significant for the French Canadians. Statistics showed a definite relationship between length of residence in the United States and wages received. French Canadians were advancing to more skilled positions in industry by the end of the century, and many French-Canadian girls were anxious to leave the cotton mills for something better. Despite the steady upward push toward higher economic, social, and professional levels, distinction was reserved for the few and the majority had to endure the hardships that accompanied their low wage scale. It was the poverty and dirt of their "Little Canadas" in the nineteenth century that gained for them a sorry reputation when they first came to New England.

Nearly every manufacturing town where they settled had its French-Canadian quarter. The usual picture of these squalid "French-villes" dispels at once the Quebec allegation that the *émigrés* departed for love of luxury. Most of them began life in the United States in tenements and were locally referred to as "Canucks." Sanitation and cleanliness were at a minimum and the high death rate in some of the "Little Canadas" was to be expected in these overcrowded and unwholesome lodgings. Fall River and Holyoke were notorious for their "hell holes," and William Bayard Hale described French-Canadian tenements in Fall River in 1894 as not fit "to house a dog." The Slade Mill tenements, he said, were worse than the old-time slave quarters, and in the Globe Mill houses rats had driven out the inhabitants.

The first large-scale tenement dwellings in Lowell were built in "Little Canada," and the population density in these structures was claimed to surpass that anywhere in the United States outside the Fourth Ward in New York City. Darkness, foul odors, lack of space and air, shabby surroundings, all these were universal tenement characteristics, to which the French Canadians had no exclusive claim, but their quarters were repeatedly singled out as among the worst or most ill-kept in New England. Mill owners, nevertheless, apparently kept their lodgings in better condition than private exploiters who later purchased them. The Granite Mills in Fall River had the best maintained houses in town and vacancies there were rare. If the French Canadians were provided with good housing, commented a Salem investigator in 1873, they were too proud a people not to keep it that way. This, alas, did not always prove true.

French Canadians, as well as Irish, were a problem to the health authorities. They were frightened by compulsory vaccination and did not understand why wakes were prohibited during a period of epidemic disease. The Lowell Health Department made an earnest effort to reach its "Little Canada." School children there were generally vaccinated free of charge and parental opposition was attributed more to the necessity of caring for the child's sore arm than to prejudice against vaccination. Detailed child-care instructions were printed in French and English and a medical inspector was sent into the district with two boys acting as interpreters. Disease was widespread among French-Canadian children and infant mortality high, much of it due to improper feeding and ignorance. The Health Department deplored the laziness and indifference of parents who failed to send for the ward physicain when their children were ill. People who could afford a funeral better than they could preventive measures were hard to get along with, wrote one health officer despairingly.

These humble and insalubrious beginnings were the common immigrant lot. There was, happily, a brighter side for the French Canadians. The impression is all too common that the farmer lives an idyllic and healthful life, but evidence often reveals the simple life as a synonym for mere subsistence. In moving to the mill towns of New England, the French Canadians enjoyed better food than in Quebec and many wrote home that they ate meat every day. "The proud housekeeper," wrote Archambault in his novel, *Mill Village,* "was the one who would place five pounds of fried pork chops and a half peck of boiled potatoes before an invited guest." Such a housekeeper was luckier than most, but the French-Canadian laboring man in Massachusetts consumed about five pounds of food per day in 1886, a pound and a half more than his confrere in Quebec. The Massachusetts Bureau of Statistics of Labor compared French-Canadian family and boarding-house diets in Holyoke, Lawrence, Lowell, Montreal, Rivière du Loup, and Quebec and found both nutritive value and quantity considerably in favor of Massachusetts.

Clothing also showed improvement. The French Canadians were quick to adopt the American mode and sometimes sacrificed food or home comforts for fashion. Sewing machines were not unknown in homes of French-Canadian workers and seemed to have a beneficent influence on the aspect of the whole household. French Canadians were reputedly well dressed, but there were relatively few silks and satins. Necessity at times drove economy to the extreme of avoiding walking to save shoe leather or wearing outgrown garments when there were no younger children to inherit them.

Toward the end of the century, the "Little Canadas" were being abandoned to other immigrants. The coming of the street railway was an important factor in enabling workers to quit the tenements, and in towns such as Worcester and Marlboro where textiles where not the predominant industry, French-Canadian home ownership made progress. Investment in real estate was regarded as an indication of stability and an

excellent way to train the French Canadians in economy through the habit of saving to pay off mortgages. The property requirement for voting by naturalized citizens in Rhode Island was an added stimulus there to the purchase of real estate, but general progress toward home ownership was slow. In view of the French-Canadian reputation for thrift, this pace is disappointing.

Frugality was a Quebec trait which on occasion excited the jealousy or envy of others. The first savings of French Canadians usually went to the church, and their fine record for financing church properties is in contrast to their slower private advancement, at the same time demonstrating their willingness to sacrifice for their faith. The amazing feature about their religious, educational and philanthropic institutions is that they were paid for by small contributions, mostly from the working class, with very few large donations. Saving was encouraged by the clergy, and toward the end of the century special savings institutions for French Canadians began to appear in New England. Holyoke's second coöperative bank was founded in 1889 to enable French-Canadian workers to buy homes on a monthly installment plan; it was the first Franco-American financial institution in the United States. Woonsocket's Institution for Savings soon had to employ French-speaking clerks to take care of French-Canadian accounts, and Aram Pothier, later Governor of Rhode Island, served in that capacity. In 1900 the first *caisse populaire,* a form of credit union, was founded in Quebec, and this movement soon spread to the United States. Another Quebec habit which promoted savings was the family system, whereby children turned over their earnings to their parents.

French-Canadian thrift, nevertheless, has probably been overestimated. Early *émigrés* had little confidence in banks or investments, their mistrust justified by such experiences as the fraudulent New England Investment Company and the loss of savings deposits in bank failures. The average annual surplus among French-Canadian families in Massachusetts in 1875 was only $10.59, and they saved less than any other ethnic group in the state at that time. Although saving doubtless increased with improvement in occupation, the estimate made by Father Hamon in 1890 that a French-Canadian worker with a family of four children should have about $80 a month left after deduction of major expenses seems high. One of the great mistakes in estimating ability to save has been simply to multiply daily wages by the number of persons working per family and to deduct the cost of living, without regard to age, occupation, or steadiness of employment. Furthermore, both Father Hamon and Ferdinand Gagnon, father of Franco-American journalism, repeatedly exhorted their compatriots to economy instead of spending money on picnics, carriage rent, circuses, and trips to Canada.

The close of the nineteenth century found the French Canadians a settled people in New England numbering over half a million. By this time they were experienced in industry and, where statistics distinguished the older residents from the new, they had proved themselves able to compete with other workers in New England. It must not be forgotten that the steady influx of new arrivals from Quebec, who yet had to pass through their period of orientation, held back the general average of the group. Instances were even known of French Canadians replacing other French Canadians at lower wages. It required time to learn to demand the same working and living standards as native-born citizens in the United States, but unbeknown to themselves, the French Canadians were conforming to the usual immigrant pattern, starting at the lowest level and surmounting it in the second and third generations. Meanwhile their United-States-born

descendants were growing up bilingual, thus better equipped for broader participation in American life.

Their economic situation gradually improved, freeing them from complete preoccupation with ethnic survival. It became almost the breath of life to the newly forming mutual benefit societies and the Franco-American press. Unlike European immigrants, French Canadians did not sever the bond with the land of their birth, for Quebec adjoined New England and visits, newspapers, and education in the province were easily accessible. Their dual loyalty, so openly avowed, puzzled Americans and often became suspect when reinforced by aloofness from public schools, non-French churches, and organizations. Thus, friction in the new environment was not confined to labor competition.

Within the limits of the century the French-Canadian migration into New England was still in a state of flux. It had, however, transplanted almost in its entirety the French-Canadian parish, with separate French churches, schools, and homes for the needy. Indeed, theirs was a splendid record in caring for their own. It was too soon to foretell the extent of change from their traditional ways until more Franco-Americans had experienced a generation of life in the United States. The old melting-pot theory has been somewhat discredited in recent years, but economic forces have remained a persistent assimilator. The twentieth century ushered in great change for French Canadians in Quebec, now become the most highly industrialized province of Canada, and it may give the Franco-Americans a chance to guide their Canadian cousins along the path of ethnic tenacity in an industrial world.

Norwegians on the Prairie

EUGENE BOE

Although the bulk of the Scandinavians reached American shores between the Civil War and the end of World War I, about 40,000 immigrants from Norway, Sweden, and Denmark came to the United States before 1860. The Scandinavians tended to settle in the midwestern plains states (Illinois, Wisconsin, Minnesota, Iowa) and unlike most minority groups had relatively little difficulty with "native" Americans. In fact, they were more quickly accepted by the majority than either the Germans or the Irish, the other two major European minorities of the mid-nineteenth century. One Norwegian traveler expressed the existing feeling in a letter to his compatriots at home. "Never," one of the native Americans had told him, "have I known people to become civilized so rapidly as your countrymen; they come here in motley crowds, dressed up with all kinds of dingle-dangle just like the Indians. But just look at them a year later: they speak English perfectly, and, as far as dress, manners, and ability are concerned, they are quite above reproach."

No minority group was more enthusiastic about its initial American experiences. Letters to the old country rhapsodized over equality and freedom found in the United States: employees and employers wore similar clothing, wages were higher, and abundant quantities of land were available for those willing to work hard. Food was so plentiful that America seemed "the land of Canaan." "Just think what an impression it would make on a poor highlander's imagination," a Norwegian wrote home, "to be told that some day he might eat wheat bread every day and pork at least three times a week!"

The Scandinavians did encounter some of the difficulties that plagued recent arrivals of other ethnic origins. Land was not always as fertile as had been anticipated and some found turning wilderness into farms too strenuous. Homesickness, however, created the greatest difficulty. Regardless of abundant economic opportunities and relative equality of treatment by other whites, many of the newcomers had not anticipated the strength of attachments to family and friends in the old country.

In the following selection Eugene Boe, grandchild of an early settler, reconstructs the modern Norwegian saga of the great migration from old-country farm village to American prairie through a sensitive and personal account of his own family's experiences.

In contrast to the smiling social democracy it is today, Norway in the last century was an overpopulated land of sharp class distinctions. The government, an insular monarchy, allowed only a privileged few any political expression. The clergy were aloof to the blunt realities of poverty and injustice. Nature had yielded her blessings in scant measure, but nothing was done to help or encourage the tens of thousands struggling to survive on little scraps of barren soil. Neighbor had quarreled with neighbor for every square foot of those steep, stony, stumpy upland meadows and the plots staked out were too small to support a family. Indebtedness was inevitable, the grip of creditor on debtor strangulating. Stills on the farms were legal and too many of the luckless could find their only consolation in drink.

In the early decades of the nineteenth century reports began drifting in from across the Atlantic that painted the New World in the colors of the Promised Land. A trickle of migrations from Norway to America started in the 1830s. Most of these emigrants set out for the frontiers of Illinois and Wisconsin, where land was available. Their letters home and the eyewitness accounts of visiting missionaries fanned the flames of discontent back in the Old Country and provoked new waves of emigration.

The Indian treaties of 1851 opened up fresh lands for settlement. By the late 1850s Norwegians were swarming into Iowa and the southern counties of Minnesota. When Minnesota shed its territorial status in 1858 for statehood, it early on established an Immigration Department that employed Norwegian-American journalists to prepare pamphlets for circulation in Norway. This literature praised the exhilarating climate, the beauties of prairie and woodland and lakes, and the potential riches of the new state. Verily, the publicists sang, this was the Land of Canaan, "glorious new Scandinavia."

In 1862 President Lincoln signed the Homestead Act. After January 1, 1863, any person who was twenty-one years old and was either a citizen or had applied for citizenship could file a claim for a quarter section (160 acres) of land and come into ownership of that land after five years' occupation of it. A claimant need have only fourteen dollars for the filing fee.

The government land offices and transportation packagers spread the word throughout the Scandinavian countries and the urge to emigrate became epidemic. The Norwegian government and church opposed any exodus of its people. Massive leave-takings were a reproach—and a shout to the world that much was wrong in the little kingdom. They also threatened the country with a kind of self-inflicted genocide, since only the strongest and the youngest of its sons and daughters—the perpetuators of the race—would take up the challenge to escape. The antimigrationists pictured America as a land ridden with poisonous snakes, bloodthirsty animals, and dangerously wild men. In a song called "Oleana" they ridiculed Ole Bull, the distinguished Norwegian violinist who had tried to build an ideal community of emigrants in Pennsylvania:

Salmon hopping from brook to kettle,
    Cakes that rained out of the heavens,
And the little roasted piggies
    That politely asked one to have some ham. . . .

Emigration Fever was called "the most dangerous disease of our time, a bleeding of the Fatherland, a Black Death."

Osten and Henrik Boe (Bö) were two young men who caught the fever. With their parents and three sisters they lived on a tiny *gaard* (farm) near the village of Vang. Vang is in the district of Valders, on the southeastern coast of Norway. Behind it the land sweeps upward steeply into a wide, flat sugarloaf of mountains.

The Boes, like their neighbors, subsisted on a little patch of ground that also had to nourish a cow and a few chickens. Finding enough food for mere survival consumed most of the family's energies. The limited rations of milk, eggs, and potatoes were supplemented only by fish taken from a lake nearby.

In the spring of 1864 Osten and Henrik were twenty-five and twenty-one years old, respectively. Since childhood they had heard the tales of a big open country far across the seas. It is doubtful that word of the Homestead Act had reached their hamlet. It was enough for them to be told of a land where bread and meat were plentiful, where neighbor helped neighbor and there was the chance to breathe and stretch. They had also heard the shocking accounts of the way the red man had slain many of their countrymen in the southern counties of Minnesota. But that uprising had occurred two years earlier and the Indians were peaceful again.

For years the brothers had been saving the trifling sums they were paid for helping local fishermen. Now they had enough put by for the modest fare to take them on their long voyage. A group of Valders folk were setting sail from the port of Drammen and Osten and Henrik would be on that boat.

The brothers were leaving with the blessing of their parents. (Later the daughters were also to go.) The moment of parting must have been painful all around. These farewells were as final as a funeral. Parents and children alike knew they would not lay eyes upon one another again in this world. For the old folks the New World was as fabled and elusive as the lost Atlantis or the Kingdom of Heaven itself. Only the young had any chance of surviving the journey and they would never take that long, long trail back to the Old Country.

One can only imagine that parting. . . .

All morning the parents of emigrating sons have been carrying provisions aboard a sailboat bobbing in the little harbor under a cheerful April sun. Now it is high noon, the boat is loaded, and the captain is eager to set sail.

Osten and Henrik pick up the crude rucksacks that contain all their worldly trappings. The two young Vikings stand sturdy and straight as a brace of Norwegian spruce.

Each is as blond as the sun. Osten has a curve of scar on his forehead; it looks like the souvenir of a Heidelberg duel but was actually inscribed by a skate. (In a turn of exhibition skating he had leapt over a horse but the point of one skate stuck in the ice and then flew back to gash him over the right eye.) He walks up the ramp with a slight limp incurred in a skiing accident. Both of these minor imperfections will be with him the rest of his long life.

The sailboat skims across the fjord toward the open sea. It rounds a peninsular cliff and the harbor with the waving parents is lost. Now the old folks must reverse the path back to their village and lonely huts. Fortunately it is spring and the light will hold nearly around the clock until the end of summer. Now, too, is the busiest time, and with fewer hands to help, those left behind will be too burdened to sorrow. The acute sense of loss will not be felt until the long black winter night sets in.

The sailboat hugs the coastline, pitching around those southernmost extremities of land curved like the tip of a tongue. Sweeping off to starboard—fleetingly—is the magnificent fjord-serrated western coast. Then the fjords, the high wooded cliffs, the silvery cascades of waterfall, and finally the long vertebrate of snow-crowned mountains slip away into the mists. The boat becomes a solitary sail on the North Sea.

Later the voyage would bring terror and prayers for God's deliverance. But as Norway fell back from them irrevocably, the voyagers were filled with the anguish of leaving. As one dialect poet of Telemark wrote:

Farewell now, o valley of Soljord
Farewell to church and woods and home.
Farewell to parson and parish clerk,
    To kith and kin, and the lovely gardens of
    home.
Would to God this were undone!
    For the old home lies there grieving.
Turn about, hasten, hasten away.

But with this anguish sometimes went expressions of criticism for a fatherland that had failed its neediest. In the words of one peasant bard:

Farewell, thou Mother Norway, now I must
  leave thee!
Because thou fostered me,
  I must give thee many thanks.
All too sparing were thee in providing food
  For the throng of thy laborers,
Though thou givest more than enough
  To thy well-schooled sons.

Those who made the crossing by sailboat (steamboats became the usual mode after the late 1860s) spent long wretched weeks on the high seas. Winds were contrary. Storms nearly overturned the vessels time after time and dumped almost enough water inside to sink them. Mold formed on all the rations. The flat bread, or *skriva brod* (a thin-sliced, yellowish-brown bread), dried mutton and ham, *primost* (a brown cheese in cake form made of whey, sugar, and cream), and *gjatost* (goat's cheese) had to be scraped and dried regularly. Seasickness, pneumonia, dysentery, and typhoid fever were common ailments. It was an unusual voyage that didn't have death itself for a fellow traveller. When someone died, the body was wrapped in sails (or a big stone was tied to the feet) and consigned to the ocean.

Each evening the captain of the boat, as devout as all the poor peasants aboard, conducted devotionals. The wooden masts might be creaking and the boat listing dangerously to windward but the good captain would be heard. "We should all be grateful to God," he intoned, "for all His gifts to us, who are so unworthy. We should be grateful to our Lord and Creator that He lets His sun rise on us so many times. It is the Almighty Who decides everything for the best. As long as He gives life and strength, we shall not fear the future. . . ."

The boat carrying Osten and Henrik took eight weeks to arrive in Quebec City. To the brothers it was stranger than a dream, this first breath of the New World. They had never been near a real city before. Why, this Quebec with its bustling waterfront must be as big and busy as Kristiania (today's Oslo) or Bergen! So many people, thousands of them, chattering away in a language you couldn't understand. Such strange people, too! Especially those black-faced men loading and unloading the boats. Neither teacher nor pastor had ever told them the world had people with black skins. Caroline Soliah, who was to meet and marry Osten Boe on the prairies of western Minnesota, made the voyage from Norway the following year and she always recalled her terror as a nine-year-old child seeing those black men on the Quebec waterfront.

The two young men slept on the wharves under the open sky for two nights. Then they were herded like swine into a canalboat that took them 150 miles down the St. Lawrence to Montreal. In Montreal they boarded the immigration car—with its steerage accommodations—of a westward-bound train. Crowded and caged, they rattled for days through the Canadian forest and across the breadth of Michigan. At Grand Haven a steamboat took them over Lake Michigan to Milwaukee. Another train, also equipped with an immigrant box car—and then wagons—carried them across Wisconsin to the old French fur-trading town of Prairie du Chien and finally to Decorah, in the northeastern corner of Iowa.

Decorah had been settled a few years earlier by immigrant Norwegians from Voss, Telemark, Sogn, and Valders. New arrivals from those districts always found a welcome there. They joined the households of the earlier immigrants, whose hospitality had no limits. Here the newcomers got their first real indoctrination into the ways and possibilities of America. From their hosts they might pick up a few words of English to help them in any dealings with Yankee tradesmen or civil servants. Visitors shared the labors of the family and able-bodied males could usually earn a day's wages working as peripatetic hired hands. It was a marking-time interlude in a kind of staging area that gave the emigrant a chance to get his bearings and to plan his next move.

Osten and Henrik soon became restless in the Decorah settlement. They were too late for it. It was a little too formed, too picked over. Stories of a newer colony of Norwegians had been reaching their ears. These most recent emigrants were settling the village of Northfield, in the new state of Minnesota.

Eager to break fresh ground, the brothers quit Decorah one day in the late spring of 1865 and began the northwesterly trek of 150 miles to Northfield. They traveled the entire distance on foot. For Henrik it would be the end of the journey. For the sixty-odd remaining years of his life, Northfield was home. There he prospered as a hardware merchant. There he married, established a home, and fathered three children who all entered professions. And there, one day in 1876, he was eyewitness to the hair-raising robbery of the Northfield bank by the Jesse James gang.

The charms of the pleasant little Norwegian-American community wore thin on Osten. Village life lacked something vital. He dreamed of land . . . of a plot of ground he could call his own, of taming it, growing things on it. He listened intently to the tales of homesteading to the north and west, of rich farmland in an open country.

One April day in 1868, when the snow was off the ground at last, he set off on foot for St. Cloud. To reach this little town on the Mississippi River he followed oxcart trails in a north-by-north-westerly direction. It took him nine days to hike the 125 miles of rough terrain. As a prospective homesteader he went to the government land office in St. Cloud, where he was shown maps of surveyed areas. Now he must decide where he wanted to settle and go to inspect the quarter sections in that area that were available for claim. When he came back and paid his filing fee, the land he had chosen would be registered in his name. Six months later he could take possession of his land. If he never left it for five years, he could have a deed to the land.

Osten chose the township of Aastad, Minnesota, because it was the farthest point out of the immigrant thrust in 1868. Only two settlers had filed claims there and no land had been broken beyound it. Aastad lies some 135 miles north and west of St. Cloud. It measures 6 miles square with 36 sections of 640 acres each. Its soil is rich black alluvial loam. The township is a gently rolling prairie punctuated with marshes, creeks, thickets, and thirty clear lakes. Its western edge flattens out and sweeps into the rich valley of the Red River of the North.

The Great Northern and Northern Pacific railroads had not put down their tracks yet. It would be a decade before those caravans of prairie schooners would come creeping like a fleet through the endless sea of green and golden grasses, their canvas tops gleaming brightly in the shimmering light. There was only the old Red River oxcart trail, the St. Paul-Pembina artery of a diminished fur-trading industry. The landscape was a trackless wilderness, immense, beautiful, uncluttered.

Again Osten is on foot. The rucksack and quilt are strapped to his back and he carries an axe to clear the jungle of undergrowth, the snarls of hazel and plum brush and vines. The air is filter-pure and the sky as blue as if it had just been scoured and painted. He passes forests primeval and lakelets and sloughs that hold a mirror to the sky, mounds and relics of prehistoric people, wild roses entwining with the grasses in a thick carpet. As he walks through the deserted land the spirits of antiquity seem to keep him company. His trail takes him closer and closer to the geographical heart of this vast continent, past the point where there is any tree, house, or living creature to break the terrain. The cathedral-like silence deepens as the path bears westward. At night he lies down with the vaulted heavens for a roof overhead. The moon swings above the landscape in solemn grandeur and the North Star is his guiding light. Finally, one sweet morning in May, there is *his* prairie . . . billowing into slopes, rising in low hills, then leveling off to sink into the interminable plain.

This last, roughest segment of his four-hundred-mile hike from Decorah has taken a fortnight of hard pushing. Now Osten is home—at last. But for him the end of the emigrant journey is only the beginning of the immigrant pioneer ordeal.

In the nineteenth century and the early decades of the twentieth century a million Norwegians emigrated to America. Most of them followed in the tracks of Osten and Henrik, pressing westward. (To immigrants, as Archibald MacLeish has remarked, America was "the west and the winds blowing.") When the valley of the Red River of the North was settled, it had the largest concentration of Norwegians outside of Norway. Its great bonanza farms began to harvest millions of bushels of wheat annually and it became known as the Breadbasket of the World.

The wonder is not that so many of these first settlers succumbed, but that so many survived. A partial catalogue of the trials that beset them would show such entries as grasshopper plagues, blizzards, long Arctic winters, stupefyingly hot shadeless summers, prairie fires, earthquakes, cyclones, tornadoes, electrical storms, the devastation of blackbirds and gophers and the chinch bug, hail storms, torrential rains that turned the grain to rot, poor seed and ignorance of good farming practices, oxen running wild, horses and cattle driven insane by mosquitoes, nerve-shattering winds, droughts, crop failures, money panic ("Need brings dogs into bondage," said the bankers), lost or stolen livestock, stem rust in the spring wheat, the constant threat of attack by Indians, killing strikes by pneumonia and influenza and tuberculosis and black diphtheria and typhoid fever, death by freezing, backbreaking labor without end, and the aching loneliness.

For many, the challenge exceeded the limits of human endurance. Perhaps of all the groups who became Americans only our black brothers—those involuntary immigrants who were brought here in chains— were more sorely tested. Many who could

not endure the life simply lay down and died. Others took their own lives. (My grandparents and their neighbors could swap horror tales of going into their barns and finding strangers hanging from the hayloft.) Still others found the release of madness.

But those who neither perished, nor committed suicide nor went mad achieved a kind of indestructibility. They lived on and on and on, many of them into their tenth decade and beyond, active, alert, and cheerful. They truly believed it was God's will that had kept them alive so long and that it would have been profane to be idle or to have wished for an earlier grave.

Not long ago a pair of old settlers who had homesteaded in Otter Tail County celebrated their eightieth wedding anniversary. They were 105 and 102 years old. To the best of all available records, they had been married longer than any other couple in the history of the United States.

The first child born on the Aastad prairie recently granted the *Fergus Falls Daily Journal* an interview. She was ninety-six years old at the time and still presiding over her home. Nothing that the reporter could ask her, nothing in the flow of reminiscences that the question unleashed, could distract the sprightly little lady from the fact that she had a cake in the oven. Three times in the course of the interview she went to the kitchen to check on its progress.

Osten stood on the treeless prairie. The buffalo grasses brushed against the calves of his legs. The plain was so wide that the rim of the heavens cut down on it in a 360-degree circle. He might have wished for some woodlands to remind him of home. But this land was *his* and it would always have a value beyond any riches it might yield. Possession of land made him one with the Norse chieftains. Land had dignity and stability. It stood for the permanence of family and it was something that could be handed down through the centuries.

First he must have a roof over his head. There was only one ripple in the terrain. Into the tough sod he plunged his axe. He hacked out pieces of earth a foot or so wide and began piling these on top of one another to make his dugout in the side of the hillock. It was a one-room sod hut, a home built of dirt, literally a hole in the ground. The walls were dirt, the roof was dirt, and the floor beneath him was dirt. Time brought a few refinements. Tamarack poles supported the roof. Rough windows and doors were cut in the sod walls. Clay steps led to the entrance. The walls, after several years, were boarded up and whitewashed and a floor was put in.

The furnishings were primitive. For sleeping there were mattresses of straw and the used straw was taken out regularly and burned. Benches for eating were made of logs split in half, their legs fastened on with wooden pegs. There was a table and eventually a cupboard with shelves and an open hearth.

Osten lived in this earth house for ten years. Then he built a one-room log house and three years later a large frame house. To the sod hut he brought his bride, the spirited seventeen-year-old girl he had met at Sunday services in a neighbor's granary during his fourth summer on the prairie. Here four of his nine children were born—and died: two in infancy, and two young daughters who, as victims of the dreaded black diphtheria, choked to death in his arms.

In winter blizzards the snow often packed against the door and drifted over the roof, imprisoning the family for days. In the spring, before there were floors, the earth beneath them would give a jar, then another jar, and gophers and garter snakes would surface to share their humble quarters.

When he looked back on that experience, Osten's fondest memories of that first home in the new country were of the winter nights when he lay warm under Caroline's patchwork quilts. A candle burned in the hollowed-out turnip and the hearth ablaze with cow dung gave off the most beautiful colors. Lying there awake he'd gaze out through the wooded slats at the moonlight putting its dazzling shine on the boundless white sea of crusted snow.

So simple were the earliest tools of the prairie that the Egyptian farmers of two thousand years ago would have been quite at home there.

In the custom of penniless immigrants, Osten helped his neighbors for two years before touching his own quarter section. The few dollars earned bought a team of oxen. By giving a neighbor another helping hand, he was able to borrow a one-bottom walking plow. The sod was extremely tough of fiber and fought hard against uprooting. Yielding finally, it gleamed and glistened under the summer sun, a rich black substance that promised great fertility.

His first growing season Osten seeded five acres of wheat. The grain was sown broadcast by hand and when it was mature it was cut with a scythe. When it was bound he carried it by wagon fifty miles over the roadless void to Alexandria, where the nearest grist mill was. The journey took three days each way and at night he slept in the wagon. In Alexandria the "liquid gold" turned into flour, which he bartered for food staples, items of clothing, and a couple of crude farming tools.

The next season he plowed and planted a few more acres. And so the process continued in successive years. The new acres were put to barley, oats, rye, clover, flax, and potatoes as well as wheat. Summers, when the grain was growing, Osten—walking with a wagon—would make several trips to Ten Mile Lake to cut down trees that would be hauled back to build the log barn, to be planked for fences, and to be used for fuel. These trips took a day of travel each way and a day to fell the trees.

After he had prospered beyond the bartering stage, Osten sold his wheat to elevator operators who shipped it to the flourishing new flour mills in Mineapolis. When he acquired cows, butter was churned on the farm and shaped into pound slabs that were stamped with lovely flowered figures made from a wood press. These were sold to the creamery in town.

Threshing machines, reapers, binders,

separators, and other laborsaving implements came along. But for Osten and his fellow homesteaders the farming life remained an unremitting burden from dawn to darkness. Always there were the farmerly chores of plowing, seeding, cultivating, harvesting, threshing, binding, milking, building fences and planting trees, feeding and doctoring the livestock, horses, and oxen.

But a farmer like Osten had to wear many other hats. He had to be carpenter enough to build his own home and furniture, sleds, skis, ox yokes, and harrows. He had to be something of a cobbler to make and repair the family's shoes and boots. And he must hunt and fish—not recreationally, as a sportsman, but from need to fatten the family larder. (Long before tall "fish stories" became an entertainment, Osten, who was as incapable of an exaggeration as of a lie, would tell about going to the slough on the edge of his property and pulling up messes of pike and pickerel by the pitchfork.)

In later years Grandma Caroline spent long hours in quite advanced crocheting, embroidering, and crewel work. Watching the needle flicking away, I'd sometimes tease her, "Grandma, I guess you've always had it easy, haven't you? Even back on the farm?" The fun of it was her serious denial. "Oh, no. Surely I was busy."

Surely she was busy, indeed. Besides feeding five children and a husband three meals a day and morning and afternoon "lunches," she spun yarn, wove cloth, sewed and darned and knitted and patched the family's wardrobe, made rugs and bedding, washed and ironed, kept the home sparkling clean, tended the orchard, put up preserves and dried fruits, took care of the chickens, often did the milking, churned the butter, baked, and made the candles (by dipping a wick of twisted cord into melted tallow) and soap (from ashes and greases and lye). Then, too, vast reservoirs of energy—and time—always had to be allocated to treating her children's ailments and superintending their religious training.

With all their industry and persistence, many homesteaders like Osten and Caroline were rather accidental farmers. They knew so little about what they were doing. Help from sources like agricultural extension colleges was decades away. Their only strategy was trial and error. They did not learn about crop rotation, for instance, until their soil was nearly exhausted. They were blessed with some of the richest farm land in the world, but what they had gained in natural resources was so frequently offset by disasters they could neither predict nor control. . . .

They came like dive bombers out of the west. They came by the millions with the rustle of their wings roaring overhead. They came in waves, like the rolls of the sea, descending with a terrifying speed, breaking now and again like a mighty surf. They came with the force of a williwaw and they formed a huge, ominous, dark brown cloud that eclipsed the sun. They dipped and touched earth, hitting objects and people like hailstones. But they were not hail. These were *live* demons. They popped, snapped, crackled, and roared. They were dark brown, an inch or longer in length, plump in the middle and tapered at the ends. They had transparent wings, slender legs, and two black eyes that flashed with a fierce intelligence.

So came the grasshoppers, like one of the seven plagues of Egypt, and the devastation they wrought was homeric.

Blanketing the ground like snow, they devoured everything in sight but the implements in the fields. They ate every blade of grass, every stalk of grain, the roots of vegetables, the bark on the trees, the clothes on the line, the hickory handles on forks, even leather saddles and boots. Boys who went barefoot and barelegged had their feet and legs eaten raw.

The hoppers left only the holes in the ground. Before calling it a season they seeded the plowed fields with tiny eggs that looked like a fine, dry sawdust, laying enough of them to pollute a continent. Next summer a fresh invasion ravaged the countryside. And the summer after that.

Osten and his neighbors set up smudge pots. They put coal tar on sheet iron. Two men would walk through the fields holding either end of a long stick scooping the hoppers into burlap sacks held open by a wooden barrel hoop. Bounties were paid according to weight. But the hoppers—which were really Rocky Mountain locusts—were seemingly as unconquerable as the cockroaches that infest urban dwellings today. Osten remembered that they were so thick in the wagon ruts that the juice from their crushed bodies would run in streams down the wagon tires. Only chickens and ducks could eat them, but a diet of hoppers turned the yolks of eggs red and gave the eggs such a strong taste they were nearly inedible.

So critical was the situation that Governor Pillsbury proclaimed a day of prayer in April of 1878. The next day, as history still records, a polar wave struck and froze every grasshopper in the state stiff. And no replacements ever flew in.

The devout, among them my grandparents, always cited this as irrefutable proof of the power of prayer.

Inside the dugout Osten heard the raging wind. The howl and whine terrified his young wife and set their infant daughter to screaming. In its fury he could see it driving waves of snow across the fields. He knew what was happening and he knew that before it got any worse he must somehow find his way to the barn and milk the cows.

The barn was no more than fifty yards from the dugout. But so great were the clouds of driving snow that he could not dimly locate it. In fact, he could scarcely see his hand in front of him. He took a coil of rope from inside, fastened one end of it to the door, and began walking in the direction of the barn. If he could just hold onto the rope, he would be able to retrace his steps to the hut.

The foaming, fuming storm blasted him off his feet again and again. The snow stabbed his face like icy needles and slashed his clothing with the force of nails. He wandered for hours, losing all sense of time, before finding the barn. Then it took all the strength of his mighty arms to open the door against that maniacal wind.

Osten was trapped in the barn for three days and three nights. The wind howled across the open plain at seventy-five miles per hour and the temperature dropped to forty degrees below zero. He drank the milk from the cows and jumped up and down and beat himself to keep from freezing to death. There were times, he confessed later, when he thought how nice it would be if he could bring himself to kill the animals and wrap himself up in their skins.

Such were his memories of the Great Blizzard of 1876.

The cold was always an overpowering fact of life, as inevitable as the coming of those long, gray, sunless, skyless days of winter itself. It still is. But nowadays there are ways of sidestepping it (Hawaii and Arizona being two popular options among the natives). The snow often comes in early October and keeps falling sometimes until May. There can be a month of days when the thermometer never makes it up to the freezing mark, while plummeting to thirty-five or forty below at night.

The cold dominates my father's earliest recollections of life on the farm and school. It was always dark when he got up and made his way with a kerosene lantern to the barn to help with chores. Sometimes he put on two suits of long underwear, two flannel shirts, two pairs of pants, a vest, a heavy coat, and two or three pairs of woolen mittens. Even so, it was impossible to keep warm. He walked the mile or so, sometimes through deep drifts, to the one-room schoolhouse, slapping his hands and jumping in place. But frequently his fingers and toes were frozen on arrival, and a good part of the school day would be spent thawing them by rubbing them with snow and ice water.

Dad recalls being trapped in the school

overnight by a blizzard and that the teacher and children chopped up the pine desks and benches and burned them to keep warm. As the flames lowered, they threw in all their books to keep the fire going.

The snow fell and fell and fell, piling up to the top of the roof so that all that was visible in this great universe of whiteness was the smoking chimney. The breath hung frozen in the air and skin that touched an iron implement would be ripped off. Livestock and horses lost during a blizzard were not found until the spring thaw uncovered their frozen corpses. When Osten and Caroline's daughters died of black diphtheria, they were buried in the snow and not brought to their permanent graves until spring softened the earth again.

The spring thaw, when it came, often flooded the fields like a reenactment of the biblical rain of forty days and forty nights.

Nothing sustained the tension in life like the threat of the "fairen," or prairie fire. It struck usually in the autumn, when the grasses were dry. Anything could set it off—a hunter dropping a match, a bolt of lightning, even a spark from a chimney or passing train. Fanned by a good breeze, it became a holocaust. It blazed across the countryside, scorching hay, fences, cattle, poultry, clothing, faces, bodies, homes. The flames leaped ten and twelve feet high. They painted the sky red and sped across the horizon like a race horse. The roar of the fire sounded like an express train or the thundering of an angry Thor.

When Osten and his neighbors had frame houses to protect, they plowed a series of furrows around their homes as a firebreak. The furrows were broken some yards apart and the grasses between them were burned to keep the fire away. Further afield they fought the fires with wet grain sacks, flailing away rather futilely at the speeding monster.

Burns, frostbites, diseases, and all other ailments were treated with home remedies. These *landnamsmen* and their families survived without doctors. They had no alternative. Doctors did not exist in that part of the country in those days. Later, when they were available, my grandparents and their children still seemed to get along without them very well. To this day my father, a robust seventy-seven year old, thinks doctors should be visited only in time of real emergency, as with a broken leg or an attack of smallpox. Live right, keep moving, and stop thinking there's anything wrong with you, according to Dad, and you won't need to be running to doctors' offices.

Children of those early settlers even got themselves born without a doctor's helping hand. The women all took turns serving one another as midwives, and they seemed to have remarkable antennae for detecting when an expectant mother's time was nigh. All nine of Grandma Caroline's children were delivered with the help of midwives.

The nearest thing to a doctor was the itinerant "medicine man" who traveled from farm to farm with a line of salves, oils, "inhalers" for catarrh, liniments, and other health aids. He traveled his route with wagon and horse and made the rounds about once a month when the weather was good. His arrival always created excitement because he was not only company but a glamorous stranger who came from far beyond the horizon. In the practice of frontier hospitality he was always given supper and shelter for the night.

Dad has vivid memories of Naftalin, a Jewish peddler, whose grandnephew was a recent mayor of Minneapolis. Besides "medical" supplies, Naftalin's wagon was loaded with objects of fascination such as combs, shoelaces, handkerchiefs, reading glasses, pocket knives, and mouth organs. When supper was over, Naftalin entertained the family with a mouth organ recital.

Grandma had quite fixed notions of how to deal with common complaints. Goose grease was rubbed on the neck and chest for sore throats and chest congestion and a wool cloth was wrapped around the greased areas to induce heat. Severe chest colds called for a rubdown with skunk oil. Carbuncles and boils got treated with poultices of sweet cream and flour or of dried bread that was crumbled, softened, and mixed with sweet milk and crushed herb leaves. Ginger tea was drunk "to bring out" measles and a multi-herbal tea was administered for "building blood" and curing flu. Castor oil was taken for stomach-aches, constipation, and cleaning out the system.

Dentistry was as unknown as medicine. To ease the pain of an exposed nerve, a tiny wad of cotton saturated with strong liniment was rubbed on the cheek and put near the infected area. When teeth became badly infected, they were yanked out, usually with a shoemaker's or carpenter's pincers.

In the wake of a good rain mosquitoes arrived by the millions. Grandma always applied sweet cream to relieve the itching and bandaged badly bitten arms and legs.

Suffering was borne with remarkable fortitude. This might in part be attributed to the fatalism of the Norse mind. But it more reflected the conviction that everything that happened in this world was in accordance with the will of God. To complain would be to invite the wrath of the Lord, who would send a punishment that would really be something to complain about.

The settlements were all homogeneous and self-contained. The immigrant invasion of that part of the country was overwhelmingly Scandinavian, but the separate components of Scandinavia did not become a melting pot in the New World. A township like Aastad remained exclusively Norwegian. The Swedes and Danes and Finns kept to themselves in communities that had names like Swedish Grove and Dane Prairie and Finlandia. The different groups could have made themselves understood to one another and might have found they had much in common. But these exchanges did not occur.

Even those first settlers who eventually left their farms to live in town—as did my grandparents after thirty-four years—managed to reestablish this separateness in a new community. The county seat, Fergus Falls, in the early 1900s was a polyglot village of Poles, Germans, Irish, Scotsmen, New England Yankees, and Dutch, as well as Scandinavians. But the various Scandinavian populations touched no other group but themselves. Each had its own Lutheran churches, newspapers, and social fraternities, with little or no cross-pollination. My grandfather and my grandmother lived more than sixty and eighty years, respectively, in this country, but there's no evidence they had more than glancing contact with anyone who was not Norwegian.

Ironically, the most contact my grandparents had with non-Norwegians was with the Chippewa Indians. Grandma, especially, was not fond of the Indians, but it had nothing to do with the pigmentation of their skin. An old Indian trail meandered close to the edge of their fields and during summers nomadic Chippewas wandering across the prairie would lay themselves down to sleep near the barn or even pitch a skin tent beside the slough, with half-naked children dancing around the evening fire.

They were a peaceful people, but Grandma would be terrified to hear them creeping up behind her when she was busy at the kitchen stove. Always they asked for pancakes and coffee. Grandma did not begrudge them the food and drink they begged. But trespassing on other people's property! Stealing into homes without knocking! Once it was pointed out to Grandma that these were minor impertinences compared with what the white man had done—and was still doing—to the red man. But Grandma was having none of this argument. She had not contributed to any ill treatment of Indians. Right was right. And that was that.

But the Indians got off lightly compared with the Swedes. How Grandma could have formed her impressions of the Swedes is difficult to imagine, because to the best of our knowledge she had never known a Swede in her life. Nonetheless, her warning could not have been firmer: never trust a Swede. At this remove it is impossible to recall any of her exact quotes on the subject. But the essence of her counsel was that the Swedes were a strange, cold, selfish, sneaky lot and that any contact with them could only have unhappy consequences.

Had Grandma been the only one with an anti-Swedish bias, it could have been dismissed as a personal idiosyncracy. But the prejudice was general. I remember walking in Fergus Falls one day with my uncle and stopping to talk with a man who served with him on the hospital's board of directors. At some point in the conversation the man good-naturedly remarked, "The trouble with you Swedes—." Reddening, my uncle interrupted, "Please don't call us Swedes."

When the Nazis invaded Norway at the beginning of World War II, the Norwegian community was stunned and outraged. It soon became apparent that Sweden had no intention of compromising its cool neutrality to come to the aid of her neighbor and the wrath of the Norwegians fixed as much on the Swedes as on the occupying enemy.

Grandma accepted the fact of Swedish noninvolvement with resignation. She closed her eyes and shook her head knowingly. What else, after all, could you expect from the Swedes?

In the midst of excruciating hardship, Osten and Caroline could see God's blessings all around them. When drought or hail or prairie fire or insect war had taken the food out of their mouths, they could still articulate the twenty-third Psalm and believe it. "The Lord is my shepherd, I shall not want. . . ." Even when poverty, disease, or death overtook them, they could see divine purpose being fulfilled. They must thank God, for God governed best. He sent them suffering and tribulations only to test their faith.

Their faith was their abiding comfort, and that faith alone enabled them to endure the perversities of fate. This time on earth was but a preparation for the heavenly home which would be their eternal abode. While they struggled through this mortal phase, a welcome was being prepared for their arrival in heaven. Ultimately they would assemble with God in the eternal mansion, where they would find everlasting joy and contentment in beholding God's face.

In the years before the first church was built, the little colony of settlers gathered each Sunday in one another's dugouts. The host would read a passage from the Bible and give his interpretation of it. Then there would be prayers and hymns. When the group came to my grandparents' hut, there was always the singing of Osten and Caroline's favorite hymn, "Den Store Kvede Flok" ("The Big White Flock," signifying angels).

As years passed, the growing community had the services of a *klokker*. The *klokker* was not an ordained minister but a kind of peddler of spiritual wares who carried the Good Word from farm to farm. He knew the Bible, he could give sermons, and he had the authority to baptize.

The coming of the *klokker* was a great event. This was God's emissary on earth. Nothing was too good for him. The devoutness and hospitality of the family must shine forth so that God would receive a good report of them. They might be living on *grot* (a mixture of flour and water) and eggs, but one of the laying chickens must be killed to feed the *klokker*. Taking his leave, he would often say, "I'll be at your house next Friday if not Providentially detained." The coy reference suggested that at any moment God might see fit to recall him for some heavenly mission. But the *klokker's* gift for survival on this planet proved quite as remarkable as that of his flock's.

The church, when it was built, was like an oasis in the desert. All week long Osten and Caroline and their neighbors were sustained by the thought of Sunday, when they would travel three miles to gather in the little wooden structure and hear the Word of God proclaimed. Nobody ever felt "not up to" attending these services and no inclemency of weather could deter anybody. In sub-zero temperatures, with the wind lashing against their faces and driven snow blinding the vision, they crossed the countryside by open sleigh to perform their sacred duty. In the church they sat enthralled for two hours or more while God's spokesman described the rosy hereafter that awaited the pious, and, in even more vivid detail, the fires of hell that would consume infidels and transgressors.

Grandpa was in his eighties when I was born. My memories of him are dim but they mostly seem to involve religion. For much of his waking time in those last years he studied the Bible and his *hus postil,* which was a book of sermons and devotionals. He also read every word of the *Decorah-Posten,* a Norwegian-language daily which is still being published, and the *Ugeblad,* a local weekly. Both these publications ran prayers and inspirational essays and news of the Norwegian Synod of the Lutheran Church.

At family dinners it was the custom for the youngest to give the blessing for the food. For a while I was the youngest grandchild and in my five-year-old mind I'm sure I thought I had found one all-purpose grace that would see me through all those family dinners. It went:

God is great, God is good.
　We will thank Him for this food.
By His hand we all get fed,
　Give us Lord our daily bread.

Grandpa suffered this grace a few times before taking up the matter with my mother one Sunday. "Doesn't he ever learn any other blessings?" he asked. The tone of reproof was not lost on Mother, who saw to it that I learned some new ones.

Mother herself had discovered early on just where Grandpa's values lay. Not long after she and Dad were married, Grandpa summoned the family to a conference in his home. He indicated that he had important business to discuss and no one should be absent. Mother assumed it could only mean that the children were about to receive some portion of their inheritance. Like most young newlyweds, she and Dad could have used any financial help that came their way.

Indeed, when the family was assembled

around the dining room table, Grandpa said he had a special gift for each of them. Then, with all the majesty of a feudal lord dispensing parcels of a fiefdom to deserving vassals, he handed out copies of a paperbound book he had bought through a mailorder house. The title of the book was *All Through Grace.* Across the span of nearly half a century, Mother can still savor the disappointment that nearly reduced her to tears. She never opened her copy of *All Through Grace.*

Religious fervor coalesced with social hunger. These first immigrants were starved for companionship. Neighbor was separated from neighbor by too much space and the workday was too consuming to allow for visits back and forth. But Sundays all the community met at church and after services were over no one was in a hurry to start home. In nice weather the congregation lingered for hours on the grounds, socializing and sharing with one another the food each family had brought. In winter if a blizzard should trap them in the unheated church overnight, it was an adventure rather than a catastrophe. They had their devotion, their singing, and their fellowship, after all, to keep them warm.

Otherwise only a funeral could break the week-long isolation. There were those who even attended funerals in churches outside the township, where they mourned the deaths of people they had never known in life. To some this might suggest a morbid streak in their natures, but a more plausible explanation was that funerals promised human contact. After the deceased was put to rest, the mourners moved from the graveside to the survivors' home where there would be refreshments and conversation, however subdued.

In the time of harvest everyone came together to give one another a helping hand. One day they would all be at Hans's farm and the next at Eric's and then Olaf's. While the men were busy in the fields, the women chatted over their sewing and quilting and crocheting. The men hunted and fished together to fatten the provender. As time went on, and there were additional hands around the farm to help with the work, there might be an occasional berry-picking expedition in summer or a brilliant winter day that would inspire a cross-country skiing jaunt to a neighbor's house or a skating party on the slough. May 17 was Norwegian Independence Day, a holiday always commemorated with folk songs and dances and feasting.

But the seventeen days of Christmas was the time of the year that brought everyone together in sustained revelry. All work came to a halt except for such inescapable chores as milking the cows and feeding the animals and chickens. Neighbors visited back and forth in a kind of festival of open houses. A major feature of these celebrations was the practice of *Yulebooking,* which translates as "Christmas fooling." Adults and children alike tried to disguise themselves in strange-looking odds and ends of clothing and homemade masks. Then they'd present themselves at their neighbors' houses and it would be up to their hosts to guess who in the world these visitors could be.

Thomas Sajord was an immigrant born in the same hamlet in Norway as my grandfather. He came to America in 1870 and worked as a farm hand for a time before becoming a private secretary to a United States senator. In 1899, from Washington, he wrote an open letter to the *St. Paul Pioneer Press* which was addressed to the Valderses (people from the district of Valders in Norway) of the Twin Cities. "Couldn't these good people have a reunion some time this spring?" he asked. "These good people" welcomed the idea. In June of that year a reunion was held in Minneapolis at which there were songs and speeches, feasting and games, and much informal visiting among long-separated fellow clansmen. This was the beginning of the Valders Lag and the entire *lag* movement.

The Valderses met again the next year and in 1901 a permanent society called the Valdris Samband was organized. Natives of other districts began similar organizations. Andrew Veblen, a professor of physics at the University of Iowa, became the first president of the Valdris Samband. In his *Valders Book* he characterized the *lags* as "for auld lang syne societies." But they were more than that. Over the years they published thousands of pages of biographical and historical material about their members and origins and they collected charitable and memorial gifts to be given to their ancestral community.

When the Valders Lag was held in our town, my grandfather's house—like the houses of the other local Valderses—would be open to Lag members who came from other parts of the state, Iowa, or the Dakotas. Nobody ever had to stay at a hotel. The same was true wherever this *lag* or any of the other *lags* were held.

Today the *lags* are fading from the scene. Their founders are dead and so are most of their children. Succeeding generations, for the most part, have never bothered to learn the language and simply do not have that much interest in perpetuating their ties to the Old Country.

It was the church that provided most of the opportunities for social outlets. There were, however, purely fraternal organizations, such as the Sons of Norway. A story, perhaps apocryphal, is told of the troubles one community had in getting a Sons of Norway chapter started. Supposedly the charter ruled that it was necessary to have one hundred members signed up before a chapter could be formed. This community had ninety-nine candidates pledged. Everybody hunted and hunted for that hundredth Norwegian that would put them in business. But he couldn't be found. It remained for an Irishman to supply the solution. "Why not take the ninety-nine Norwegians," he suggested, "and add one Swede and just change the name to Sons of Bitches?"

However these people got together, it was always without the social lubricant of drink.

They were rigidly opposed to the use of alcohol for any purpose whatsoever. It's a safe speculation that my grandparents—and everybody they knew—went to their graves without a drop of hard liquor ever having moistened their lips. If a doctor had prescribed whiskey to alleviate some pain or affliction, they would have ignored the prescription and suffered in silence.

The evils of drink were promulgated, of course, from the pulpit. But why had the clergy fixed on this one transgression to underscore so emphatically? The Bible warns against drunkenness, among other sins of excess. But it also extols the salubrious effects of wine taken in moderation and it makes clear that the fermented juice of the grape flowed at the marriage at Cana and many other occasion. But these men of the cloth could not be softened by such references. Many of them, ironically, were grossly overweight because they were always ready to eat when food was set before them, and this could be many times a day in making their rounds. But it didn't seem to occur to them that they were guilty of gluttony, another sin deplored in the Good Book.

According to an old Christmas custom in Norway, the lady of the house gave wine to each member of the family Christmas morning while everyone was still in bed. For this ceremony my grandmother used chokecherry wine made from berries gathered on the farm. The amount of wine each of us received was a mere soupçon—as symbolic as the taking of Communion—and hardly enough to relax the central nervous system of an ant. A bottle of wine in Grandma's house lasted longer than the bottle of vermouth of someone who drinks his martinis very, very dry.

Just before my father went off to World War I, he daringly brought home a case of beer from the local brewery and invited Grandpa to drink a farewell bottle with him. To his surprise, Grandpa accepted. "And I'll have another one with you when you come back," said Grandpa. But probably nothing short of sending a son off to foreign battlefields could have persuaded him to down anything as heady as even that insipid local beer.

There was one member of the family who did like his drop. But excuses were made for him. During a prairie fire he had risked his life to save some newly born calves from a burning barn. He carried to the grave the scars of his bravery. And being both a man of God and a man of substance, Uncle Eric could be forgiven if he sometimes refreshed himself from the bottles he kept up in the attic.

As a young bride my mother was unwittingly introduced to one of those bottles during a family picnic. A bee had stung her and she was crying from the pain. Uncle Eric was the one who had something more than sympathy to offer. "Come with me, little girl," he said, "I've got some special medicine for bee sting." He took her up to the attic. There on a long table was a row of decanters apparently containing magic elixirs for the cure of various afflictions. Each had a different label: Croup, Catarrh, Summer Complaint, Appendicitis, Gallopping Consumption, Gout, etc.

From the decanter labeled Bee Sting Uncle Eric poured a generous dosage of the "medicine" into a glass of lemonade he had carried upstairs and told her to drink it slowly.

Mother immediately began to feel better and soon she was telling Uncle Eric what a wonderful time she was having. She says she was never afraid of being stung again by a bee at Uncle Eric's, remembering how pleasurable could be the cure.

The groaning board known as the smorgasbord came long after the early prairie years. In the beginning the immigrants had simple, monotonous diets. They ate whatever they could raise or catch or maybe barter in exchange for a hogshead of flour. Early menus featured bread, oatmeal, smoked fish and fish soups, cheeses like *primost* and *gjatost,* pemmican (dried meat mashed into a paste with fat), buttermilk, sour milk on boiled potatoes, and *spky kjot*—the shavings off a leg of lamb or beef that had been dried and smoked and were almost too tough a challenge for a regular knife.

In season game was plentiful, as there were always quail and pheasants and prairie chickens to be flushed out of the long grasses and ducks in the slough. On special occasions there was (and still is) *lutefisk,* a dried cod whose odor in the cooking has sent strong men fleeing from the house. When a family could afford to eat into its capital, so to speak, a chicken was killed or a hog or a cow was butchered for home consumption. Two meat specialties were *lub,* a blood sausage, and *rulapulsa,* a meat roll made of beef flank stuffed with pork steak and usually sliced cold. Dried apricots and prunes and apples formed the basis of the fruit soups so dear to the palates of all Scandinavians. Lingonberries and herring, two other staples of the Norwegian diet, were imported from the Old Country. Lingonberries were bought by the barrel.

By modern nutritional standards, the immigrant diet was "heavy" and deficient in key vitamins and minerals. Meat and potatoes became the essential table. Cream, butter, and milk high in dairy fat content were consumed daily in large quantities, but nobody had heard of cholesterol counts and nobody ever seemed to die from hardening of the arteries. Orange juice, leafy green vegetables, and salads were unknown to my grandparents.

In common with most people who abstain from alcohol, each of my grandparents developed a prominent sweet tooth. When she could afford the time and a few conveniences, Grandma developed into an accomplished bread and pastry chef. Some of the confections that came from her kitchen— such as the delicate rosettes with their topping of Devonshire-thick cream and lingonberries and her *Krumkage* and *Berliner Kranser*—can't be found anywhere today. Her *flot brod* was renowned. So was her

lefse, a potato-flour pastry which is eaten half-raw and speaks eloquently for the sturdiness of the Norwegian digestive system.

It was said of Grandma that she kept things so clean you could eat off her floors. It's been said of others, of course. But it was said of her even when her floor was the smooth earth of the dugout.

Cleanliness was a virtue held in high esteem by all her contemporaries. It ranked just behind godliness, where the Bible had placed it. "Cleanliness is next to godliness...." For them it was a virtue unto itself, unrelated to hygiene. The Scriptures recommended it and that was sufficient reason to practice it.

Some higher judge will have to rate Grandma on her godliness. But with cleanliness, it was almost possible to root for the dirt, so uneven was the contest. "Everything should be so clean," she often said, "that the king could come and visit and there would be no room for shame." (Grandma never entirely adapted to the sea change that had borne her from a monarchy to a republic.)

On the farm no domestic chore took precedence over her making of the soap. She scrubbed and scrubbed at everything. When each object and surface in the house had been scoured, she went outside and scrubbed down the cows with a brush. She said this was a practice brought over from the Old Country but many thought she invented it. She had different skirts for scrubbing, dusting, and cooking and these she'd change during the course of the day as she moved from one task to the next. Whatever else she might be doing, the dust cloth was rarely out of her sight.

Grandma spent the last years of her life in a house that was far too big for one person. She was on everybody's mind, but there didn't seem to be any solution to the problem. She was determined to hold her ground and not move in with any member of the family. Hiring a housekeeper to live with her was out of the question because of Grandma's standards of immaculateness. Several attempts were made to install a married couple in an upstairs apartment who would live there rent free in exchange for keeping an eye on Grandma. But the lodgers had barely unpacked their bags before the family began hearing reports of untidiness and accumulating filth.

I was last in Minnesota for any extended time in the spring of 1946. I had just come out of the army and was catching my breath before going back to college in the East. Grandma was in her ninetieth year then and still in charge. But we worried about her, especially her being alone at night. It was decided, as a makeshift solution for those weeks while I was at home, that I would sleep at her house.

For the first night's vigil I came armed with what I thought were newsy tidbits that would interest her. I would tell her about meeting her pastor on the street, how Mother's flowers were progressing, and the results of Dad's fishing trip. But Grandma's attention was hard to hold. We sat in the living room and the inevitable dust cloth was in her hand. In mid-sentence I would be deserted by Grandma's sudden flights from the room. Dim as was the light, her sharp eye had spied a speck of dust on the bannister in the hallway or on the rungs of one of the dining-room chairs. And of course it had to be erased that instant.

I finally gave up and retreated to my book. But I could feel Grandma's eyes on me and knew she had something on her mind.

"Eugene," she said (she always pronounced it Jew-gin), "come. You must help me."

The problem was in the kitchen. When she mopped the floor, she could only reach so far underneath the refrigerator. Her bones were too brittle now for her to get down on her hands and knees and push the mop all the way back. But she knew there must be dirt way under, against the baseboard.

"But Grandma," I said, bending over, "it looks spotless."

No, there had to be dirt way back there.

"But if you can't see it, Grandma, and I can't see it, what does it matter?"

Like Hilary's Mt. Everest, it was there—and had to be conquered.

Down on hands and knees, pushing the mop hard against the baseboard, I felt the top of my head being patted. Grandma had never been demonstrative and this uncharacteristic stroke of affection surprised me. When I looked up, she was beaming her gratitude.

"Oh, I wish I could do that," she sighed. It was the only time I ever heard an expression of envy from her.

A thrift born of early poverty was natural among these people. But here again Grandma set rather a record. Long after circumstances had rendered such economies ridiculous, she was patching and repatching ten-cent washcloths. She saved every piece of string and tin foil and every paper bag that came into the house. She salvaged bits and pieces from worn-out clothing items, even socks and mittens. No piece of wrapping paper was ever discarded; if it had contained fish or meat from the market she scrubbed it until it was clean and odorless. Even when he was going to high school in town, my father says he was still wearing underwear made out of flour sacks.

Her eyes opened wide with wonder when she saw something new in anybody's house. It might be just a lamp or a whatnot shelf but she would always remark, "Surely that must be expensy." To save ourselves the implied criticism of extravagance—and Grandma any fears she might have of our impending bankruptcy—we learned to play down new acquisitions. A wise strategy was to infer that something had been gotten cheap at a fire sale, through coupons, won in a contest, or as a birthday present. One could almost hear Grandma's sigh of relief.

Social security was still decades away. But Osten was able to retire in 1902 when he was in his early sixties. Though he might not have looked or felt it, he was—by any reasonable standards of the day—a prosperous man. He owned two farms, which he rented out. He moved his family into a house he had built on the edge of town with enough land for gardens and an orchard and to keep a few cows, chickens, and horses.

"Town" was Fergus Falls, six miles from the original homestead. Fergus Falls is one of the loveliest small cities in the middle of America. Set in a natural amphitheater of low hills, it is a green, green city lavishly endowed with parks and groves and tree-lined avenues and flowers (even the street lamps sprout nosegays). The city has five lakes and is bisected by a meandering tributary of the Red River of the North.

In common with so many heirs of the landed immigrants, not one of the five children of Osten and Caroline who lived had any desire to remain on the farm, though one of the daughters was to marry a farmer. America must hold out something different from the grueling experiences their parents had been through. They themselves had suffered enough hardships to know that a farmer's life, in that time and place, promised little more than an ordeal.

Moving to town meant moving into a peopled world. It meant activity and excitement, companionship with other young persons, learning English, completing their schooling, careers... getting on with the process of Americanization. The two sons were interested in business—and eventually both would reap modest fortunes as merchants. Unlike so many of the Scandinavian girls who emigrated to those parts on their own or who were the daughters of laborers, my aunts were spared the necessity of becoming servant girls in the homes of the well-to-do burghers. (Such girls worked out as either a *barnepige*—someone who took care of the children—or as a *tjenestepige,* one who worked as a maid-of-all-service.) Osten's daughters could think of taking up nursing or secretarial work or hat making, because the means were available for their training.

Thus, the children of Osten and Caroline found a larger landscape. At about the same time, the children of Osten's brother and sisters were doing the same. And the children of all these children extended themselves further. The progression is typically American and what, in essence, most of us think America is all about. The sociological wordsmiths of our day call it upward mobility.

More than a century has passed since the April morning on which the two young brothers set out from that forgotten hut five thousand miles away. Their quest was mainly for meat and bread. In their wildest fantasies they could not possibly have dreamed that the seed from their family tree—flowering now unto its fifth generation—would be so fruitful in the New World... that it would bear surgeons, lawyers, writers, musicians, professors, farmers with large landholdings, politicians, successful businessmen, a college president, and a state governor.

In his ebbing years Osten occupied himself quietly. Much of the time when he wasn't studying God's Word he was marveling at God's wonders in the physical world around him. He especially loved birds and developed an almost encyclopedic knowledge of those birds that were indigenous to that area. He talked to the robins, people said, and the robins sat in his lap and talked right back to him.

He was also devoted to the animals he kept. Of these he had a particular fondness for a pair of white mares named Nancy and Lady, who pulled him in the buggy on his errands downtown. Nancy and Lady were a pair of sluggish beasts, but Osten had taught them the one trick of rearing up on their hind legs. And somehow he had trained them to do this the moment he untied them from the hitching post in front of the creamery or the feed mill store or wherever. The idea, as my father explains it, was that some passerby would assume that Osten had a pair of high-spirited, runaway horses on his hands and would come hollering, "Whoa, whoa!" But in all truth, says Dad, Nancy and Lady were so fat and overindulged they could not have been goaded into running anywhere. Such was the ingenuousness of Osten's deceits!

Osten fretted that his youngest grandson was not learning Norwegian. Not because knowledge of the language would enable them to communicate better or because the boy was being culturally deprived. No, Osten's concern was that without facility in the language, this grandson could not be confirmed in Norwegian at the Bethlehem Lutheran Church.

I was just starting school then and nothing was less enticing than the study of Norwegian. To be able to speak Norwegian, I reasoned, meant you were going to speak English with a Norwegian accent. And that would be fatal. To speak with an accent of any kind was to invite the mockery and abuse of one's peers—a punishment far outweighing all possible benefits.

I never regretted not having been confirmed in Norwegian any more than I would regret it if I had never been confirmed at all. But the neglected opportunity to learn the language of my forebears now seems like such a high price to have paid for a silly conformity.

Osten died in the summer of 1928, at eighty-nine. Death came simply from the accumulation of years. Caroline, who was seventeen years his junior, lived nearly another twenty years; she died a few months short of her ninety-first birthday in April of 1947.

The death of Osten shattered Caroline as no other blow ever had. Years later, as her daughter lay dying of cancer—a beautiful woman, taken in her prime, whose sunshine made the flowers bloom in January—she could stand by the deathbed and say quite matter-of-factly, "Now, Berte [Bertha], you must make your peace with the Lord." Once more she could acquiesce to the Divine Will, though this was the daughter who had stayed home, who gave up marriage to care for her parents in their old age, and whose death would deprive her of that support and companionship. Nobody could remember ever having seen Caroline cry before, but with Osten's death the tears of a lifetime flowed openly. This tribulation was nearly more than she could bear. This time God had tested her and found her wanting.

They had been through so much together, these two parallel pillars, and had borne it all without a whimper. Except for the Great Blizzard and the times Osten went to the lake forest for logs, they had never in the fifty-five years of their marriage been out of each other's sight longer than two hours. Never had they raised their voices to each other in argument or anger. Together these constant companions had survived so many disasters, so many varieties of privation and discomfort. And it had all been sufferable because of their faith—and each other.

The obituaries of Osten and Caroline—and so many other pioneers of that time and place—praised their kindness, courage, charity, and "fine Christian character." Their patience, honesty, and stamina might also have been noted. The faces on the faded photographs shine with goodness; they are open and guileless and have a touching, childlike innocence.

What eclipses the memory of my grandparents' wondrous piety is the fact that they actually managed to live so much of their religion. They inherently abided by the Golden Rule. No one can recall any word or deed of theirs that would have given them anguish had it been turned back upon themselves. With their children they were severe disciplinarians, but when punishment was dispensed, the pain was clearly mutual.

And how industrious they were! Now industry is no longer necessarily synonymous with virtue. We must question the consequence of industriousness, whether the result of an effort is truly serving man or just adding to the glut of production that threatens to poison man's body and stifle his spirit. But there can be no questioning the end of *their* industriousness, which was the maintenance of life itself through the growth of the soil.

If lightness and laughter were not their dominant assets, their experiences had hardly been the sort to promote levity. Humor came to them late in life and then quietly. Not much that had happened to them had been a laughing matter. Nor would it have crossed their minds that they were expected to find anything in this world funny. Their duty, as they conceived it, was to endure what must be endured—uncomplainingly.

The corner of the world they touched is a more civilized place for their having passed this way.

And so they came and went, the first sons and daughters of that cruel prairie. The long, hard day's journey into night had a stop—finally—and they are all gone now, these builders and tamers, gone gently into that last wakeless sleep, where surely they dream of the eternal mansion with gates flung open, its towers resplendent in the celestial morning.

The Italian Americans

RUDOLPH VECOLI

Over 5,000,000 Italians have moved to the United States, four-fifths of this total arriving between 1880 and 1920. They came primarily from southern Italy and established colonies in every part of the country. They could be found as laborers on construction gangs, peons on farms, in the fisheries, in the mines, in the stockyards. "Little Italies" sprang up in Boston, New York, Philadelphia, New Orleans, San Francisco, Chicago, and numerous other American cities. Like almost all of the other minority groups Italians were victims of vicious stereotyping and accused of being "volatile," "unstable," "undesirable," and "largely composed of the most vicious, ignorant, degraded and filthy paupers, with something more than an admixture of the criminal element." Because most Italians worked at unskilled, low-paying jobs, they lived in crowded and unhealthy quarters. At the end of the nineteenth century 417 Italians in one Chicago district had bathtubs in their apartments while 13,943 did not; in a Sicilian area in New York City 1,231 people were squeezed into 120 rooms; one-third of the families in Philadelphia's Italian area had one-room apartments, only a few had toilets and those were in outdoor shacks, and almost none had bathtubs.

Aside from the miserable living conditions Italians endured, more than any other white group they suffered greatly from vigilante justice. Between 1891 and 1914 Italian-Americans were lynched in New Orleans, murdered in Colorado, beaten in Mississippi, and shot by mobs in Illinois. Frequently they were considered criminals by nature. Accordingly, vigilante action was undertaken for the good of society. Hostility toward them reflected more than the usual animosity minorities have come to expect in America. At the turn of the century the Italian served, as one Connecticut observer reported, as "the symbol of all the recent immigrants who spoke no English and blotted the native landscape."

The newcomers and their descendants, though at a slower pace than immigrants from other European nations, gradually rose from poverty and unskilled jobs to approach the average American white population's income and occupational distribution. Italian-Americans still lag behind the general Caucasian educational level, but the younger members of this ethnic group are closing the gap. Anti-Italian stereotypes are less prominent than in the past, but negative references to Italian-Americans as criminal and violent types still permeate the public media.

From *The Center Magazine* (July/August 1974), a publication of the Center for the study of Democratic Institutions, Santa Barbara, California. Reprinted by permission.

Unlike earlier generations, the Italians are now vigorously defending themselves against such bigotry. In the article that follows Professor Rudolph Vecoli discusses these and other aspects of the Italian-American experience in tracing the history of this enclave from its nineteenth-century beginnings to its present-day situation.

Any discussion of the characteristics of the Italian American ethnic group must begin with a consideration of the history of that immigration which spawned it. Since the unification of Italy in 1860, more than twenty-five millions have emigrated from that ill-favored land, and of these at least half have settled permanently in another country. The Italian immigration to the United States was thus part of a much larger movement of people in search of work and bread denied to them at home. While northern Italians emigrated in great numbers to northern Europe and Latin America, the predominant majority of those who came to the United States were from the southern regions and Sicily.

For historical reasons, the *Mezzogiorno* (the South) was more traditional, backward, and poor than the north. The *contadini* (peasants) were the mudsill of a still largely feudal society. Oppressed and exploited by *signori* and *borghesi* alike, they were despised as *cafoni* (boors). Illiterate, unschooled, lacking self-confidence, the peasantry was preindustrial in culture and mentality. Not a very good preparation for grappling with life in America's urban jungles?

In emigrating, the motive of the *contadini* was not simply to escape from grinding misery; rather it was to improve their family's lot by earning money with which to buy land back in their village. Thus, most came to America, not with the intention of settling permanently, but to work, save, and return after several years with a few hundred dollars. Like the Chinese, to whom they were often compared, the Italians were sojourners. The predominantly male and youthful character of the immigration reflected this purpose.

Of the millions who emigrated, about half in fact did return to their villages in Sicily, Basilicata, Campania, some having accom-

plished their mission, others having met defeat. But even those who remained in America often continued to nourish thoughts of the day they would go back to their *paese*. The persistence of this sojourner mentality was an important condition affecting the Italian immigrant's adjustment. Why learn English, why become a citizen, why Americanize, if one were going back to the old country—if not this year, next? In the villages of southern Italy today one finds these "Americani" who after fifty years returned to live on their Social Security benefits.

The Italians for the most part provided raw manpower for the American economy. Although there were artisans among them— barbers, weavers, stonecutters—who entered more specialized occupations, the typical immigrant took up the pick and shovel. These were the legendary dago ditchdiggers who built the nation's railroads, dams, subways, and cities. Having displaced the Irish, they contested with Negroes, Mexican Americans, and Asiatic immigrants for common labor jobs. It would be difficult to find worse examples of exploitation than those experienced by the Italians in the decades before World War I. Driven by sadistic bosses—sometimes at the point of a gun— living in boxcars and shanties, eating wretched food, killed and maimed by explosions and accidents, the immigrants labored twelve and more hours a day in all kinds of weather. Most endured this purgatory passively so that of the $1.50 daily wage they might save fifty cents.

The Italians were doubly exploited: by the capitalist system on the one hand, and by their more experienced, enterprising countrymen on the other. These so-called *padroni* served as middlemen between the workers and their American employers. The swindles and extortions perpetrated at the expense of the immigrants by these "bosses," who also served as bankers, saloonkeepers, and politicians, were legion.

From such grim beginnings, the Italians slowly gained a toehold in America. As they entered the building trades and factories, they brought over their wives and brides-to-be, established families, and settled permanently in America's cities and mill towns. World War I, which sealed off the immigrants from Europe, and the immigration legislation which followed gave a new quality of stability to these "Little Italies." Grouping themselves along certain blocks according to provinces or even villages of origin, the *contadini* re-created in the shadow of the factory chimneys much of the rural, folk life of southern Italy. Change penetrated slowly into these closed neighborhoods.

One of the striking characteristics of the Italian ethnic group has been the relative stability of its residential patterns. Italian Americans of both first and second generations are still highly concentrated in the regions of their original settlement. More than two-thirds are in the north Atlantic Seaboard states stretching from Massachusetts to Maryland; a third are packed into the New York-New Jersey metropolitan area. Italian Americans may be the most highly urbanized ethnic group in the country; over ninety per cent live in urban areas and less than one per cent in rural farm areas. Coming from an ancient urban culture, the immigrants had rejected efforts to convert them into American farmers; they preferred the crowded tenement districts to the wide open spaces. This preference for urban living is still a distinctive trait of the Italian Americans.

Certainly the Italian American neighborhoods have not been impervious to changing population patterns, land uses, and the suburban exodus. Especially since 1945 many of the old neighborhoods like Boston's West End and Chicago's Near West Side have been wiped out by "urban renewal" projects. However, one can still find Italian enclaves in the North End of Boston, South Brooklyn, the South Side of Philadelphia, the West Side of Cleveland, and in many other cities as well. In part, this attachment to the inner city is a matter of the limited resources of blue-collar families; but more important is the preference for the dense texture of social relationships despite declining municipal services, rising crime rates, and all the other deteriorations of urban America. Row houses with false stone fronts, handkerchief lawns with statues of the Madonna, decal flags in the windows, groceries replete with Italian delicacies, corner bars, social clubs, and churches—this is their social world. Those who have moved out, or who have been moved out, express poignantly their feelings of displacement and nostalgia for the old neighborhood.

Residential stability has been ascribed to the strength of family bonds among Italian Americans. Obviously a relationship in which children feel a compelling obligation to remain physically close to aging parents does not encourage mobility.

Pride of home ownership also rooted the Italian American family in the neighborhood. For many the purchase of a house (or, better, a duplex which would yield rent) was the main achievement of years of struggle and work in America. It was the crowning accomplishment for which many sacrifices, including the children's education, were often made. In a sense it was the American fulfillment of the peasant's dream of owning land which would make him independent and self-respecting. Since the Italian American often invested his leisure time in the maintenance and improvement of his house, it became more than simply a piece of property to him.

For these reasons the Italian Americans have clung to their neighborhoods with extraordinary tenacity. Developers have coveted their land for luxury apartments; planners have sought to break up their "ghettos"; federal housing programs have encouraged the flight to the suburbs; the Catholic Church has failed to come to the aid of the beleaguered communities; and their own politicians have betrayed them. Yet if many

"Little Italies" have fallen before the bulldozer, others have survived. Not only have they survived, but the communities that organized themselves in the fight against freeways, redevelopment, and residential invasion by other groups have revitalized themselves in the process.

Inevitably since the Italians were often the largest white ethnic element left in the inner city, they became locked in bitter conflict with the incoming groups—blacks and Puerto Ricans—over living space. Struggles over turf are, of course, nothing new in American urban history. When the Italian immigrants arrived they had to fight for the right to walk down certain streets and to live on certain blocks. Gradually they dispossessed the Irish of neighborhoods, and now they, in turn, have been slowly retreating for several decades before the black and Puerto Rican advance.

Surely this process of residential succession has not been peaceful. Widespread violence has broken out in the Bronx, Cleveland, Philadelphia, and elsewhere. As the urban housing market tightened, the Italian resistance has stiffened. The incoming groups following the path of least resistance found it easier to penetrate the ethnically mixed middle-class areas, flowing around and encircling the Italian American islands.

The contention for housing, as well as jobs and schools, has engendered racism on both sides, hatred born of fears and frustrations. Much Italian American community organization in fact has been inspired as a defensive measure against encroachment by blacks and Puerto Ricans. For this the Italian Americans have been branded racists. But do those who live in the suburbs or in guarded apartment buildings have the right to point their finger at the efforts of working-class neighborhoods to maintain their integrity and security? The tragedy is that the urban minority groups (blacks, Puerto Ricans, Italians, and others) are all victims of a corrupt, manipulated real estate market and of a wrongheaded and inadequate federal housing program.

If the Italian Americans appear to have been more resistant to the lure of suburbia than most other ethnic groups, they have not been entirely immune to the *Better Homes and Gardens* version of the American Dream. Actually they have been engaged in a slow migration outward from the city center for more than half a century. Moving along certain corridors they finally crossed over into the suburbs. This process did not necessarily break up and disperse the ethnic community. Such suburban settlements as Melrose Park outside Chicago became an extension of the city neighborhoods, differing little from them in their essential characteristics. However, after World War II more second-generation Italian Americans made the leap into the ethnically mixed suburbs. This migration by upwardly mobile persons meant a sharper break in community ties and life-style than had previous movements.

The suburbanization of Italian Americans has been little studied, but it is my impression that the suburb has been no more effective as a melting pot than was the city. However, ethnicity in the suburbs tends to express itself through middle-class institutions, e.g., in the country club rather than the athletic club. Suburban migration was thus an expression of the growing class differentiation among Italian Americans, particularly the second generation. While those who remained in the old inner-city neighborhoods tended to be blue-collar workers (lower middle class), the suburbanites represented the emerging professional and business element (upper middle class). These sharpening class distinctions among Italian Americans were yet another major development of the last thirty years.

Until World War II, the Italian Americans remained solidly proletarian. Many had established themselves in the skilled trades as barbers, bakers, tailors, masons. An even greater proportion had entered the ranks of semiskilled factory workers and coal miners. However, the Italians were still more likely to be found in the category of laborers than was any other European immigrant group.

Despite this predominantly blue-collar character, a class of small businessmen had emerged whose restaurants, groceries, saloons, ice and coal deliveries catered for the most part to an ethnic clientele. From such modest beginnings, there came in time construction firms, trucking companies, and import and wholesale houses, particularly in foods and liquors. Many early Italian American fortunes also had their initial source in the operations of the aforementioned *padroni*. Ambitious young Italians were also quick to take advantage of what Daniel Bell has called a "curious ladder of social mobility." The rackets, gambling, petty extortion, thievery provided an entrée for them into organized crime, an activity in which they soon rivaled their Irish and Jewish competitors. Prohibition was a boon to the Italians, who took naturally to home distilling. Not a few Italian families began their climb to affluence through bootlegging. Meanwhile professional men were relatively scarce. The few physicians, druggists, and lawyers among the immigrants were joined in time by the first college graduates among the American-born.

The modest mobility realized by Italian Americans between the two wars was reflected in the low levels of their educational attainment. College and even high-school education was then the prerogative of the children of the small businessmen and professionals. The sons and daughters of the workers rarely continued in school beyond the school-leaving age, most commonly fourteen years. Not only economic necessity, but a basic distrust of American schools by immigrant parents was evidenced in the preeminence of Italian children during these years in dropout and grade retardation rates.

Despite major obstacles, the Italian Americans by the nineteen-twenties had begun to move into better-paying industrial jobs and various kinds of business enterprise. Within the ethnic group, a rudimentary social structure was beginning to take shape as significant differences in wealth and status developed. The prospects for an accelerated social mobility appeared good. Then the Great Depression struck. As a still largely marginal ethnic group, the Italian Americans were particularly vulnerable and suffered especially high rates of unemployment. Because of their frugality, family cohesion, and peasant resourcefulness, the Italians weathered the crisis, but, along with other Americans, they achieved little upward mobility during the nineteen-thirties.

Since World War II, Italian Americans have achieved a breakthrough in social mobility for two basic reasons—the sustained boom of the American economy, and the coming of age of the second generation. Yet as recently as 1950 the occupational structure of the Italian Americans continued to be one of a broad base of blue-collar workers with much thinner strata of professions, businessmen, and white-collar employees. Among the first generation there was a strong persistence in the manual occupations and a definite underrepresentation in the higher status occupations, while the occupational profile of the second generation continued to bear a striking resemblance to that of their immigrant parents. Like them, the American-born were concentrated in the skilled and semiskilled industrial jobs. A much higher proportion of the second generation, it is true, had begun the climb in the corporate bureaucracies as clerical and sales workers.

Two decades later, the situation had changed dramatically. In a 1969 survey of major occupation groups by ethnic origin, the Italian males were only slightly underrepresented among profession and technical workers as compared with the total population. They also lagged somewhat behind all other groups (except Spanish) as managers, officers, and proprietors; but they led in the category of clerical workers. The proletarian heritage of the Italians was reflected in their strong showing as craftsmen and foremen, ranking second only to Poles. Again as operatives and laborers, they were second only to the Spanish.

The realization that a college degree was

the key to high-paying and high-status jobs seems to have overcome the traditional skepticism about higher education on the part of Italian Americans. Meanwhile, a new affluence permitted even the children of blue-collar workers to attend, if not Ivy League universities, at least the state and community colleges. Second- and particularly third-generation Italian Americans are entering institutions of higher education in unprecedented numbers.

Still an analysis of the educational attainment of Italian Americans discloses a mixed picture. A 1969 survey reported that the Italian Americans had completed on the average 11.3 median years of school; that a majority (54.3 per cent) had not graduated from high school; that while 20.7 per cent had attended college, only seven per cent claimed four or more years of college. In each of these measures of educational attainment the Italian Americans ranked behind all other ethnic groups, except the Mexicans and Puerto Ricans. However, if the comparison is restricted to the twenty-five to thirty-four years of age group then the disparity between Italians and other groups becomes much less. It is in the thirty-five and over age group that the relative lack of formal education among Italians is most vividly demonstrated.

Status, power, and income are the trinity of rewards for upward mobility. Of these, income is the most easily measurable. Here we are confronted with the paradox that while the Italian Americans tend to be underrepresented in the higher categories of occupations and educational attainment their income levels are comparable, if not superior, to those of other ethnic groups.

On all three counts, then—occupation, education, and income—the Italian Americans (and particularly the younger members of the second generation) appeared to be effectively closing the gap which had for many decades separated them from most other Americans. However, this upward mobility was obviously not being experienced equally by all members of the ethnic group. Inevitably the differences are expressed in con-sumption patterns, life-styles, politics—in sum, the difference between "Little Italy" and suburbia.

In America, the Italians have lived up to their reputation as individualists. Despite their numbers and resources, the Italian Americans have created nothing comparable to the Jewish social services, the Polish parochial school system, the Finnish coöperatives, or the Slovak fraternal organizations. The Italians' indifference to organizations and institutions has been attributed to their intense attachment to the family. The family in south Italian culture has in fact dominated the individual's interests and loyalties. It has been his exclusive means for socializing, mutual aid, and other functions. Hence there has been little need felt for voluntary associations. The family continued to play this primary role for the immigrants.

The provincial identities of the immigrants also militated against the emergence of community-wide institutions. The *contadini* had little feeling of Italian nationalism. For them, the village was the true *patria*. For them, the world extended only as far as the sound of the bells in the *campanile,* a mentality that came to be known as *campenilismo.* Those from other towns, even across the valley, were *forestieri* (strangers), to be viewed suspiciously.

Bringing these attitudes with them, the *paesani* formed residential clusters in American cities and organized mutual-aid societies which provided sick and death benefits and celebrated the *festa* of the patron saint. Such mutual-aid societies proliferated in the "Little Italies" across America. The Order of the Sons of Italy in America never attained the strength of such fraternals as the Polish National Alliance or the First Catholic Slovak Union.

Intragroup conflicts have not been peculiar to the Italians but they appear to have been a greater obstacle to unity. In addition to the regional antagonisms between "northerners" and "southerners" (or Calabrians and Sicilians), there were, among Italians, bitter fights between nationalists and radicals, religious and anticlericals, Fascists and anti-Fascists. Italian nationalists tried to organize the immigrants into patriotic societies and cultural organizations. Italian socialists tried to re-create the workers' institutions then emerging in Italy—study circles, consumers' coöperatives, and labor unions. Italian priests tried to establish churches and schools. None had more than limited success with the mass of Italian immigrants, who remained wedded to a cynical and fatalistic view of the world.

The Catholic Church did not provide the organizational structure for community-building for the Italians that it did for the Irish and Poles. Not only did the Italians find an American Catholicism alien to their religious traditions and many American Catholics hostile to them, the immigrants also brought with them an indifference toward institutional religion born of a long history of neglect and abuse by a reactionary clergy. Italian national parishes thus emerged slowly, suffered from financial anemia, and seldom had parochial schools. Italians could not see why they should pay for an education that was offered free in the public schools.

Since 1945, the Italian Americans have been developing a more elaborate pattern of organizations and institutions. Perhaps with the loosening of family and neighborhood ties, there has been greater need for formal associations. Increased organizational activity also reflects the growing class differentiation among Italian Americans. Within the "Little Italies," the *Società di San Rocco* of the first generation and the Black Knights Athletic Club of the second still occupy their dingy storefront quarters. But the upwardly mobile types no longer feel comfortable in such surroundings. Whether they have felt excluded by "American" organizations or because they have felt more comfortable "with their own kind," middle-class Italian Americans have pursued a course of organizational parallelism, creating professional, business, service and social clubs with an ethnic character. In Chicago, for example, there are Italian American organizations of lawyers, doctors, dentists, teachers, and policemen, as well as fraternal and cultural associations.

It would seem that upward mobility, at least for a good many persons, generates a need to identify more rather than less strongly with their ethnic group. Italian American identity among the second and third generations, however, has little to do with Italy. There may be a sentimental attachment to the old country, but it is usually accompanied by complete indifference toward contemporary Italian politics and culture. Rather, ethnic affirmation is an expression of the need for group identity and support in this American pluralistic society. The participation of second- and third-generation persons has reinvigorated old organizations such as the Sons of Italy and more recent ones like UNICO. Under this youthful leadership Italian Americans have demonstrated a new enthusiasm and capacity for associational activity. However, the old attitudes die hard. Recent efforts to establish an umbrella organization, a National Congress of Italian American Organizations, were wrecked upon the rock of traditional discord. Unity still evades the Italian Americans.

A new commitment to the Catholic Church on the part of Italian Americans, noted in recent years, has been described as a process of "Hibernization." To a greater degree than their immigrant ancestors, the second and third generations appear to approach the Irish American model of the Catholic who is respectful to priests, contributes to their support, and sends his children to parochial school. The recently discovered enthusiasm of Italian Americans for parochial education must be viewed in the light of the racial conflicts and other problems assailing the public schools. However, a new religiosity does seem to have accompanied the Italian American's rise to middle-class status. Certainly the Church plays a more active and constructive role in the ethnic community than it did in the past. Anti-clericalism, along with anarchism and socialism, seems to have all but disappeared among Italian Americans.

Yet some evidence suggests that the Italian American has not simply become an ersatz Irish Catholic. Studies of religious attitudes and behavior among various Catholic ethnic groups indicate that the distinctive Italian religious heritage persists beneath an apparently homogeneous surface. Italian Catholics are more likely to take a position on an issue—such as contraceptive practices—which is at odds with the teachings of the Church. Compared with Irish and Polish Catholics, they are also less regular in church attendance and participation in the sacraments. Southern Italian traditions such as the *festa* have not only survived, but are undergoing a revival. In these mixtures of piety and carnival, thousands gather each year to honor the Madonna or a patron saint.

The Italian priests who accompanied the immigrants to America were a mixed lot. Some were men of great dedication and ability. More were of mediocre quality. And not a few were mercenaries, if not worse. They were not welcome in many dioceses. A native-born clergy emerged slowly because religious vocations were few in the early years. Italian parents preferred to have their sons become doctors or lawyers. Since the nineteen-forties, an increasing number of Italian Americans have entered the priesthood. These second- and third-generation priests are a new breed. Some, like James Groppi, are deeply involved in the civil-rights and peace movements. Others, like Geno Baroni, have become articulate and militant spokesmen for the needs and aspirations of the Italian American communities.

But in seeking a positive response from the Church, such priests have often met the same resistance from the hierarchy as did their forerunners a half-century ago. The Americanization credo espoused by the Church toward the end of the nineteenth century still holds sway today. The American Irish have fought doggedly to maintain their power within the Church as they have in city halls across the country—and with considerably more success. A longstanding grievance of Italians and other ethnic Catholics has been the lack of proportional representation in the American hierarchy. Until the appointment of Francis Mugavero, a son of Sicilian immigrants, as Bishop of the Diocese of Brooklyn in 1968, Italians had occupied the bishoprics of only a few minor sees.

By the nineteen-seventies the informal arrangements of the "Little Italies" no longer sufficed for an increasingly middle-class population. New organizations were formed and old ones rejuvenated to serve more complex needs. Rather than insulating the ethnic group from the outside world, these institutions were designed to express the views of Italian Americans and to promote their interests in the larger society. But whether these organizations spoke for or represented the blue-collar Italian Americans of the inner city was a moot question.

What in Italian Americans is still distinctively Italian? On the face of it, very little. The language was first to go. The immigrant spoke not Italian, but a score of dialects, often mutually unintelligible. Out of this linguistic chaos emerged an Italian American jargon, a mixture of dialects and Italianized loan words like "giobba" (job), "groceria" (grocery), and, of course, "isaboxa." For the second generation this rich, melodious speech—burlesqued on stage, screen, and radio—was a badge of inferiority. The reaction to the Alka-Seltzer commercial, "Datsa some spicy meatball," suggests that it still is.

Not surprisingly, the children of the immigrants refused to speak it (except perhaps at home) and shied away from studying Italian on the rare occasions when it was offered in the schools. Although more than four millions claim Italian as a mother tongue, effective bilingualism among Italian Americans has in fact been rare. The current resurgence of ethnicity seems to be bringing increasing numbers of young people of the third generation to the formal study of the Italian language.

The cultivation of *Italianità* in America has been the preoccupation of the few truly cultured immigrants, the nationalist propagandists, and the newly rich but unlettered *prominenti*. Through the *Società Dante Allighieri*, the Italy-America Society, and the *Casa Italiana* of Columbia University, they extolled the glories of ancient Rome and the Renaissance. But the bombastic rhetoric about the "genius of Italy" had little meaning for the mass of immigrants. After all, "Italian language and culture" were alien to them. Except for an occasional socialist or priest the immigrants lacked intellectual leadership. The task of cultural and linguistic maintenance so vigorously pursued in such ethnic communities as the German and Ukrainian were largely neglected among the Italians. The schools, colleges, and cultural centers which such groups created appeared beyond the resources of the sons of Italy.

To speak, then, of an Italian American cultural heritage is not to refer to "high culture" but rather to an urban culture which is a compound of southern Italian and American working class folkways. It is in this anthropological sense that one can speak of an Italian American culture today. Its core values are the primacy of personal relationships and of right behavior within these relationships. An unwritten code specifies the reciprocal obligations among members of the immediate family, relatives, and friends. Within the primary group, emotional intensity characterizes these relationships, and, because emotions are not really repressed, feelings of love, hate, anger erupt freely. The purely contractual, legalistic, or economic relationship which is so typical of American society is foreign to such a value system.

At the risk of caricaturing Italian American culture, one can catalogue what appear to be its salient qualities: the obligation of loyalty to family and friends; the emphasis on domesticity (enjoyment of the home and family); the dominant role of the male; the importance of cutting a fine figure (*fare bella figura*); the overflowing hospitality; the passion for good food and drink; the respect for authority figures. If these values are particularly characteristic of blue-collar Italian Americans, they have not disappeared from the behavior of middle-class ethnics. While the more colorful expressions of this lifestyle may be attenuated among the upwardly mobile who self-consciously seek to behave "properly," one often finds the ethnic pattern of emotional responses not far beneath the surface.

To conclude from structural pluralism that cultural assimilation is an accomplished fact is to be deceived by appearances. The institution itself—whether it be a formal dinner, a debutante ball, or a club meeting—is an empty form. What is crucial is what actually takes place: How do people behave? What is the conversation about? How much do people eat or drink? What are the feeling tones? Having attended quite a few ethnic functions over the past few years, I can certainly tell an Italian banquet from a Norwegian banquet by the noise level, to say nothing of the food.

Given the proletarian character and general illiteracy of the Italian immigration, it was not to be expected that the "Little Italies" would nourish intellectual pursuits. Educated persons were regarded with mistrust; in the old country, the priest and professor had been among the exploiters. Immigrant parents prized education solely for its utilitarian value; reading in itself was thought to be an idle, and perhaps injurious, pastime. Not surprisingly, few writers and scholars as compared with professional athletes and popular entertainers emerged from the "Little Italies."

Until recently, therefore, the analysis and interpretation of the Italian American experience have been undertaken largely by "outsiders." It is only within the past quarter-century that a significant number of Italian

Americans have entered the fields of the social sciences, journalism, and belles-lettres. In the process, not a few were "de-ethnicized," to use Joshua Fishman's inelegant but descriptive term. They rejected their identity and ties with the Italian American group.

But in the last decade a new involvement of educated Italian Americans with their history and cultural heritage has manifested itself. For example, in 1966 the American Italian Historical Association, the first such organization of a professional character, was founded by a group of historians and sociologists. The establishment of the A.I.H.A. signified the beginning of an intensive exploration of the Italian American experience such as had not been undertaken before. New ethnic publications such as *Fra Noi* and the *Italian American National News* appeared as vehicles for intragroup discourse. Most of those engaged in these discussions were themselves second- and third-generation Italian Americans. The fruits of such self-scrutiny are the insightful writings of Gay Talese, Mario Puzo, Nicholas Pileggi, and Alexander DeConde, to mention only a few.

The emergence of an Italian American intelligentsia, if we may use such a pretentious phrase, is itself a function of the coming of age of the ethnic group. The entry of second- and third-generation persons into the professoriat as well as the growth of a college-educated audience were preconditions for such a development. Novels, historical studies, and journalistic writings are raising to the level of consciousness the common experiences and values which comprise the Italian American heritage.

If one were to construct a scale of the intensity of the bigotry to which American minority groups have been subjected, the Italians would certainly be somewhere in the upper ranges, along with the Irish and the Chinese, although several cuts below the American Indians, blacks, and Mexican Americans. Arriving in an age of hyper-racism, the Italians were not considered "white labor." Because they were Latin, Catholic, and poor they were viewed with contempt by Protestants, and not much more sympathetically by their Irish co-religionists. Denounced by organized labor as strike-breakers, by conservatives as anarchists, by eugenists as an inferior breed, the Italians were "undesirables."

While certain ethnic stereotypes, such as that of the jig-dancing, drunken Irishman or the hook-nosed, rapacious Jew, have dimmed with time, that of the Italian as a bloodthirsty criminal has shown amazing persistence. Brigands with stilettos in their teeth titillated nineteenth-century Americans, just as Mafia cutthroats do their descendants today. The stigma of criminality which greeted the immigrants at Ellis Island is carried by their grandchildren half a century later. The typical Italian American, as Alistair Cooke demonstrated recently, is, in the minds of many, Al Capone. The figure of the Italian gangster—exploited for decades in pulp magazines, books, and motion pictures—has imbedded itself deeply in the American imagination. I would wager that a content analysis of the mass communications media for the period from 1924 to 1974 would reveal that more than ninety per cent of the references to Italians have been with respect to criminal activities.

Since the nineteen-fifties, the American television-viewing public has been exposed to thousands of hours of "factual" and "fictional" portrayals of the Mafia, Cosa Nostra, the Mob, and the Syndicate. The Senate investigations led by Estes Kefauver and John L. McClellan, with the assistance of Robert Kennedy and J. Edgar Hoover, popularized the notion of a mysterious organization which controlled organized crime in America and which in turn was dominated by Italians. The mass-circulation magazines, drugstore paperbacks, and television quickly picked up on this theme as a seller. *The Godfather* was the culmination of a literary genre; its success was predictable. But Mario Puzo, writing from the inside, turned the story into an

Italian American *Fiddler on the Roof*. Aside from the incidental mayhem, *The Godfather* is really a melodrama about family solidarity and the heavy burdens which fall upon the shoulders of the patriarch. I am surprised no one has made a musical out of it.

All of this began to grate upon the nerves of Italian Americans. Hypersensitive ethnics? Perhaps. But think of the reaction to a television series based on the exploits of Irish alcoholic priests, black pimps, or Jewish slumlords. These stereotypes also have a basis in reality. The Italian Americans have been long-suffering, grinning, and bearing the latest joke about "cops and wops" or "dicks and dagos," but underneath they have been doing a slow burn.

The Mafia syndrome may perhaps be best understood as an expression of the neo-nativist psychology of the postwar decades. Certainly the obsession with this nebulous sinister conspiracy bears all the hallmarks of what Richard Hofstadter called "the paranoid style in American politics." A secret and alien organization, replete with exotic rituals and elaborate hierarchy, with its own code of morality to which members are sworn by blood oath, is gnawing at the vitals of the Republic. In other times, it was the Masonic Order, the Catholic Church, the Mormons, the Communists. In the nineteen-sixties, it was the Cosa Nostra. Seen in this light, Joseph Valachi's revelations may perhaps be best interpreted as belonging to that genre of confessional literature beginning with Maria Monk's *Awful Disclosures*. As in those other episodes of nativism, national tensions were running high; the Mafia provided a villain which could be safely attacked as the source of the major evils in American life. Politicians could earn votes by doing so; publishers could sell books; moviemakers fill theaters; TV networks secure high ratings. So everybody was satisfied, except it was the Italians' turn (again) to be the heavies.

Does this mean that the Mafia has been trumped up by the mass media? No, if by Mafia one means the undoubtedly strong presence of Italian Americans in organized crime. Perhaps, if by Mafia is intended some international conspiracy which, octopuslike, extends its coils into all areas of American life. Criminal enterprise has been for Italians, as for other ethnic groups, an important ladder of upward mobility. Undoubtedly a criminal element did accompany the mass migration from southern Italy. But need it be said that the Italian did not import crime into America? Gambling, prostitution, drug traffic, were all flourishing when they arrived. Italian criminals simply found a particularly favorable environment in the rampant political and police corruption of American cities. They also demonstrated that the cohesiveness of the south Italian family provided an effective basis for criminal organization. As Francis A. J. Ianni and others have pointed out, the Mafia is more a kinship group than an army or business corporation. The relationships among criminal groups around the country are not formal and contractual, but familial, based on ties of blood and marriage. To note this is in no way to ennoble what is, to say the least, a highly antisocial way of life. But it does point up the role of fantasy in many portrayals of the Mafia.

Most Italian Americans would probably deny the existence of the Mafia and say, "If there are Italian criminals why don't they put them in jail, but stop this business about Mafia and Cosa Nostra." However, given the dense network of social relationships, not a few law-abiding Italian Americans do have a friend, a cousin, or even a brother who is tied in with the "mob". Growing up in neighborhoods where the rackets provided a livelihood for many, bookmaking seems like a relatively innocent occupation. Many feel that the alleged Italian gangsters have been unjustly hounded and persecuted. In fact, since the police and F.B.I. were singularly unsuccessful in securing convictions of those they described as "Mafia chieftains," they pursued a policy of harassment, mass arrests, and illegal wiretaps. Meanwhile, the congressional hearings into organized crime resembled, in their imputation of guilt by association, the infamous McCarthy hearings. Yet these systematic violations of civil liberties elicited little protest from American liberals. Is it any wonder that Italian Americans tend to feel that the concerns of American liberalism exclude them?

In the nineteen-fifties, Harry Golden remarked that although they were perhaps the most vilified ethnic group in the country, the Italians shrugged their shoulders and went on eating spaghetti and drinking wine. By the nineteen-sixties the Italians had had it. The anger generated by the Mafia issue found expression in defense organizations which adopted the militant rhetoric and tactics of the times. Founded in 1966, the Italian Anti-Defamation League (forced to change its name to Americans of Italian Descent because of a lawsuit by the Anti-Defamation League of B'nai B'rith) brought pressure on the mass media to stop typecasting Italians as criminals. It also pressed for more appointments of Italian Americans to high government positions.

A more effective and spectacular protest was mounted by the Italian-American Civil Rights League. Founded in 1970 by Joseph Colombo, Sr., himself reputed to be a Mafia leader, the League directed its activity against the harassment of alleged Mafia figures by the F.B.I. On June 29, 1970, an Italian Unity Day sponsored by the League gathered a crowd of fifty thousand in Columbus Circle. Waving Italian and American flags, sporting "Italian Power" and "Italian Is Beautiful" buttons, they wildly cheered speeches which proclaimed that Italians would no longer suffer discrimination and insult silently. Within a few months, the league had enrolled more than sixty thousand members and had raised more than two million dollars. It had also demonstrated that militant protest worked for the Italians as well as for other groups.

After the League's persistent picketing of the New York F.B.I. offices, the Nixon Administration, in July, 1970, ordered the Justice Department to stop using the terms Mafia and Cosa Nostra. The same pressure

tactics worked with the National Broadcasting Company and the newspapers. Even *The New York Times* gave in after initial resistance. At the second Unity Day rally in 1971 Joseph Colombo was shot, and the League melted away. But the League had tapped deep wells of resentment and frustration in the Italian American communities and had shown that these could be mobilized.

Italian Americans have been slow to rise to political power for many of the same reasons which slowed their economic and social progress. The immigrants were for the most part apolitical. Few had had the right to vote in Italy. The expression, *ladro governo,* summed up their view of government. Military conscription and taxation robbed them of their sons and their money. The machine politics of American cities confirmed their cynicism. In America as in the old country, a man needed a friend with influence. The *padroni* were such "friends" for a price. Because of political indifference related to the sojourner mentality, many immigrants failed to become citizens even after living for decades in America. For many years, the Italian Americans counted for little in politics on any level.

The Italian politicians went to school to the Irish who provided "American" models in politics as other fields. But the antagonism between the Irish and the Italians drove an increasing number of the latter into the Republican Party. So it was that Fiorello LaGuardia, an urban progressive, was elected on a Republican ticket. LaGuardia was a singular phenomenon and the only Italian American political leader of major stature to emerge between the wars. During the nineteen-thirties, Franklin D. Roosevelt and the New Deal brought the Italian Americans solidly into the Democratic Party.

The election of John O. Pastore, son of an Italian tailor, as governor of Rhode Island in 1946 and then as United States senator in 1950 signaled the beginning of a new era in Italian American politics. In succeeding years, other Italian Americans were elected governors and senators. The number of Italian American congressmen increased steadily, and Italian Americans played a larger role in state and municipal politics. The leadership of the second generation was vital to this political maturation.

Italian Americans, however, were still conspicuous by their absence in the national councils of government. In the nineteen-sixties, Italian names first began to appear in the Cabinet and among White House staffers: Anthony J. Celebrezze, Secretary of Health, Education and Welfare in Kennedy's Cabinet; Jack Valenti, special assistant to Johnson; and John Volpe, Secretary of Transportation in Nixon's first Administration. These appointments reflected a new sensitivity to the Italian American vote on the part of the nation's political leaders. (Italian Americans are deriving particular satisfaction from the fact that none of the major figures involved in Watergate bears an Italian name. Segretti was a small fish. But two sons of Italian immigrants—John Sirica and Peter Rodino—are responsible for bringing the guilty to justice.)

As they moved into the middle class, a significant portion of the Italian Americans began shifting their support to the Republican Party. This conservative trend was accelerated by the turmoil of the nineteen-sixties. The "Black Revolution," urban riots, student uprisings, anti-Vietnam war demonstrations, drugs, and sexual liberation, all left the Italian Americans angry, troubled, and confused. Their natural bias for stability had been reinforced by the "American" values of patriotism, respect for constituted authority, and concern for property rights. Now it appeared to them that these values were being desecrated by college kids burning draft cards; hippies smoking pot; and blacks rioting and looting in the ghettos. Italian Americans generally lined up behind "our boys in Vietnam" and "law and order" at home.

Italian Americans, particularly the blue-collar workers in the urban neighborhoods, saw the civil-rights and black power movements as a direct threat. The increasing violence and crime in the inner city created tensions and anxieties about physical safety. Black demands for access to jobs, housing, and schools frightened and angered the Italians. It seemed that the blacks were after *their* houses, *their* jobs, and *their* schools. "The niggers expect to have it all handed to them on a silver platter, after we've worked our asses off to get where we are," was a common attitude in "Little Italy."

The liberal response to the urban riots further antagonized the Italian Americans. The War on Poverty appeared to them to be a capitulation to violence. Who was going to pay for all these welfare programs? Feeling the bite of increased taxes, the Italian Americans felt they were being handed the bill for America's racial problem, and, as one said, "My old man never owned no slaves."

Suddenly the Italian Americans appeared on the scene as black-lashing bigots and hawkish hardhats, throwing rocks at Martin Luther King, beating up peace marchers, and organizing vigilante groups. While there was truth in the characterization, the mass media failed to interpret the deeper sources of alienation among such working-class white ethnic communities. Italian Americans were not simply racists opposing black progress out of prejudice. Rather they were themselves hurting from the decay of the cities, the deterioration of public services, the increasing danger to person and property, and the chaos in the public schools. Many blue-collar families faced with rising inflation and job insecurity were struggling to stay above the poverty lines. Dropout and drug addiction rates were high among Italian American youth.

These Italian American families, first- and second-generation, left behind in the "Little Italies" felt abandoned and powerless. No one in City Hall, Washington, or the foundations was interested, it seemed, in *their* problems. The federal programs of the nineteen-sixties, by focusing on the black ghettos while neglecting urgent if not comparable needs in the "Little Italies," heightened the hostility of the Italian Americans. Basically, then, the Italian Americans were being driven into reaction by the neglect and indifference of the political and intellectual elite which was not even aware of their existence.

In the last few years, things have begun to change, partly due to the rediscovery of white ethnicity, but more importantly because the Italian Americans have shown a new sophistication in using their substantial political clout. The 1969 mayoralty election in New York City revealed the potential of the Italian American vote. Though Lindsay won by a plurality, John Marchi (a north Italian) and Mario Procaccino (a south Italian) split fifty-eight per cent of the vote between them. In the gubernatorial election the following year, Nelson Rockefeller assiduously courted the Italians, while Arthur Goldberg commented disdainfully that he would not stoop to ethnic politics. Rockefeller won a resounding victory, largely because of a dramatic shift of Italian votes into the Republican column. Shortly after, both state and city governments became much more responsive to the Italian Americans in funding community programs and making appointments.

The days when the party bosses could count on the Italian districts were over; the Italian American vote was in nobody's pocket. The old political loyalties were strained, if not broken, and it was not clear in which political direction the Italian Americans would be drawn. George Wallace's mixture of populism and racism had a strong appeal, but he made only modest inroads in the Italian working-class neighborhoods. However, the takeover of the Democratic Party by the McGovernites alienated a great many Italian Americans. The proportional representation principle which gave control of the Democratic Convention to youths, blacks, and women (or so it seemed) made no provision for the white ethnic groups. Fewer Italian Americans were delegates than in previous conventions. The Democratic Party's apparent permissiveness on the issues of drugs and

sexual liberation further repelled the moralistic Italians. Meanwhile, Nixon was directing a well-oiled "symbolic" campaign toward the white ethnics. In 1972, large numbers of Italian Americans either stayed at home or went out and voted for Nixon.

Whether in the future Italian Americans will turn to reaction or progressivism appears to depend in part on the effectiveness of the ethnic leadership in dealing with the problems of the blue-collar workers. The social class differentiation among Italian Americans has produced a political cleavage within the group. As the more successful withdrew from the "Little Italies," they have lost touch with the lower-middle-class Italians. Their organizations and pressure groups have addressed themselves to the concerns of the upwardly mobile: How do we open up executive suites or university faculties to Italian Americans? The needs of their hard-pressed ethnic brothers have been forgotten. The overnight success of the Italian American Civil Rights League revealed the vacuum of leadership in the old urban neighborhoods.

There are hopeful signs that the Italian Americans may yet develop the commitment, leadership, and expertise they need in order to rebuild their communities. Enlightened Italian Americans increasingly recognize that professional skills and intelligence must be used in the service of the ethnic group. Community-affairs specialists, long a profession among American Jews, are just beginning to staff such organizations as the Joint Civic Committee of Italian Americans in Chicago and the Italian American Coalition in New York City.

Community organizers, themselves of the second and third generations, are bringing a blend of social engineering and urban populism to bear on the problems of working class ethnics. Geno Baroni through the National Center for Urban Ethnic Affairs, funded by the Ford Foundation, is spreading the gospel of community organization up and down the land. In some cities, smart operators like Mary Sansone in Brooklyn, Steve Adubato in Newark, and Paul Asciolla in

Chicago, are mobilizing Italian American communities to cope with all the pressures which threaten them. Better schools, better police protection, day-care centers, clinics, loans for home maintenance, fighting freeway takeovers—these are some of the specific issues they are confronting. The basic talk, of course, is to organize the communities politically so that they can get a hearing at City Hall or in Washington. It seems to be working.

Without claiming powers of prophecy, one can predict that the trends described above will continue into the foreseeable future. Italian Americans will comprise a viable ethnic group for many decades to come. The torch has been passed from the first to the second generation. And, given the resurgence of ethnic consciousness, the chances of strong continuity into the third and perhaps fourth generations appear good.

Also, the future of Italian Americans is very much tied in with the future of America's cities. As a highly urbanized ethnic group, its orientation, whether progressive or reactionary, will have a major impact on the politics of the cities. Conversely, the acceptability of policies dealing with urban problems will affect the political temper of the Italian American communities.

The process of class differentiation will continue to sharpen social and cultural differences within the ethnic group. Tensions and conflicts as between the upper-middle-class Italian Americans and working-class Italian Americans can be expected to intensify. The challenge to ethnic leaders will be to bridge these differences.

The rate of upward mobility of Italian Americans will increase as their level of educational attainment continues to rise. As their pressure for a larger share of the jobs and power in business, government, education, and the Church grows, the outlook is for increased rivalry with the entrenched ethnic elements, particularly the Jews and the Irish. On the other hand, the Italian blue-collar workers will be subjected to more intense competition from blacks, Puerto Ricans, and other newcomers, for jobs, residential areas, and institutional facilites. Thus the outlook at both the upper and lower rungs of the social ladder is for increased group conflict.

Finally, in the resolution of these problems and conflicts the Italian Americans will no longer be passive. They have discovered the need for community organization, social activism, and militant protest as each situation warrants. From the ranks of the ethnic group is emerging a new leadership, university trained but close to the grass roots, able to articulate the group's position and to guide it to constructive actions.

Given the opportunity, because of their long history as an urban people, because of their heritage of tolerance, because of their propensity for stability, I believe the Italian Americans have a particularly creative role to play in the true renewal of the American cities.

The East European Jewish Migration

LEONARD DINNERSTEIN

Jews have been in the United States since 1654. By 1790 they numbered perhaps 1,200 and sixty years later about 15,000. Spread thinly throughout the land they had little difficulty finding a place for themselves in the greater society and were accepted as individuals or in small groups. During the middle of the nineteenth century Jews from the German states of Europe entered the United States along with Protestant and Catholic Germans and they, too, were absorbed easily. By the 1880s, however, East European Jews started coming in the hundreds of thousands. A changing industrial society, Pan-Slavism, and continual pogroms proved too difficult a combination to combat, especially while opportunities existed in the United States.

The colonial Jews—mostly Sephardim from the Iberian Peninsula and Brazil—settled mainly in the port cities of Newport, New York, Philadelphia, Charleston, and Savannah and engaged in shopkeeping and mercantile activities. Many chose to assimilate into the dominant community, married gentiles, and raised their children as Christians. The Jews who were a part of the mid-nineteenth-century influx also gravitated toward cities but they did not remain exclusively in the East. Many a Jew put a pack on his back, traveled in different sections of the country, and finally settled down in places as different as Greenville, Mississippi; Boise, Idaho; Columbus, New Mexico; Cleveland; Atlanta; Dallas; and Los Angeles. Other Jews, however, went directly to New York, Cincinnati, Chicago, Philadelphia, and Detroit, and immediately set down roots. As a result, the families of the mid-nineteenth-century Jewish migration were spread throughout the United States. They, too, engaged in the traditional commercial activities usually associated with Jews, but they also had children who were trained for the professions. The German Jews achieved a level of prosperity well above those of other ethnic groups. In 1890, when the majority of American Jews were still of Sephardic or German extraction, the Hebrew community was considerably more prosperous than the national average. Two-thirds of all Jewish families in the United States had at least one servant, while over 90 percent of the American population failed to earn enough money to maintain a family in moderate circumstances. But the massive influx of Eastern European Jews, most of them poor, was already operating to lower the aggregate wealth of American Jewry to the point where this ethnic minority became collectively an underprivileged group.

The new migrants differed in several ways from their predecessors. They came in the hundreds of thousands and could not disappear into the American population with relatively *little notice. They were also more Orthodox in religion, bizarre in dress, and determined to settle in Jewish enclaves and perpetuate Orthodox customs. They also tended to concentrate in a few localities. More than 70 percent remained in New York City and the surrounding area. They threatened the security of the Americanized Jews who had already moved into the middle class and who feared, correctly, that the newcomers might stimulate waves of overt anti-Semitism in the United States which would victimize all of the Jews.*

Most knew how to read and write Hebrew or Yiddish, and the men had some urban and vocational skills. But the opportunities originally available to them were as unskilled or semiskilled laborers, and for years they were plagued with poverty and occupied cheap tenements on New York's Lower East Side.

The story of their experiences, and ultimate accomplishments, is discussed in the following selection.

INTRODUCTION

Jewish migration to the United States in the nineteenth and twentieth centuries may be divided into three groups: the German, the East European, and the Central European. During the first period of heavy Jewish immigration to the United States, mainly during the pre-Civil War years but roughly from the 1840s through the 1870s, about 50,000 Jews arrived from the German states. They engaged almost exclusively in trade and commerce, many starting off as peddlers and some moving up quickly into banking and department stores. The second and most important wave, from the 1870s through 1924, came primarily from Eastern Europe. Responding to the economic uprooting of society and the frequent pogroms of the late nineteenth and early twentieth centuries, more than 2,000,000 Jews left Russia, Galicia, Rumania, and Hungary for the great trek to the United States. These people included artisans, skilled workers, small merchants, and shopkeepers. They and their descendants have made the greatest impact of all the Jews in the United States and are the subject of this essay. The third group, from Central Europe, numbering about 365,000, came to America between 1925 and 1953, with approximately 132,000 in the years between 1948 and 1953. Some of these people emigrated for economic reasons, but the overwhelming majority were victims of Hitler's rise to power in Germany. In the 1930s

Nazi persecutions and brutalities forced many German Jews to leave the country, and after the Second World War some concentration camp victims and the displaced refugees were granted opportunities to resettle in the United States. This third group quickly moved into the Jewish mainstream in the United States. They made major impacts in the American scientific and intellectual communities.

Before the Second World War these Jewish groups were quite different and easily identifiable: by income, education, jobs, residence, and organized associations. In the past twenty-five years, however, the differences have diminished considerably because of a vast leap in both educational and income levels of American-born Jews. It would be quite difficult, if not impossible, today to distinguish among the descendants of the previous generations of Jewish immigrants. In terms of life-style, occupation, and income the overwhelming majority of Jewish families are in the middle and upper middle class and their breadwinners occupy professional, technical, and managerial positions.

CAUSES FOR EMIGRATION

The Jews left Eastern Europe for much the same reason that most other peoples left their states—grinding poverty at home made them yearn for a decent life elsewhere. In Russia 94 percent of the Jews lived in the "pale of settlement," a huge belt of land in Western and Southwestern Russia and the Ukraine stretching from the Baltic to the Black Sea. Jews could live outside of this area only by special permission. Within the pale their population increased from 1,000,000 in 1800 to 4,000,000 in 1880 and this expansion constricted the possibilities of economic opportunities. In Rumania they were regarded as aliens, while in Galicia Jews suffered from economic boycotts and other manifestations of hostility.

During the 1870s the industrial revolution began to make a significant impact in Russia. That impact was greatest within the pale, where industrialization took place most rapidly. The Russian government, which had earlier set numerous restrictions on Jews, feared their influence, especially after industrialization began. Jews actively engaged in trade and commerce, which attracted many of the gentiles once they were forced off the land. Competition for positions in a tight economy heightened Christian-Jewish tensions. Industrialization also stimulated the movements of Jews and gentiles from rural to urban areas to seek employment. The city of Lodz, which had eleven Jews in 1797, counted 98,677 one hundred years later and 166,628 in 1910. Warsaw's Jewish population leaped from 3,521 in 1781, to 219,141 in 1891. Industrial expansion also led to a major flight of people to the west. Many Jews went to Germany, France, and England in Europe, and to Argentina, Canada, South Africa, and Palestine. More than 90 percent of the Jewish migrants, however, wound up in the United States.

Other factors also propelled the Jewish exodus. As in the case of emigrants from other nations, flight was impelled by specific items like the unsuccessful Polish uprising of 1863, the Lithuanian famine of 1867–69, the Polish cholera epidemic of 1869, and by the predisposition of young people to try their fortunes in a new world, and the developing political ideologies of Zionism and socialism which made traditional modes of thought and behavior too confining. Many Jews were outspoken socialists. They envisioned a new democratic social order with a more equitable distribution of the nation's wealth and resources. Anti-Semitism, which rose in intensity as Pan-Slavism gripped the Eastern Europeans, however, provided a unique reason for the Jewish migration. Jews were not Slavs and therefore stood as an impediment toward nationalistic unity. The assassination of Tsar Alexander II of Russia in 1881 by a group of socialists spawned a wave of pogroms against the Jews which continued intermittently until the First World War. Major pogroms occurred in 1881, 1882, 1903, and 1906, and hundreds of others have been recorded. These pogroms, often inspired by government officials, resulted in wanton and brutal assaults upon Jews and their property. Russia also codified and curtailed Jewish rights after Tsar Alexander's assassination. The May Laws of 1882 restricted the numbers of Jews that might attend Russian universities and the kinds of occupations Jews might pursue. They could not rent or own land outside of the towns and cities nor could they keep their shops open on the Christian sabbath or on Christian holidays.

American letters and money sent by earlier immigrants, along with the advertisements from railroad and steamship lines anxious to transport emigrants, further stimulated migration from Eastern Europe to the New World. Promising economic conditions in the United States, combined with increased persecutions and deprivations in Russia, Galicia, and Rumania, expanded the exodus to the West, as revealed in the following figures:

   1870s—   40,000
   1880s—   200,000+
   1890s—   300,000+
   1900–14— 1,500,000+

PATTERNS OF SETTLEMENT

Over 90 percent of the more than 2,000,000 Jews who left Eastern Europe between 1870 and 1924 went to the United States. Unlike many other immigrant groups, the Jews mostly traveled with their families. During the years 1899 to 1910, females made up 43.4 percent of the total number of Jewish immigrants and children 24.7 percent, the highest figure for any arriving peoples. During the same period males constituted 95.1 percent of the Greek immigrants and 78.6 percent of the southern Italians. Only the Irish had a larger percentage of females than the Jews (52.1 percent), but it is believed that many of them came alone to work as domestics. Statistical estimates indicate that 71.6 percent of the Jews came from the Russian empire, including Latvia, Lithuania, and Poland; 17.6 percent from Galicia in the Polish area of the Austro-Hungarian empire; and 4.3 percent from Rumania.

Most of these people landed, and remained, in New York City. In 1870 the city's Jewish population had been estimated at 80,000; in 1915 almost 1,400,000 Jews lived there. The newcomers found friends, relatives, jobs, and educational opportunities in New York City, and, in any case, few had the money to travel elsewhere. Moreover, the Orthodox knew that they could find *kosher* butchers which would allow them to maintain Jewish dietary laws, and jobs where they would not have to work on the sabbath. To be sure, those who landed in Boston, Philadelphia, or Baltimore, or even those who made their way to Chicago and other cities, found small Jewish communities in which they could settle. Chicago, in fact, had 200,000 Jews by 1912. But the major center, by far, for East European Jews was New York.

Most of the immigrants who chose to live in New York City settled originally in a small section of Manhattan Island known as the Lower East Side. The boundaries of this ghetto lay roughly within the blocks bordered by Fourteen Street, Third Avenue and the Bowery, Canal Street, and the East River. The heart of the district, the tenth ward, housed 523.6 people per acre at the beginning of the twentieth century. In the 1890s Jacob Riis, an enterprising reporter, observed that "nowhere in the world are so many people crowded together on a square mile" as in the Jewish quarter. Within the Lower East Side numerous subdivisions could be identified as streets housing primarily Russian, Galician, Rumanian, or Hungarian Jews. The area contained 75 percent of New York City's Jews in 1892, 50 percent in 1903, and 23 percent in 1916.

The tenements where the Jews lived can best be described as dark, dank, and unhealthful. One magazine described the dwellings in 1888 as

great prison-like structures of brick, with narrow doors and windows, cramped passages and steep rickety stairs. They are built through from one street to the other with a somewhat narrower building connecting them. . . . The narrow courtyard . . . in the middle is a damp foul-smelling place, supposed to do duty as an airshaft; had the foul fiend designed these great barracks they could not have been more villainously arranged to avoid any chance of ventilation. . . . In case of fire they would be perfect death-traps, for it would be impossible for the occupants of the crowded rooms to escape by the narrow stairways, and the flimsy fire-escapes which the owners of the tenements were compelled to put up a few years ago are so laden with broken furniture, bales and boxes that they would be worse than useless. In the hot summer months . . . these fire-escape balconies are used as sleeping-rooms by the poor wretches who are fortunate enough to have windows opening upon them. The drainage is horrible, and even the Croton as it flows from the tap in the noisome courtyard, seemed to be contaminated by its surroundings and have a fetid smell.

Two families on each tenement floor shared a toilet. In the summer months the heat and stench in these places were unbearable and the stagnant air outside provided little relief.

The first Jewish immigrants, despite their toil, earned barely enough to subsist on. As a result it was not uncommon to find parents, children, other relatives, and some boarders in a two-, three-, or four-room apartment. The boarder may have paid three dollars a month for his room and free coffee, but that came to 30 percent of the family's ten-dollars-a-month rent. Looking back, the prices of four cents for a quart of milk, two cents for a loaf of bread, and twelve cents for a pound of *kosher* meat may look ridiculously cheap, but when one reckons this on an average weekly income of less than eight dollars, the picture is quite different.

Fortunately for the Jews, their earnings increased sufficiently after a few years in this country so that they did not have to rot in the slums for an interminable period. "It was judged to be a ten-year trek," Moses Rischin tells us, from Hester Street, on the Lower East Side, to Lexington Avenue, in the more fashionable uptown area. The tenements, of course, did not disappear, but their inhabitants continually changed.

Most of the immigrant Jews from Eastern Europe resided first on the Lower East Side and the Hebrew population in that area of the city peaked at more than half a million in 1910; by the 1920s fewer than 10 percent of New York's Jews still lived there. The completion of the subways in the early part of the century opened up vast tracts for settlement in upper Manhattan, Brooklyn, and the Bronx (other boroughs of New York City), and the Jewish working class, anxious and able to take up residence in better neighborhoods, moved away.

Jewish immigrants in Boston, Chicago, and other large cities had initial experiences similar to those who remained in New York. In most other places where Jews went, the tenement areas were smaller or nonexistent, the neighborhoods less congested, and the opportunities to live in more healthful surroundings considerably better. East European Jews who went south or west had experiences considerably different from their brethren who went to the urban areas of the Northeast and Chicago, but they constituted fewer than 5 percent of the entire migration.

Over the years the children and grandchildren of the newcomers moved out of these cities to surrounding suburban areas or flourishing new communities where economic opportunities beckoned. Most of the subsequent growth in the American Jewish population took place in the states closest to New York: Pennsylvania, New Jersey, and

Connecticut, with two major and a few minor exceptions. After World War II job opportunities and a pleasant year-round climate drew hundreds of thousands of Jews to California, especially the Los Angeles area, and many older people first visited and then retired in Miami Beach, Florida. The growth of the Jewish population in California and Florida is primarily a phenomenon of the past thirty years.

LABOR AND BUSINESS

East European Jewish immigrants differed from most of the other foreign-born arrivals in the late nineteenth and early twentieth centuries in that 95 percent of them came from urban rather than rural areas. Their urban origins resulted in the development of skills and talents which would aid them greatly in the United States. An 1898 survey of the Russian pale of settlement found that Jews owned one-third of all the factories in the area and that Jewish workers concentrated in the clothing (254,384), metal-working (43,499), wood-working (42,525), building (39,019), textile (34,612), and tobacco (7,-856) industries. The skills they acquired there were also in demand when they reached the United States.

An American survey of the occupations of immigrants entering the United States between 1899 and 1910 listed 67.1 percent of the Jewish workers as skilled compared with a general figure of 20.2 percent for all newcomers. In his study, *The Promised City*, Moses Rischin indicates that

Jews ranked first in 26 out of 47 trades tabulated by the Immigration Commission, comprising an absolute majority in 8. They constituted 80 per cent of the hat and cap makers, 75 per cent of the furriers, 68 per cent of the watchmakers and milliners and 55 per cent of the cigarmakers and tinsmiths. They totaled 30 to 50 per cent of the immigrants classified as tanners, turners, undergarment makers, jewelers, painters, glaziers, dressmakers, photographers, saddle-makers, locksmiths, butchers, and metal workers in other than iron and steel. They ranked first among immigrant printers, bakers, carpenters, cigarpackers, blacksmiths, and building trades workmen.

In the United States the Jewish immigrants found jobs in distilleries or printing, tobacco, and building trades, while significant numbers of others started out as butchers, grocers, newspaper dealers, or candy store operators.

The majority of the Jewish immigrants, however, found work in the needle trades, which were—because of the increasingly efficient methods of mass production and the existence of a mass market—undergoing rapid expansion. The arrival of the East Europeans with their particular talents coincided with this vast growth. By the end of the nineteenth century Jews had just about displaced the Germans and Irish from the industry. In New York City the development of the clothing industry transformed the economy. In 1880 major clothing manufacturers numbered only 1,081, or 10 percent of the city's factories, and employed 64,669 people, or 28 percent of the city's work force. By 1910 the borough of Manhattan (which before the consolidation of the five boroughs in 1898 had been New York City) had 11,172 clothing establishments, which constituted 47 percent of the city's factories. The industry employed 214,428 people, slightly more than 46 percent of Manhattan's workers. In 1890, 60 percent of the employed immigrant Jews worked in the garment industry and on the eve of the First World War more than half of all Jewish workers, and two-thirds of Jewish wage earners, were still to be found in the industry. The Jewish influence was so great that the manufacturing of wearing apparel in the United States came to be regarded as a Jewish endeavor. Hebrews not only labored in the garment factories; they also worked their way up to supervisory positions and the bolder ones opened their own establishments. Before the Second World War it was estimated that Jews controlled 95 percent of

the women's dress industry, 85 percent of the manufacturing of men's clothing, and 75 percent of the fur industry.

Initially, the owners were German Jews who at first looked down on their East European coreligionists and exploited their labor. Many of the early twentieth-century factories were nothing more than reconverted lofts and tenements or else small areas of workers' apartments. Many garments were actually finished in home sweatshops. Workdays lasting from 4:00 a.m. to 10:00 p.m. in these hovels were not uncommon, and wages averaged $6.00 to $10.00 a week for men and $3.00 to $5.00 for women. (Children also worked on these garments and in other industrial areas as well. Naturally, they earned lower wages than adults.) Because of the seasonal nature of the work, few had a steady yearly income. The annual wage of the average garment worker came to $376.23 in 1900, $1,222 in 1921, and $873.85 in 1930.

Low wages, appalling working conditions, and the insecurity of workers' positions prompted many to think about union organization. Among the Jewish immigrants were many socialists and members of the Russian Jewish Bund who had tried to improve social conditions in Europe. Many of these men also provided the backbone for unionization in the garment trades in the United States. The International Ladies' Garment Workers Union was founded in 1900 but not until the major strikes of clothing workers in 1909 and 1910 were significant victories won and the union firmly established. In Chicago 40,000 garment workers struck in 1910 and in New York 20,000 waist and dressmakers went out from November 1909 through February 1910. In July 1910 as many as 60,000 cloakmakers struck. The strikes attracted wide attention in the press, among social workers, and throughout the Jewish community. The workers won a victory when in July 1910 a "Protocols of Peace" set up a Board of Arbitration, a Board of Grievances, and a Board of Sanitary Control. Four years later the cloakmakers formed the core of the new Amalgamated Clothing Workers of America, a union which had its origins in Chicago with a less effective group, the United Garment Workers of America.

The International Ladies' Garment Workers and the Amalgamated were the two major Jewish unions in the United States. Because of the socialist heritage of so many of its participants, the two unions were concerned not only with improving labor conditions but with a vast program for improving the living conditions of all of its members. The unions were responsible for ending sweatshops, raising wages, and improving working conditions. They also pioneered in the development of a large number of auxiliary services for members. They built housing developments, established educational programs, maintained health centers, provided pensions, set up vacation resorts, developed a system of unemployment insurance benefits long before the state and federal governments assumed this responsibility, and opened banks giving services at significantly lower cost than other financial institutions. The Jewish unions, in sum, initiated social reforms which other labor organizations adopted. Aside from the ILGWU and the Amalgamated, the only other powerful labor union made up primarily of Jewish workers and leaders was the United Federation of Teachers (now the American Federation of Teachers) which galvanized New York City's schoolteachers in the 1960s and propelled its president Albert Shanker, to the forefront of labor leadership in America.

EDUCATION AND SOCIAL MOBILITY

Despite the benefits obtained by and from the labor unions, Jews had no desire to remain in the working class. Their ambition to "get ahead" knew no bounds and as soon as possible they, and/or their children, strove to move up to more lucrative and prestigious occupations. As early as 1900, American-born sons of Russian Jews constituted six times as many lawyers and seven times as

many accountants as were to be found in their parents' generation but only one-third the number of garment workers. As the years passed, this tendency became even more pronounced. Jewish workers also tried to become manufacturers. Many of those who started out as peddlers eventually moved into small retail outlets and some of the latter then expanded into larger emporiums. It was the rare community, in fact, that did not have some Jewish storekeepers. Random samplings in different decades through the 1940s showed anywhere from 31 to 63 percent of the Jews engaged in trade. In one study of the South the author noted, "It is said, 'If there is a Jewish holiday, you cannot buy a pair of socks in this whole country,' a remark which illustrates how complete the control of the retail dry-goods trade by Jews is supposed to be."

The entertainment industry also provided an avenue of advancement for some immigrant Jews. In 1905 it was estimated that half of the actors, popular songwriters, and song publishers in New York City were Jewish. Within a few years Jews also pioneered in the motion picture industry.

The Jews made great economic and social advances because educational and business opportunities were available to the more enterprising and because the masses of East European Jewish immigrants considered it necessary to "Americanize" their children and have them learn the language and customs of the new country as quickly as possible. From their beginnings in this country, the East European Jews also showed a passion for education and professional advancement unique in American history. Members of other immigrant groups, before or since, have not been as zealous in their quest for knowledge. The newcomers themselves were forced to do manual work, but whenever possible they encouraged their children to remain in school, attain an education, and move up in the world. As Samuel Gompers, leader of the American Federation of Labor, observed, "The Jews were fairly ravenous for education and eager for personal development. ... All industrial work was merely a steppingstone to professional and managerial positions.'' Jewish parents wanted their children in high-status positions where they could operate on their own and not be subject to the bigotry of employers. Jewish boys strove to become doctors, lawyers, dentists, accountants, and teachers. They also opened pharmacies and other retail businesses. In these occupations Jewish parents felt their children would be both prosperous and independent at the same time. In 1903 it was estimated that Jews comprised about half of New York City's 5,000 to 6,000 physicians and thirty-four years later 65.7 percent of the city's lawyers and judges, 55.7 percent of its physicians, and 64 percent of its dentists. In the 1960s Jews still made up a majority of these professions in New York City.

Statistics of Jewish occupational categories for other cities are similar. By the 1930s only one-third of all Jewish workers were still engaged in manual jobs while two-thirds were in white-collar positions. The figures for non-Jews were just the reverse: two-thirds in manual occupations, one-third in white-collar jobs. Jews also moved into professional positions at a much faster rate and in much higher percentages than non-Jews. In the 1930s eighteen out of every 1,000 Jews in San Francisco were lawyers and judges, while sixteen were physicians. For every 1,000 gentiles the figures were five and five, respectively. Similarly, in Pittsburgh fourteen of every 1,000 Jews were lawyers and judges, thirteen were physicians, while the corresponding figures for non-Jews were five and four, respectively.

The tendency for Jews to seek and obtain the highest status positions in American society has not diminished in recent decades. In 1955, some 55 percent of all gainfully employed Jews, compared with 23 percent of non-Jews, had professional, technical, managerial, executive, or proprietary positions while in 1967, 51 percent of the Jews, compared to 23 percent of the Catholics and 21 percent of the Protestants in the United States

were classified as professionals. Among younger Jewish adults the figures for professional occupations were even higher. With higher status occupations came higher incomes. In 1967 the Gallup Poll found that 69 percent of the Jews had incomes over $7,000 a year but only 47 percent of the Catholics and 38 percent of the Protestants claimed earnings of that level or higher. By 1971, 60 percent of the Jewish families where the head of the household was between thirty and fifty-nine years old had annual incomes exceeding $16,000.

But money alone does not tell the whole story. Since the end of World War II not only has there been an almost complete disappearance of Jewish young men in blue-collar jobs, but Jews in increasingly larger numbers have shunned retail businesses—frequently owned by their fathers—to seek careers and greater personal satisfaction as journalists, writers, scientists, architects, engineers, and academics, as well as the traditional favorites of the Jewish immigrants: lawyers and physicians. Discouraged earlier by family preferences and gentile bigotry from seeking careers where they would have to be employed by others, the enormous expansion of opportunities in the 1950s and '60s made previously unheralded vocations or fields formerly difficult to enter more attractive and more accessible.

CULTURAL AND RELIGIOUS LIFE

The East European Jews, despite their poverty, arrived in this country with certain advantages. They had a strong commitment to a religion which rigidly dictated much of their daily behavior and gave their lives a structure and continuity which helped them to overcome problems of displacement in a new society. Moreover, unlike other immigrants to the United States who may have been poor at home but who otherwise ''belonged,'' the Jews had been minorities wherever they had dwelled in Europe. As a result they had acquired a knowledge of how to move deftly among the dominant groups who, at best, tolerated them or, at worst, despised them. They had learned how to survive under a variety of hostile conditions and this experience served them well in the United States where they also had to struggle with adversity. Another important advantage that the Jews had brought with them can best be described as a middle-class view of life. They were ambitious, self-disciplined, and intellectually curious. A number of them had been socialists and participants in the revolutionary movement in Russia and Poland. Most had lived in small towns and villages and were attuned to what might now be considered the urban style of life.

The culture that the Jews brought with them to the United States survived in New York City. In recent decades attempts have been made to transplant it, as well, to Miami Beach and Los Angeles. In Boston, Chicago, and other cities where the Jews initially dwelled, they composed too small a percentage of the population to make much impact on the community. They may have had their own food stores and shared an affinity for literature, music, art, and religious observances, and perhaps even were more socialistically inclined than their neighbors, but in time their tastes and views blended with the dominant values of their respective communities, and today outside of the strongholds of the remnants of East European Jewish orthodoxy in New York, Chicago, Pittsburgh, Los Angeles, and Miami Beach, about the only thing left to distinguish Jews from everyone else in the United States is the Reform Temple.

In New York City, however, an East European Jewish culture flowered for decades and still lends a distinctive tone to the life in this vast metropolis. Cafés abounded where Jews would sit around and *shmooze* (talk) for hours over cups of coffee or glasses of hot tea. "For immigrant Jews," one chronicler reminds us, "talk was the breath of life itself." Discussions during these get-togethers ranged over a wide spectrum of topics and no one ever felt the necessity to refrain from participation because of a limited knowledge of the topic under consideration. The cafés gave the Jewish East Side a flavor—"a Yiddish Bohemia, poor and picturesque"—and their patrons included the most intellectual and articulate Jewish actors, poets, playwrights, journalists, and politicians of the day.

Jews also relaxed in the theater. The coming of the East European Jews not only spawned a Yiddish theatre in the ghetto but also stimulated vaudeville and the Broadway stage. They also pioneered in the radio industry and virtually founded the motion picture industry.

Jews throughout the United States have been known for their patronage of the arts and their interest in literary endeavors. Between 1885 and 1914, for example, over 150 Yiddish daily, weekly, monthly, quarterly, and festival journals and yearbooks appeared in New York City, including the daily *Forward* which is still published today. Cultural centers were established wherever sufficient numbers of Jews congregated. Typically, the Cleveland Jewish Center had a gym, a roof garden, a library, classes in Hebrew language and literature, a scouting program, art classes, political forums, sewing and baking clubs, etc.

Owners of art galleries and concert halls (about one-third of whom in New York City are Jewish) know that the larger a community's Jewish population the more likely it will be that their showings and musicales will be rewarded with large audiences. Jews are also heavily represented in every aspect of radio and television production. They purchase more books and attend more poetry readings than non-Jews and have also been among the major book publishers in New York City.

For the recent arrivals, however, the single most important cultural institution was the synagogue. Unlike the German Jews who came before them and worshiped, for the most part, in Reform temples barely distinguishable from Unitarian churches, the overwhelming proportion of the East Europeans maintained a devout orthodoxy during their first years in the United States. The numbers of synagogues proliferated in geometric proportion. In 1870 there were 189 Jewish congregations in the United States, the majority peopled by German Jews. By 1906 there were 1,769 and twenty years after that 3,118. In New York City alone the number of synagogues increased from 300 at the turn of the century to 1,200 in 1942. Usually these places of worship were no more than converted store fronts or private homes which came into being because one group of men had an argument with another group and then stormed out to find someplace else to pray. Since the end of World War II Americanized Jews have tended to worship in distinguished and substantial edifices but, aside from New York, Miami, and the four or five other cities in the country with large Jewish populations, it would be rare to find a community with even half a dozen Jewish temples or synagogues.

In the Jewish ghettos early in the twentieth century, shops closed on the Sabbath and the men and women, separated by curtains, prayed in the neighborhood synagogues. On the most holy days of the Jewish year, generally in September, 95 percent of the East European Jewish families went to the synagogue. As the Jewish immigrants and their children assimilated and Americanized, this percentage dwindled considerably. Although no statistics on high holy day attendance are available, it would be a safe guess to say that today the figure is at best 50 percent. All we can assert with accuracy, however, is that "all surveys of religious commitment, belief, and practice in the United States indicate that Jews are much less involved in religious activities than Protestants, who are in turn less active than Catholics." Nevertheless, it is still true today that the New York City public schools are closed for the major Jewish holidays because Jews constitute a majority of the teachers and their absence would create severe administrative headaches. Furthermore, on the Jewish holidays many of the city's businesses are closed, restaurants in commercial areas are nearly empty, and the mass transportation system has no more than half, if that many, of its usual patrons.

GERMAN vs. EAST EUROPEAN JEWS

The East European Jews who arrived in the United States in the late nineteenth and early twentieth centuries encountered an unreceptive American Jewry. The American Jews, descended mostly from the German migrations of the middle of the nineteenth century, had achieved a secure middle-class position in the United States. They were doctors, lawyers, bankers, manufacturers, and merchants. They had established or developed some of the leading department stores in the country like Macy's and Sears Roebuck. In addition, they had made every effort to appear indistinguishable from the more prosperous gentile Americans.

The coming of the East European Jews threatened the security of the German Jews. One of them wrote, in 1893, that the experience of the United Jewish Charities in Rochester, New York, "teaches that organized immigration from Russia, Rumania, and other semi-barbarous countries is a mistake and has proved a failure. It is no relief to the Jews of Russia, Poland, etc., and it jeopardizes the well-being of American Jews." The Americanized Jews felt little kinship with the newcomers and also feared that their presence would constitute a burden on society and stimulate an outburst of anti-Semitism. When the *Hebrew Standard* declared, on June 15, 1894, that "the thoroughly acclimated American Jew . . . is closer to the Christian sentiment around him than to the Judaism of these miserable darkened Hebrews," it probably expressed the dominant sentiment of American Jewry at the time.

Despite their antipathy, the Americanized Jews realized that the gentiles in the United States lumped all Jews together and that the behavior of the Orthodox would reflect on everyone. As Louis D. Brandeis later phrased it,

a single though inconspicuous instance of dishonorable conduct on the part of a Jew in any trade or profession has far-reaching evil effects extending to the many innocent members of the race. Large as this country is, no Jew can behave badly without injuring each of us in the end. . . . Since the act of each becomes thus the concern of all, we are perforce our brothers' keepers.

One should not minimize, however, the fact that the American Jews also had a paternalistic sympathy for their East European brethren and therefore, since they could not contain the stampede from Russia, Galicia, and Rumania, they set about, after an initial display of coldness, to improve the "moral, mental and physical conditions" of the immigrants.

Once they decided to facilitate assimilation by assisting the newcomers, the American Jews spared no efforts and "few human needs were overlooked." Of all immigrant groups none proved so generous to "their own kind" as did the Jews. Money and organizational talent combined to provide hospitals, orphan asylums, recreational facilities, and homes for unwed mothers as well as for the deaf, the blind, the old, and the crippled. Educational institutions were also established and the "zeal to Americanize underlay all educational endeavor." Part of this Americanizing process also resulted in the building up of the Jewish Theological Seminary in New York City to train Conservative rabbis. The American Jewish establishment could not tolerate orthodoxy but recognized that the East European immigrants would not come around to Reform Judaism. Conservatism provided an acceptable compromise since it preached American values while retaining the most important orthodox traditions.

Another of the projects resulted in an attempt to disperse the immigrants throughout the United States. The Americanized Jews did not want the newcomers to congregate in one massive ghetto. Between 1901 and 1917 the Industrial Removal Office dispatched 72,482 East European Jews to 1,670 communities in forty-eight states. Nevertheless, many of those transplanted eventually returned to New York. In fact, of the 1,-334,627 Jews who did arrive in New York City between 1881 and 1911, 73.5 percent remained there.

The most important and lasting agency set up by the Americanized Jews to help—and lead—their brethren was the American Jewish Committee. Ostensibly formed as a result of the outrageous pogroms in Russia between 1903 and 1905 and dedicated to protecting the civil rights of Jews wherever they were threatened, the American Jewish Committee came into being in 1906 primarily because the established Jewish community in the United States wanted "to assert some control over existing Jewish institutions and mass movements." As Louis Marshall, one of the American Jewish Committee's leading members and its president from 1912 to 1929, put it in 1908, the purpose of those who formed the organization was "to devise a simple and efficient instrument which might deal quickly, and at the same time deliberatley, and with an understanding based on experience, with the problems that might present themselves from time to time."

The American Jewish Committee, composed of wealthy Jews, exercised great influence politically "through private contacts with men in power." Since Jacob Schiff, Cyrus Adler, Louis Marshall, Felix Warburg, Oscar Strauss, Julius Rosenwald, Mayer Sulzberger, and others of their stature dealt regularly with the most prominent Americans of their generation, the Committee "on the whole, acted effectively in the interests of American Jewry." The American Jewish Committee, as one scholar has pointed out, "offered American Jewry a vigorous, disciplined and highly paternalistic leadership as well as a program of Americanization," but its members looked down upon the East Europeans and expected them to follow its leadership. This did not occur. Perhaps if the Committee had been more democratically organized it might have served as a bridge to the newcomers and won them over. But as one of the group said, "let us get away from the idea that the American Jewish Committee must be representative and that its members must be chosen in some way by the vote of the Jews in this country. No great moral movement has been undertaken and carried through except in just such a manner in which we are doing our work."

The enormous assistance provided by the Americanized Jews to the immigrants was accepted with reservations. The established Jews showed disdain for the East Europeans and their culture and the recipients of their largesse felt like beggars and poor relations. The charity may have been given out of a sense of obligation but it did not come with warmth and kindness. And the leadership provided by the American Jewish Committee definitely smacked of elitism which the immigrants would not tolerate. As soon as the East Europeans could provide their own network of charitable and welfare organizations they did so. It would be a long time before they would look upon their "benefactors" without a jaundiced eye.

ANTI-SEMITISM

The German and East European Jews in the United States recognized the vast gulf that separated them socially, economically, and culturally but gentiles did not. The coming of the new Jews intensified latent anti-Semitic feelings among gentile Americans and, as the German Jews had originally feared, this hostility erupted in public. The German Jews felt the sting first. In 1877 a prominent Jewish banker was barred as a guest from a resort hotel that had previously accepted his patronage. As the nineteenth century came to a close, German Jews also found themselves excluded from private schools, prominent social clubs, and other resorts. In 1890 the editors of The American Hebrew sent around a questionnaire to prominent Americans in-

quiring why gentiles were so hostile to Jews and one university president responded that "All intelligent Christians deplore the fact that the historical evidences for Christianity have so little weight with your people."

The East European Jews were not affected at first by social anti-Semitism but in the early years of the twentieth century the bigotry became acute. In rapid succession crude slurs, journalistic reports, and supposedly learned commentaries lambasted the Jews. A letter to the editor of the New York Herald complained that "these United States are becoming rapidly so Jew ridden... ," while a faculty member at Teachers College in New York wrote to a colleague and asked him to "please do me the favor of not coming to the banquet tomorrow night, as I have invited a friend who does not like Jews." A magazine writer asked of the Russian Jew, "is he assimilable? Has he in himself the stuff of which Americans are made?" University of Wisconsin sociologist E. A. Ross claimed that "the lower class of Hebrews of eastern Europe reach here moral cripples, their souls warped and dwarfed by iron circumstance... many of them have developed a monstrous and repulsive love of gain." Finally, University of Berlin Professor Werner Sombart's prediction "that in another hundred years the United States will be peopled chiefly by Slavs, negroes and Jews," was prominently featured in one of the leading American periodicals of the day.

In view of these prejudices it is no wonder that outside of the garment district and other Jewish-owned establishments Jews had little chance for obtaining decent jobs. Many help-wanted advertisements specified "Christian only," and real estate agents preferred gentile clients. To combat this discrimination one of the older American Jewish fraternal organizations, B'nai B'rith, which had been founded in 1843, established its Anti-Defamation League in 1913. The League over the years has proved quite successful in combating anti-Semitism.

Despite the efforts of the Anti-Defamation League, schools and employers continued discriminating against Jews. Quotas in higher education began in the 1920s and became more rigid during the depression years of the 1930s. As late as 1945 the president of Dartmouth College defended regulations which kept Jewish students out of his school, but he was probably the last outspoken advocate of an already waning policy. Beginning with World War II more opportunities opened to practically all skilled white people and the growth of the economy, the passage of state laws forbidding discrimination in employment and entry into universities, and a generally more tolerant spirit in the land led to widened economic and occupational opportunities for Jews. Law firms, scientific organizations, universities, and businesses needing the very best talent available hired goodly numbers of Jews who were among their few qualified applicants.

Bigotry did not disappear completely. The executive suites of America's largest corporations contain relatively few Jews and one still reads of prominent Jews being denied admission to country clubs. On December 14, 1973, *The Wall Street Journal* ran a story on Irving Shapiro, the new chairman and chief executive of Du Pont and Company, the world's largest chemical concern. Well into the article the author noted that being a lawyer, a Jew, and a Democrat were not helpful to Mr. Shapiro in his rise to prominence within the firm (although his talents, of course, overrode these "handicaps") and then tellingly, "Mr. Shapiro's official biography is noticeably lacking in the kind of club affiliations that adorn those of his colleagues."

LEGISLATION AND POLITICS

There were never any specific laws in the United States regarding East European Jews, but their arrival contributed to the movement for immigration restriction. The major American laws keeping out aliens passed Congress in 1921 and 1924 and these set quotas for groups based on a percentage of their population in the United States in 1910

and 1890, respectively. Such laws were designed to drastically curtail southern and eastern European migration to this country. The Jews, being the second largest immigrant group in the early twentieth century, were obviously one of the major targets of this legislation. As early as 1906 an Italian American had been told by a member of President Theodore Roosevelt's immigration commission that the "movement toward restriction in all of its phases is directed against Jewish immigration. . . ." The Irish, the English, and the Germans who constituted the majority of nineteenth-century immigrants to the United States received the largest quotas. No religious test was allowed by this legislation. Consequently, Jews born in Germany were counted under the German quota and Jews born in England came in under the English quota even though their parents might have come from Russia or Rumania. Subsequent legislation affecting the East European Jews came in 1948 and 1950 when some of the persons displaced by the German policies of the 1930s and the Second World War were allowed to come into the United States under special provisions. Current immigration regulations in the United States make no statement about religion and have done away with quotas based on national origins. Present legislation gives preference to immigrants with close relatives in the United States and to those who have occupational skills in demand in this country.

Jews in the United States have never been legally restrained from pursuing any social or economic interests that struck their fancy. Many states originally restricted voting rights to adult males who believed in the divinity of Jesus Christ, but these were abolished in all but a few states by the beginning of the nineteenth century.

The East Europeans, like other whites, voted after becoming citizens (which took only five years after entering the United States), but they registered and voted in much higher proportion to their numbers than did members of other ethnic groups. They took stands on political issues of concern to them and supported candidates for office who appeared to be in harmony with their own views. A number of Jews have been elected to high political office, such as governor of a state or United States senator, but before the Second World War almost all of these people were of German background. In the past score of years, however, Jews of East European background have achieved similar prominence. The best known of these are United States Senators Jacob Javits of New York and Abraham Ribicoff of Connecticut, and Governors Milton J. Schapp and Marvin Mandel of Pennsylvania and Maryland, respectively. Numerous Jews who were born, or whose parents were born, in Russia, Rumania, and Poland have been elected to the United States House of Representatives and the various state legislatures.

Although Jews have supported Republicans, Democrats, and socialists, since the New Deal era the vast majority have been loyal Democrats both with their votes and their financial contributions. In fact, their contributions are so lavish and their votes so important that policies affecting American Jews—and especially Israel—have to be taken into account by the leading Democratic politicos. So devoted to the Democrats are the Jews that in Richard Nixon's overwhelming re-election victory in 1972 they were the only white ethnic group in the nation that gave a majority of its votes to the Democratic nominee for President, George S. McGovern, although not by the overwhelming support usually accorded Democratic candidates. A few Jews, notably Max Fisher of Detroit, also lubricated Republican coffers. As a result, an anti-Israel policy simply would not be politically acceptable to most of the elected officials in Washington.

SUMMARY AND CONCLUSION

The East European Jews have accomplished great things for themselves in the United States. Most of them arrived on the brink of poverty around the turn of the century and their descendants have risen to comfortable and secure middle-class positions in American society. They can live where they like, work almost any place where they have the necessary skills, and worship—or not—in any manner that pleases them. This almost total freedom has resulted in a good deal of interfaith marriage and a slackening of religious and ethnic ties. During the past decade one out of every three Jewish marriages has been with a non-Jew.

Overt anti-Semitism, with the exception of the controversy between blacks and Jews arising out of the 1967 and 1968 schoolteachers' strikes in New York City, has subsided considerably during the past few decades, and recent laws have forbidden discrimination on the basis of race, creed, or national origins in employment and housing. These laws are not always observed, but they do indicate that the state and federal governments are putting up formal barriers against wanton bigotry. Ironically, diminished discrimination loosens the ties that bind ethnic minorities. The educational system, especially at the college and university levels, inculcates a national culture and a national way of thinking and it is the rare individual who, after being subject to such exposure, can be completely comfortable again in a strictly ethnic setting. With each succeeding generation of educated Jews, therefore, the ties to the traditional culture are weakened. Most American Jews today are products of the American education system and work and live in areas with people of varying ethnic backgrounds. Only some of the Jewish immigrants and their children can still be found in ghettos. And with each passing year their numbers fade.

Also on the wane is Orthodox Jewry. The attachment to the traditional faith was strong among the immigrants and their children but later generations found it a burden. Only a tiny fraction of American Jews keep the Sabbath and only a few more observe the dietary restrictions. Outside of New York, Los Angeles, Chicago, and Miami Beach, the Conservative and Reform branches of Judaism hold sway in temple memberships while the way-of-life practiced by practically all American Jews is in the Reform tradition. Thus attendance at religious services is sparse except at the beginning of the Jewish New Year and the Day of Atonement, and a middle-class life-style, almost totally devoid of ethnic flavor, is vigorously pursued.

In the early 1960s one American rabbi said, "Today there is little that marks the Jew as a Jew except Jewish self-consciousness and association with fellow Jews." It is difficult to assess the strength and significance of this self-consciousness. If one "feels" Jewish and seeks out other Jews for companionship, the ties are still there. Jewish identity has also been reinforced by the emergence and travails of the State of Israel. It is impossible, of course, to predict for how many generations such sentiments will sustain American Jewry.

As the Jews become Americanized, strains and dissimilarities between the German and Russian elements have disappeared. When Hitler began persecuting Jews in Germany, and especially in the past score of years, when differences in income and life-styles have narrowed considerably, there have been few if any clashes between Jews of German and East European ancestry in the United States. In fact, one might say that with each succeeding generation there is less and less difference among all American Jews regardless of their grandfathers' native lands. Class, geographical location, education, occupation, and income would be more appropriate categories for demarcation than German-Russian or Orthodox-Reform background. The only exception to this generalization would be the American Council for Judaism, whose members are primarily of German-Jewish ancestry. It is supported by only a fraction of 1 percent of the American Jews and it differs considerably from other Jewish organizations in its regard of Israel as just another foreign country with which American Jews should have no special relationships.

Still another aspect of the migration and its subsequent impact in the United States is the fantastic influence that East European Jews have had on the academic, intellectual, medical, political, and cultural life in the country, especially since the end of the Second World War. Whereas in the 1930s it was rare to find Jews, let alone those of East European descent, on the faculties of American colleges, in more recent times Jews whose parents or grandparents came from Russia, Poland, and Rumania adorn the most prestigious American universities. It would be difficult to name them all, but even a cursory cataloging would include sociologists Daniel Bell, Nathan Glazer, and Seymour Martin Lipset of Harvard University (all, by the way, graduates of New York City's City College in the 1930s); Harvard historian Oscar Handlin; and Yale Law School Dean, Abraham Goldstein. Also on the Harvard faculty is the Russian-born Nobel Prize winner, Simon Kuznets. Herbert Stein, one of President Nixon's chief economic advisers; former United States Supreme Court Justice and Ambassador to the United Nations, Arthur Goldberg; the discoverer of the vaccine to prevent polio, Jonas E. Salk; film-maker Stanley Kubrick; musician Leonard Bernstein; violinist Yehudi Menuhin; playwrights Arthur Miller and Neil Simon; and artist Ben Shahn are only a few of the others of East European Jewish descent who have made their mark in the United States. In fact, the East European Jews and their descendants have made a much greater impact, and in a wider range of activities, than people from any of the other contemporary group of immigrants.

And yet, despite their absorption into American society, it is still true, as Jacob Neusner wrote in 1973, that "to be a Jew in America is to be in some measure different, alien, a minority." The dominant culture in the United States is still intolerant of differences among groups of people and of non-Christians loyal to a foreign state or a different faith. This, of course, presents great difficulties to the various ethnic minorities in the United States. On the one hand "cultural pluralism" is celebrated in song and spirit from every official podium while deviation is regarded as a sign of subversion and inferiority. This schizophrenic conflict affects all American minorities and to be a non-WASP is to be somehow marginal and alien. For most Jews who are prosperous, employed, and ensconced in comfortable homes, these feelings are rarely discussed, but the fierce American-Jewish devotion to the State of Israel suggests that even in the United States Jews do not feel absolutely secure. Somehow they feel that loyalty to a Jewish state is necessary. Whether it is because of an attachment to the heritage and traditions of Jewry or because of a sense of being part of the same group, or even because they fear that someday they or their descendants might have to flee the United States and take refuge in Israel is impossible to say. But we do know that the sense of identification with Israel is strong and this, in a very specific way, differentiates Jews from other Americans.

The Polish-American Community

WILLIAM I. THOMAS and FLORIAN ZNANIECKI

The Poles are one of the most significant of the twentieth-century minorities. Only the Italians and Jews outnumbered the 875,000 Polish immigrants who came to the United States between 1870 and 1924. Most of the newcomers settled in the cities of Buffalo, Chicago, Milwaukee, Pittsburgh, Detroit, and New York and took on available laboring jobs; some migrated to mining areas and farming communities; they lived in crowded quarters and worked for barely livable wages. In the Shenandoah coal mines Polish children worked ten hours a day, six days a week, and took home $2.68 for their efforts. Adult wages were not much better.

The following selection is taken from The Polish Peasant in Europe and America, *a pioneering effort in social research and theory. This multi-volume work by William I. Thomas and Florian Znaniecki explores the organization of the Polish peasant society undergoing fundamental social change. Psychological responses, social processes, class, migration, vagabondage, law breaking, tradition, alienation, assimilation, cultural values, patterns of social control, prejudice, efficiency, and happiness are among the subjects treated in Thomas and Znaniecki's analysis. The chapter reprinted below focuses on the roles played by vocation, benevolent societies, religion, and the ethnic press in creating a cohesive ethnic community.*

The tide of Polish immigration grew continually until 1914. The number of returns to Poland was also, indeed, increasing, but these on the average did not exceed 30 per cent of the arrivals. The population of the old Polish colonies (in Pittsburg, Buffalo, Cleveland, Detroit, Chicago, Milwaukee, etc.) rivalled that of Polish cities in Europe, Chicago with its 360,000 Poles ranking after Warsaw and Lódź as the third largest Polish center in the world. Outside of these, numerous new colonies have developed, for the most part founded by immigrants sufficiently familiar with American conditions to search for work away from the traditional centers, but recruited later chiefly from Europe. Since the beginning of the present century hundreds of new colonies were founded in the East, which originally had only a few old and small Polish settlements. Some of them have developed rapidly. Thus, according to Polish sources, one-third of the population of

From William I. Thomas and Florian Znaniecki, *The Polish Peasant in Europe and America*, II (2 vols., New York: Alfred A. Knopf, 1927), pp. 1511–49. Reprinted from the Dover Publications edition published in 1958.

New Britain, Conn., is Polish and the Polish parish in that city is among the most flourishing and best organized. In the far West the development has been slower, in the South quite insignificant.[1]

The process by which Polish colonies appear and grow can thus be observed in detail during the last 20 or 30 years. It seems to present a uniformity of outline which permits us to construct a general sociological scheme of the development of a Polish-American community applicable with some variations to all such communities except agricultural colonies, which we have not had the opportunity to study, and a few of the oldest and largest groups which originated under different conditions and are now organized around several centers, thus presenting a greater complexity of life than the smaller settlements, each with one main social center.[2]

When a Polish immigrant finds work which pays well and promises to be permanent in a locality where there is no Polish settlement yet, he usually tries at once to attract his friends and relatives from other Polish-American communities. His motives are evident. He has been accustomed to such social response and recognition as only a primary group with old social bonds and uniform attitudes can give, and however well he may be adapted to American economic and political conditions he seldom is at once accepted as a member by an American primary-group (or by a primary-group of some other immigrant people). Even if he were he would miss the directness and warmth of social relations to which he has been accustomed in his own group. Sometimes, indeed, he does not succeed in attracting any one. Then if he does not leave the place driven by loneliness, he becomes gradually absorbed in the American milieu. Usually, however, a small group of Polish workmen is soon formed; and their first attempt, partly for economic, partly for social reasons, is to have a Polish boarding-house. Often some one of them who has some money and a wife in America assumes the initiative, brings his wife as soon as his situation seems settled, rents a large apartment and takes the others as roomers or boarders. It may happen that a bachelor marries some Polish girl he knows, with the understanding that they are going to keep a boarding place. Sometimes under such conditions a wife or a fianceée is even brought from Europe. Frequently, however, the initiative comes not from an individual but from the group; all the workmen put some money into renting and furnishing the apartment and induce one of their number who has a wife or fiancée to bring her. In this case they buy their own food and the woman only cooks it and cleans the house, receiving for these services a small sum from each ($1 to $2 a week) and by tacit understanding feeding herself and her children on her boarders' superfluous food.

If the locality has a permanent industry the small Polish colony continues to grow, partly by invited, partly by independent arrivals. Almost every individual or small family once settled attracts new members from the outside, however large the colony may already be, provided the economic conditions are favorable. The reason why, even when there is a Polish group formed, its members still invite their friends and relatives to come is once more to be found in the desire for response and the desire for recognition. As long as the Polish immigrant is isolated among Americans or immigrants of different nationalities he welcomes the arrival of any Pole. But even among people of the same nationality and the same class the desires for

[1]There are no reliable official statistics of the Polish population in this country. According to the data privately collected by Mr. Stanislaw Osada of Chicago for a work which he is preparing under the title "Polonia Americana," there are about 1,200 Polish parishes with a membership of nearly 2,000,000. The number of Poles not directly connected with parishes may be estimated roughly at about 1,000,000.

[2]The following typical scheme of development of Polish-American colonies was outlined to us in its main features in private conversation by the Rev. Priest Syski of Boston, who has observed Polish American life very closely and intelligently for many years. We are also using materials collected by ourselves. Our explanation of the social process here described is based in a large measure on the results of our preceding volumes.

response and recognition are not satisfied as fully as among relatives or friends. Relatives are on the average more satisfactory than strangers, those who come from the same community in Poland or from the same town in America are next best and tend to keep together more closely than those born or reared in different parts of the country; friends with a long past of common interests are more united than recent acquaintances. Each individual desires the fullest response and the widest recognition possible. He may accept provisionally whatever he finds but very soon begins to desire more. On the one hand he is ready to lavish his social feelings on any one within his reach, if he has only a few possible objects; but, on the other hand, when his social milieu widens and he can select the objects of his social feelings more consciously, he becomes more reserved and discriminating. Thus when a mere acquaintance comes into a colony formed of close friends and relatives, or when a group of immigrants coming from the same community is joined by an individual born in a different part of the country, the newcomer feels like an outsider. He naturally tends to call in his own relatives and his own friends, or people from his neighborhood. It often happens that a Polish colony is divided into several distinct groups which, though more closely connected with one another than with their American milieu, still look at one another with some mistrust and even a slight hostility. As we shall see later this division is soon overcome by cooperation for common purposes and does not exist in the older colonies, except that immigrants who have recently come from the same communities always associate with each other more willingly than with those who lack the same early neighborhood connections and sometimes a colony—or a parish in a large colony like Chicago—is composed principally of immigrants from some one of the provinces of Poland, Posen, Silesia, Galicia, the Congress Kingdom of Lithuania. The fact that the emigration from these provinces started at different periods has probably something to do with this phenomenon.

Dissensions between immigrants are also indirectly a factor in the growth of new colonies, for when relatives, friends or acquaintances have quarreled each party wishes to be independent and to bring more relatives, friends or acquaintances to satisfy the social needs formerly satisfied by the other and to furnish additional support against it. As long as the existence of the new colony is not quite assured, the colony is naturally recruited more from the unsettled part of the population of other Polish-American communities than from the new immigrants, since the former can more easily risk moving temporarily to a new place. There are many instances of new settlements springing up in connection with an increased demand for labor in a given locality and suddenly disappearing after a relatively short time, if the labor conditions grow worse, a factory goes bankrupt, or a mine or lumber field is exhausted, etc. But if a colony lasts for several years, after having attracted chiefly the shifting and unsettled Polish-American elements from other colonies it usually begins to depend more on European immigration, since there are always many members who maintain their connections with Poland. The influx of new immigrants thus often becomes for a time the most important factor in its growth. Later when the community is definitely settled marriages and births—at first relatively insignificant—gradually acquire the predominant importance.

In this respect it must be remembered that from the standpoint of the traditional family system the family group should tend to be as numerous as possible and that this old conception perfectly harmonizes with the view of the Catholic Church according to which many children are to be considered a ''blessing of God.'' Of course the family system loses much of its power through emigration, but it remains still strong enough, at least in the first generation, to prevent any rapid decay of this attitude, which is one of the oldest and most deeply rooted family attitudes. We may add that the immigrant seldom knows any means of preventing childbearing except abortion, which is considered shameful—probably because resorted to mostly by unmarried girls—and sexual abstinence, which the peasant considers hardly worth while merely in order to limit his family. Moreover the economic conditions here favor the growth of large families. For although the children cannot be utilized economically as early as they are on a peasant farm in Poland, still there is seldom any real difficulty in bringing them up, for the average wages of an immigrant are certainly sufficient to support a large family on the scale to which he has been accustomed in the old country, if not on a higher one. When the children grow up they are expected to preserve family solidarity at least to the extent of turning over to the family most of their earnings, so that whatever expenses the family incurs to support them until working age are treated as an investment of the family funds from which a return is expected. Furthermore, a large family is considered normal, for the social and economic status of the second generation will probably be above that of the first here, whereas in the old country a too numerous family often means a division of the property into such small parts that the children are unable to maintain the economic and social level of their parents. And if we realize that the power of the parish is here, as we shall see presently, greater than in Poland and that the parish favors for obvious reasons a rapid growth of the population, it will not be surprising that social opinion maintains the old standard of "propagation" and the prestige of a family group grows with the number of its children. Of course in cases of individual disorganization all these factors may cease to work. Generally, however, they work well enough to make the Polish immigrants at least as prolific as the peasants in the old country. Propagation has been even emphasized recently as a patriotic duty to both Poland and the local colony.[3]

[3]We know an intelligent Pole, a relatively recent immigrant, who has been very successful in business and who openly says he desires to fulfill his national duty by returning to Poland with twelve children and a million dollars for each of them.

Along with the growth of the new colony goes progress in unity and cohesion. In the beginning the group of Polish immigrants is naturally more or less scattered territorially, particularly when the locality has several factories or mines, since every workman tends to live near his working place. There are no interests to keep it together, except the personal ties of relationship and friendship between particular members of marriage groups and the general feeling of racial solidarity. But individuals always appear in every group—usually those who have had some experience in other Polish-American colonies—with whom the feeling of racial solidarity and perhaps also the desire to play a public rôle becomes motives for starting a closer organization. A "society" is established invariably whenever the colony reaches 100 to 300 members. . . .

The first purpose for which such a "society" is usually established is mutual help in emergencies (sickness, death, and, more seldom, lack of work). For however vague many be originally the bond of racial solidarity between the members of a new colony, it never fails to manifest itself at the death of a member. Usually a severe sickness or disabling accident also provokes sympathetic feelings and the desire to help. Just as in matters concerning the increase of the family, so in cases calling for communal solidarity there are in the conditions surrounding the new Polish-American colony factors that are able to counterbalance in some measure and for a certain time the disorganizing influences of the new milieu. The workman who has no productive property and is hired by the week is evidently more seriously affected by misfortune than the peasant farmer or even the manor-servant hired by the year. Yet during times of prosperity his increased earning power makes him more able to help others in case of need and more willing to do so, since money has less value for him than in the old country, particularly after he has once resigned himself to considering his earnings as a means to live rather than as a means to acquire property. Further, the group of workmen constituting a Polish-American colony is isolated and cut off from all wider social milieux, instead of constituting, like a group of working men in Poland, an integral part of a larger society disposing of some wealth. Private charity from wealthy people, which in the country districts of Poland still remains a valuable source of help in emergencies, is thus necessarily very limited in this country. As to public charity, an appeal to a charitable institution is considered even in Poland a mark of social downfall; it is even more of a disgrace in the eyes of Polish immigrants here because of the feeling of group responsibility which is imposed, or thought to be imposed by the American milieu. The immigrant has been accustomed to see the wider social group hold every narrower social group within its limits responsible for the behavior of every member; the village praises or blames the family as a whole for the activities of an individual, the parish does the same with reference to the village group, the wider community with reference to the parish or village. The American population is supposed to do the same—and, of course, in some measure actually does the same—with reference to the foreign colony in its midst. Every Pole who accepts the help of American institutions is thus considered not only disgraced personally as a pauper, but as disgracing the whole Polish colony. If in spite of this social attitude many relatively self-respecting individuals do not hesitate to claim assistance from American institutions, it is because they misinterpret the meaning of this assistance and consider it as being *due* to them, taking the institution as part of the whole American social and political system on which they place the blame for the evil befalling them. And thus they expect all kinds of relief and benefits as a perfectly normal method of redressing their grievances. But such misinterpretations are found mainly in unfamiliar situations, and help given in ordinary sickness or after a natural death preserves the traditional character of charity, from whatever source it comes. No individual who has preserved some self-respect will accept it from an American institution

unless his traditional conceptions have been obliterated owing to the new conditions and to insufficient contact with the Polish-American group.

Originally, during the early stages in the evolution of a Polish-American community mutual help is exercised sporadically, from case to case, by means of collections made for the benefit of the individual or family in distress. Naturally, the more settled and well-to-do members of the community on whom most of the burden falls are eager to substitute for this unregulated voluntary assistance a regular system of mutual death and sickness insurance, and thus favor the establishment of an association which will diminish their risks. The very fact that such a regulation of mutual assistance is necessary shows, of course, that the old naïve and unreflective communal solidarity, where each individual had rightful claims on the help of every other individual in a degree dependent on the closeness of their social connection, has been radically modified. As a matter of fact, most of the individuals who under the old system would be the first to be called to assist a member—his nearest relatives and old neighbors—are not here; their function has to be assumed, at least in part, vicariously by relative strangers who in Poland would never be asked to interfere. In the eyes of these, the help which they have to give appears not as a natural duty to be unreflectively performed but as, we might say, an artificial duty, the result of abnormal conditions. And this attitude communicates itself gradually even to those who under the old system would always be obliged to help, as friends and close relatives. The duty to help cannot be disclaimed entirely, for the member in distress is at least a fellow-countryman; but it is no longer connected with the very foundation of social life. Mutual insurance is a reflective solution of this difficulty. It is the best method of escaping the conflict between the rudiments of the old attitudes of communal solidarity, strengthened by the feeling of group responsibility, and the individualistic unwillingness to endorse claims for assistance which no longer seem rooted in the very nature of things. Since communal solidarity was a universal social institution among Polish peasants and the new individualistic attitude develops in all immigrant colonies, it is clear that the institution of mutual insurance, being the effect of this combined cause— pre-existing institution and new social attitude—must be found everywhere in Polish-American society. The individual's own tendency to have a fund assured for himself or his family in case of sickness or death is in the beginning only a secondary matter. It assumes, however, increasing importance as the institutions of mutual insurance in a given community grow in economic power and social opinion begins to appreciate this growth and to require that every individual be adequately insured, while, on the other hand, as we shall see later on, the individual's feeling of responsibility for other members of the colony decreases with the numerical and social progress of the latter. In the older and larger colonies the individual's desire to be insured plays, therefore, perhaps even a greater part in the development of mutual insurance associations than his desire to insure others.

But the "society" founded in a new colony is much more than a mutual insurance institution. Not only does it bring the scattered members of the colony periodically together, thus actively encouraging social intercourse, but it becomes the social organ of the community, the source of all initiative and the instrument for the realization of all plans initiated. This is probably the most important of its functions. In a peasant village there is no need for such an organ, for the territorial concentration and the close social cohesion of the village make direct individual initiative and immediate spontaneous cooperation of the concrete group possible from case to case. For the old country community, the *okolica* which includes a number of villages, the ready institutions of the commune and, in certain matters, the parish are more than sufficient to effect such changes as the community is legally entitled and practically able to introduce into the tra-

ditional system. Thus the cooperative organization which in Poland corresponds to the Polish-American "society," though it may exercise a strong influence over the primary community in which it exists and works, seldom acts as the organ of this community in proposing or realizing plans concerning the community as a whole except, of course, in its own special line of interest—establishment of cooperative shops for public use, public artistic performances, etc. The Polish-American community on the contrary, is too loose socially and territorially to do without an organ and has no old, political or religious centers which could play this rôle, while it needs organized initiative much more than the old Polish community whose activities can run for a long time more or less smoothly in the established channels of the traditional system.

Thus in a new Polish-American colony it is the "society" which assumes the care of the hedonistic interests of the group by organizing balls, picnics, etc., of its intellectual interests by giving theatrical representations, inviting lecturers, subscribing to periodicals; of its religious interests by arranging religious services to which some priest from an older Polish colony is invited. It is a center of information for newcomers, visitors, travellers; it sends to the press news about any opportunities which the locality may offer to Poles. It acts as a representative of the colony in its relations with the central institutions of Polish-American society, and eventually also with American institutions which try to reach the Polish community for political or social purposes. Thus all the campaigns for funds for Poland and for American Liberty Loans were waged in small communities by these associations. Finally, the great work of the society, through which it assures the permanence of the social cohesion of the colony, gains extraordinary prestige and security, though at the same time resigning its exclusive leadership, is the foundation of a parish.

When studying this most important Polish-American institution we should again be careful not to ascribe too much significance to its external form and official purpose. Just as the "benefit society" is much more than a mutual insurance company, so the Polish-American parish is much more than a religious association for common worship under the leadership of a priest. The unique power of the parish in Polish-American life, much greater than in even the most conservative peasant communities in Poland, cannot be explained by the predominance of religious interests which, like all other traditional social attitudes, are weakened by emigration, though they seem to be the last to disappear completely. The parish is, indeed, simply the old primary community, reorganized and concentrated. In its concrete totality it is a substitute for both the narrower but more coherent village-group and the wider but more diffuse and vaguely outlined okolica. In its institutional organization it performs the functions which in Poland are fulfilled by both the parish and the commune.[4] It does not control the life of its members as efficiently as did the old community for, first of all, it seldom covers a given territory entirely and is unable to compel every one living within this territory to belong to it; secondly, its stock of socially recognized rules and forms of behavior is much poorer; thirdly, the attitudes of its members evolve too rapidly in the new conditions; finally, it has no backing for its coercive measures in the wider society of which it is a part. But its activities are much broader and more complex than those of a parish or of a commune in the old country.

Its religious character is, of course, important in itself since there is a certain minimum of religious ceremonies—christenings, weddings, funerals—which are considered absolutely indispensable even by the least religious among the immigrants and which are sufficient to justify the existence of a church and a priest in the eyes of all of them. The

majority consider the Sunday service—at least the mass—and even more the Easter confession as also essential. But all these purely religious needs could be satisfied almost as well and at less expense by joining the local Irish-American church with an occasional visit from a Polish priest for confession and a sermon. It would even seem to be the wiser course, since the Irish-American clergy, coming from a better social class, better controlled by its bishops and by American society and having to compete with the Protestant churches, are on a much higher intellectual and moral level than the Polish-American clergy, recruited from an uneducated milieu and exercising their power without any competition and practically uncontrolled except by the Polish-American society which not only does not have very high standards but is bound by its own interests to support them even while criticizing them.[5] If the Poles with few exceptions refuse to join Irish-American parishes it is because what the Polish colony really wishes in establishing a parish is not merely religious services but a community center of its own.

Of course a church is for many reasons best fitted for this purpose. The religious activities, even when religious interests are weakened, still constitute a very good foundation for community organization, first because every member, man, woman or child, can share in them, secondly because among the Polish peasants, where the mystical current is very low and heterodoxy therefore very rare, religion is less apt to give birth to struggle and competition than political or economic activities. The church organization is familiar to every member of the community, it has firmly established forms and well-trained professional leaders, and it introduces at once a contact between the activities of the community and a world-wide system of activities—all advantages which in

---

[4]Mr. Bronislaw Kulakowski, of New York, first attracted our attention to the social rather than religious character of the Polish-American parish. He identifies it sociologically with the old Slavic commune. We cannot, however, follow this analogy to the end, since in the preceding volumes we have studied only the modern social organization of the peasants.

[5]The American Catholic Church does not dare to interfere too much with the education and morals of Polish priests lest the latter emancipate themselves from the control of Rome altogether and join the Independent Polish Church.

any other field of social cooperation could be gained only after long efforts. The church building with its annexes is a traditional object of the æsthetic interest of the community and can easily become a *locus* for all important common activities, to which its more or less marked sacred character imparts a kind of superior sanction and official meaning.

But it is clear that the Irish-American church, though on the religious side its organization is similar, can never become for the Polish community anything more than a religious institution; its framework cannot be successfully utilized by the Poles for other social purposes, since they do not feel "at home" in a parish whose prevalent language and mores are different and with whose other members they have no social connections. The parish is not "their own" product, they have less control over its management than over that of a Polish parish which they have founded by free cooperation, they get little encouragement for the various common activities which they wish to initiate and obtain little prestige by their achievements; they cannot use the parish system to satisfy their desire for personal recognition, and so on. In short, unless they are already Americanized individually they do not get out of the English-speaking Catholic parish any satisfaction of their "social instinct." Of course if they are not numerous enough to establish a parish of their own, many join the nearest Irish-American church, which then becomes an important factor of their Americanization. But in this case a large proportion—all those whose religious interests are not particularly strong—remain outside of all religious life.

It is a mistake to suppose that a "community center" established by American social agencies can in its present form even approximately fulfil the social function of a Polish parish. It is an institutuion imposed from the outside instead of being freely developed by the initiative and cooperation of the people themselves and this, in addition to its racially unfamiliar character, would be enough to prevent it from exercising any deep social influence. Its managers usually know little or nothing of the traditions, attitudes and native language of the people with whom they have to deal, and therefore could not become genuine social leaders under any conditions. The institution is based on the type of a "club," which is entirely unknown to the Polish peasant. Whatever common activities it tries to develop are almost exclusively "leisure time" activities; and while these undoubtedly do correspond to a real social need, they are not sufficient by themselves to keep a community together and should be treated only as a desirable superstructure to be raised upon a strong foundation of *economic* cooperation. Whatever real assistance the American social center gives to the immigrant community is the result of the "case method," which consists in dealing directly and separately with individuals or families. While this method may bring efficient temporary help to the individual it does not contribute to the social progress of the community nor does it possess much preventive influence in struggling against social disorganization. Both these purposes can be attained only by organizing and encouraging social self-help on the cooperative basis. Finally, in their relations with immigrants the American social workers usually assume, consciously or not, the attitude of a kindly and protective superiority, occasionally, though seldom, verging on despotism. This attitude may be accepted by peasants fresh from the old country where they have been accustomed to it in their relations with the higher classes, but it is apt to provoke indignation in those who, after a longer stay in this country, have acquired a high racial and personal self-consciousness. In either case the result is the same. The immigrant associates his connections with the American institution with humiliation, submitted to willingly or unwillingly, whereas in his own Polish institutions not only his self-consciousness is respected, but he expects and easily obtains personal recognition. Of course his priest has also a strong attitude of superiority, but this is fully justified in the peasant's eyes by his sacral character.

We see that the parish as instrument for the unification and organization of the Polish-American community is thus quite unrivalled. The radical elements among Polish immigrants have sometimes tried to oppose its influence by establishing a lay community center, for instance, a theater. But except in large colonies such as Chicago, Detroit, Milwaukee, Pittsburgh or Buffalo, where community life is too complex to concentrate itself entirely around parishes, these efforts seem to have met but little success, since even the majority of those who are opposed to the control of the clergy—the so-called "national" party—still group their local life around the church and cooperate in parish activities.

However, the establishment of a new Polish-American parish meets with many obstacles. The parish has to be recognized and its rector appointed by the bishop. But the bishop, usually an Irish-American, is not inclined to favor the development of foreign-speaking parishes within his diocese. His opposition is further stimulated by the local Irish-American priest who wants the Polish sheep in his sheepstall, and by the Polish priest of the nearest Polish-American parish who expects them to come to his church on important occasions or to build a chapel and invite him or his vicar to come once or twice a month to perform the services. The latter solution is usually accepted provisionally as long as the colony is relatively small and poor. But if the Polish parish is not near enough, or if the colony increases rapidly, or if its "society" is strong and ambitious and has active and independent leaders, the matter is soon taken up again. Sometimes the opposition of the bishop is broken by an appeal to Rome, where the Polish-American clergy has influential connections due to the order of the Redemptionists. . . . Sometimes a different weapon is resorted to, particularly if the colony has many "free-thinkers." (A very moderate degree of heterodoxy is usually enough to earn this name.) These suggest the establishment of an "independent" parish, *i.e.,* a parish which, while pre-

serving most of the traditional Catholic dogmas and ceremonies, does not belong to the Roman Catholic Church and does not recognize the authority of the Pope nor of the Roman Catholic bishops. The proposition may be accepted by the community. In fact there are at this moment nearly 50 "independent" Polish parishes unified into a "Polish National Church," whose head is Bishop Hodur of Scranton, Pa., besides an unknown number of isolated independent parishes which have not joined this church. The establishment of an independent parish is easy if the community agrees, for any member of the Roman Catholic clergy who is willing to emancipate himself from the Roman Catholic Church is acceptable as priest. The Polish National Church requires also the rejection of a few dogmas, the chief of which is belief in Hell and the use of Polish instead of Latin during the mass; but among the young vicars, who are often badly treated by their rectors, many would gladly accept an invitation to become the rector of an independent parish. More frequently, however, the American Catholic bishop, in view of this danger of heresy, yields to the demand of the Polish colony and recognizes the new parish and appoints a priest for it.

When the parish has been organized the mutual help association to which this organization is due ceases to be, of course, the central and only representative institution of the community, for the leadership naturally passes into the hands of the priest. But it does not surrender entirely any of its social functions; it simply shares the initiative in communal matters and the representation of the community with the priest on the one hand, and on the other hand with the other associations which now begin to appear in rapid succession. The establishment of the parish opens new fields of social activity, widens the sphere of interests and calls for more and better social cooperation. For *the ideal of the development of the community,* which did not consciously exist while the community had no organ and was only vaguely conceived and intermittently realized during the period when the local mutual help "society" played the leading rôle, becomes now clearly formulated as the common ideal of the whole group and relentlessly pursued. The existence of a framework for the permanent organization of the community in the form of a parish produces both a tendency to utilize this framework to the full extent of its possibilities and a corresponding desire to see the community grow in numbers, wealth, cohesion and complexity of activities. While individualistic motives—economic reasons with those whose living depends on the Polish colony, desire for wider recognition with those who fulfill public functions, etc.—may give a strong additional incentive to individual activities tending to realize this ideal, the chief foundation of the latter is social. It is the same "community spirit" which makes the individual identify his interests with those of his group in the "we"-feeling which makes the mass of the population of a state desire its expansion. We shall see the fundamental part which this aspiration to have one's group grow plays in the development of all Polish-American institutions.

The priest, far from limiting the activities of local associations, favors their development and utilizes them consistently as instruments for all purposes connected with the progress of the parish. While in Polish country parishes the chief method of obtaining the cooperation of the community in matters connected with the church is an appeal to the large mass of parishioners directly or through the parish council, in Polish cities the help of religious "fraternities" is largely used for such purposes as special religious celebrations and pilgrimages, æsthetic improvements of the church building, development of church music and song, organization of charities, etc. In America this system of collaboration of organized groups is extended in two ways. First, in addition to religious fraternities, which are for the most part initiated by the priest himself for purely devotional purposes and remain under his complete control, lay associations with economic

or cultural purposes, and more or less independent of the priest, are also expected to contribute to the aims of the parish. Secondly, these aims are no longer limited to matters of cult and charity, but embrace all fields of social life.

Immediately after the completion of the church or even before, the parish school is organized. Usually the church is planned as a two-story building, the lower story including class rooms and halls for small meetings. Sometimes a private house is rented or bought for school purposes. Both arrangements prove only provisional usually, for the growth of the parish sooner or later forces it to erect a special school building. There are many parishes—five in Chicago alone—whose school is attended by more than 2,000 children. The teachers are mainly nuns of the various teaching orders, though sometimes priests and lay men-teachers are also found, particularly in the larger colonies. Polish and English are both employed as teaching languages, the proportion varying in different schools.

We cannot study here the much discussed question of the educational inferiority or superiority of parochial schools as compared with public schools. Good or bad, the parochial school is a social product of the immigrant group and satisfies important needs of the latter. The most essential point is neither the religious character of the parochial school, nor even the fact that it serves to preserve in the young generation the language and cultural traditions of the old country; it is the function of the parochial school as a factor of the social unity of the immigrant colony and of its continuity through successive generations. The school is a new, concrete, institutional bond between the immigrants. Its first effect is to bring them territorially together, for it has been noticed that proximity to the school—where the children must go every day—is considered even more desirable than proximity to the church. Further, the education of the children is an interest common to all members, just as the religious interest, and this community is fostered by the participation of the parents in all school celebrations and festivities. But even more important than this unification of the old generation is the bond which the parish school creates between the old and the young generation. Whereas children who go to public school become completely estranged from their parents, if these are immigrants, the parish school, in spite of the fact that its program of studies is in many respects similar to that of the public school, in a large measure prevents this estrangement, not only because it makes the children acquainted with their parents' religion, language and national history but also because it inculcates respect for these traditional values and for the nation from which they came. Moreover the school is not only a common bond between all the members of the old generation but is also considered by the young generation as their own institution thus fostering their interest in the affairs of the Polish-American colony. The parochial school is a necessary expression of the tendency of the immigrant community to self-preservation and self-development.

Some large and wealthy parishes have gone further still and established high schools. One—the parish of St. Stanislaus Kostka in Chicago—has even founded a college which is, however, only a little more than a high school. In these cases some economic help from other parishes is expected and obtained, so that these institutions though located within the territories of certain parishes are already in a measure part of the superterritorial Polish-American system. Quite above the territorial parochial organization are such educational institutions as seminaries for priest and for teachers, and the College of the Polish National Alliance in Cambridge Springs, Pa.

The social attitudes manifested with reference to questions of public charity and social work in general are interesting. It has been noticed that as compared, for instance with the Jewish charitable institutions, the Poles in America have little to show in this line. Care for orphans and care for the old and incurable are practically the only problems which are more or less seriously dealth with; in other fields initiative is rare and realization insufficient. The few charitable institutions belong for the most part to the superterritorial system, and seldom to territorial communities. They are due to the personal efforts of a few leading members of Polish-American society acting through the church and influenced by Christian principles rather than to the recognition of altruistic obligations by the society at large. In a word, no social need to take care of the weak seems to be felt by Polish-American communities. This seems strange in view of the old traditions of social solidarity and of the fact that in the beginning of the development of a new colony, as we saw above, assistance is invariably given to the needy. The more coherent and self-conscious the community becomes, the less is it inclined to bother with the misadapted and the disabled. This is simply a manifestation of the tendency of the group to self-preservation, made possible by the facility of excluding the weak members from, or more exactly, of not including them in the community system. As long as the community is small and loose, scattered among Americans, any "fellow-countryman" belongs to it by the same right as any other, and common national origin connected with the feeling of group responsibility before American society is sufficient to maintain the obligation to help in distress. But when the community has grown large and has more or less concentrated itself territorially and created by social cooperation a system of institutions, it becomes more exclusive. It is no longer sufficient to be a Pole and to live in the given locality in order to be considered a member of the community, the subject of social rights and the object of social responsibility. The individual must voluntarily cooperate in the construction and development of the social system of the community, join the parish and one or more of the local associations, contribute economically to common aims and take part in common activities. Unless he does this he is an outsider with reference to whom the community has no obligations and for whom it does not feel responsible before American social opinion, because it is proud of its positive achievements in social organization and, imagining that American society knows and appreciates its work, does not think that this appreciation can be counterbalanced by any individual cases of despondency or pauperism which may be found among the Poles not actually belonging to the organization.

In a new form we find here the well-known old method of dealing with the undesirable individual—the method of severing all connection between this individual and the group. But in groups whose social unity is chiefly based on ties of kinship or on the exclusive control of a given territory the undesirable individual is primarily the anti-social individual, and the individual who is merely inefficient is seldom explicitly qualified as undesirable and, with rare exceptions, is kept within the group, unless the solidarity of the latter has been weakened as a consequence of social disorganization; whereas in a group whose social unity is the result of conscious efforts the mere inability or unwillingness to participate in these efforts is sufficient to disqualify the individual. Nothing shows more clearly the difference between the old organization which we have found among the peasants in Poland and the Polish-American social system than the fact that the same phenomenon—ignoring or dropping the inefficient and misadapted—which there was a sign of weakness and decay is here a mark of strength and growth. The moral reason by which the Polish-American community justifies its apparent egotism is found in the very basis of its organization. The latter is socially and economically an organization for self-help; its first purpose is to prevent the individual from becoming a burden to the community, and the individual who does not choose to avail himself of the opportunities which this organization offers voluntarily resigns all claims to the help of the group. If the latter still feels obliged to assist in some measure the orphans, the old and the incurables, it is only in so far as it feels that the system of mutual insurance is not yet efficient enough to cover these cases adequately.

Of course since the Polish-American community tends to ignore even the merely inefficient, we cannot expect it to take any care of the demoralized. The contrast is striking between the intense reformatory activities found in Poland . . . and the entire lack of interest in reformatory work in this country. Individual demoralization is either ignored or the demoralized individual is simply dropped at once. No one bothers about the innumerable cases of family decay, juvenile delinquency, alcoholism, vagabondage, crime. Few know the full extent of the demoralization going on among American Poles. We expect that the study of demoralization which constitutes the second part of this volume and is based on American sources will be a painful surprise to most of the constructive elements of Polish-American society. Here again the contrast with peasant communities in Poland is instructive. The latter could not get rid of demoralized individuals unless demoralization had proceeded as far as crime. Thus, they had to make efforts to control their anti-social members. Further, the community was the only social milieu of the individual, and the closeness and complexity of social contacts were such that every action of the individual more or less affected the group, whereas here the Polish-American community can easily cut off a harmful member by excluding him from its organizations or, in radical cases, giving him up to American institutions. The problem is solved as soon as raised. But it seldom has to be raised at all, for the Polish-American community does not claim to absorb the individual completely; it is not necessarily and directly affected by everything he does in his private circle or in his contacts with American society. It needs only a part of his activity for its social purposes, and as long as he remains able to perform this part and does not draw others into conflict with American social opinion and law, it matters little to the parish or the local association what else he does or does not do. In Polish country communities the interest of the group is to know everything about the individual and to control his entire behavior, whereas the interest of the Polish-American community is to leave out of consideration anything in the individual's past and present which has no direct bearing on his positive social obligations so as not to impair the growth of its institutions by scrutinizing too closely the private life of those who can be useful in its public affairs. Of course there is gossip, which represents a degenerate remnant of the social opinion of the primary group. The clergy still, though vaguely and impersonally, preach against sin in private life and continue to exercise some of their old reformatory influence through confession. A few idealists from the old country, imperfectly adapted to local conditions, and some religious or political *revoltés* disclose through the press the private life histories of certain prominent members of Polish-American communities. In general, however, by a tacit understanding individuals enjoy immunity from social control in all except their social activities in Polish-American institutions.

This does not mean, however, that the Polish-American community does not attempt to extend the field of its control. The method reflectively or unreflectively used for this purpose can perhaps never completely subordinate all individuals in all respects to the influence of the group, but is very efficient as far as it goes. We may characterize it as aiming 1) to attract every individual into the sphere of public activities and to open for him the way to social prominence in some field; 2) to institutionalize as many activities as possible. The first tendency is manifested very clearly. By multiplying indefinitely associations and circles, and by a very active propaganda exercised through all possible mediums, nearly all the members of the parish—men, women and young people— even those who for some reason or other have not yet joined the parish or have dropped

out, can become in some way connected with the system and thus acquire a minimum of public character. This public character grows whenever an individual is, even if only momentarily, connected as public functionary with some scheme for common action—religious ceremony, entertainment, meeting, bazaar, collection for a social purpose, etc.—and this increased public importance is every year attained by a large proportion of the community. The highest degree of public dignity is, of course, the share of those who are elected officers in associations or become members of permanent committees or directors of institutions; and if we realize that every association has from 6 to 20 officials, that every committee numbers on the average 10 members and that some large parishes have more than 70 associations and committees while even a small parish has at least a dozen of them, we see that every active and fairly intelligent individual of whatever sex and age, is sure of becoming some time a public dignitary; and even if the existing organization does not give him enough opportunities, he can always initiate a new institution and gain recognition as organizer and charter member.

By thus giving the individual favorable attention and inducing him to take voluntarily a place "in the limelight" among the leaders, the community controls him better than by making him a passive object of its "ordering and forbidding" regulations, particularly when the latter cannot be physically enforced. The conscious purpose of the multiplication of public "dignities" is to interest personally as many members as possible in the development of the community and to give everybody a chance to get recognition. But the individual who believes himself elected for his positive qualities, who feels that public opinion is interested in his behavior (and usually exaggerates this interest), and who knows that the community expects him to be and to remain superior to the average, usually tries to adapt his behavior, if not his character, to these expectations. It happens, of course, that an individual placed in a responsible position with opportunities for abuse cannot withstand the temptation, particularly if the position is too far above his intellectual and moral capacities, as is sometimes the case with officials of the great super-territorial institutions which have outgrown the level of their leaders. Such cases are, however, rare in territorial communities and small local institutions, and the often ridiculous vanity and importance of the innumerable "public dignitaries" are more than offset by their positive qualities. This moralizing influence of "public dignities" is, of course, noticeable only with members of the communities who owe their positions to election and are raised above the level by social opinion. Positions which are obtained by appointment and superiorities based not upon the recognition of the community but upon other factors, such as the sacral character of the priest, economic supremacy, "jobs" in American institutions, fail to produce the same effect, for the individual considers himself independent of the community and above social opinion.

The other method of extending social control—institutionalization of activities—is evidently involved in the very organization of the community. The church and church associations institutionalize religious activities, the mutual insurance associations certain economic interests, and the parish school education. This method is further extended to other fields. Thus public entertainments under the auspices of local associations or parochial committees play a large part in the life of a Polish-American colony and are gradually taking the place of private entertainments; and if we remember that a hall, a picnic, a theatrical representation or a concert with a mixed program—song, music, recitals, speeches require much time and energy in its preparation, we see that by this means a large proportion of individual activities are transferred from private to public life and subjected to social control. A custom which has an old origin but has been developed to an unprecedented extent during the war—the custom of making a collection

for some public purpose at all weddings, christenings, etc.—gives even to private entertainments some institutional meaning. Among the local associations we find theatrical and literary circles and even circles for sewing and crocheting in common at periodical meetings. Informally and unreflectively, buying and selling have become more or less a public matter, for every Polish-American shop is a meeting-place for the neighborhood, where private and public matters are discussed. It would seem that the best way to institutionalize all leisure-time activities would be to introduce the Anglo-American principle of clubs. Strangely, however, the club does not seem to thrive in Polish-American communities. A few associations (particularly the *sokol,* a gymnastic organization) have, indeed, become clubs by acquiring houses of their own which are continually open to members, establishing reading rooms, dining-rooms, billiard rooms, gymnasiums, etc., but the use made of these club arrangements is still very limited. Attempts have been made to establish clubs for young people, and some have been successful; but the failures are more striking than the successes, for they show that for the Polish immigrant, just as for the Polish peasant in the old country, the institutionalization of leisure time activities is still indissolubly connected with the excitement of public meetings.

The double tendency to draw as many personalities and activities as possible into the sphere of public attention culminates in the press. The wealth of printed material bearing on the local life of Polish-American colonies is surprising, particularly if compared with the limited use which primary communities in Poland make of the press. Whereas the popular press there is mainly an instrument for the unification and centralization of many primary communities into a wider community, here its predominant functions are to express, perpetuate, control and unify the social life of each particular primary community. Of course professional publications and those connected with the super-territorial Polish-American system have other purposes similar to those of the popular press in Poland; but even these, the newspapers in particular, have to serve in some measure the interests of the local communities within which they are published.

The desire of the Polish-American community to give its personalities and activities official publicity and to have them recorded for the future manifests itself at first chiefly, as in Poland, in correspondence addressed to the Polish newspapers which are published in neighboring Polish-American centers or are the organs of super-territorial institutions. But very early it begins to show a tendency to have a press of its own in the form at least of commemorative pamphlets and sheets— statutes and yearly accounts of associations, programs of meetings, records of successive steps in the organization of the parish, etc. Publicity has to remain on this stage until some local newspaper is started which, of course, is possible only when the colony is numerous or is a center of several small colonies scattered in the neighborhood. The local newspaper originates in various ways. Sometimes it is started as a political organ connected with an institution which is strong enough to support it and make it an instrument of propagation; in these cases it usually develops into a super-territorial publication serving the interests of a party of cooperative organization and only secondarily those of the local community. Such has been the history of several newspapers which have come to play an important rôle in Polish-American national life. Sometimes the priest initiates the publication of a paper devoted at first chiefly to religious matters, and then the printing-office may be used also for the publication of religious pamphlets and books. Such a paper, to which the parish or at least its religious associations are usually made to contribute in some form, either becomes slightly secularized and, by paying attention to all local affairs, fulfils the function of a community organ, or continues to serve the more exclusively professional interests of the church in general, and in this case may obtain a country-wide circulation; or it com-

bines both the local and the professional religious functions, as in the case, for instance, with the organ of the Polish National Church, published in Scranton, and with several Roman-Catholic papers. In other cases the newspaper is supported by some business man—banker, real estate agent, owner of a printing-office—and then it is an instrument for advertising his business or helping to raise his standing in American circles. But often, particularly in the larger American cities, where there is the hope of obtaining advertisements from American firms, the foundation of a newspaper is a free personal enterprise, motivated by idealistic reasons or by the desire for recognition, or treated as purely private business. Then the newspaper cannot be anything else than an organ of the community, for its circulation and its very existence depend entirely on the way it expresses the social life of the group.

Through this organ not only the attention of which the public personalities and activities are the object is continually revived (for the paper prints, of course, all the records of public institutions, meetings, etc.) but many individuals and facts which otherwise would remain private and would be at most objects of unregulated gossip are drawn into the circle of official public interest. The newspaper becomes a factor of prime importance in community life, for it partly reorganizes the degenerated and disorganized social opinion which, as we have seen in our first volumes, was the main factor of unity and control of the primary group in the old country. It does this on a new basis which is not perhaps as solid as the old, for social opinion is no longer formed by the community directly in personal contacts but indirectly through the instrumentality of print and through the medium of the editor, whose own personality constitutes an incalculable factor of variation. And yet when the old standards by which the community spontaneously selected and judged phenomena of public importance are no longer strong enough to assure without conscious regulation a unified and consistent social opinion, the concentration of news in a specialized organ which standardizes it before spreading it around is probably the only way of substituting some uniformity, order and public spirit for the chaos of gossip.

An interesting development in the same line is the so-called "album" of the parish, a commemorative publication which in older parishes is issued on important anniversaries by the parish committee presided over by the priest and contains an illustrated history of the parish up to date, with brief records of all the institutions included within its limits, collective photographs of all the associations, portraits and short biographies of the most prominent members and families, etc.—in short, a perfectly standardized synopsis of everything which social opinion considers worth knowing and remembering about the community.

Simultaneously with this process of social organization of the Polish-American group its territorial concentration goes on. There is, of course, a certain minimum of concentration preceding the establishment of the parish and resulting from the tendency of the immigrants to be sufficiently near one another for frequent social intercourse. But this tendency alone cannot completely counterbalance the desire to live near the place of work and results only in drawing together the Poles who work in the same or neighboring factories and shops. In large cities the obstacle of distance is only partially overcome and if the colony grows fast each separate neighborhood tends to become the nucleus of a separate parish. This is, for instance, the case in Chicago, where we find three large Polish neighborhoods, each including several primary parish-communities—located on the north side, around the stockyards, and in South Chicago—and a number of smaller ones, each constituting an independent primary-community. If the colony remains small, relatively to the size of the city, it may not form any territorially concentrated communities even after parishes have been established. This is the case in New York, where no exclusively Polish neighborhoods exist.

This situation, however, is rare; usually the majority of the members of a parish gather around their church and school. This process is consciously fostered by the parish committee and the priest who endeavor to select the location for the church as close as possible to the centers where most of the Poles work and also take care to choose a neighborhood where rent is low and real estate cheap. If the choice has been successful the process of territorial concentration begins at once. The original population of the district is slowly but ceaselessly driven away, for an Irish, German or Italian tenant or houseowner who sees Polish families take the place of his former neighbors and knows that they have come to stay near their parish-center soon moves to a more congenial neighborhood. At the same time a Polish real estate agency or, on a higher stage of social organization, a building association or a cooperative savings and loan bank pursues a campaign among the Poles which leads to a progressive transfer of houses and vacant lots into Polish hands. The campaign favored by the parish leaders from social considerations is evidently also good business, for the same reasons which make the neighborhood of the Polish church less valuable for other national groups raise its value for the Poles. The very growth of concentration produces new factors of further concentration. Polish shops, originally selling everything indispensable for the household and later specializing as various businesses—groceries, liquor, shoes, clothes, photographs, books, banking, undertaking, contracting—attract Polish customers and consciously contribute to the Polonization of the neighborhood. In the older colonies the entire practical business of the immigrants living near their social center is transacted exclusively with Polish firms. Later still, Polish professional men, chiefly lawyers and physicians, settle in the colony or at least have offices there. Curiously, the Jews who in Poland almost monopolize small trade in provincial localities, here relatively seldom settle within a Polish neighborhood; though they try to reach

Polish customers also, they evidently, with rare exceptions, do not wish to limit the sphere of their business to one immigrant group.

The evolution of the Polish community in this country is thus in a sense the reverse of the evolution of primary peasant communities in Poland. Whereas territorial vicinity is there the original foundation of community life, and all social organization is built upon this basis, here reflective social organization becomes the main factor of territorial concentration. When, however, the latter has been in a considerable measure achieved the process is reversed again and social organization, just as in Poland, begins to depend on territorial neighborhood.

This is well exemplified by the history of secessionist groups. The latter exist in every community, for the subordination of all social life to the parish system always meets some opposition, particularly because it leads to a supremacy of the clergy. The reason for opposition is more or less a matter of principle, but no doubt personal antagonisms often contribute to its development. The secessionists form an organization independent of the parish system and often attempt to create a territorial center away from the church in the form of a "national home" as locus for common activities. But since religious activities are not included, and the group lacks the means and the framework for establishing a regular school, and the parish is a well-known old country institution, whereas the national home is an entirely new thing, the latter does not exercise the same attraction as the church in the way of territorial grouping, though it may become an important center of social organization. Therefore in older communities the concentration of the Polish-American colony around the church is usually accepted and utilized by the secessionists who by establishing their social centers near the parish center and developing their activities within the territorial community introduce new complications into Polish-American life.

There are two important types of se-

cessionist groups—the "nationalists" and the socialists. We shall study these groups in the next chapter as components of the superterritorial Polish-American organization where they play a very important part, more important, indeed, than those groups which are integral parts of the parish system. But there is no doubt that as elements of the territorial organization of the community they are relatively weak. The only way in which they can obtain predominance in community life is not by opposing another local organization to the parish organization but by becoming a part of the parish organization and controlling it. This is naturally often the case with "independent" parishes; but there are also Roman-Catholic parishes in which "nationalistic" organizations have the upper hand even in the parish activities. These parishes—as, for instance, the Holy Trinity in Chicago—are usually characterized by a more democratic spirit, a greater independence with reference to the theocratic policy of the clergy, and the higher intellectual and moral level of their priests; and of course the parish as a form of community organization is strengthened by the cooperation of its more liberal elements. But the parishes are more numerous in which the "nationalist" associations resign themselves to the rôle of forming a minority opposition *within* the parish, while acknowledging some common interests with the majority, and there remain a large number of communities where nationalist associations stay *outside* of and in permanent opposition to the whole parish system. The institutions initiated or controlled by socialists are still more consistent and active in struggling for a lay community organization. Thus the parish can seldom if ever permanently monopolize all the social life of the community, particularly as its opponents have usually most of the intelligent members of the colony on their side. And even if it succeeds in overcoming active opposition, it cannot prevent the increasingly rapid growth of associations which, while not aiming to supplant it as community center, wish to remain free and separate from the parochial system, and do not care to cooperate in its development. To this class belong, besides some mutual help organizations, many of the gymnastic, educational and professional societies. In every large community there are thus a number of small social circles whose functions are independent of those of the parish. Nevertheless, the latter continues to keep its hold through religion and primary education upon individual members of those circles, with the exception of the socialists and a few free-thinkers.

The Japanese-American Experience: 1890–1940

ROGER DANIELS

In 1942 apprehensive Californians culminated nine decades of anti-Oriental agitation by encouraging John L. DeWitt, commanding general of Western Defense Command of the United States Army, to recommend relocation of all Japanese and their descendants living in the state to detention camps farther inland. Eugene Rostow later characterized these places as "little better than concentration camps." While Americans of Japanese descent were deprived of their citizenship rights, the much larger contingent of this ethnic group residing in Hawaii remained free, as did German and Italian aliens on the mainland. Clearly, race prejudice rather than considerations of national defense dictated the policy of incarceration. The Japanese, along with the Jews and in contrast to other immigrant enclaves, incurred ill-feeling by rising too rapidly above their economic and social beginnings in this country. Both minorities, the best educated and most upwardly mobile of the immigrant groups, evoked similar types of hostility. They were labeled shrewd and hard working but essentially untrustworthy. Hence, in the aftermath of the "sneak attack" on Pearl Harbor, Japanese-Americans were regarded as a fifth column. Roger Daniels in the following essay shows how the decision for internment grew out of the history of the Japanese settlement in California. He focuses on the type of life the newcomers made for themselves and the difficulties made for them by the bigotry of other Californians.

After the war anti-Japanese sentiment declined. Before 1905, when victory over Russia made Nippon a threat to American interests in China, Japan was well regarded as a protégé of the United States. During the cold war, when China was considered our chief foe in the Far East, and Japan once again came under our wing, the old paternalism reasserted itself. Improvement in relations between these nations enhanced the status and image of Japanese already here, and of the 100,000 arrivals since 1950. In 1948 a proposition on the California ballot to make the alien laws harsher was defeated at the polls, the first time an anti-Japanese referendum in that state ever failed to secure a majority vote. Four years later the 1913 Alien Land Act, which had been passed to prevent Japanese residents from owning land, was declared unconstitutional by the California Supreme Court. In 1952 the McCarran-Walter Immigration Act lifted the ban on Asian entry and the exclusion of Asians from citizenship. By the 1960s public opinion polls disclosed that most people now considered Japanese immigrants (Issei) and their offspring (Nisei) desirable citizens, trustworthy human beings, and loyal Americans. Japanese-Americans responded well to their recently acquired favorable standing and their new acceptance accelerated the pace and extent of assimilation. By the 1950s they had attained a higher educational level than did Caucasians, and currently nearly 90 percent of third-generation members of this ethnic minority go to college, a proportion equaled only by Jews. An even more crucial measure of assimilation, interracial marriage records, show that contemporary Nisei are choosing white spouses about half the time.

According to the Census of 1940 there were 126,948 Japanese Americans in the continental United States; they comprised less than one-tenth of 1 percent of the total population. Had they been dispersed evenly throughout the country—as Secretary of State William Jennings Bryan once proposed—there would have been about forty individuals in each American county. But, like almost all other ethnic groups throughout our history, the Japanese Americans tended to cluster. Almost nine out of ten lived in one of the three Pacific Coast states, with nearly three-quarters of the total found inside the borders of California. Within that state too, there was clustering. More than one-third of the state's Japanese Americans were in Los Angeles County, while six other counties (of a total of fifty-eight) accounted for almost another third. But even in the area of highest concentration of their population—Los Angeles County—persons of Japanese origin were a tiny minority. Out of every thousand Angelenos, sixteen were Japanese. How was it then that such an infinitesimal portion of the whole population could inspire such fear and hatred in the rest of the American people? How could such a group provoke so totalitarian a response from a government dedicated to "life, liberty, and the pursuit of happiness"? These are the questions that this book seeks to answer. As will become obvious, the answers are more to be sought within the larger society than by an examination of the minority. In the final analysis, one must explain the culprits, not the victims. But an understanding of the victims is necessary. The evacuation of 1942 did not occur in a vacuum, but was based on almost a century of anti-Oriental fear, prejudice, and misunderstanding.

The immigrants from Japan who began to arrive in the United States in significant numbers after 1890 (Japan had legalized emigration only in 1885) already had two strikes against them. The western United States in general and California in particular had learned to despise Orientals before this Japanese migration began. Immigration from China, starting at about the same time as the gold rush of 1849, had created an entirely new strain of American racism from which the Japanese Americans were to suffer greatly. The anti-Orientalism of California and the West was separate from but certainly related to the general prejudice against colored people—"the lesser breeds without the law" as Kipling put it—which was endemic to white Americans from almost the very beginning of our history. Similar prejudices, usually called nativism, were exhibited even against white people if they happened not to speak English or practiced a non-Protestant variant of Christianity. But even within the general ethnocentric intolerance of American society, anti-Orientalism was something special.

The earliest Chinese immigrants were not particularly mistreated. Their outlandish costumes and unique appearance—apart from "color" most Chinese men wore their hair in long pigtails, or queues—added merely another exotic note to the polyglot cosmopolitanism of gold rush San Francisco. The fantastic boom then in progress made any addition to the labor force welcome, and these earliest immigrants found a ready-made economic niche. (The Chinese characters for California can also be translated "golden mountain.") This economic attraction—what historians of immigration call "pull"—coupled with the "push" of Chinese peasant poverty and the existence of cheap and frequent trans-Pacific sail and steamship transportation produced a steady stream of Chinese migration to the United States, as the tables below show.

Relatively speaking, the Chinese were a large fraction of the population of the West in the years after the Civil War. In 1870 Chinese comprised perhaps 10 percent of California's population and almost a fourth of the population of its metropolis, San Francisco. The economic impact of the Chinese was even greater than their numbers would suggest, for almost all of them were adult males who competed with white workingmen for jobs. This competition first asserted itself in the mining districts, but became really acute after the completion of the Union-Central Pacific Railroad in 1869, which had employed some 10,000 Chinese laborers to construct its western leg. From an economic point of view the almost unanimous hostility with which far-western workingmen viewed the Chinese was quite rational. Chinese labor was cheap labor, and far-western labor had been, due to its scarcity, expensive labor. The result of this competition was a popular anti-Chinese movement, led for a while by the immigrant demagogue Dennis Kearney. His rallying cry,

"The Chinese Must Go," is a good shorthand description of the whole movement. Originally the sole property of Kearney's third-party movement, the Workingmen's party, a Chinese exclusion policy was soon appropriated by both Democrats and Republicans, first at the state and regional levels, and then nationally.

But the protest was not solely economic. Based upon the legitimate and understandable economic grievances of western workingmen against what they considered unfair competition (one is reminded of present-day California farm workers' resentment of the importation of Mexican nationals on a temporary basis), the movement soon developed an ideology of white supremacy/Oriental inferiority that was wholly compatible with the mainstream of American racism. Not only did "John Chinaman," as he was often called, "work cheap and smell bad," but he was also subhuman. California courts refused to accept his testimony; municipal ordinances were passed to harass him; the state legislature tried to stop his further immigration; and the California constitution itself, as rewritten in 1879, had an entire anti-Chinese section which, among other things, called upon the legisature to

prescribe all necessary regulations for the protection of the state, and the counties and towns . . . from the burdens and evils arising from the presence of aliens who are and may become . . . dangerous and detrimental to the well-being or peace of the state, and to impose conditions upon which such persons may reside in the state, and to provide the means and modes of their removal.

Apart from "legal" discrimination, the Chinese suffered greatly from individual and mob violence. Since they lived in isolated mining camps or in segregated urban ghettoes, assaults against Chinese were usually witnessed only by other Chinese, whose testimony was inadmissible in court. In a sense, California courts declared an open season on Chinese, who were subjected to everything from casual assault (cutting off a pigtail was a popular sport) to mass murder. The worst

IMMIGRATION OF CHINESE
TO THE UNITED STATES

Years	No. of Immigrants
To 1860	41,443
1861–1870	64,301
1871–1880	123,823

CHINESE POPULATION, BY CENSUS

	United States	Pacific States	California
1860	34,933	—	34,933
1870	63,199	52,841	49,277
1880	104,468	87,828	75,132

single California atrocity occurred in Los Angeles during a one-night rampage in 1871 in which a white mob shot, hanged, and otherwise murdered some twenty Chinese. Other similar mob violence took place throughout the state, and indeed, throughout the West. Outside California the bloodiest outbreak took place in Rock Springs, Wyoming, in 1885 in a massacre of Chinese, originally employed as strikebreakers in a Union Pacific coal mine; twenty-eight were killed and fifteen wounded, and damage to property came to nearly $150,000.

Some employers, outside the West, saw the presence of Chinese as an opportunity. They were brought to New England to break a shoemakers' strike, and some fantastic schemes were hatched to use Chinese as substitutes for newly freed and fractious Negroes on southern cotton plantations and as a solution to the vexatious "servant problem" that troubled the upper middle class in Gilded Age America. But, in essence, the Chinese question was a western question, and largely a California problem at that.

The West, however, could not solve the problem; to put an end to immigration from China, federal power was required, and by the early 1870s western legislatures and western political parties were petitioning Congress to end Chinese immigration and adopting planks calling for Chinese exclusion. An exclusion bill passed both houses of Congress in Rutherford B. Hayes's administration, but received a Presidential veto. In 1882, however, Chester Alan Arthur reluctantly bowed to Congressional feeling and signed a compromise exclusion bill, barring all Chinese for ten years. The ten-year ban was renewed by Congress in 1892 and then made "permanent" under the progressive administration of Theodore Roosevelt in 1902. A regional problem had required a national solution; that solution was certainly easier to achieve than it might have been for two quite separate reasons. It was easy for most Americans to extend their feelings about the inferiority of the Negro to all "colored races"; in addition, China was a weak, defenseless nation, and the protests of its government did not have to be taken seriously. Chinese exclusion represented the first racist qualification of American immigration policy, although it would not be the last. In addition, the whole anti-Chinese episode in our history served as a kind of prophetic prologue for what would befall immigrants from Japan.

Significant immigration from Japan actually started about 1890. The census of that year enumerated 2039 Japanese in the entire country, more than half of them in California. According to the not always accurate immigration data of the federal government, about 25,000 immigrants came in the 1890s, 125,000 in the peak period of immigration between 1901 and 1908, and then about 10,000 a year until the Immigration Act of 1924 barred further immigration from Japan. During the entire period fewer than 300,000 Japanese were recorded as entering the United States. In comparison to the total immigration picture—between the end of the Civil War and 1924 some 30 million immigrants came to the United States—this is a very small number indeed. But even the 300,000 figure greatly overstates what some publicists like to call the "yellow flood." Cheap and rapid trans-Pacific transportation made it possible for a number of individuals to go back and forth many times. Others were students and "birds of passage," that is, sojourners rather than immigrants. A brief population table will put the demographic data into clearer perspective (see table below). Yet, as we shall see, this tiny population became the focus of local agitation, national concern, and international negotiation and insult. But before we consider the furor that was raised over them, we ought to look at the immigrants themselves.

Immigrants from Japan (hereafter called Issei, from the combination of the Japanese words for "one" and "generation"; their children, the American-born second generation, are Nisei; and the third generation are Sansei) came to the United States for exactly the same kinds of reasons that other immi-

JAPANESE POPULATION, BY CENSUS

	Japanese in U.S.	United States Population	Japanese in California	California Population
1890	2,039	63,000,000	1,147	1,200,000
1900	24,326	76,000,000	10,151	1,500,000
1910	72,157	92,000,000	41,356	2,400,000
1920	111,010	106,000,000	71,952	3,400,000

grants came: for economic opportunity and to escape sever economic and social dislocations at home. The Japan which they left was rapidly undergoing its own industrial revolution. (According to W. W. Rostow, the Japanese economy "took off" between 1878 and 1900.) Unlike many other contemporary immigrant groups however, emigration for the Issei did not mean rejection of the old country. Most of them maintained an interest and a pride in the accomplishments of Japan, a pride that they publicly exhibited on such traditional occasions as the Emperor's birthday or on the occurrence of special events like Admiral Togo's victory over the Russian fleet during the Russo-Japanese War.

For many of the Issei generation, the United States itself was not the first stop. The first significant trans-Pacific migration of Japanese was to the kingdom of Hawaii, where they provided cheap agricultural labor on the semifeudal sugar plantations of the American economic elite. During the period of heaviest immigration (1900–1908) more than 40,000 of the Japanese entering the United States came via Hawaii. The attraction of the United States vis-à-vis Hawaii was simple: wages were higher, hours were shorter, and economic opportunity more abundant. But whether they came by way of Hawaii or directly from Japan, the Issei generation started at the bottom of the economic ladder. Few came with any significant amount of capital; the vast majority were young adult males without family ties. One Issei recently told an interviewer:

I grew up in a farm in Japan. My father owned a fairly large piece of land, but it was heavily mortgaged. I remember how hard we all had to work, and I also remember the hard times. I saw little future in farm work; my older brothers would later run the farm, so at my first good chance I went to work in Osaka. Later I came to California and worked as a laborer in all kinds of jobs. However, for the first five years I had to work in the farms picking fruit, vegetables, and I saved some money. Then I came to live in the city permanently.

This immigrant's experience was, if not typical, common. Most of the Issei came from the Japanese countryside rather than the city; most seem to have come from somewhere above the lowest socioeconomic strata of the population; and most exhibited that combination of energy and ambition which has made the Japanese Americans the most upwardly mobile nonwhite minority in the United States. (If the Japanese had been white Protestants, the tendency would be to attribute their success to what Max Weber and others have called "the Protestant Ethnic." That is, that the "Puritan traits" of honesty, industry, zeal, punctuality, frugality, and regularity advanced the growth of capitalism by promoting rational, systematic economic conduct. Apart from the Japanese, the American ethnic group that best exemplifies these traits are the Jews.) Whatever its cause, the spectacular economic achievement of the Issei generation—especially within agriculture—was an important causal component of the animosity it engendered.

This achievement can be best seen in California, where the bulk of the Issei settled. By 1919 about half of the state's 70,000 Japanese were engaged in agriculture. They controlled over 450,000 acres of agricultural land, some of it among the most fruitful in the state. Although this amounted to only 1 percent of the state's land under cultivation, the labor-intensive agricultural techniques which the Issei brought from Japan produced about 10 percent of the dollar volume of the state's crops. The historian of Japanese American agriculture, Masakazu Iwata, has ably summarized the contribution the Issei made.

First they filled the farm labor vacuum and thus prevented a ruinous slump. . . . Then as independent farm operators, the Japanese with their skill and energy helped to reclaim and improve thousands of acres of worthless lands throughout the State, lands which the white man abhorred, and made them fertile and immensely productive. They pioneered the rice industry, and planted the first citrus orchards in the hog wallow lands in the San Joaquin Valley. They played a vital part in establishing the present system of marketing fruits and vegetables, especially in Los Angeles County, and dominated in the field of commercial truck crops. From the perspective of history, it is evident that the contributions of the Issei. . . . were undeniably a significant factor in making California one of the greatest farming states in the nation.

Most of the Issei farmers achieved a steady but unspectacular prosperity; one Japanese immigrant, however, had a career that reads like a Horatio Alger story, George Shima (he Americanized his name) came to the United States directly from Japan in 1889 at the age of twenty-six with less than $1000 in capital. The son of a relatively prosperous Japanese farm owner, he worked first as a common laborer and then rather quickly became a labor contractor who specialized in marketing the services of his countrymen to white agriculturalists. He invested his profits in hitherto unused land, starting with a leasehold on 15 acres. Working in partnership with other Issei, Shima created his own agricultural empire, specializing in potatoes, then a new crop in California. By 1909 the press was referring to him as the "Potato King" of California. By 1913, when a Japanese graduate student surveyed his holdings, Shima controlled nearly 30,000 acres directly, and, through marketing agreements, handled the produce raised by many

of his compatriots. By 1920 it was estimated that he controlled 85 percent of California's potato crop, valued at over $18 million that year. He employed over 500 persons in a multiracial labor force that included Caucasians. When he died, in 1926, the press estimated his estate at $15 million; his pallbearers included such dignitaries as James Rolph, Jr., the mayor of San Francisco, and David Starr Jordan, the chancellor of Stanford University. In 1909 he bought a house in one of the better residential sections of Berkeley, California, close to the university. A protest movement, led by a professor of classics, demanded that he move to an Oriental neighborhood. Shima held his ground, although he did erect a large redwood fence around the property, as he told the press, "to keep the other children from playing with his." Even an Issei millionaire could not escape the sting of discrimination.

Most of the Issei, whether they lived in the city or the country, did not offend the housing mores of the majority; they lived the segregated life typical of American minority groups. Those who did not go directly into agriculture usually started out as common laborers or domestic servants. Like their rural fellow immigrants, they too demonstrated upward social and economic mobility. Starting with almost token wages—in 1900, $1.50 a week plus board was standard—these immigrants quickly learned English and the "ropes," and moved into better-paying jobs, although several thousand remained domestic servants. Since California trade unions almost universally barred Orientals from membership, work in manufacturing, the building trades, and many other occupations was closed to them. The typical pattern for urban Issei was to establish a small business—a laundry, a restaurant, a curio shop—or to go to work for an Issei businessman who was already established. A great many of these businesses catered to the immigrant community; others provided specialized services to whites (for example, contract gardening) or served as retail marketing outlets for Japanese agriculturalists, usually specializing in produce or flowers. A smaller group—and one that was to arouse special concern after Pearl Harbor—went into commerical fishing; more than any other group of Issei entrepreneurs the fishermen were in direct economic competition with white businessmen. Most other Issei formed a complementary rather than a competing economy. Their businesses employed almost exclusively members of their own ethnic community at lower wages and longer hours than generally prevailed.

If Californians and other westerners had been the rational "economic men" of nineteenth-century classical economic theory, there would have been no anti-Japanese movement. The Issei subeconomy neither lowered wages nor put white men out of work. Its major effect, in fact, was a lowering of the cost of fresh fruit and vegetables for the general population, and Issei agriculture was one of the bases which allowed California's population to expand as rapidly as it did, from less than 1.5 million in 1900 to almost 7 million in 1940. But race prejudice, of course, is not a rational phenomenon, even though in some instances, as in the anti-Chinese movement, it does have a certain economic rationale. Nothing more clearly indicates the nonrational, inherited nature of California's anti-Japanese movement than the fact that it started when there were fewer than a thousand Japanese in the entire state.

The anti-Japanese war cry was first raised by elements of the San Francisco labor movement in 1888, and for the first two decades of agitation labor took the lead, as it had done against the Chinese. In 1892 the demagogue Dennis Kearney returned to the hustings and unsuccessfully tried to base a political comeback on the slogan "The Japs Must go!" and in the same year a San Francisco newspaper launched a self-styled journalistic "crusade" against the menace of Japanese immigration. These first moves were abortive: in 1892 probably not one Californian in ten had even seen a Japanese. But they were indicative of things to come. Just eight years later the real anti-Japanese movement began.

At a meeting sponsored by organized labor, the Democratic mayor of San Francisco, James Duval Phelan, effectively linked the anti-Chinese and anti-Japanese movements. The major purpose of the meeting was to pressure Congress to renew Chinese exclusion, but Phelan pointed out a new danger:

The Japanese are starting the same tide of immigration which we thought we had checked twenty years ago. . . . The Chinese and Japanese are not bona fide citizens. They are not the stuff of which American citizens can be made.

Another speaker at the same meeting was the distinguished sociologist Edward Alysworth Ross, then teaching at Stanford University. Ross rang some changes on Phelan's remarks and made a common analogy with the protective tariff: If we keep out pauper-made goods, he asked, why don't we keep out the pauper? In those years few academics championed the cause of labor (Ross would soon lose his job at Stanford because of his economic views), but most of those who did were opposed to immigrants in general and Oriental immigrants in particular. Although their grounds for this objection were ostensibly economic, most flavored their arguments with racist appeals. The same could be said for most American socialists in the years before 1920. From staid Victor Berger of Milwaukee to flamboyant Jack London of California, socialists insisted that the United States must be kept a white man's country.

These arguments of the left quickly found echoes in the more traditional segments of the political spectrum. During the summer of 1900 all three major political parties—Republicans, Democrats, and Populists—took stands against "Asiatic" immigration, and at the end of the year the national convention of the American Federation of Labor asked Congress to exclude not only Chinese, but all "Mongolians."

Agitation of this sort continued sporadically until 1905; in that year the anti-Japanese movement escalated significantly. The reasons for the escalation are to be sought both inside and outside the United

States. On the world scene, the startling triumph of Japan over czarist Russia in both land and naval battles effectively challenged, for the first time, white military supremacy in Asia and raised the specter of the yellow peril. At home, heightened immigration of Japanese—45,000 came between 1903 and 1905—made the "threat" of Japanese immigration much more real than it had been five years before. In February the San Francisco *Chronicle,* a conservative Republican paper and probably the most influential on the Pacific Coast, began a concerted and deliberate anti-Japanese campaign. The first front-page streamer, THE JAPANESE INVASION, THE PROBLEM OF THE HOUR, set the tone for the whole campaign. In addition to the usual economic and racial arguments, arguments that stressed a lowering of the standard of living and the impossibility of assimilation, the *Chronicle* injected two new and ugly elements into the agitation: sex and war. The paper insisted that Japanese were a menace to American women and that "every one of these immigrants ... is a Japanese spy."

A little more than a week after the *Chronicle's* campaign started, both houses of the California legislature unanimously passed a resolution asking Congress to limit the further immigration of Japanese, Included in a long bill of particulars were statements that

Japanese laborers, by reason of race habits, mode of living, disposition and general characteristics, are undesirable.... Japanese ... do not buy land [or] build or buy houses.... They contribute nothing to the growth of the state. They add nothing to its wealth, and they are a blight on the prosperity of it, and a great and impending danger to its welfare.

The legislature was obviously reacting in a sort of racist conditioned reflex, a reflex conditioned by decades of anti-Chinese rhetoric. Within a few years the tune of the anti-Japanese song would change: the new refrain would stress not Japanese pauperism but Japanese landholding. The 1905 legislature had one other distinction: it limited itself

to an anti-Japanese resolution. For the next forty years, every session of the California legislature would attempt to pass at least one piece of anti-Japanese legislation.

A major factor in the introduction of these bills was the existence of anti-Japanese organizations and pressure groups which sprang up throughout the state from 1905 on. In May of that year the first of these organizations, the Asiatic Exclusion League, was set up. In effect, the League and its immediate successors were appendages of the powerful San Francisco labor movement. But the anti-Japanese movement appealed to more than labor; in December 1905, two California Republican congressmen, using League arguments, introduced similar Japanese exclusion bills into Congress. Although these bills never got out of committee, they produced one significant reaction: a leading southern politician, Oscar W. Underwood of Alabama, pledged that on this race question the South would support the Pacific Coast.

Despite this momentary national attention, the anti-Japanese movement failed to attract any publicity outside the Pacific Coast in 1905. When national and international notoriety did come, in the very next year, it was not immigration but school segregation that drew the spotlight. In May 1905, in response perhaps to the *Chronicle's* continuing crusade, the San Francisco School Board announced that it intended sometime in the future to order Japanese pupils—native and foreign-born removed from the regular schools and placed in the already existing school for Chinese. The stated reason was so that "our children should not be placed in any position where their youthful impressions may be affected by association with the Mongolian race." (The use of the term "Mongolian" was dictated by an old California school law which permitted exclusion of children of "filthy or vicious habits," or "suffering from contagious diseases," and segregation in separate schools of American Indian children and those of "Chinese or Mongolian descent." The law made no provision for Negro children.) But like so many pro-integration statements of intent today, these segregationist sentiments were left purely verbal, and no national or international notice was taken of them.

A year and a half later, the school board acted, and ordered the segregation to take place. In the meantime the famous San Francisco earthquake and fire of April 18, 1906, had taken place, and, in the chaotic conditions that followed, the anti-Japanese movement changed from peaceful if bigoted protest to direct action. Japanese restaurants, laundries, and other business establishments were picketed and boycotted, and in many instances businessmen, employees, and even white customers, were physically abused. By the fall of 1906 assaults upon individual Japanese were too frequent to have been accidental. Most of those who suffered were humble immigrants, but a distinguished party of visiting Japanese seismologists was stoned and otherwise attacked in various parts of northern California. More typical was the complaint of a laundry proprietor, as put forth in the stilted English of an employee of the Japanese consulate:

I am proprietor of Sunset City Laundry. Soon after the earthquake the persecutions became intolerable. My drives [of slow, horse-drawn laundry wagons] were constantly attacked on the highway, my place of business defiled by rotten eggs and fruit; windows were smashed several times. . . . The miscreants are generally young men, 17 or 18 years old. Whenever the newspapers attack the Japanese these roughs renew their misdeeds with redoubled energy.

Apparently there were never any convictions of whites for assault on Japanese during this period, although several Japanese were punished when they tried to defend themselves. It was in this atmosphere that the San Francisco School Board promulgated its segregation order on October 11, 1906. It was apparently unnoticed in the rest of the United States, and even the San Francisco papers gave it very little space. But nine days later the segregation order was front-page news in the Tokyo newspapers, and from that moment on the anti-Japanese movement was both a national and an international problem.

The Japanese government, always solicitous about the welfare of its citizens abroad, naturally protested. (Hilary Conroy has pointed out that the chief motivation for this solicitude "was the protection of her own prestige as a nation.") These protests, raising as they did the question of American-Japanese friendship, naturally disturbed many Americans, but few were disturbed as mightily as President Theodore Roosevelt. Roosevelt had been aware of the growing anti-Japanese agitation on the West Coast and as early as 1905 had privately expressed his disgust with the "idiots" of the California legislature. In response to the Japanese protests of October 1906, he dispatched a Cabinet member to investigate the school situation in San Francisco and privately assured the Japanese government of American friendship. But even before the report was in, Roosevelt publicly denounced the San Francisco proposal. In his annual message of December 2, 1906, the President asserted, falsely, that Japanese were treated, in most of the United States, just as most Europeans were treated. He went on to denounce the action of the school board as a "wicked absurdity" and then proposed that the naturalization laws—which provided for the naturalization of "free white persons and persons of African descent"—be amended to permit the naturalization of Japanese.

Roosevelt thus differentiated sharply between Chinese and Japanese. As we have seen, he signed the Chinese Exclusion Act of 1902, and strongly reiterated his opposition to Chinese immigrants in 1905. The reason Roosevelt discriminated between Orientals was because of the different relative military strengths of China and Japan. As he himself put it in his 1906 message, "the mob of a single city may at any time commit acts of lawless violence that may plunge us into war." Japan was strong, so its immigrants must be treated with respect; China was weak, so its immigrants could be treated as the mob desired. But, it should be noted, Roosevelt quickly retreated from his advanced position on Japanese naturalization; he soon discovered that Congress would not permit it, and he never again publicly proposed it.

Shortly after his annual message, Roosevelt received and published the report on San Francisco schools from his Secretary of Commerce and Labor Victor H. Metcalf. It was something of an anticlimax for most of the nation to discover that the whole furor had been raised over a grand total of ninety-three Japanese students distributed among the twenty-three public schools of San Francisco. Twenty-five of these students had been born on American soil, and since they were American citizens, the federal government could do nothing for them. Separate but equal facilities had been condoned by the United States Supreme Court in *Plessy v. Ferguson* (1896), so segregation of American citizens was perfectly legal. But for the sixty-eight school children who were subjects of the empire of Japan, the government could do something. They were protected by a stronger shield than the Constitution: the 1894 treaty between Japan and the United States, which guaranteed reciprocal "most favored nation" residential rights to nationals of both countries. Secretary of State Elihu Root himself, working with Department of Justice lawyers, prepared a federal desegregation suit directed against the San Francisco School Board.

At the same time, however, the federal authorities entered into discussions with the Japanese government designed to alleviate what they considered the real problem— continued immigration from Japan. In a complicated series of maneuvers Roosevelt, at a personal interview at the White House, persuaded the San Francisco School Board to revoke the offending order, managed to restrain the California legislature from passing anti-Japanese legislation relating to schools and other matters, and began an exchange of notes with Japan which collectively became known as the Gentlemen's Agreement of 1907–1908. The Japanese government agreed to stop issuing to laborers passports that would be good in the continental United States (Japanese labor was still wanted on Hawaiian sugar plantations), but it was agreed that passports could be issued to laborers who had already been to the United States and, most significantly, "to the parents, wives and children of laborers already there."

Roosevelt and his subordinates apparently failed to realize that under the provisions of the Gentlemen's Agreement thousands of Japanese men resident in the United States would send for wives, and that these newly married couples would increase and multiply. They presented the Gentlemen's Agreement to the hostile California public as exclusion. When, under its terms, the Japanese population of California continued to grow, first largely from the immigration of women and then from natural increase, Californians and others concerned about the Japanese problem insisted that they had been betrayed by their government in Washington. Instead of easing racial tension in California, the Roosevelt administration, in the final analysis, exacerbated it. The subsequent sessions of the California legislature, in 1909 and 1911, witnessed persistent attempts, usually led by Democrats, to pass anti-Japanese legislation. The measures were defeated, one way or another, by Republican majorities in both houses under pressure from national Republican administrations concerned about the possible effects of this legislation on relations between Japan and the United States. In 1913, however, a different situation prevailed. Republicans still controlled the California government, but the Democratic administration of Woodrow Wilson was in charge nationally. California Republicans, who during three elections had suffered Democrats' slurs about their national party's position on the Japanese question—in the 1908 election one Democratic slogan was "Labor's choice [is] Bryan—Jap's choice [is] Taft"—now saw a chance to make political capital and embarrass their opponents. In this whipsaw of the politics of prejudice the Japanese issue once again became an international affair.

By 1913 California politics had become dominated by progressive Republicans, and one of the chief architects of progressivism, Hiram W. Johnson, sat in the governor's chair. Two years previously, cooperating with a national administration of his own party, he had "sat upon the lid" and prevented passage of significant anti-Japanese measures. With a Democratic administration, Johnson quite early foresaw, as he wrote his most trusted adviser, a "unique and interesting" situation and "one out of which we can get a good deal of satisfaction." What the wily Johnson foresaw came about. A popular antialien land bill, designed to forbid "aliens ineligible to citizenship" (that is, Asians) from purchasing land, moved rapidly through the California legislature, with Johnson doing some behind-the-scenes stage-managing. Johnson arranged a public hearing in the spacious Assembly chamber in Sacramento, and seems also to have planned a "spontaneous" demonstration by farmers. The leading "farmer" was, in fact, a former Congregational clergyman, Ralph Newman, who made an appeal that ended:

Near my home is an eighty-acre tract of as fine land as there is in California. On that tract lives a Japanese. With that Japanese lives a white woman. In that woman's arms is a baby. What is that baby? It isn't a Japanese. It isn't white. It is a germ of the mightiest problem that ever faced this state; a problem that will make the black problem of the South look white.

The specter of interracial marriage or sex, although often raised by extremists, was not really a significant factor; Japanese rarely married or cohabited outside their own ethnic group. What had changed was the perceived nature of the Japanese threat. No longer the pauper immigrant, but an increasingly successful entrepreneur, Newman's image—the Japanese possessing the white woman— could be interpreted as the sexualization of a different kind of usurpation, the yellow man's taking of what the white man conceived to be his rightful place in society. With this kind of send-off, the anti-Japanese land bill seemed assured of passage.

Back in Washington, Woodrow Wilson and his Secretary of State William Jennings Bryan were faced with persistent diplomatic protest in the very first weeks of their administration. They were reluctant to intervene, as both Roosevelt and Taft had, for three reasons. First, they feared, correctly, that the Republican California administration would reject their pleas. Second, each of them had expressed and still held distinct anti-Japanese sentiments. Third, both of them, like most Democrats of their time, held strongly Jeffersonian states' rights views, and were much more reluctant to intervene in the internal affairs of a state than were their Hamiltonian Republican predecessors. But national power brings responsibility, and Wilson and Bryan at least made an effort to moderate the California action. Bryan went all the way to California, addressed the legislature, caucused with followers, all to no avail. The Alien Land Act passed both houses overwhelmingly and was quickly signed by Johnson.

Although passage of the Alien Land Law of 1913 was a great psychic triumph for the Californians—after almost a decade they had finally thwarted Washington—it served very little real purpose, as the more astute California politicians (including Hiram Johnson) knew at the time. Japanese land tenure was not seriously affected by the law; although it prohibited further ownership by Japanese aliens, it did permit leasing. It was quite simple for the attorneys who represented Japanese interests in California to evade the alleged intent of the law in many ways. The simplest was through incorporation so that control was ostensibly held by whites. For the growing number of Issei who had American-born children, things were even easier; they simply transferred the stock or title to their citizen children whose legal guardianship they naturally assumed.

When the truth about the impotence of the

bill dawned on many Californians, their bitterness against the Japanese and their own government merely increased. The years that followed, however, were years of war, and during part of that time Japan was on our side, or at least fighting the same enemy, Germany. During those years anti-Japanese activity, organized and spontaneous, was at a minimum. The years after the war, however, saw the anti-Japanese movement go over the top and move from triumph to triumph.

How representative of white California were the exclusionists? The best possible measure of the popularity of the anti-Japanese position came in 1920, when a stronger Alien Land Act, one that prohibited leasing and sharecropping as well as land purchase, was put on the California ballot as an initiative. It passed by a margin of more than 3 to 1. Few of the more than six hundred thousand California citizens who voted for the measure can have been in any way actual or potential competitors with Japanese farmers; the measure carried every county in the state, and did well in both urban and rural areas. The simple fact of the matter was that Californians had come to hate and fear Japanese with a special intensity.

Late in 1919 this hate and fear became focused in one omnibus anti-Japanese organization—the Oriental Exclusion League. Although it had a vast number of cooperating organizations, four of them provided the real clout: the California Federation of Labor, the American Legion, the State Grange, and the Native Sons and Daughters of the Golden West. This curious coalition agreed on little else—the Legion and organized labor were almost always on opposite sides of the fence—but it did formulate an anti-Japanese program about which they could all agree. They had five basic demands, four of which were quickly achieved.

1. Cancellation of the Gentlemen's Agreement
2. Exclusion of picture brides
3. Rigorous exclusion of Japanese as immigrants

4. Maintaining the bar against naturalization of Asians
5. Amending the Federal Constitution to deny citizenship even to native-born Asians

The picture brides, about whom the nativists were so bitter, need some explanation. Under the Gentlemen's Agreement, as we have seen, Japanese men already in the United States were given the right to bring in wives. The Japanese government was reasonably careful about granting such passports, and usually went far beyond the terms of the agreement. To ensure that these women immigrants would not become public charges, the husband or prospective husband was often required to present evidence to a Japanese consulate in California showing that he could support a wife, before her passport would be issued. In many instances the prospective bridegroom would return to Japan and bring back a bride. In other instances, however, friends and relatives at home would do the selecting for him. A proxy wedding would take place; a picture of the bride would be sent to California, followed, eventually, by the bride herself. As shocking as this seemed to the American ideal of romantic love, marriages arranged in such a manner were quite common in Japan and not infrequent among some European immigrant groups. The matchmakers, or go-betweens, took pride in their work, and, in fact, their reputations depended upon the success of the marriages they arranged. To the Japanese this seemed natural; to most Americans, unnatural; but to many Californians this age-old method of mate selection seemed just another aspect of a massive and diabolical plot to submerge California under a tide of yellow babies.

The California reaction to the picture brides, to the creation of yellow American citizens, can only be described as paranoid. One leading exclusionist, V. S. McClatchy, former publisher of the Sacramento *Bee* and a director of the Associated Press, once assembled "indisputable facts and figures" which demonstrated that America's Japanese population unless checked, would reach 318,000 in 1923, 2 million in 1963, and 100 million in 2063. One female exclusionist was sure that California was being "Japanized" in the same way as the South was being "Negroized"; she warned her fellow Californians about "Japanese casting furtive glances at our young women." Cora W. Woodbridge, a state legislator and an officer of the California Federation of Women's Clubs, dismissed the Issei woman as "a beast of burden up to the time of the birth of her child [who], within a day or two at most resumes her task and continues it from twelve to sixteen hours a day." Even more outrageous to the convinced exclusionists were the white allies of the Japanese, who were called "Jap-lovers" and "white-Japs, who masquerade as Americans, but, in fact, are servants of the mikado." All this emotion, remember, was generated at a time when there were only 70,000 Japanese in the state; they amounted to one Californian in fifty. But Californians were convinced that they were threatened. After passage of the 1920 Alien Land Act, which inhibited the growth of the Issei agriculture but did not cripple it, the state had used all its alternatives. As had been the case with the anti-Chinese movement, the goals of the exclusionists could only be achieved with federal power

California, of course, had allies. Most other western states, but particularly Oregon and Washington, had anti-Japanese movements of their own and passed similar alien land laws. In addition, most southern senators and representatives stood ready to support their fellow "beleaguered" whites. But a western and southern bloc cannot carry Congress. National support had to be organized. Much of the support came from two of the major California pressure groups. At the national level both the American Legion and the American Federation of Labor worked hard for exclusion. But even more crucial support came, however indirectly, from Japan itself. Sometime between the be-

ginning of the Russo-Japanese War and the end of World War I the Japanese became, in the eyes of most Americans, villains. Aggressive actions by Japan, particularly its demands against China and its conflict with the United States in Siberia during the short-lived occupation of parts of Soviet East Asia, helped cause American public opinion to turn against Japan, thus providing more support for the exclusionist position.

But at least equally important was the growing racist feeling in the United States, a feeling exacerbated by both the postwar retreat from internationalism and the domestic upsurge against "un-American" ideas and individuals. Intellectual racists like Lothrop Stoddard and Madison Grant warned of a "rising tide of color" that menaced white civilization; the second Ku Klux Klan, focusing its attack on Catholics, Jews, and foreigners, gained brief power and pseudo-respectability in much of the Midwest and some of the East. These two factors, added to the persistent anti-Japanese propaganda and organizational activity of the western exclusionists, eventually created a climate of opinion that made exclusion possible.

Perhaps the key organizational meeting, at the national level, was held in the caucus room of the United States House of Representatives on April 20, 1921. Called by Senator Hiram Johnson and the rest of the California delegation, it united one senator and one representative from each of twelve other western states into an informal executive committee to push exclusion through Congress. The group insisted that the West was being "invaded." Their argument is worth quoting at length.

The process of invasion has been aptly termed "peaceful penetration." The invasion is by an alien people. They are a people unassimilable by marriage. They are a people who are a race and a nation unto themselves, it matters not what may be the land of their birth.

Economically we are not able to compete with them and maintain the American standard of living; racially we cannot assimilate them. Hence we must exclude them from our shores as settlers in our midst and prohibit them from owning land. Those already here will be protected in their right to the enjoyment of life, liberty, and legally acquired property. . . .

The alternative [to exclusion] is that the richest section of the United States will gradually come into the complete control of an alien race. . . . A careful study of the subject will convince anyone who will approach it with an open mind that the attitude of California, and other states . . . is not only justifiable but essential to the national welfare.

But before this powerful Congressional group could get into action, the Supreme Court of the United States made things a little easier for the exclusionists. As we have seen, Japanese and other Asians were considered aliens ineligible to citizenship. This presumption stemmed, not from any constitutional bar, but from the naturalization statute, which, after the Dred Scott decision of 1857 and the Fourteenth Amendment, had been rewritten to permit naturalization of "white persons" and aliens of African descent. Although in some jurisdictions—most significantly Hawaii—courts had naturalized Japanese and other aliens, prevailing practice had been to bar them. This practice was challenged by Takao Ozawa, born in Japan but educated in the United States. The court conceded that he was "well qualified by character and education for citizenship."

Ozawa's counsel, George W. Wickersham, who had been Attorney General under William Howard Taft, argued that in the absence of any specific Congressional provision barring Japanese, they were eligible for citizenship, and he pointed out that the original language, which went back to 1790, had spoken of "free white persons." The original intent of Congress, Wickersham insisted, had not in any way been aimed at Japanese or other Asians. The court unanimously rejected Wickersham's argument, and confirmed the denial of citizenship to Ozawa. This decision meant that Congressional exclusionists could now safely use the time-honored "aliens ineligible to citizenship formula" and did not have to resort to a spe-

cial Japanese exclusion act, as had been the case with the Chinese.

For tactical reasons, the exclusionists bided their time; exclusion of Japanese would come, not through special action, but as a part of the general restriction of immigration which the nativist climate of the 1920s made a foregone conclusion.

What became the National Origins Act of 1924 originated in the House of Representatives in late 1923. After much backing and filling the House Committee on Immigration—under the chairmanship of a West Coast representative, Albert Johnson of Washington—came up with a frankly racist quota system whose basic aims were to reduce greatly the volume of immigration in general and to all but eliminate "non-Anglo-Saxon" immigration from eastern and southern Europe. As reported by the Committee and passed by the House, the bill also contained a section barring all "aliens ineligible to citizenship." (Had the quota system, which was based on the number of individuals from each country reported in the 1890 census, been applied to Japan, the result would have been a maximum of 100 immigrants a year.).

In the Senate, however, exclusionists did not control the Immigration Committee, and the bill reported to that body provided for a Japanese quota. While the debate was in progress Secretary of State Charles Evans Hughes suggested to Japanese Ambassador Masanao Hanihara that a letter from him containing an authoritative description of the Gentlemen's Agreement would be helpful in combating the drive for exclusion, which neither government wanted. Hanihara complied. In the course of the letter to Hughes, which was made public, Hanihara spoke accurately of the possible results of exclusion as opposed to a token quota.

I have stated or rather repeated all this to you rather candidly and in a most friendly spirit, for I realize, as I believe you do, the grave consequences which the enactment of the measure retaining [the aliens ineligible to citizenship] provision would inevitably bring upon the otherwise

happy and mutually advantageous relations between our two countries.

At the time Hanihara's note was made
public by Hughes, it seemed possible that the
Senate, usually more sensitive to the international implications of its actions, would reject the exclusion provisions of the House
bill. But in a shrewd but utterly unprincipled
tactical stroke, Senator Henry Cabot Lodge
of Massachusetts, seizing upon the phrase
"grave consequences," made the language
of the Japanese ambassador's friendly note
seem to be a "veiled threat." "The United
States," he insisted, "cannot legislate by the
exercise by any other country of veiled
threats." Once the matter had been made a
question of national honor, reason flew out
the window. Senators who had previously
expressed themselves as favorable to a
Japanese quota or a continuation of the Gentlemen's Agreement, now, for what they said
were patriotic reasons, joined the exclusionist side of the debate. On the key
roll call, the Senate vote was 76–2 against
the Japanese.

With the passage of the Immigration Act
of 1924 all but one of the basic demands of
the anti-Japanese movement had been met.
Although many individual exclusionists continued to agitate for a constitutional amendment that would deprive Nisei of their citizenship, such an amendment was never seriously considered by Congress. But, after a
campaign of nearly a quarter century, exclusion had been achieved, the immigration
question had been settled. The exclusionists
were exultant: "I am repaid for my efforts,"
wrote former California Senator James D.
Phelan who had been an exclusionist from
the beginning; "the Japs are routed."

But left in the wake of the rout was a sizable immigrant community with a growing
number of citizen offspring. At the time of
the Gentlemen's Agreement male Issei had
outnumbered females by better than 7 to 1;
the years of largely female immigration after
1908 had somewhat redressed that balance,
but many thousands of older Issei were

doomed to bachelorhood if they remained in
America. Despite the halt in immigration,
the Japanese population of the United States
continued to rise (the slight drop in total
population between 1930 and 1940 would
soon be reversed by the births of Sansei,
which were just beginning), as the table indicates:

JAPANESE POPULATION, CONTINENTAL
UNITED STATES

	Total	Alien	Native	% Native
1920	111,010	81,383	29,672	26.7
1930	138,834	70,477	68,357	49.2
1940	126,947	47,305	79,642	62.7

The Japanese American community was
thus really becoming two communities in the
years after 1920: the Issei community, alien
and somewhat Japan-centered, and the Nisei
community, native and distinctly American-
oriented. As the years passed, the first grew
steadily older and smaller—absolutely and
relatively—while the second matured and
saw its influence grow. But during most
of these years the overwhelming majority of
Nisei were children. In a typical Issei family,
children were born in the years 1918–1922
to a thirty-five-year-old father and a twenty-
five-year-old mother; this meant that the numerically most significant group of Nisei
were coming of age between the years 1939
and 1943. Even without any external crisis,
generational conflict surely would have
arisen between the Issei and their children.
As John Modell has observed:

[The Nisei] had inherited from his parents a remarkable desire to succeed in the face of hardship, but had also learned the American definition
of success, by which standard the accommodation
made by his parents could not be considered satisfactory.

The older immigrant generation and their
American children had many conflicts, but
essentially these conflicts were over life
style. The Issei, like many immigrant groups
before and since, tried to re-create a Japanese

society in America, but the image of Japan which most of them held was static. They remembered, as immigrants usually do, the Japan of their youth, not the emerging, industrializing Japan of the twenties and thirties. Since the United States deliberately tried to keep them separate by both law and custom, the Issei were probably better insulated against Americanization than were contemporary immigrant groups from Europe. Within the Issei community almost all the institutions—the press, the church, and the other associational groups—were Japan and Japanese-language centered. At the same time, membership in a broad spectrum of Americanizing institutions was denied to them. Had the immigrant generation been eligible for naturalization and at least potential voters, certain opportunities would have been open to them.

On the other hand, despite their own cultural isolation, the Issei insisted that their children not only accept education but excel in it. The Nisei thus went to school and were subjected to the most powerful Americanizing influence; fortunately for them, their number in any school was generally so small that the classrooms they attended were truly integrated. Therefore, they participated, from early childhood, in at least a part of American society; despite the general anti-Orientalism of western American society, the schools themselves seem to have been, almost without exception, more than fair to the Nisei children. At least part of the explanation for this was the exceptional behavior and aspiration of the Nisei children; from the very first they charmed their American teachers and ranked quite high in scholastic achievement. That these achievements were not always appreciated by the rest of society is perhaps best illustrated by the case of John Aiso, now a judge in Los Angeles. He was the Los Angeles winner in the American Legion oratorical contest one year, but the authorities of that organization sent the second place finisher, a Caucasian, to represent Los Angeles in the national finals in Washington.

Outside school, however, the Nisei faced a society that rejected them regardless of their accomplishments. Fully credentialed Nisei education majors, for example, were virtually unemployable as teachers in the very schools in which they had excelled. Whatever their skills, most Nisei were forced into the ethnic economic community; their parents expected and accepted this—shouldn't children follow in the footsteps of their parents?—but the Nisei resented and chafed at the low wages, long hours, and lack of status which jobs in the ethnic community entailed. As one Nisei wrote, in 1937:

I am a fruitstand worker. It is not a very attractive nor distinguished occupation. ... I would much rather it were doctor or lawyer ... but my aspiration of developing into such [was] frustrated long ago. ... I am only what I am, a professional carrot washer.

The almost total lack of economic opportunity outside the ethnic community had closed down the horizons for this young man. He went on to say that the zenith of his aspirations was to save some money and get a business of his own, which would probably be a fruit or vegetable market. Other Nisei were similarly "trapped" in agriculture, gardening, curio shops, and other aspects of the economic ghetto. Despite what Modell calls their "American definition of success," all but a very few of the maturing Nisei generation found that their "safest recourse" was within the ethnic economic structure.

There was generational political and cultural conflict as well. Most of the Issei identified with Japan. Their organizations—for example, the Japanese Chamber of Commerce of Los Angeles—tended to support or at least find a rationale for Japanese aggression. In a 1931 publication the Chamber complained of "China's oppressive policy toward the Japanese" and insisted that the purpose of Japanese troops in Manchuria was "purely to protect the life and property of our countrymen" and that "we possess no political ambition." Similar treatment was given to what the Japanese liked to call the "China incident" of the mid-1930's.

The Nisei did not share in these sentiments. It was not so much a case of opposing the interests of Japan, although there were a few members of both the immigrant and second generation who participated in such anti-Japanese activities as picketing Japanese ships in the late 1930s. It was simply that the vast majority of the Nisei were almost wholly American-oriented and simply did not concern themselves with things Japanese. As early as the 1920s they began to form their own organizations; there were Japanese American Young Republicans and Young Democrats and even some all-Japanese American Legion posts. What was to become the most important of the Nisei organizations —the Japanese American Citizens League (JACL)—formally came into being in 1930 and had arisen out of a number of local and regional organizations of the second generation.

Even if there had been no war crisis, the JACL was on a collision course with the organizations of the older generation. Since it was an organization for citizens, the older generation was barred; since it stressed Americanization and minimized even cultural ties with Japan, its goals were somewhat repugnant to many of the Issei, especially to the community leaders. The JACL creed, written in 1940, perhaps best expresses the orientation of the more articulate Nisei on the eve of World War II, and is worth quoting in full.

I am proud that I am and American citizen of Japanese ancestry, for my very background makes me appreciate more fully the wonderful advantages of this nation. I believe in her institutions, ideals and traditions; I glory in her heritage; I boast of her history; I trust in her future. She has granted me liberties and opportunities such as no individual enjoys in this world today. She has given me an education befitting kings. She has entrusted me with the responsibilities of the franchise. She has permitted me to build a home, to earn a livelihood, to worship, think, speak and act as I please—as a free man equal to every other man.

Although some individuals may discriminate against me, I shall never become bitter or lose faith, for I know that such persons are not representative of the majority of the American people. True, I shall do all in my power to discourage such practices, but I shall do it in the American way—above board, in the open, through courts of law, by education, by proving myself to be worthy of equal treatment and consideration. I am firm in my belief that American sportsmanship and attitude of fair play will judge citizenship and patriotism on the basis of action and achievement, and not on the basis of physical characteristics. Because I believe in America, and I trust she believes in me, and because I have received innumerable benefits from her, I pledge myself to do honor to her at all times and all places; to support her constitution; to obey her laws; to respect her flag; to defend her against all enemies, foreign and domestic; to actively assume my duties and obligations as a citizen, cheerfully and without any reservations whatsoever, in the hope that I may become a better American in a greater America.

This hypernationalism, as we have seen, did not spring from the Nisei experience or accurately reflect the current status of the second generation. It was, rather, an expression of expectations, a hopeful vision of what the future would be like. As many historians of immigration have observed, when the second generation becomes patriotic, quite often it tries to become 200 percent American. A good part of this overreaction is compensation and a conscious rejection of an alien heritage that is seen as retarding the aspirations of the second-generation group concerned. Another factor is surely the belief, conscious or unconscious, that if only it protests its loyalty loudly enough, the majority will come to believe its protestations. In addition, of course, many of the Nisei had become so thoroughly Americanized that they actually believed the creed as written, although one wonders how the "professional carrot washer" with his frustrated ambitions felt about the "wonderful advantages . . .

liberties and opportunities such as no individual enjoys in this world today.''

But, whatever its basic cause or motivation, the superpatriotism of the JACL availed the Nisei little. They were prepared to defend America "against all her enemies," but when war came American identified them as the enemy. They tried, in many ways with success, to be better Americans than most of their white fellow citizens, but when the chips were down their countrymen saw only the color of their skin and remembered only that their parents had come from the land of the rising sun.

IV

ETHNIC MINORITIES IN CONTEMPORARY AMERICA

Today the descendants of those who came in the great migrations from Europe and Asia are relatively free of persecution. With the passage of time they have fled the slums, acquired political power, and dropped their foreign ways. First-, second-, and third-generation Americans enter college, move to the suburbs, and occupy remunerative positions. Discrimination against these groups in country clubs, trade unions, and universities has diminished and in some places has disappeared. Unfortunately the latest entrants from Latin America, the West Indies, and Puerto Rico and at least two indigenous ethnic groups, the Indians and blacks, have not made similar gains.

Within the past decade there has been renewed interest in the miserable existence of the 750,000 surviving Indians. Sympathetic national figures like the late Robert Kennedy and his brother Edward have critically re-examined reservation life and the Department of the Interior's Indian Bureau policies. The chief of the Bureau of Indian Affairs himself acknowledged that agency programs had yielded few significant results. In 1964 he stated that unemployment on the reservations averaged 40 to 50 per cent, that nine out of ten Indians lived in housing "far below minimum standards of comfort, safety, and decency," and that the average age at death on the reservation was forty-two years. Fortunately for the Indians, however, a younger generation of militants has tried to unite their beleaguered minority with other downtrodden groups in an effort to improve conditions. In 1968 some of them joined the Christian Leadership Conference's Poor People's March on Washington, a radical break with the red man's traditional isolation, and in 1969 some took over Alcatraz, the federal prison in San Francisco Bay, because, they claimed, the land had belonged to their ancestors. In the past few years the struggle for recognition of Indian rights and improvement of living conditions on the reservations has intensified. The American Indian Movement spearheads this "red power" insurgency by publicizing the miserable existence of their people, by raising Indian consciousness, and by seeking to unite the different tribes in an organization committed to redressing Indian social and economic grievances. The militant leaders' quest for long-delayed justice has focused on opposition to the Bureau of Indian Affairs and on fulfillment of the long series of broken treaties whose violations have robbed Indians of wealth and land. Rifts between older and more conservative factions and younger and more militant groups have created considerable internal friction in this ethnic minority and resulted, in 1974, in violent confrontation and death in the "Second Battle of Wounded Knee."

The plight of the Spanish-speaking Americans, the most recent migrants to the United States, is less severe than the problems of the Indians, but it represents another chapter in the long history of injustice toward minority groups in America. Uninhibited by the quota system established by Congress in 1921 and 1924, Western Hemisphere and non-mainland American citizens—Mexicans, Puerto Ricans, West Indians, and Cubans—have constituted the majority of the new arrivals in th past half-century.

Mexicans began to enter the United States in large numbers at the turn of the century, when railroad and agricultural expanison in the Southwest and Far West created a demand for cheap, unskilled labor. The low wages paid for seasonal agricultural and construction labor appealed to the dismally poor Mexicans. Depression in the 1930s stemmed immigration for a decade but manpower shortages after World War II revived the inflow from Mexico. Americans of Mexican origin, the largest of the Spanish-speaking minorities, currently number about 8,000,000. Most of these newcomers came originally as agricultural laborers on the farms in the Southwest and on the Pacific Coast. Today four-fifths of this ethnic minority live in the Southwest. Many entered under the *bracero* agreement made between the Mexican and American governments. Lasting between 1942 and 1964, this program arranged for temporary seasonal employment by fixed contracts guaranteeing a minimum number of working days, adequate wages, and suitable living accommodations. The terms of the agreement were widely violated. Wages were low, living conditions abysmal, and many of the laborers did not go back to Mexico. Hundreds of thousands became permanent, if illegal, resident aliens, faced with the choice between poverty in their homeland and exploitation in America. In the Far West and the Southwest, Mexican Americans have been an "untouchable" caste, occupying the bottom rung of the occupational and income ladder. Their status and income paralleled that of the blacks in other areas of the country. Like other immigrants who started out as agricultural laborers, they made the transition to industrial employment and urban life. By the 1950s Mexican-Americans made up 20 percent of California's auto workers, half of the members of the building-trades union, and a majority of those working in the state's garment factories. This Spanish-speaking minority began to shift from agricultural to industrial jobs and from rural to city living during World War II. By 1950 two-thirds of those of Mexican ancestry resided in cities, and today about four-fifths of the Mexican-Americans dwell in urban areas.

The Mexicans had a more difficult life in the United States than most immigrant groups. Most of the entrants were poor and illiterate refugees from a traditional rural culture. Their mixed Spanish and Indian ancestry subjected them to the American caste system and narrowed their opportunities for economic and social advancement. White Protestants in Texas, California, Arizona, and other states of settlement disdained the Mexicans' Roman Catholicism and dark complexions. Unaccustomed to such prejudice in their home country, the newcomers confronted a raw and ugly situation of racial and religious bigotry. In June 1943 friction between the Anglos and the Mexican-Americans triggered the "Zoot Suit" riot in Los Angeles. While walking in a slum area surrounded by the Mexican barrio, a group of sailors were assaulted. The victims claimed that their assailants were Mexican youths, and for a few nights following the initial fight gangs of sailors went into the Mexican-American ghetto and beat up every zoot suiter (young man affecting the then faddish ensemble of baggy trousers with high waist and cuffs, long coat with wide shoulders, and broad-brimmed hat) they could find. The Los Angeles police did nothing to stop the attacks, and it took intervention by the Mexican government to get military leaves cancelled and thus halt the mob action.

Mexican-Americans are still an underprivileged minority, but their economic status has been upgraded by their movement to the cities and to industrial employment. They constitute one-third of those below the poverty level in Texas and New Mexico and one-fourth of the poor in Arizona and Colorado. This poverty is largely the result of rural living. Mexican-Americans still dwelling in the countryside have an average yearly family income well below the poverty line. The United Farm Workers Union, led by César Chavez, is currently trying to organize the grape and lettuce pickers in California in order to ameliorate the dismal conditions of Spanish-speaking agricultural workers. At this writing his union is locked in a bitter struggle with the farm owners and the Teamsters Union, and the outcome of the conflict is still in doubt. Mexican-Americans in urban areas, such as the towns and cities of California, are considerably better off. In fact, by 1972 they had an aggregate median family income of $8,759, higher than the $6,864 for blacks but lower than the $11,549 for Anglos.

After World War II large numbers of Puerto Ricans began moving to the mainland. In 1940 there were fewer than 70,000 Puerto Ricans on the East Coast, but overpopulation and poverty in Puerto Rico, postwar prosperity in the States, and quick, low-cost air travel induced hundreds of thousands to emigrate. By 1957 the chief port of entry, New York City, housed 550,000 Puerto Ricans. The new arrivals grouped in Brooklyn, the South Bronx, and East Harlem. They took jobs in light industry, in the garment factories along Seventh Avenue in Manhattan, and in hotels and restaurants. Color, culture, and language held back their progress toward wealth and higher status in much the same manner as it did the Mexicans. The problem of bigotry was even worse for the Puerto Rican because of friction between the Spanish-speaking and black communities in New York City. Puerto Ricans, never before subject to racial prejudices, quickly learned the ethnic pecking order and attempted to distinguish themselves from the blacks. Nonetheless, white Americans rejected them on racial grounds and blacks resented them for adopting conventional prejudices and feared their competition for jobs and living quarters.

The 750,000 Cubans who live in the United States are unique among American minority groups. Unlike most other immigrants, many were among the political, social, professional, and economic leaders in their homeland until shortly before they left. According to one study, 70 per cent of the refugees from Castro's Cuba were professional, skilled, or white-collar workers, almost 40 percent had some college education, and 80 percent had yearly incomes above those earned by the average Cuban. But their privileged position abruptly disappeared when Fidel Castro seized power. Unable or unwilling to adjust to the reorganized society, about 5 percent of the population—or those who had something to lose by the revolutionary character of the new Cuba—fled to other nations. Most came to the United States and the majority of these remained in and around Miami, Florida. Once in this country they encountered conditions similar to those that other minorities had experienced, but because they had been educated and had marketable skills—and the federal government made efforts to assist them—adjustment proved less difficult than it had for so many other groups. In 1971 the 350,000 Cubans in the Miami area, one-third of the metropolitan population there, had an average annual income of over $8,000, more than half owned their own homes, and 91 percent had automobiles. The Cubans ran most of the area's best nightclubs and restaurants and controlled 30 percent of all new construction in Dade County. In 1962 half of the Cubans in the Miami area had received some form of welfare; seven years later fewer than 10 percent required public assistance.

The postwar influx from Latin America was in part responsible for curbing unlimited immigration from the Western Hemisphere. The immigration bill of 1965, which abolished the national-origins provisos that had existed since 1921, allotted each nation a 20,000 yearly ceiling on immigrants, and preferences for visas allowing American entry were given to close relatives of citizens and resident aliens and those whose occupational skills were most in demand in the United States. This law also resulted in a gradual increase in newcomers from 296,697 in 1965 to 400,063 in 1973 and caused a shift in the geographical origins of recent arrivals. In 1965 the numbers coming from northern and western Europe exceeded those from eastern and southern Europe, but the reverse had occurred by 1973. The biggest increase in sources of immigration was from Asia. In 1965 approximately 7 percent of the immigrants came from the Far East. By 1973 this part of the world contributed 124,160, or 32 percent, of the total number admitted. Outside the Western Hemisphere the largest number of immigrants by country of birth was the Philippines (30,799), followed by Korea (22,930), Italy (22,151), China and Taiwan (17,297), and India (13,124). These latest arrivals are now going through the same experiences as their predecessors: newly transplanted Chinese work in garment factories in New York's Chinatown for wages as low as 65 and 75 cents an hour. This latest wave also threatens to end the traditional low crime rate among those of Chinese ancestry. The Asians have congregated in urban ghettos and generally labor in jobs with little pay, status, or satisfaction, and with marginal prospects of advancement. But the "brain drain" which has attracted European professionals to the United States also lured to this country Asian, especially Filipino, Indian, and Indonesian, graduate students, doctors, nurses, and engineers.

Aside from the long-term sources of migration, postwar movement to America has been affected by temporary transfers of large numbers of refugees. This type of immigration began with the War Brides Act of 1946, which eventually enabled 120,000 alien spouses and children of American soldiers to settle here. Another 600,000 immigrants entered the United States under the Displaced Persons laws of 1948 and 1953. This legislation permitted the arrival of World War II refugees, many of them Jews who survived Hitler's concentration camps and genocide policy. Congressional acts opened the gates or gave grants of assistance for 30,000 Hungarians who fled their country after the abortive revolution of 1956, for 31,000 Dutch Indonesians after Indonesia became an independent nation in 1957, for 500,000 Cubans who were allowed to leave by the Castro regime, and for 13,000 South Vietnamese who escaped after the 1974 downfall of their American-aided government. These groups, unlike the other types of immigrants, were usually middle class in origin or occupation. Except for the World War II displaced persons, they were mainly casualties of left-wing governments. Leftists who sought refuge here from right-wing dictatorships, as in the case of those attempting to flee the Chilean coup of 1973, were denied entry.

The contemporary era has also witnessed the greatest upheaval in black-white relations since the Civil War. Whites have felt increasingly guilty for society's ill-treatment of the black man and have gradually altered established policies (too gradually from the black point of view). President Harry S. Truman desegregated the armed forces and public facilities (schools, transportation, recreational areas, etc.) in Washington, D.C. In the 1950s the United States Supreme Court reversed a sixty-year-old policy by declaring segregation in public facilities unconstitutional. In 1957 Congress passed its first civil rights act since 1870. Subsequently Presidents John F. Kennedy and Lyndon B. Johnson expressed their concern for the plight of all minority groups and prodded Congress to pass additional legislation supposedly guaranteeing voting rights, access to public schools and housing facilities financed with federal funds, and job training. Despite these endeavors, many blacks saw little change or material progress in their own lives. They grew even more uneasy after the promise of federal assistance turned out to be insignificant. False hopes and unfulfilled promises spawned the growth of radical black leaders like Malcolm

X, H. Rap Brown, and Eldridge Cleaver, who demanded immediate and full equality. Failure of the whites to respond to what they considered hasty and costly reforms led to urban riots, especially in the blistering summer days when affluent whites retreated to their air-conditioned homes or seashore resorts while blacks simmered in the heat of closely packed urban ghettoes.

President Johnson's National Advisory Commission on Civil Disorders reported in 1968 that the United States was a racist society. It recommended a massive infusion of federal funds to be spent for decent housing, improved educational and recreational facilities, and job training. The billions of dollars necessary to implement these proposals staggered the vast majority of the white public and members of Congress. Instead of grappling with the basic causes of discontent, members of both federal and state legislatures advocated harsher law enforcement. The slogan "Law and Order" had the appeal of immediate action at a cheap price and inspired enthusiasm in Americans still shackled to a heritage of racist repression.

The slow pace toward material and social equality is a fundamental but not total explanation for racial conflict today. Statistical studies in *The Negro American* (Talcott Parsons and Kenneth Clark, eds., New York: The Daedalus Library, 1965), the most complete study of black society in the United States, indicated that blacks were improving their incomes and occupational status (that is, increasingly more blacks were moving into white-collar jobs and middle-class status), but at a slower rate than whites. More recent figures released by the Department of Labor indicate that between 1959 and 1967 blacks living in cities were slowly closing the family income gap between white and black families. No gains were registered in increasing the proportion of males in white-collar occupations, but substantial advances (a 12 percent increase) occurred in the proportion of female white-collar workers. These figures disclose the root of the American blacks' grievance against white society. Until the 1960s they were making agonizingly slow gains in status and wealth while many lower-class whites were striding rapidly into a comfortable middle-class existence. By the late 1960s they seemed to have begun to close the income and status gap, mostly because of a considerable upgrading of the status and income of females. In the 1970s, however, the income gap between whites and blacks has been widening, civil rights laws have not been as vigorously enforced as in the past, and the black portion of college students has diminished. The slow pace of advances in the 1960s and the present reverses have convinced many blacks that their position in American society is deteriorating, but this realization has not as yet evoked the militant protests reminiscent of the 1960s. Even during the era of gains in the 1950s and '60s certain aspects of black society actually worsened.

Mass movement to the city and the advances made by black women, amidst the comparative stagnation of income and vocational improvements among black men, have intensified the disintegration of the black urban family. In 1959 some 23 percent of such families were headed by women. Eight years later the total was 30 percent. In 1959 only 71 percent of black children in the city lived with both parents; in 1967 as few as 61 percent lived with both parents. Leaving aside issues of justice or humantiy, the simple necessity for social stability demands that these trends be reversed. The nation will not have domestic peace until the most volatile element in the black community, the young males, are confident of their vocational and familial future.

SELECTED BIBLIOGRAPHY

For the contemporary period there are two good comparative studies. Oscar Handlin's *The Newcomers: Negroes and Puerto Ricans in a Changing Metropolis* (Cambridge, Mass.: Harvard University Press, 1959) is excellent. Nathan Glazer and Daniel Patrick Moynihan have analyzed five groups (Irish, Italians, Jews, blacks, and Puerto Ricans) in New York City in *Beyond the Melting Pot* (2nd edition; Cambridge, Mass.: M.I.T. Press, 1970).

Indians are discussed in David A. Baerreis, ed., *The Indian in Modern America* (State Historical Society of Wisconsin, 1956), and Vine Deloria, Jr., *Custer Died for Your Sins: An Indian Manifesto* (New York: Macmillan, 1969).

On what it is like to be black in the United States see Claude Brown, *Manchild in the Promised Land* (New York: New American Library, 1965) and *The Autobiography of Malcolm X* (New York: Grove Press, 1965). Especially insightful for the more recent period is Sam Levitan, William B. Johnston, and Robert Taggert, *Still a Dream: The Changing Status of Blacks since 1960* (Cambridge: Harvard University Press, 1975); this book shows how little progress blacks have actually made during the past two decades.

The best history of the Mexican-Americans is still Carey McWilliams, *North from Mexico,* originally published in 1949 but reissued (New York: Greenwood Publishers, 1969) with a new introduction. A more recent survey is Matt S. Meier and Feliciano Rivera, *The Chicanos* (New York: Hill and Wang, 1972).

The most recent survey of the Puerto Ricans is Joseph P. Fitzpatrick, *Puerto Rican Americans* (Englewood Cliffs, N.J.: Prentice-Hall, 1971); a study of the Cubans who arrived in the United States between 1959 and 1962 is Richard R. Fagen, Richard A. Brody, and Thomas J. O'Leary, *Cubans in Exile: Disaffection and the Revolution* (Stanford: Stanford University Press, 1968).

The 1970s have also witnessed the response of white ethnics to the public attention received by racial minorities and Hispanic-Americans. As a reaction Michael Novak wrote *The Rise of the Unmeltable Ethnics* (New York: Macmillan, 1972), which analyzes the culture of Italian and Slavic Americans. Novak's contention that these groups wish to retain their heritage intact is debatable but his arguments are provocative.

What the Indians Want

ALVIN M. JOSEPHY, JR.

In contrast to its stance on black civil rights, the administration of Richard Nixon (1969–74) initially attempted to redress long-standing Indian grievances. The Bureau of Indian Affairs was reorganized with a new head and other policy makers who put Indian needs above bureaucratic procedures or pressures from other interest groups. Appropriations for the Bureau and federal expenditures for Indian programs increased dramatically and Indians were given access to influential administration policy makers. This new departure began in 1970; within a year it had been reversed. The result was a rise of expectations followed by bitter disappointment, culminating in an Indian march on Washington and violent conflict on the reservations. The promise of improved living conditions and just treatment was blighted by pressure from white business interests who feared that the new policies would prevent exploitation of mineral deposits, water rights, and land opportunities in Indian territories; by infighting between the Bureau and the Department of the Interior and Congress; by conflicts between government-imposed tribal councils, responsive mainly to white commercial groups, and red people seeking to protect their remaining sources of wealth; and by friction between "mixed bloods," who usually dominated the political establishments on the reservations, and younger, more radical militants, frequently "full bloods," who accused the councils of selling out and oppressing the tribes in order to feather their own nests. Alvin M. Josephy, Jr., a student of Indian affairs, describes these tragic events and current struggles in the essay that follows.

To most non-Indian Americans, the Indian occupation and destruction of the Bureau of Indian Affairs Building in Washington, D.C., last November, and in recent weeks the seizure of 11 hostages and the succeeding dramatic events at Wounded Knee, S. D., the kidnapping of the city's mayor and shootout at Gallup, N. M., the burning of the courthouse at Custer, S. D., and the scattered—but spreading—rash of similar violent confrontations between Indians and whites in different parts of the country have been shockers.

Indians *that* militant? Coming out of the

quiet of 100 years of the subjugation and inoffensiveness of "out of sight, out of mind" reservation life; tearing up a Government building in the nation's capital to convert it into a defensive fortress; threatening, if attacked, to kill whites and be killed themselves because (as the Sioux and Cheyennes once cried at the Little Bighorn) "it's a good day to die"; proclaiming goals of Indian sovereignty and Indian independence and asking for intercession by the United Nations; acting, in fact, for all the world like modern counterparts of all the Indians who fought back desperately against the ferocity and injustices of the white invaders of their lands in the 17th, 18th and 19th centuries and went down fighting as patriots—who would have believed it in 1973?

The most shocked, by far, has been the Nixon Administration, which believed genuinely that it had made a historical reversal of the tragic course of Federal-Indian relations and was giving American Indians, at last, everything they asked for. The Indians had been saying for years that it was about time that they be allowed to manage their own affairs on their reservations and not be governed like colonial subjects by Department of the Interior bureaucrats with yes-and-no power over everything that was important. They wanted the Government to continue to act as trustee, protecting their lands and rights that were guaranteed to them in treaties they considered sacred; but if they were to break the terrible grip of poverty and low standards of education, health and other fundamentals of life that made existence so desperately hopeless for them, they wanted an end to unworkable policies and programs imposed on them by unknowledgeable white bureaucrats in Washington and the ability, instead, to devise and carry out the programs which they knew, better than others, that their people needed and could make work successfully.

Some called it freedom, some called it self-determination. But no President listened to them until 1970. In July of that year President Nixon finally sent a special message to Congress, announcing a new national attitude toward Indians—at least, on the part of his Administration. He would give the Indians the self-determination they had asked for, making them self-governing on their reservations in the same way that all other Americans were self-governing citizens of their cities, towns and counties. At the same time, like a bank that acts as a trustee for a person's money or property, the Federal Government would continue to act as trustee for the Indians, protecting the land and resources that they owned.

Nor, at first, were these simply words. The President followed up his message by sending enabling legislation to Congress (which the Congress has not yet passed) and ordering a thorough "shaking up" and restructuring of the Bureau of Indian Affairs, the agency in the Department of the Interior charged with carrying out Federal Indian policies and programs, to provide mechanisms through which the tribes could take over the management and direction of their own affairs from the bureaucracy.

Though this sudden turn of events seemed hard for Indians to believe, their incredulity began to give way to enthusiasm as the Administration drove on in the new direction. Accessibility to the highest levels of Government was given to Indians by the assignment of two of the President's White House aides, Leonard Garment and his assistant, Bradley Patterson, as troubleshooters, with an open door in the Executive Office of the President to aggrieved Indians and a directive to help Indians push the bureaucrats to carry out the intent of the new policy. Another expediting mechanism, the National Council on Indian Opportunity, chaired by Vice President Spiro Agnew and composed of eight Cabinet-level officials and eight nationally prominent Indians, established another line of communication between the Indian people and the very top of the Government. Its function was to act as a watchdog over all Federal-Indian relations and see that the Government carried out effectively the policies the Indians wanted.

The failure of Congress to enact the legislation sought by the Administration (more about those bills later); some damaging resistance and politicking by various old and new bureaucrats and officials in the Department of the Interior (more about that, too); and minor and temporary differences among some of the Indians over certain policies (which were eagerly played upon and magnified by opponents of Nixon's Indian policy in Congress and the Administration, and which also will be expanded upon below) had the effect of hobbling the drive to carry out the President's goal of self-determination. But under Louis R. Bruce, the new, sympathetic Commissioner of Indian Affairs, son of a Mohawk and a Sioux, who soon became beloved by most Indians in the country, the Bureau was "shaken up" and reorganized to prepare itself for true Indian self-determination by becoming a service, rather than a managing, agency. Brilliant and dedicated young Indians were brought in to head Bureau activities as policy makers, and for a while in late 1970, before the political hobbling began to trip them up, they gave to Federal-Indian affairs a freshness, vitality and optimism that were unprecedented in the Bureau's long and dismal history.

With all these things, including most importantly the publicly stated objective of the President, going for them, the Indians soon began to feel that maybe this time there would be no broken promises. Despite the absence of the enabling legislation which the Administration had requested, ways were found to turn over full management of their affairs to two tribes, the Zuñis in New Mexico and the Miccosukees in Florida. Dozens of other tribes, preparing to follow the Zuñi and Miccosukee example, acquired control over certain activities on their reservations, including in some cases their schools, contracting with the Bureau for funds with which to operate what they took over. At the same time, Federal spending for Indians was increased dramatically. The Bureau's appropriations rose from $243 million in fiscal 1968 to more than $530-million in fiscal 1973, while over-all Federal expenditures for Indians (including funds for Indian programs in such agencies as the Office of Economic Opportunity and the Department of Health, Education and Welfare) climbed from $455 million to $925-million in the same period. The Bureau also undertook studies to persuade the Administration and Congress to add wholly new appropriations for the provision of education, health, welfare and other services to so-called urban Indians, now estimated to number almost half a million, who live in cities and do not share in most tribal programs, though their needs are often equal to those on the reservations.

On many other fronts—from increased scholarships for higher education and support of Indian cultural activities to accelerated economic development programs—steps were taken to give tribes what they wanted and to ameliorate or end long-festering situations. High on the list of such actions were the settling of the land claims of the Alaskan Natives (a complicated, land-and-money compromise that satisfied most of the Natives, though in the long run it may prove not to have been in the best interests of all of them) and the return to several tribes—including the Taos Pueblo in New Mexico, the Yakimas in Washington and the people of the Warm Springs reservation in Oregon—of sacred or other desired pieces of land which the Indians felt had been unjustly taken from them and which they had been struggling for many years to regain. Each of these actions resulted largely from the personal interest of the President, the Vice President and the White House aides charged with special attention to Indian affairs and reflected, at the least, the wish on the part of the White House to strengthen Indian faith in the Administration.

Then why, in the face of all this, did the sudden explosion occur at the Bureau of Indian Affairs Building last November that seemed to say, also at the very least, that there was no faith, only a desperation and hatred so deep that the Indians were ready to kill and be killed in the nation's capital? The answer lay both in the long, dishonorable history of this nation's treatment of Indians, which could not be overcome in so short a time, and in new frustrations and injustices that undermined and threw into question among many Indians the genuineness of the President's policy.

From the start, the enunciation of that policy and the incipient efforts to implement it seriously disturbed some of the top officials of the Department of the Interior, various people in the Office of Management and Budget, who question and approve the conduct of, and budgeting for, Indian programs, and certain members of the House and Senate Committees on Interior and Insular Affairs, who are responsible in Congress for Indian legislation. The reason for their wariness and distress is not hard to fathom. It has often been said, with considerable truth, that there is big money in "Indian business." The Indian tribes still own more than 55,000,000 acres which, with their water, minerals, timber, grazing lands and other natural resources, represent a sizable portion of that part of the nation's territory which is still largely unspoiled, unexploited and unpolluted. For many years the acquisition of these resources has been the objective of numerous non-Indian users, whose pressures and tactics, often questionable if not outright fraudulent, have brought them into serious conflicts with the Indians. Inevitably, the conflicts have turned the white interests for help to Senators and Congressmen of the Interior Committees and to friendly officials of the Department of the Interior of other agencies of the Administration, and almost as inevitably the Indians have suffered.

Most of the conflicts concern matters falling within the interests of agencies of the Department of the Interior and the two Interior Committees in Congress—land, water rights, mineral deposits, grazing ranges, rights-of-way, etc. Indeed, some of the chief usurpers of Indian resources have been Department of the Interior agencies themselves, like the Bureau of Reclamation which has diverted Indian water to non-Indian reclamation projects and built dams that flooded Indian lands, as well as the National Park Service and the Bureau of Land Management. The Department—and indirectly the two Congressional committees concerned with its activities—therefore wears two hats. As trustee of Indian resources, it is bound by law to protect tribal holdings; at the same time, its own agencies and various private interests (who, incidentally, have more votes and can contribute more campaign funds than Indians) must also receive sympathetic representation by the Department and its solicitors.

The conflict of interest has worked increasingly against the Indians, but in truth it has been to the liking of Western interests, some of the officials of the Department, and various Congressmen and Senators. It has kept Indians and Indian resources under their thumbs, so to speak, permitting them to exercise control over the course and disposition of the conflicts. Any move toward self-determination, any restructuring of the Indian Bureau that permitted the Indians to edge closer to decision-making authority over their own affairs (i.e., to get out of control), was something to oppose.

Perceiving this conflict of interest, the President nevertheless sent to Congress in the package of seven Indian bills he wished passed a proposal to establish an Independent Trust Counsel to represent the Indians in conflicts with Interior or other Government agencies. This has resulted in one of the first strains of Indian resentment, for not only has Congress predictably failed to enact the proposal, but the Administration, with the passage of time, has given scant evidence that it had a sincere commitment to this or any of its other Indian bills or really wanted them passed.

Meanwhile, grabs for Indian resources have reached the dimension of a massive assault by all sorts of conglomerates and huge industrial combinations. Tribe after tribe has become split into factions, as the Government has encouraged and aided coal companies to strip-mine Indian lands, much of them held sacred by the traditionalist Indians (those loyal to their ancient ways and spiritual beliefs); power companies to build monster, polluting generating plants, transmission lines, railroad spurs and truck highways on the reservations; and real-estate and industrial-development syndicates to erect large projects among the Indian settlements for the use of non-Indians.

Conflicts with a marked antiwhite as well as anti-Government character have broken out over many of these developments. Angry groups of Indians, composed not only of young activists but of all elements of the people, have protested the Bureau of Reclamation's diversion to a non-Indian irrigation project of the water of the Truckee River, the only major source of water for Pyramid Lake in Nevada, which is practically the entire reservation and the main supplier of income and livelihood to a Paiute tribe but which consequently is now drying up. Other Indians have become inflamed by strip-mining and power-plant developments on the Hopis' sacred Black Mesa in Arizona, on Navaho lands in Arizona and New Mexico and on the Crow and Northern Cheyenne reservations in Montana. Still others have fought white real-estate developments on a number of Southwestern reservations. These, and other white intrusions have been accompanied, moreover, by frictions that have made them worse: Indian water rights have been won away from tribes by deceit; leases have been signed secretly; their terms have been unfair; and even those terms have not been lived up to and are not enforced.

The method by which leases for Indian-owned resources are approved and signed has exposed another—and extremely serious—source of Indian anger. Prior to their military defeat by white men, all tribes had centuries-old methods for governing themselves, some by councils of wise and respected civil headmen and chiefs, others by hereditary religious or clan leaders. But in 1934 the Federal Government imposed on almost every tribe a uniform system of tribal councils—styled in the white man's way—that named the top tribal officers. Council members were supposed to be elected democratically by the people, but in practice the new system was so alien to large numbers of Indians that majorities of them on many reservations have refused consistently to vote in tribal elections and continue even today to regard the councils as institutions of the white man rather than of their own people.

The gap thus created between the tribal governments and the Indians who did not accept them was bad enough in the past—indeed, it has been another inhibiting factor in Indian development for a long time—but the move to give Indians self-determination, together with the greatly increased funds that have been appropriated for Indians in recent years, have worsened the situation by increasing the power and financial resources of the councils and tribal officers and, in effect, creating small political and economic Indian "establishments" on many reservations. The present Administration, looking for leaders who will run a tribe's affairs, has encouraged this development. But the system has resulted in accelerating the growth of corrupt little tyrannies, composed sometimes of the tribal councils and their friends and relatives, sometimes simply of the tribal chairman and his treasurer. These, acting in collusion with Government officials, the white interests desiring to exploit the reservation resources and the tribal lawyers (usually white men, but in all cases persons who *must* be approved by the Secretary of the Interior), have come to serve almost as willing arms or accomplices of the Federal Government.

The people's antagonisms to their tribal governments (sometimes exacerbated by added irritations, such as white-oriented mixed bloods who do not speak the tribe's language but who rule highhandedly over full bloods) have split many reservations. The Brûlé Sioux on South Dakota's Rosebud reservation have seethed for many years over a series of allegedly corrupt tribal officials. On the neighboring Pine Ridge reservation, the frustrations of Oglala Sioux who tried unsuccessfully to oust their tribal chairman, Richard Wilson, a mixed blood charged with corruption, nepotism and with being a puppet of white interests, were a major contributing cause of the outburst at Wounded Knee. Crows, Northern Cheyennes, Hopis and Navahos have had serious internal divisions over the secretive leasing activities of their tribal leaders, and numerous other groups, including the Mohawks in New York State, the Cherokees and other tribes in Oklahoma, and Indians at Tesuque in New Mexico and in Minnesota, Nebraska, the Northwest and throughout the Dakotas, have been in conflict with their governments.

The truth is that on few reservations today are the tribal leaderships fully accountable, or responsive, to the people (few Hopis knew about the leases to strip-mine Black Mesa or even today can find out what happens to the lease money paid to the tribe by the Peabody Coal Company). And the laws governing the Indians are still such that the people of few tribes possess the legal or political powers to "throw out the rascals" or reform their systems of government. Yet when they complain to the Bureau of Indian Affairs, they are told with utter hypocrisy that, because of the Indians' wish for self-determination, the Government will no longer interfere in internal tribal matters. But every Indian knows that the leases that threaten their reservations and are bringing them into conflict with white exploiters had to be approved by the Government, that in most cases it was the Government that first brought the white companies to the tribal chairman and lawyer, that the Government advised the chairman in the writing of the leases, and that it, finally, encouraged him to sign it.

The result of this—and of a number of allied developments—has been the growth of opposition, often sparked by activists, traditionalists and Indian landowners, against the reservation power establishments, whose members are termed derisively "Uncle Tomahawks" or "apples" (red on the outside, white on the inside), because they are viewed as tools of the white interest and betrayers of their own people. The problem has become more serious as the white intrusions have increased and become more insensitive to Indians and their ways of life, and as efforts by the Indians generally to bring them under control or stop them have been frustrated. Recognition of the Government's role in directing the Indian power establishment, even while it talked of self-determination, took on the coloration of anger over betrayal and, together with the developments that were occurring in Washington and on different reservations, began to set the stage for an Indian explosion.

In Washington, as noted, invigorating changes had begun to be made in the Bureau of Indian Affairs. It was not long, however, before storm signals were flying there too. Old-liners in the Bureau began to drag their heels, sabotage directives and engage in politicking against the new young Indian policy makers and their restructurings. The old bureaucrats who felt that their jobs and petty authority were threatened turned in three directions for help: they whipped up fears and jealousies among reservation tribal chairmen against the young Indian "militants," who, they said, had come to the Bureau from the cities, did not know the problems of the reservations and were instituting policies that would hurt the reservation Indians. Their charges were false, but they served for a time to arouse opposition among some tribal chairmen against Commissioner Bruce and any changes in the Bureau. At the same time, the old-liners appealed to members of the Senate and House Interior Committees, warning them that control over the tribes was slipping away, and to higher officials of the Department of the Interior, complaining of gross inefficiencies on the part of the allegedly inexperienced newcomers.

All these forces were strong enough to combine, in 1971, to halt the efforts to achieve the goals of President Nixon's message. Within the Department of the Interior, the line of authority in Indian affairs moved upward from Commissioner Bruce to Harrison Loesch, Assistant Secretary for Public Land Management under Secretary of the Interior Rogers C. B. Morton. Loesch, a stong-willed, determined man, who knew practically nothing about Indians and announced when he assumed office in 1969 that he had never been on an Indian reservation, became really the top Indian-affairs official in the Department. This put the Indians at a disadvantage for Loesch, who comes from Colorado and had good relations with Colorado Congressman Wayne Aspinall, chairman of the House Interior Committee, was more in tune with Western interests—whose eyes were on Indian resources—than he was on the tribes, and failed at any time to give evidence that he was in sympathy with the President's Indian policy.

Responding to the pressures of all those who, from intent of ignorance, objected to what the Bureau was doing, Loesch and the Department, with Congressional backing, took Bruce's powers from him, transferring them to a new Deputy Commissioner, John O. Crow, an unpopular old-liner, himself part Indian but one who had been associated with a discredited policy of the nineteen-fifties that would have ended the reservations, and who was removed from the Bureau in the nineteen-sixties by Secretary Stewart Udall. The Bureau's new policies, including the granting of self-management to the tribes, were halted; the whole thrust toward self-determination was shunted aside, and even the White House aides, Garment and Patterson, and the Indian members of the National Council on Indian Opportunity felt politically helpless. An almost instantaneous, united and highly vociferous Indian reaction throughout the country, however, resulted in second thoughts. A partial reversal followed, but the damage was done. Although Bruce's powers were somewhat restored to him, Loesch and his aides constantly undetermined Bruce and frustrated many of his objectives, hamstringing and immobilizing those in the Bureau who tried to get self-determination back on the main track of Indian affairs.

As a result, during 1972, Federal-Indian relations, off to so excellent a start in 1970 following the President's message to Congress, deteriorated rapidly. The Indian activists, many of them well educated, living in cities and familiar with the ways of the whites, lost patience with the establishment leaders on the reservations, who seemed to them to be playing willing stooges to a double-dealing Federal Government. Many of the activists joined the militant American Indian Movement and used every occasion to demonstrate and force confrontations with offending whites. They were, in truth, given many opportunities. Despite the increased Federal appropriations, services were not being delivered with any more efficiency to the Indians, nor were the added funds making a noticeable impact on age-old reservation problems. (The Government was spending almost $2,000 for each reservation Indian, yet the average annual income of each Indian *family* remained considerably below that figure.) To Indians who were aware of the affluence and high standards of living in the rest of the country, the continuation of the grinding poverty, the denials and the frustrations of families on the reservations were intolerable, as were the leases which the tribal leaders approved and which threatened their lands, resources, health, and continued existence as Indian peoples.

In addition, the prejudices, atrocities and injustices against Indians continued. In the Puget Sound area, for instance, Hank Adams, a courageous Assiniboin-Sioux and well known Indian intellectual, who had been leading a struggle for the Indians' treaty-guaranteed fishing rights in that region, had been shot and seriously wounded at night, and no one was arrested, In western Nebraska, Raymond Yellow Thunder, an elderly Sioux, was stripped of his pants by white tormentors, humiliated for fun before a white audience, then murdered and left in the cab of a pickup truck. In Philadelphia, Leroy

Shenandoah, an Onondaga veteran of the Green Berets and a member of the honor guard at President Kennedy's funeral, was brutally beaten and shot to death by police who justified the act as "excusable homicide." In California, Richard Oakes, a Mohawk known to all Indians as the leader of the occupation of Alcatraz Island, was slain by a white man whom the law treated lightly. In Custer, S.D., Wesley Bad Heart Bull, a Sioux, was killed and a white gas-station attendant was accused in the slaying. When the dead Indian's mother protested that the white man faced a maximum of only 10 years in prison if he were convicted, she herself was arrested by the white authorities and held on a charge calling for a maximum sentence of 30 years in prison.

Such incidents were neither new nor unique, but now they fed fuel to a fire that was rising. Neither the Federal Government nor state or local officials nor their own tribal leaders seemed willing or able to protect the Indians. Out of feeling of betrayal, of promises broken anew, the descent on the national capital, known as The Trail of Broken Treaties, was organized during the summer and early fall of 1972. Several Indian groups, as well as individuals from different reservations and cities, joined to send three automobile caravans from Los Angeles, San Francisco and Seattle across the country to Washington, D. C. The plan was to arrive there just before the national election, to bring the Indians' demands to the attention of the country, and to President Nixon and his opponent, Senator McGovern. The groups agreed that the mission would be peaceful. Church groups and others donated money, and the caravans started off in October, stopping at reservations and Indian centers along the way and picking up holy men, mothers and fathers with their children, young couples, old people, anybody who would come. There was no idea of violence; to some it was even a holiday, a great adventure, a chance to leave the reservation for the first time and see the rest of the country.

The caravans included large contingents of young members of the American Indian Movement, a confrontation-experienced group. The leading architect of the undertaking, however, was Hank Adams, the Puget Sound fishing-rights leader, who had run unsuccessfully in last year's Washington State Congressional primary (though garnering more than 10,000 votes). Adams helped organize the caravan from Seattle and was head of a group called the Survival of American Indians Association. As early as 1971 he had chaired a committee which had framed a 15-point program for a new national Indian policy "to remove the human needs and aspirations of Indian tribes and Indian people from the workings of the general American political system and . . . reinstate a system of bilateral relationships between Indian tribes and the Federal Government." When the Washington-bound caravans paused in Minneapolis and St. Paul, the 1971 proposals for a new Indian policy became the foundation for a set of 20 demands, calling principally for the reinstitution of a treaty-making relationship between the U.S. and the "Indian Tribes and Nations."

The events that ensued in the nation's capital reflected possibly the ultimate in bad faith on the part of the Government. On Oct. 11, Harrison Loesch had issued "specific directions" that the Bureau of Indian Affairs was "not to provide any assistance or funding, either directly or indirectly" to the Indians coming to see the President. Before the caravans' arrival, however, Robert Burnette, a Rosebud Sioux, former executive director of the National Congress of American Indians and author of "The Tortured Americans," together with other Indian advance organizers in the capital, persuaded Loesch to change his mind and offer certain facilities to the Indians while they were in Washington. Although President Nixon would be in California, the organizers won promises that the Indians would be able to meet with policy-making officials of the Government, including White House representatives of the President, to discuss their grievances and proposals.

But these expectations were soon destroyed. Living quarters arranged for the Indians were inadequate and rat-infested. The top officials they expected to see turned out to be Harrison Loesch, Bradley Patterson from the White House and lesser figures who angered them by their disdain and patronizing. Bitterness reached the boiling point when the Indians were barred from entering Arlington Cemetery to visit the graves of Indian heroes, including that of Ira Hayes, a Pima and one of the famous Marine flag-raisers at Iwo Jima in World War II. Finally, the explosion came. The Indians had been told they could move into the auditorium of one of the Government buildings. Just before they got to the building, someone locked the door—the rumor being that Loesch had ordered them kept out. The Indians hastened to the Bureau of Indian Affairs Building and, after a conference, were told that they could stay there. When the guard was changed, however, the new shift, apparently ignorant of the agreement, tried to oust the Indians. A scuffle ensued, the guards themselves were ousted and the Indians took possession of the building, remaining in control of it for almost a week.

The damage they did, by some estimates more than $2-million, reflected their anger and frustration as well as their determination to defend the building against attack, laying down their lives, if necessary, like Indians of the past who fought for their people. It was not a hollow gesture. Once the building had been occupied, Department of the Interior officials showed almost unbelievable insensitivity. Refusing to meet with Indian negotiators until the building had been evacuated, Secretary Morton unknowledgeably termed the occupiers a "small, willful band of malcontents." A few tribal chairmen were induced to hurry to Washington to condemn the occupiers. The chairmen's presence angered the Indians even more. Led by Hank Adams and tribal religious leaders, some of the occupiers humiliated the chairmen denouncing them as traitors to their people. Thereupon the chairmen, saying that

all Indians supported the aims of the Trail of Broken Treaties but hoped there would be no violence, returned to their reservations. More seriously, the Government brought busloads of armed men and won court permission to oust the Indians by force if they did not leave the building peaceably.

The final deadline was 6 P.M., Nov. 6, the eve of Election Day. Most of the damage inside the building occurred that afternoon as the Indians prepared barricades of business machines and furniture and weapons to defend themselves. Dynamite, rumored to have been supplied by Black Panthers in Washington, who had been inside the building to pledge solidarity with the Indians, was said to have been placed on the top floor to blow up the structure; the corridors and office floors were littered with papers from files, providing the makings of a conflagration; and Molotov cocktails had been prepared. The solicitors and other officials of the Department of the Interior must have known that a pitched battle, with many casualties on both sides, threatened the nation's capital, yet at 5 P.M. on the day before the American people were to go to the polls, they were still determined to risk a national tragedy, with enormous historical consequences, by storming the building.

The disaster was averted at the last minute by a stay from the U.S. Court of Appeals and the intervention of the White House. That evening Leonard Garment, Bradley Patterson, Louis Bruce, and Frank Carlucci, then Deputy Director of the Office of Management and Budget, began the first of several negotiating sessions with the Indians that led eventually to the peaceful evacuation of the building and an agreement by the White House to consider the Indians' 20-point program.

The Indians left Washington, some of them taking cartons of documents from the files; the Government did consider the 20 points and turned them all down, and a new—and still undefined—chapter opened in Federal-Indian relations.

As the tribal chairmen had stated, most

Indians in the country approved of the aims of the caravans, though they disapproved of the destruction of the building. The entire affair, including the taking of Government documents, however, angered many members of Congress, as well as officials of the Administration, who regarded the episode as reflecting an ungratefulness on the part of Indians generally. The Government, Secretary Morton announced soon afterward, had tried things the Indian way; now it would do things its own way. That sort of punitive mood against all Indians has not yet died in Washington, and it remains to be seen whether punishment will come and, if so, what form it will take. Initial indications of the way the Administration will henceforth conduct its relations with the tribes do not bode well for the Indians.

John Crow and Harrison Loesch were fired, but so was Commissioner Bruce, who angered his superiors by staying inside the occupied building with the Indians one of the nights. Loesch, meanwhile, has been hired as a staff counsel by the Senate Committee on Interior and Insular Affairs, where, if he is of a mind to, he can wreak a terrible revenge on the Indians. In the White House Leonard Garment and Bradley Patterson have been told to "get off their Indian hobby horse" and turn to other things, and restructurings inside the Executive branch foretell abandonment of all the hopes and promises held out by the President's message to Congress in 1970. A new acting Commissioner of Indian Affairs, with little power, will report to Secretary Morton, who will also have little power, for he, in turn, will report on the "human affairs" of Indians to Secretary Caspar Weinberger of the Department of Health, Education and Welfare, and on "land and resource affairs" to Secretary Earl L. Butz of the Department of Agriculture. Both those men, in turn, will report to John Ehrlichman in the White House. This decision-making power over Indian affairs is further complicated by the appointment of John C. Whitaker as Under Secretary of the Interior, with authority over Indian affairs,

and the ability, apparently, to report directly to Ehrlichman, bypassing Secretary Morton, whom Indians are already calling "Secretary of his limousine."

All of this raises new questions for the Indians in dealing with the Government: Whom do they see? Who will see them? Who can speak with authority? Who will have the last word in decisions? It also suggests a diffusion of Indian affairs throughout the bureaucracy and a blending of Indian interests with those of non-Indians (will they be "packaged" into programs for the population as a whole?). If this occurs, what happens to the special and unique Federal-Indian relations, concerned with treaties, treaty rights, trustee functions guaranteed services, etc.? And, finally, what happens to self-determination and to the reservations, the sacred lands and their resources, the tribal organizations, and the tribes themselves? In short, what happens to the Indians as Indians?

These questions are unsettling to the tribes, filling them once more with fears for the future, and, worst of all, persuading them that they may be facing another heart-breaking turnaround of Indian policy. Nor are their fears groundless. The Presidential impoundments of funds appropriated by Congress, being felt by other elements of the population, are already striking hard at reservations, where health, education and development programs, begun and expanded so optimistically with the increased appropriations of recent years, are being cut down or abruptly ended before they have had a chance to accomplish their intentions. Community development, preschool training, road building, medical services, scholarships—every aspect of the Indians' plans to lift themselves from poverty and helplessness—are being affected. And as they protest and demonstrate with the only method they have to call attention to their plight, the method itself hardens the attitude of the white law-enforcement agencies toward them in a manner that recalls the 19th-century use of troops against their forefathers, and further divides the Indians between the fearful ones, the venal ones and the determined patriots.

Must the "Indian problem" (really the white man's problem) go on then, with more human misery and suffering, for another generation? It is abundantly clear that it need not. As a first step, the Nixon Administration can—indeed, must—restore the policy of tribal self-determination as enuciated in the President's message of 1970, halting the diffusion of Indian interests throughout the Government, supporting again the goals of former Commissioner Bruce, and establishing accessibility for aggrieved Indians to a decision-making center in the White House. It must, in addition now, go further by enabling the Indian peoples to attain true political freedom and liberties that will permit them to establish forms of government of their own choosing on their respective reservations, letting them run their own lives and make their own mistakes as do the citizens of any other community. Only in this way will responsible, and responsive, governments emerge, able to protect their people from exploitation, abuse and injustices. The principles, if not the terms, of the Trail of Broken Treaties' 20 points must also be seen from the Indian viewpoint as viable guidelines for the protection of their lands and resources. It may be necessary to take the route of executive order, rather than go through Congress, to set up some sort of independent trust counsel and free the Indians from the stranglehold of Interior and its committees in Congress. But however it can be most rapidly accomplished—and even President Nixon once acknowledged its urgency—the committed goal must be the immediate and strict observance of treaty guarantees and trustee obligations by the Federal Government.

Finally, poverty and its attendant demoralizing ills among Indians on and off reservations must be attacked and broken without inhibition. The Government has responded with billions of dollars for aid and rehabilitation programs for suffering peoples, including its former enemies, everywhere in the world. The same is certainly due its own citizens, the American Indians. A massive, long-range public-works program, supplying tens of thousands of Indian jobs, could provide roads, housing, water and sanitation facilities, schools, hospitals, utilities, and other improvements needed and desired by the Indians. Numerous other programs, devised by the people themselves who know better than the whites what they need and can carry out successfully for their own development, await only Federal funding.

But will the Administration listen to the Indians and respond wisely to their new crisis? Only President Nixon himself now has the power to supply the answer.

THE FIRST AMERICANS

According to the U.S. census of 1970, the Indian population of the United States today, including Eskimos and Aleuts, is approximately 843,000, with some 480,000 of them living on or near reservations and the rest in cities or rural communities. Their heaviest concentrations, as estimated in 1972, are in Arizona (117,000), Oklahoma (84,000), New Mexico (82,000), Alaska (59,000) and California (49,000). At the time of the first white settlements in the early sixteen-hundreds, it is estimated that about one million Indians lived in what is now the United States. Studies still under way suggest that many Indians were wiped out in epidemics of Europeans' diseases before the tribes even came in contact with the white frontier settlers, and that the actual figure may therefore have been considerably higher. Today, Indians are increasing at a faster rate than that of the over-all U.S. population.

By treaty and other obligations, the Bureau of Indian Affairs serves 267 Federally recognized Indian land units, including reservations, colonies, rancherias and communities, and 35 groups of scattered public-domain allotments and other off-reservation lands. Indians also live on state-recognized reservations and on lands which are no longer, or never were recognized as reservations by the Federal Government or a state. —A. M. J. Jr.

Black America:
Still Waiting for Full Membership

JUAN CAMERON

Today the Afro-Americans face ambivalent prospects. During the late 1950s and 1960s, blacks made significant civil rights gains. Congress passed its first civil rights bill since Reconstruction in 1957, and in the next decade followed through with additional legislation designed to protect political rights and advance residental, educational, and vocational integration. Municipal and state legislatures and commissions apparently guaranteed blacks long-withheld citizenship rights and laid the groundwork for integration in housing and schools. The private sectors, particularly labor unions, large corporations, and colleges, enrolled sizable numbers of blacks as members, employees, and students, and less appreciable but important increases were registered in managerial and faculty posts. Nevertheless, the current situation is less hopeful than it appeared a few years ago despite the fact that bourgeois blacks continue to make progress in getting more education, better jobs, and higher income, and a greater percentage of the race is now in the middle class. On the other hand, those in the lower income, educational, and occupational strata, who still compose a majority of the race, are losing ground. As a result, the gap between black and white unemployment rates, income levels, and entry into college has widened. Residential and school integration has also increased; divorce and desertion rates in the black family have risen; federal, state, and local governments are less active on behalf of civil rights; and the waning commitment to civil rights and the recession of the mid-1970s severely diminished the treasuries and hence the ability of civil rights organizations like the NAACP and the National Urban League to fight for racial equality and integration. Juan Cameron, in "Black America: Still Waiting for Full Membership," describes these recent gains and losses and their impact upon black expectations and attitudes and upon race relations in America.

... [Thomas Bradley and Frank Robinson] are not "black leaders" as the phrase is customarily used. They are leaders in various demanding professions, and they happen to be black. That Thomas Bradley should be picked as the best-qualified man to run the third-largest U.S. city, and that Frank Robinson could move from straightforward slugging to the subtleties of management are signs that—200 years late—America is making use of a great reservior of talent it long, out of prejudice, denied itself.

The young man with the keys could serve as symbol both of how far the blacks have come in the past ten years and of how far they still have to go. Sheriff Thomas Gilmore of Greene Country, Alabama, has taken command of the very jail he was thrown into in 1965 for getting blacks to register to vote. Blacks now control the county's entire political structure, from the school board to the probate judgeship. Jobs are still scarce as ever, and the average black family in Greene County has an income of about $2,500. Political power, in short, has produced no economic miracles, unless 250 subsidized housing units are considered such. What blacks have gained is a strong sense of pride. "Hopes are high among my people," says Gilmore. "The question is, how do we deliver on them."

A VANGUARD CLOSES THE GAP

This story of a drive to success by the able and ambitious, of hopes raised but still unrequited among the poor, is the story, in summary, of 23.7 million black Americans today. In the past decade, the majority of blacks have made their own way into the mainstream of U.S. life, while an underclass has remained mired behind as wards of the welfare state. Black progress can be measured in rapidly growing political power, a doubling of the college-graduation rate among the young, and dramatic increases in income. Young black families are the vanguard, and they have virtually closed the income gap between the races.

The longer the perspective, the greater the progress looks. An American born after World War II has seen the first black generals and admirals, the first black Supreme Court Justice, the first two black Cabinet officers, new black superstars in the theater, motion pictures, the record industry, and television—and, of course, the emergence of black stars in all major sports. The number of black lawyers, accountants, college teachers,

and other members of the professions almost doubled in a decade.

To most whites, this seems quite remarkable progress, a reaffirmation of the System's noblest ideals. But whites do not have, as blacks do, a profound sense of having been defrauded in the first place by the hypocrisy of a government that proclaimed all men equal and kept some locked in slavery. Even the great national drama of the Civil War, fought with so much bloodshed and passion, brought no permanent improvement in the lot of blacks, whose status was the central issue.

As laborers and skilled artisans, blacks tilled the land and built the mansions of the South but were condemned to live as second-class citizens. A "peanut gallery" was reserved for them in movie theaters. They could not try on clothing in department stores or reserve a Pullman berth. Newspapers did not use courtesy titles for blacks. "Your first name becomes 'nigger,' your middle name becomes 'boy' (however old you are) and your last name becomes 'John,'" Martin Luther King wrote in his famous "Letter from Birmingham Jail."

This train of searing humiliations has, understandably, left a bitter residue. Some blacks sound even angrier than they did ten years ago when the breakthroughs were just beginning. Many educated blacks today, particularly younger ones, vent an almost paranoic distrust and even hatred of whites. The alienation of the black underclass, if less vocal, is no less profound. It has produced almost unfathomable social and financial problems in the ghettos of the nation's cities, where blacks have been locked in a seemingly inescapable cycle of poverty and crime.

But the sometimes blinding anger is only one facet of a broader phenomenon—that more blacks are asserting themselves and shaking off old feelings of inferiority. Dr. Alvin Poussaint, a psychologist at Harvard Medical School, predicts that slogans like "Black Is Beautiful," and the adoption of African hairstyles and dress, will have a strong positive effect on the self-esteem of the new generation of blacks now coming to maturity.

"OUR FIRST HURRAH"

So will the new class of black politicians, who have gradually replaced the older civil-rights leaders as the chief spokesmen for their race. "Politics is our first hurrah," says Maynard Jackson, the flamboyant mayor of Atlanta. "It's where things are today." As mayor, Jackson can intervene vigorously at the least hint of police brutality—a major complaint of blacks for decades in Atlanta—and he has jobs and other patronage to dispense. Mervyn Dymally, the lieutenant governor of California, points out that blacks now have a lot of power in the California legislature, and this puts them in a position to bring pressure on labor unions to let in more black apprentices: "If the unions are interested in some legislation I can call them up and say, 'My people in Watts can't get into your union.' They will respond to us now because we have some political clout here."

Behind the big names like Jackson and Dymally and Senator Edward Brooke of Massachusetts lies an impressive mass effort by blacks in politics. Over 3,000 blacks serve as elected officials today, ten times as many as a decade ago. The number of black voters in eleven southern states has nearly doubled during the past eight years, thanks in great part to the Voter Education Project now headed by John Lewis, a civil-rights pioneer who successfully made the transition from sit-ins to hard organizational work. The number of blacks elected in those eleven states has jumped from 72 in 1964 to 565 in 1970 and 1,587 in 1975. All together, blacks now hold eighteen seats in Congress and 278 in the state legislatures. Black mayors run 120 towns and cities, including Los Angeles, Detroit, Washington, D.C., Dayton, Newark, Atlanta, Cincinnati, and Gary, Indiana.

Martin Kilson, a professor of government at Harvard, points out that if black voters' influence is to be felt in state and national policy, their political leaders must appeal to a wider electorate. And so Kilson's interest, and that of many black leaders, is focused on those politicians like Bradley and Brooke who have demonstrated the ability to win elections by combining the black and the liberal white vote. Wilson Riles has twice been elected as California's superintendent of public instruction (he controls the largest chunk of the state budget), and last fall, Colorado, like California, elected a black lieutenant governor. Blacks make up less than 10 percent of the population in California and 3 percent in Colorado. The Memphis congressional district, which is 53 percent white, elected a black Congressman, and Raleigh, North Carolina, which is only 24 percent black, elected a black mayor. Less attention has been paid so far to an equally significant trend—the effort by *white* politicians to woo black voters. Governor George Wallace of Alabama has appointed a black as coordinator of highways and traffic and he has swallowed the white-supremacist rhetoric that made him a national political power.

Black economic progress can also be demonstrated by a mountain of statistical evidence. But two adverse trends have developed. One is that the growth peaked in 1969; the median income of black families is actually a bit lower now than then (while white median income edged up 6 percent). The other trend is what Andrew Brimmer, formerly a member of the Federal Reserve Board, and now a professor at Harvard Business School, calls the "deepening schism" in black America. Even while black income was drawing somewhat closer to average white income, the gap was widening *within* the black community "between the able and less able," as Brimmer puts it, "between the well-prepared and those with fewer skills." Senator Brooke points out that while 35 percent of black families now earn more than $10,000 a year, the number considered to be living in poverty still stands at almost eight million, or about a third of the black population. That figure has declined hardly at all since 1968.

There is no single explanation for the disappointing trend in black incomes since 1969. Blacks were hit harder than whites by the 1970 recession, and since then the median incomes of blacks and whites have been on roughly parallel tracks. (Whites haven't done very well either, thanks to recession and roaring inflation.) But the dramatic black catch-up seems to have ended for now.

THE MAN WHO ISN'T THERE

Black leaders blame this adverse development on the policies of the Nixon Administration, citing cuts in funds for many community-action programs, which had employed a large, well-paid corps of black managers and clerical workers. While laying off these blacks, however, Nixon and Congress vastly increased various income-support programs. Since some of these programs, such as food stamps and Medicaid, aren't reflected in the income statistics, poor families have been faring somewhat better than Census Bureau data would indicate. According to one recent study, blacks living on welfare can afford more than twice as much in the way of goods and services as welfare families could in 1947.

One continuing drag on black income, and perhaps the most important, is family instability. This is connected in turn with high unemployment rates among black males—and with the waywardness of welfare programs. If the family is intact, both husband and wife usually work, and in such households the median family income is $9,729 a year. But if the husband loses his job, a vicious chain reaction may begin. Since the family can't live on the wife's earnings alone, the husband may decamp while the wife signs up for welfare. The family is thrown abruptly from near-affluence to poverty—all the way across that "schism" Brimmer talks about.

Since 1969, the proportion of black households headed by females has increased from from 28 to 34 percent. Average income in these households is less than one-half that of households where the husband and wife are living together. During this same period, the percentage of black married women in the work force has been declining. According to the Census Bureau, this trend among black women had a "particularly strong effect on the overall black family income."

One of the wilder white misconceptions about blacks, however, is that most of them are on the dole. It is true that a black mother is twice as likely to be drawing welfare as a white mother, but 85 percent of black income is earned, compared to 86 percent for whites. The difference is in the source of the non-earned income; blacks get theirs mostly in transfers from government and whites get more of theirs from capital.

Blacks have been steadily upgrading themselves into better jobs, an effort that should sooner or later get family incomes moving up once again. The proportion of blacks holding white-collar jobs has increased by 50 percent in the past ten years. Blacks have been pouring into the trade unions, where they account for 12 percent of the total membership and a third of all new members. They are poorly represented in the union hierarchies, but their influence is growing, especially in the industrial and government unions: one-third of the steelworkers and a third of the members of the state and municipal workers' unions are black, and the percentage is about the same for the auto workers. Employment gains have been particularly noticeable where federal contracts and subsidies can be used to force employers to take "affirmative action" in hiring quotas of blacks and other minorities.

These quotas, however, are the newest friction point between blacks and whites. Black leaders charge that the Nixon Administration softened its commitment to the program, easing the pressure on corporations to comply. The bulging case loads at the federal enforcement agencies involved in the program don't seem to bear out this charge. Almost every large corporation does have a quota, or at least targets, for minority hiring.

But many corporate executives consider them a basic affront to a free society, and it may well be that they are meeting their targets grudgingly at best.

SOME ARE WINDOW DRESSING

In any event, and for whatever reason, corporations have been hiring more blacks for managerial jobs. Some 379,000 blacks are now managers, half again as many as in 1969. It is true, as blacks charge, that very few of them have risen to positions of real authority. Corporations say this is due to their lack of experience and seniority rather than to prejudice, but that is not how blacks view it. "Every nonwhite employee is seen as lowering standards," says Tony Brown, a television producer in New York. "But when I compare myself to whites in the industry who are above me, I don't think they are competent enough to work for me."

Only a few corporations—among them Cummins Engine, Xerox, and I.B.M.—have placed blacks in responsible line positions. Most black managers, even the vice presidents, have what they describe as "window dressing" jobs, or else are relegated to personnel and sales posts concerned with black markets. Black hold few directorships in major corporations and few partnerships in law and accounting firms.

Black-owned and -managed businesses, with a few exceptions like Motown Industries, H. G. Parks, Johnson Publishing, and North Carolina Mutual Life Insurance, are small and undercapitalized. Many of them, including a number of black-owned banks, are in precarious financial condition. A survey by *Black Enterprise* magazine in 1974 showed that only thirty-four of the top 100 black-owned corporations had sales of $5 million or more; all 100 companies had sales of only $601 million. Individual blacks have accumulated little personal wealth. Their family net worth averages less than $4,500, according to a 1966 Census Bureau survey, one-fourth that of whites.

Blacks have not been able to break the white noose of suburbia that encircles the inner city. Three-fourths of all blacks live in urban areas, 60 percent of them in the central city. In the decade of the Sixties this pattern showed little change. While some 800,000 better-off blacks were able to move into suburban housing—mostly in all-black areas— the black population in the inner cities grew by 3.3 million. During this same period, the white population of the inner cities dropped by two million.

Much of this polarization was doubtless inevitable, given the need of poor black migrants for cheap housing in the cities and the longing of the white middle class for single-family homes. But it was made much worse by a persistent pattern of discrimination in the sale, renting, and financing of suburban housing. A federal law against such discrimination has been on the books for ten years, but nobody has succeeded in enforcing it. Blacks who aspire to be homeowners have also been hit by a cruel economic trend: just as their incomes began rising rapidly, the cost of housing shot up rapidly too.

To make matters worse, industry has followed the move of middle-income whites to the suburbs. Effectively barred from living near the relocated businesses, blacks have found themselves shut out of jobs. Asking a black to make the daily journey to the suburbs, a Baltimore official says, is like asking him "to go to Timbuktu." In the Baltimore area, he explained, several hours of travel would be required using antiquated, expensive, and unreliable public transportation.

THE BREAK IN THE DIALOGUE

Despite all these barriers, more points of contact have developed between whites and blacks in recent years, especially in the workplace. Yet it is difficult to escape the impression that whites and blacks are not talking to each other as candidly as they did in the heyday of the civil-rights breakthroughs in the 1960s. Whites are inclined to be a bit smug about those breakthroughs, and even to give themselves quite a lot of credit for correcting age-old wrongs. But blacks would argue that very little happened until Mrs. Rosa Parks, a Montgomery seamstress, refused to move to the back of that bus in December, 1955. Change was not granted by white society but wrenched from it, and most of the victims of the struggle—though not the most publicized ones—were black.

Many blacks are now worried that the gains won at such cost will be stolen. One coming battle will be to extend the Voting Rights Act, which expires [in 1975]. Blacks have had to return repeatedly to the courts to get civil-rights laws enforced, and the federal government is spending about $360 million this year on what must be considered only a partial effort to make the laws stick. One civil-rights officer with the Department of Health, Education, and Welfare in Atlanta says: "Without this pressure from the courts and the executive, school desegregation in the South and elsewhere would disappear during the morning recess period."

As the fights over busing in Boston and Pontiac illustrate, the resistance to the acceptance of black rights is as strong in the North as it ever was in the South. Perhaps, today, more so. Mayor Bradley says, "The whole mood of whites has been affected by the cry of the reactionaries: 'We've done too much for blacks already.' "

Oddly enough, hopes are highest in that old crucible of black despair, the South. Although blacks have been leaving the South at the rate of about 100,000 a year since World War II, half of all blacks still live there. The migration hasn't ceased, but increasingly it is from rural areas to southern rather than northern cities. School integration has worked better in the South, and families are more apt to remain intact. And young black families, though starting from a lower base, have been making much more rapid economic progress.

THE ONE, TWO, THREES OF CHANGE

That veteran activist, John Lewis, also hails the rapid development of an interracial politics. In towns where Lewis was once beaten or jailed, he now gets greetings from white officials and, on occasion, a police escort. He is disturbed by some of the angry rhetoric he hears from black spokesmen in the North. "We can't afford to indulge in these outward forms of protest," he says. "We want the one, two, threes of change—things like better housing, paved streets, and traffic lights." And he adds, echoing Sheriff Gilmore of Greene County: "There is an element of hope in the South. Blacks have not given up."

The hope Lewis speaks of dims on the road northward. In the border city of Louisville, Lyman Johnson, the local president of the National Association for the Advancement of Colored People, tells how he has managed to desegregate a number of Louisville institutions during a forty-two-year fight. But real integration in schools and housing is no nearer than ever, and this elderly retired school principal says with astonishing fervor that the only way for his people to ge their due is to "destroy the system, which is rotten to its core."

In Harlem and Detroit, the mood is grim, and not only among the poor, but among middle-class students and blue-collar workers as well. The depressing hypothesis that forces itself forward is that the blacks' feeling of oppression in this white man's country has been altered not a whit by the vast change that has been and is taking place in the material conditions of black life. As one young black professional woman expressed it: "You are continually aware of your color from the time you wake up. When you walk down the street, come to your office. You are never allowed to forget it by whites."

The truth is that whites in the big cities of the North are scared half to death of blacks, and this fear and its accompanying hostility can be seen flickering in their eyes. The tragedy is that these feelings are visited most often on hardworking blacks—the only kind most whites see from day to day—who are as unlike criminals as people from another planet.

Some interesting contradictions in white attitudes are revealed by the opinion polls. The polls show that the majority of Americans are in *favor* of desegregated schools and open housing—even though whites have time and again fled both schools and communities when blacks moved in. Whites, in other words, have high principles for which they are not prepared to make much of a personal sacrifice, which perhaps is only human. To whites, it seems only rational to be wary of school integration in a city like New York, for example, where only 34 percent of the pupils in the public schools are reading at or above their grade levels, and 85 percent of those in correctional institutions are either black or of Spanish descent. Blacks who can afford to also shun poor schools and dangerous neighborhoods.

"A TANGLE OF PATHOLOGIES"

White attitudes will no doubt continue to change over time—integration even in the workplace is still a fairly new phenomenon and not without its tensions for whites as well as blacks. But a thorough transformation, a major shucking off of prejudice, probably won't happen until there is change in the black underclass, whose transgressions are dumped indiscriminately on the shoulders of every black. So the crux of the problem lies somewhere in the ghetto and the forces that created it, somehwere in what black psychologist Kenneth Clark has described as the "tangle of pathologies" there.

Unfortunately, nobody knows how to work any dramatic improvement in such an underclass, whatever the racial makeup. Better job opportunities for blacks would certainly help. James Q. Wilson, a professor of government at Harvard, has drawn up a rationale for imposing stiffer jail sentences on habitual offenders—the small group that commits more than half the crime. But many law-abiding blacks resist such a solution. Though blacks are themselves the principal targets of black crime, they have tended to view black criminals as victims of the larger society. They argue for less emphasis on jails, and more on rehabilitation programs outside prisons.

There is obviously a strong case for doing something to improve ghetto schools. Here again, unfortunately, nobody knows what might work. In a recent study, Sar Levitan, William Johnston, and Robert Taggart of George Washington University surveyed the ambitious and varied efforts that have been made to improve pupil performance in the slums. They reached this somber conclusion: "There is no proof that integration, increased outlays per pupil, more relevant curricula, or any changes have had, or will have, a rapid and significant impact."

And finally, since both crime and learning disabilities are strongly associated with broken homes, there is an argument for trying to knit together the fabric of black family life. Looked at from this perspective, the trends are getting worse. Birthrates for all black families have fallen sharply as for the population as a whole, but blacks still have larger families, especially at the lower-income levels. And as a result of rising separation, divorce, and illegitimacy rates, more than half of all black children gow up in female-headed households.

It would not seem beyond the political imagination to draw up a welfare program that encouraged work and stable families—rather than discouraging both. As the program is now designed, its incentives are skewed. In cities where the maximum welfare package is available, a husband earning $2 an hour could increase his family's income $2,158 a year by leaving them.

Nor does welfare provide an incentive to break out of the system and the degradation enveloping it. According to a recent congressional study, a woman in Detroit with three children to support would have to earn $7,350 a year to maintain the living standard welfare provides.

Blacks agree that the welfare system needs to be changed, but they helped defeat one attempt to do so, Nixon's Family Assistance Program. They suspect, not without cause, that campaigns for reform are sometimes a disguise for campaigns to cut the benefits. And they also accuse reformers of trying to impose white family patterns on blacks. This attitude inevitably seems as romantic to whites as the tendency to see black criminals as victims.

While the South seems to be moving, however haltingly, toward some sort of inter-racial society, the destination of blacks in the North is far less certain. For a while in the Sixties the idea of black separatism was fashionable among a small group. But that notion has been abandoned. The theme heard today among black leaders in many fields is that their people should strive to penetrate further the economic world that whites dominate. At the same time, however, blacks speak of continuing to build a distinct cultural image of themselves to strengthen the social and political cohesiveness of their race. These twin efforts, blacks hope, will finally open the door to their full membership in U.S. society.

TO STILL THE FIRE BELLS

At about the time the cotton economy of Greene County, Alabama, was beginning to flourish in the 1800's, the problem of black slavery was beginning to rack the nation. Thomas Jefferson foresaw the trouble that lay ahead on this issue. He heard ''a fire bell ringing in the night that awakened and filled me with terror.'' His words were a prophecy of the war, the murders, terrorism, lynchings, riots, and burnings that have occurred in this country in the century and a half since over the issue of race. While much has been accomplished in the last ten years to redress the grievances of blacks, much more still remains to be done if blacks are not to remain a rebuke to the nation's stated beliefs and ideals. The most difficult challenge will be to rekindle hope where it has flickered out. Conversely, the most encouraging sign is the hope that Greene County Sheriff Tom Gilmore sees still alive today among his people in the black belt. The problem, as he says, is how to ''deliver'' on those hopes, and so to still at last the rancor and violence that their denial has produced.

"Mexican American" and "Chicano":
Emerging Terms for a People Coming of Age

RICHARD L. NOSTRAND

The history of the southwestern part of the United States cannot be understood without examining the contribution and experience of those who came north from Mexico in the twentieth century. The maintenance of the railroads, the picking of cotton in Texas and Arizona, the digging for sugar beets in Colorado, the cultivation of a variety of fruits and vegetables in the San Joaquin and Imperial valleys of California, and the manning of machines in packing houses and industrial centers depended on the labor of the Mexicans and their children. Yet those of Mexican ancestry, like so many others who came from foreign countries to the United States, have never felt quite comfortable in this country. This self-consciousness is reflected in the fact that neither they nor other Americans have found a satisfactory term by which everyone can refer to them. In different parts of the West and at different times they have had a variety of appellations: "Mexican Americans," "Spanish Americans," "Latin Americans," "Latins," "Latinos," or "Chicanos." In the essay that follows geographer Richard L. Nostrand gives a brief history of the territorial distribution of settlement of this ethnic group and discusses the significance of these references for the Spanish-speaking minority. He explores the ethno-cultural ramifications of such usages for the minority group from the interior perspective of their own applications and from evaluations by the dominant culture of these references at various stages of their history in the United States.

Some years ago while conversing with a local resident in Las Vegas, New Mexico, I absent-mindedly inquired whether this individual were a "Mexican American." He bristled, replying that no, he was a "Spanish American." For me, this experience underscored a phenomenon which characterizes people of Spanish-Indian or Mexican descent: the existence of regional variations in self-reference terms.

"Spanish American" (sometimes simply "Spanish") and "Mexican American," together with "Latin American" (sometimes "Latin"), "Chicano(-a)," and "Mexican," are terms having the greatest currency in the American Southwest where members of this sizable minority are concentrated. They are the important terms by which "Hispanos" (used in this paper as an all-inclusive label) refer to themselves collectively. But, with

From *Pacific Historical Review*, Vol. 42, No. 3 (August 1973), pp. 389–406. Copyright © 1973 by the Pacific Coast Branch, American Historical Association. Reprinted by permission.

the exception of Chicano, they are used by Hispanos only when speaking in English; when speaking in Spanish, *mexicano* is most prevalent, although one also hears *raza* or *la raza* (literally, "the race," but figuratively, "the [our] people").

That these different self-referents exist is recognized in much of the literature concerning this minority, but there has been no attempt to synthesize this information in one place or to go beyond it and indicate which terms are currently in greater use and where. What follows is an attempt to do so, a task that must take into account certain historical patterns.

Spanish-Mexican colonization of the Southwest was not, of course, the result of one grand march to the north but of lesser enterprises separated in time and space on a distant frontier. Earliest colonization oc-

curred in the upper Río Grande Valley of Nuevo México, the result of a private venture led by Juan de Oñate in 1598 (Fig. 1). A century elapsed before missions began to be built (the first in 1700) in a second area of the present-day Southwest, northern Pimería Alta. In a score of years several settlements had been founded in Tejas (the earlier settled El Paso district was considered part of Nuevo México until the nineteenth century), and beginning in 1769 colonists converged by land and sea on Alta California. By the time of the signing of the Treaty of Guadalupe Hidalgo (1848) and the purchase of land by James Gadsden (1853)—events marking the frontier's transition to United States political status—settlements were numerous and widespread and the Mexican population numbered over 80,000.

Of the 80,000 Mexicans three-fourths

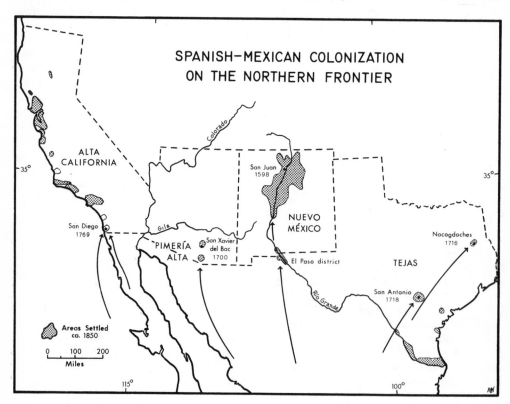

Figure 1. Spanish-Mexican Colonization of the Northern Frontier, ca. 1850.

lived in the basin of the upper Río Grande, an area made even more distinctive by certain cultural attributes. When the region was settled, some colonists practiced self-flagellation and other rites of the Penitente Brotherhood (introduced with Juan de Oñate, himself a Penitente), and all spoke Spanish. Some of these practices and certain features of this now archaic speech were perpetuated by New Mexicans in their isolation from others. Also perpetuated were the folk songs and plays brought from Iberia and transmitted orally from generation to generation. There developed an indigenous art form in which depictions of Christian saints (santos) were carved and painted—a craft which flourished in the first quarter of the nineteenth century. Thus, a folk culture with roots deep in the Spanish era was already in existence in New Mexico by the mid-nineteenth century.

Following the American takeover of the Southwest in 1848, Hispanic patterns underwent significant modification. One change resulted from the internal migration of those already residing in the Southwest, notably the movement of New Mexicans into south central Colorado (Fig. 2). A second resulted from the in-migration of Mexicans who reinforced numbers in existing settlements, or settled in new areas. From a trickle in the nineteenth century, the influx of migrants grew to a flood in the twentieth century, nearly 500,000 arriving during the 1920s alone. The two states receiving the largest numbers were Texas and California; Arizona received far fewer, and, by comparison, New Mexico and Colorado practically none. A third change resulted from the arrival in the Southwest of non-Hispanos. Even before the American period the number

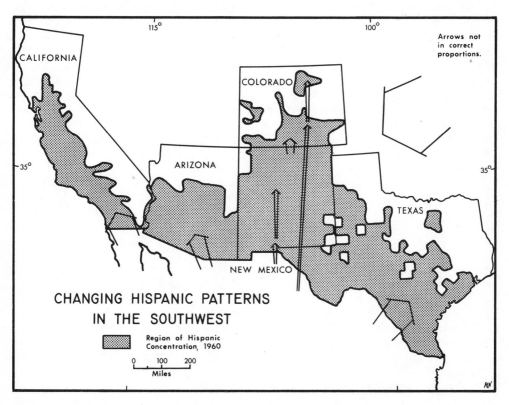

Figure 2. Changing Hispanic Patterns in the Southwest, 1850–1960.

of easterners and others who had gone to Texas and California was sufficient to engulf the resident Mexicans. Thereafter, numbers continued to swell and Hispanos were put increasingly in the minority.

By 1970 nearly 6,200,000 Hispanos (17.1 percent of the total population) inhabited the five southwestern states. An additional contingent, nearly 3,100,000 in size, had found its way to the non-southwestern states, but these Hispanos were widely scattered, many living in cities of the Middle West (notably Chicago). Thus, of the 9,300,000, two-thirds resided in the Southwest, the preponderance within the region delimited (Fig. 2). With over four-fifths of the southwestern Hispanic population in Texas and California, the pattern in 1970 was one heavily weighted to either end of the region—a complete reversal from that of a century before when three-fourths of the Mexicans lived in the region's center.

This is a distinctive yet highly diverse minority which is heavily concentrated in the more southerly Southwest. Most Hispanos are mestizo, yet some trace their lineage to Spaniards (as do certain New Mexicans), perhaps others to Indians. Most speak Spanish as a mother tongue, yet a few speak English in the home. Most are disadvantaged socio-economically, yet there are those who have advanced to a higher status. Over eighty-two percent are native-born and are, therefore, United States citizens, while of the remaining foreign-born only a small percentage have become naturalized citizens. There are, of course, vast differences in how far back the native-born can trace their ancestry in the United States—most not very far. Out of this diverse background sprang the several self-referents.

During the years of Spanish and Mexican political rule, the inhabitants of the northern frontier referred to themselves quite appropriately as "Spaniards" (*españoles*) and "Mexicans" (*mexicanos*). "Spaniard" did not abruptly disappear after 1821. Lewis Garrard, when traveling to Taos in 1846–1847, found it a "common term" (if one can

infer that what native New Mexicans were called reflected what they called themselves). On the other hand, "Mexican" increased in currency; it was the term Garrard usually used, and it was apparently prevalent everywhere on the frontier except in California. There, feelings of patriotism were "vague and contradictory," and to show autonomy within the Mexican Republic, natives referred to themselves as "Californios."

After the Mexican War native New Mexicans continued to refer to themselves as "Mexicans," but contempt for Mexicans was widespread among Anglos who used the term disparagingly. Under these circumstances, it is perhaps surprising that "Mexican" prevailed as long as it did. For, according to Erna Fergusson, it was not until World War I that "Spanish-American" was "invented" in New Mexico by those who wished to praise the readiness of natives to fight but who lacked a term for doing so. This diplomatic label rapidly caught on among Hispanos (also Anglos) in the 1920s. Significantly, this was precisely the time when relatively large numbers of Mexican immigrants were arriving—a group which the natives wished to disassociate themselves from in part because of its generally lower socio-economic status. By "Spanish American" a native meant that he was native-born of *Spanish* descent—a claim which could be made with justification if a Spanish-derived folk culture were being implied, but not if it implied a direct Spanish lineage, since most natives were mestizo.

After the Mexican War discrimination against persons of Mexican descent became especially severe in Texas (also in "Little Texas," an area in southeastern New Mexico). There, the southerner's attitude toward Negroes was carried over to the less dark Mexican, and the word "Mexican" was used with hatred. Presumably some Hispanos—like the small number of descendants of early colonists at Nacogdoches today—referred to themselves as "Spanish," still others as *tejanos,* but most called themselves "Mexicans." Thus, when "Latin American" was coined, it was probably welcomed. Just how and when this took place is not clear. It was apparently in use in south Texas prior to the founding there in 1929 of LULAC, the League of United Latin American Citizens, for that organization was formed from a merger of three organizations, one of which was the League of Latin American Citizens. This polite term did not become widespread in Texas until after World War II, however. With certain exceptions, the Hispano, when referring to himself as a "Latin American," meant that he was native-born of Mexican descent. But the educated who use this term are aware of its broader meaning to include most people of the Western Hemisphere south of the Río Grande.

Self-referents evolved somewhat differently in California. There the term "Californio" persisted among the native-born until the 1880s. Meanwhile, people calling themselves "Mexicans" were arriving from Mexico, and Californios, especially those of the upper class, behaved with animosity towards these foreign-born. In turn, both the Californio and the Mexican were alienated by the Anglo who considered each to be inferior because he was part Indian. Perhaps it was this situation that prompted the Californios to refer to themselves increasingly as "Spanish"—apparently to emphasize their Spanish descent—in an attempt to disassociate themselves from "Mexicans" in the eyes of Anglos. So important did "Spanish" become that, by the early twentieth century at San Fernando, even those born in Mexico were calling themselves "Spanish," and for an Anglo to use "Mexican" meant he had a fight on his hands. Just how widespread the use of "Spanish" among the foreign-born became is not clear, and today only a small number of Californio descendants, notably those at Santa Barbara and at other nearby places where they were in the majority for some time, refer to themselves as "Spanish."

"Mexican" was apparently the prevalent self-referent among the California-bound immigrants of the 1920s, but the term which eventually prevailed among their descendants was "Mexican American." One wonders where and when this term originated. Its use predates the Second World War after which it became prevalent in California, for there is evidence that it was being applied as early as 1930 to south Texas American citizens of Mexican descent. What one meant when using this term, of course, was that he was native-born of Mexican descent.

Perhaps even older than "Mexican American" is "Chicano." There is record of this term having been used in a Spanish-language newspaper in Laredo as early as 1911 to differentiate between a person of Mexican descent who had not been "Americanized" (the "chicano") and another who had. This term, or at least one similar to it, was also in use about 1930 when Manuel Gamio noted that immigrants from Mexico were often derogatorily referred to by the native-born as "chicamos" (spelled with an "m" rather than an "n"). "Chicano" was also used in the 1930s as a term of endearment among Hispanos. When used in these ways, the word, which in derivation is probably a dialectal form of "xicano" (from *mexicano*), was confined during these early years to the minority when speaking only in Spanish.

These usages limited only to Spanish have been greatly overshadowed by a more recent development. About the mid-1960s younger and more militant minority members who were inspired by the black civil rights movement of the preceding decade began to demand their equal rights and to organize politically to solve their social and economic problems. Like the blacks, they rejected the strategy of earlier generations which was to assimilate with the majority, and they acquired a new sense of pride in their heritage which led them to demand bilingual and bicultural educational programs and self-study centers in colleges and universities. These minority members seized upon

"Chicano" as a self-referent when speaking in English or Spanish, a phenomenon which one might speculate happened first in California where "Chicano" is most prevalent. A "Chicano," then, was someone (of Mexican descent) who identified with a new, aggressive, highly self-conscious subculture —a subculture separate from either that of the Anglo from whom the Chicano felt alienated or that of the Mexican from whom the Chicano had grown apart. Many older Hispanos resent this "slang" use of Chicano, as they call it, and are apprehensive about the Chicano movement itself.

Curiously, in Arizona and eastern Colorado no term seems to have replaced "Mexican." The relative recency with which Mexicans first settled in eastern Colorado (New Mexicans had colonized areas further west) is perhaps one reason why no term replaced "Mexican" in that area, but such cannot be said of Arizona. There (as indeed everywhere), persons of Mexican descent were discriminated against and "Mexican" was used derisively. Also, the native-born citizens began to outnumber the Mexican-born aliens in the decades after the large immigrant influx of the 1920s with the result that referring to oneself as a "Mexican" was no longer appropriate for the majority. Even so, "Mexican" persisted, although Anglos in time used it with less invective, the degree of their reproach depending on how they said the word. Thus, in two areas "Mexican" took on a double meaning; on the one hand, it embraced those who were Mexican-born and noncitizens— *everywhere* in the Southwest people of this status so refer to themselves—while, on the other hand, it included those who were native-born and of Mexican descent.

In most of the Southwest during the present century, then, several terms came to replace "Mexican" among the native-born of Mexican descent. Several reasons for this have already been suggested in the preceding discussion. In addition, certain regional differences in the Southwest suggest why given terms arose where they did. In New Mexico,

for example, relatively large numbers of Spaniards colonized early, and their descendants could look with pride to their Spanish-derived folk culture. "Spanish American" seemed an appropriated choice. On the other hand, in Texas and California (and even in Arizona), tendencies on the part of the native-born upper socio-economic class to refer to itself as "Spanish" during the nineteenth century were suppressed, for, unlike New Mexico, the number of native-born in these two areas was relatively small, and those present were engulfed by the immigrants. "Latin American" and "Mexican American" were, of course, the terms adopted. "Spanish American" and "Latin American," unlike "Mexican American," are euphemisms. Perhaps a euphemism was less needed in California where "Mexican American" took hold. Discrimination (and the correlated enmity with which "Mexican" was used) was certainly less severe there than in Texas and southeastern New Mexico. "Mexican American" seemed appropriate in California.

Thus, for various reasons Hispanic subgroups came to designate themselves by one of several terms, and within the region of Hispanic concentration, there exists today a distinct pattern of regional usage (Fig. 3). For purposes of delimiting these present regions, questionnaires were sent out and interviews were conducted. Data gathered from Hispanos in these ways are summarized in Table 1.

In order to gain an initial impression of the regional usage of the several self-referents, 395 questionnaires were sent to managers of chambers of commerce within the study area in the spring and early summer of 1969. Sending questionnaires to chamber of commerce managers had the advantage of securing quickly and inexpensively a relatively large body of data spread evenly throughout the study area. The disadvantage was that these data would be supplied by non-Hispanos. However, I reasoned that even non-Hispanos could tell me what the *prevailing* local self-referent was

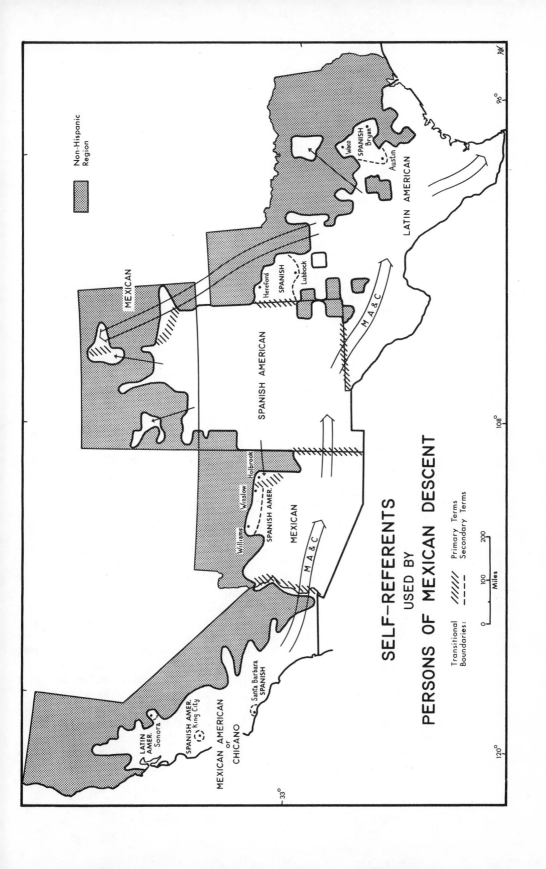

SELF-REFERENTS

USED BY

PERSONS OF MEXICAN DESCENT

Transitional
Boundaries: ///// Primary Terms
              - - - Secondary Terms

0   100   200
   Miles

Non-Hispanic
Region

Table 1. Self-Referents in English Prevailing Among Americans of Mexican Descent ("Hispanos") in the Region of Hispanic Concentration, 1969–1972

State	Mexican	Mexican American[a]	Chicano(-a)[a]	Spanish or Spanish American[b]	Latin or Latin American	Total
Arizona	9	4	3	2		18
California	5	32	23	2		62
Colorado	2	1	1	7		11
New Mexico				6		6
Texas		21	4	4	32	61
Total	16	58	31	21	32	158

SOURCE: Data compiled from 59 interviews with Hispanos and 99 questionnaires returned by Hispanos between 1969–19872.

[a]Respondents in Arizona, Colorado, and Texas noted that "Mexican American" began to be used about the early 1960s, and that "Chicano" began to be used in the latter 1960s. "Chicano" is also a self-referent when speaking in Spanish. The seemingly low scores for "Chicano" in California and Texas are explained by the fact that 20 Hispanos who gave "Mexican American" as the prevailing term among most minority members and "Chicano" as the prevailing term among younger minority members were all recorded as favoring "Mexican American."

[b]The relatively low number of Hispanos who reported "Spanish" or "Spanish American" in New Mexico merely reflects the fact that few Hispanos in that state chose to return questionnaires.

among Hispanos. I further requested that the chamber of commerce managers furnish me with names of Hispanos who might respond to the same questionnaire. In all, 295 questionnaires were returned, 46 from Hispanos, who, because they were acquaintances of the chamber of commerce managers, represented largely the "establishment" portion of their respective communities.

There were obvious places for which the data were conflicting or questionable, and these places were visited during August 1969. At that time 66 additional persons, 43 of them Hispanos, were interviewed in 39 communities located in central Texas, west Texas, eastern Colorado, central New Mexico, north central Arizona, and central California. The approach taken in the field was usually to go to the priest or minister of the local church (about one out of four of these clergymen was of Mexican descent), explain the study to him, and ask for the names of community residents of Mexican descent. A conscious effort was made to interview persons from the several socio-economic strata, although in those cases where persons interviewed had been referred to me by a member of the clergy, I was, of

course, sampling only from among church members. In these interviews (as in the questionnaires), the principal purpose was to determine which self-referent prevailed locally. This was not necessarily the self-referent the individual himself may have preferred.

An additional 16 Hispanos were interviewed during the summer of 1971 while I was teaching at the University of Arizona, and during the 1971–1972 academic year while I was undertaking research and also teaching at the University of Texas at Austin. These individuals were, for the most part, students, and by and large they represented the young, nonchurch-attending segment of the community.

While in Austin I learned that a directory of Spanish-speaking organizations had been published in July 1970. Drawing heavily on this source for potential respondents, I sent out 175 additional questionnaires in the fall of 1972 to organizations within the study area. This mailing netted 54 returns, 53 of them from Hispanos who represented mainly the middle and upper socio-economic strata. Thus, the distribution which follows is based on interviews with or questionnaires returned by 158 Hispanos from all walks of life.

"Mexican" is, of course, the self-referent of Mexican-born persons. But it is also the *prevailing* self-referent among the native born in much of Arizona and in eastern Colorado. Why this is so in Arizona remains an enigma. The spatial proximity of those who refer to themselves as "Mexicans" to those who refer to themselves as "Spanish Americans" is perhaps a reason for the persistence of "Mexican" in eastern Colorado, however. For one of Mexico's nationalistic themes after acquiring independence was the emphasis on its Indian ancestry and heritage, a development which led Ruth Barker to quip that it is more insulting to call a Mexican in Mexico a "Spaniard" than it is to call a Spanish American in the United States a "Mexican." Perhaps for this reason, the Mexicans of eastern Colorado, many of whom were descendants of those who had recently come from Mexico, rejected "Spanish American." Another explanation may be found in the fact that they were rather far removed from the areas where the other terms were popular.

"Spanish American," sometimes "Spanish," is the *primary* self-referent in most of New Mexico where its distribution corresponds to a remarkable degree with state boundaries. It is also the *primary* self-referent in places where New Mexicans settled: in south central Colorado and areas farther north in that state, and in eastern Arizona in the vicinty of Show Low, Snowflake, and Holbrook. It is of secondary use (after "Mexican") in the area west of Holbrook, between Winslow and Williams, where New Mexicans are a minority. "Spanish" is also of secondary importance where descendants of "old families" are numerous, for example, at Santa Barbara and nearby Carpinteria in California and at Nacogdoches (located outside the study area) in Texas.

When using "Spanish American" or "Spanish," New Mexicans or the descendants of "old families" mean that they are native-born of Spanish descent. "Spanish," meaning Spanish-speaking, is also used by

some in the Southwest but only as a secondary term. This is the case in two parts of Texas, one being the area roughly triangular in shape south of Waco and the other being the area between Hereford and Lubbock. (The use of "Spanish" in the later location is apparently unrelated to the influx of New Mexicans into the region, especially into the larger cities such as Lubbock.) This is also the case in King City, California, where Hispanos refer to themselves as "Spanish Americans," meaning Spanish-speaking. In King City, perhaps also in Texas, schools fostered the terms used.

The *primary* self-referent throughout the Texas part of the region is "Latin American" or "Latin" and, with one exception (of only secondary importance), its use seems to be restricted to Texas. The exception occurs in California's Tuolumne County, in the vicinity of Sonora, Tuolumne, and Standard, where a "Latin American Society" composed of persons of Mexican descent and others from Latin American countries has been organized. As a consequence, "Latin American" has become prevalent among "Anglos" in the area when reference is made to persons of Mexican descent, and it is apparently used occasionally by the latter when referring to themselves.

"Mexican American" and "Chicano" are both *primary* terms in the California regional segment, "Mexican American" being prevalent among the majority and "Chicano" among the more militant youth. Unlike the other terms, however, these two are diffusing areally, apparently from their region of greatest usage (arrows shown in Fig. 3 merely suggest apparent areal diffusion from California, and most certainly do not represent paths of movement). Promoted by the press and, with respect to "Chicano," by the rising momentum of the Chicanismo movement, these terms have gained popularity only recently, within the last half dozen years in many areas, but their spread has been rapid. Thus, "Mexican American" and "Chicano" have gained wide use in Arizona, in southern New Mexico (where the descendants of immigrants find them acceptable), and especially in Texas (where in the larger cities and the lower Rio Grande Valley they are preferred by many over "Latin American"). They have also become increasingly popular in the larger cities and agricultural areas of eastern Colorado.

The diffusion of "Mexican American" and "Chicano" portends the possible emergence of a strong sense of a common ethnic identity among Hispanos throughout the Southwest. This development, if successful, may have significant political implications, for it could help provide these peoples with the unity which earlier disagreement over terminology—and what that terminology implied helped impede. Still, many refuse to change, especially the "Spanish Americans" of New Mexico and southern Colorado, most of whom continue to take umbrage at being called "Mexican Americans."

Because they align themselves with the movement, many younger Hispanos in the region of Spanish American usage are beginning to call themselves "Chicanos," apparently ignoring the pride-in-*Mexican*-heritage connotation attached to this term by most who use it. This development suggests that "Chicano" might appear to be the best hope for a label behind which all Hispanos could unite. It is a term chosen by members of the minority; none construe it as disparaging; and it is not a clumsy combination of terms hyphenated or otherwise. But it does have its drawbacks, for, unlike "Mexican American," it is not immediately intelligible to many Americans outside the Southwest. Moreover, many Hispanos, especially those who are older, are opposed to its use as a self-referent.

That "Mexican American" and "Chicano" *are* being accepted by many is significant, however, for it indicates that this is a minority coming of age. For those who identify with "Mexican American" and "Chicano" accept, even assert (as in the case with "Chicano") their Mexican heritage. One sees a parallel with America's largest minority: When discrimination was once more overt, Negroes were "niggers" and Mexicans were either that or "meskins." To avoid these opprobrious terms, Negroes turned to "colored," a euphemism analogous to "Spanish American" and "Latin American" to which Hipanos turned. Only recently has the Negro accepted his being "black"—"Black is beautiful," he asserts. With "Mexican American" and "Chicano," so has the person of Mexican descent accepted his being "Mexican."

For Hispanos It's Still the Promised Land

PAUL AND RACHEL COWAN

At present over 12,000,000 people of Mexican, Puerto Rican, Cuban, and other Spanish-speaking origins reside in the United States. The 6,000,000 to 8,000,000 Mexican-Americans, the largest of the Hispanic groups, dwell mainly in the Southwest and the Far West, but the New York City area contains the largest concentration of the other Spanish-speaking people. The Hispanic community of New York City now numbers between 1,500,000 and 2,500,000. Puerto Ricans continue to constitute the majority, with about two-thirds of them residing in the metropolitan area, but the numbers of Cubans, Dominicans, Ecuadorians, Peruvians, and Colombians are steadily rising. The socio-economic status of the different nationalities composing the Hispano contingent vary from relatively high for the Cubans, most of them middle-class refugees from the Castro regime, to an abysmal low for Puerto Ricans. The latter enclave's annual family median income in 1970 totaled $4,969, lower than that of any other urban minority; its unemployment rate doubled that of other segments of the population; 30 percent of all Puerto Rican families in New York exist below the poverty line, and one of every two families is on relief. Compared with other groups fewer Puerto Ricans graduate from high school or college, and more of their elementary-school-age children are below grade level in reading than pupils of other ethnic backgrounds. Puerto Ricans have a higher incidence of recorded juvenile delinquency and drug addiction than the dominant groups in society, and they seem more susceptible to diseases like tuberculosis and venereal disease than those who are better off financially. The Dominicans also rank at bottom; the South American newcomers—Peruvians, Colombians, and Ecuadorians—perhaps because the trip to New York is more costly from these places than from Santo Domingo or San Juan, come from a higher social class. Most of the recent arrivals from these Latin American nations were artisans or proprietors of small businesses in their home country and have generally fared better in their new land than have the Puerto Ricans or Dominicans. In the article reprinted below Paul and Rachel Cowan trace the experiences of New York's various Hispanic peoples. They study these different groups not only by way of generalizations about life-styles and living conditions but also in a more concrete and personal manner by examining the experiences of individuals and their families.

The Rincon Ecuatoriana is one of the dozens of tiny Latin-American restaurants in Jackson Heights. We'd gone there for a meal of *seco de chivo* and *seviche de camarones*—goat stew and spicy marinated shrimp—foods we used to relish when we were Peace Corps volunteers in 1966–67 in Guayaquil, Ecuador.

It was a Sunday afternoon, and the small, spotless restaurant was crowded. As we were paying our bill, we heard two people calling us: a couple we'll call Carlos and Sonia Espinoza.

We hadn't seen them since we lived in Guayaquil. In those days, they had seemed well-established. Carlos was an influential official in the Public Works Department, a protégé of the populist Mayor Assad Bucaram. He and Sonia were students in the community-development course we taught. Now they were part of New York's huge Hispanic population—two of the city's most anonymous, most invisible people. They explained what had happened to them—and, even with its political idiosyncrasies, their story was like those of many Hispanos we interviewed; they and hundreds of thousands of Domincans, Cubans, Colombians, Argentinians and Peruvians have transformed New York's Hispanic community from a Puerto Rican "island in the city" (as writer Dan Wakefield once called it) to a "continent in the city." The majority of the Hispanic community, now estimated at 1.5 million to 2.5 million, is still Puerto Rican, but others are coming in ever-increasing numbers, and they are the focus of this article.

About eight years ago, Bucaram, Carlos's protector, was deposed by Guayaquil's oligarchy, and Carlos was forced out of work. He couldn't find another job. Soon he decided to come to New York.

He found two jobs within a week of his arrival—one as the janitor of a building in Manhattan, the other sweeping floors in a Queens toy factory. He took them both. He'd come here on a tourist visa, which meant he was legally forbidden to work. Because of his status, he toyed with the idea of divorcing Sonia—who was still in Guayaquil—and paying $1,000 to a lawyer who'd arrange a wedding between him and a Puerto Rican. (He wouldn't have known the woman. The mere fact that he was married to a U.S. citizen would have enabled him to get his green card, or residence visa.)

Sonia rejected the idea. He assured her the divorce was temporary, but she still considered it a sin. "You don't have to destroy your morality to get ahead," she wrote him. After that exchange, she began to pressure him to bring her and their 15-year-old daughter Teresa to New York. Soon he acceded.

There was a hidden reason he wanted her to stay home, she confided. He'd been so full of hope when he left Guayaquil! So certain that America would be as lavish as it seemed in the movies that starred Rock Hudson and Doris Day, in televsion programs like "Peyton Place." In fact, the city had been a room in a railroad apartment on 96th and Broadway—a place he shared with three other men. It had been interminable interborough subway rides, barely understood directions at work, back-breaking labor that he—like most of his social class—would have scorned in Ecuador. But his letters were as filled with boasts as his departure had been with hope. He exaggerated the size of his apartment, the extent of his English, the importance of his jobs. He considered those boasts harmless attempts to soothe his wife, and impress her. Now he was afraid she'd mistake them for lies.

But, she told us, she was so glad to see him that she quickly forgot her own swollen expectations. Soon she found work. Her first job was in a tiny Queens loft, a garment factory where 10 Hispanos—Ecuadorians, Colombians, Dominicans—worked nine hours a day making blouses, piecework for which they received 35 cents a blouse. In a good week, Sonia produced about 180 blouses: $63. But there were weeks when her boss, a Dominican, refused to pay her. He claimed his debts were too great. His words conveyed the implicit threat that he'd report illegal aliens (about half the workers) to the Immigration and Naturalization Service. No one complained. They all needed whatever money they could get.

In Guayaquil it's especially hard for a woman to find work. The traditions of *machismo* die hard. One reason Sonia was eager to come to the States, even illegally, was that she'd earned an advanced degree in psychology and couldn't find a suitable job at home. But the world she entered in New York was filled with garment workers, janitors, doormen, domestic servants; no one, certainly, who could provide her access to the city's professional people.

Then someone in the Upper West Side building where Carlos worked happened to tell him of a day-care center that needed a Spanish-speaking family counselor. Sonia decided to apply. She was immediately accepted for the job.

Now, with their increased income, the Espinozas could afford the material goods that provided concrete proof of their achievements. They moved to a three-room apartment in Jackson Heights and made down payments on a matched living-room set—its plush, flowered fabric carefully protected by plastic slipcovers—a color TV console with a built-in stereo, and an ornate glass coffee table. They hung drapes and placed a large painting of the Last Supper over the couch. They set a small Ecuadorian flag in the middle of the coffee table.

They opened a savings account, to which they added $20 a week. Now they could afford to send $5 every Saturday to Sonia's mother in Guayaquil. They also knew that when they returned home they could shower their friends with gifts—with the American-made shoes, slips and shirts that are testimony to a successful stay in New York.

Teresa learned English quickly. She went to a parochial school were she got a far better education than she might have in Guayaquil. Carlos and Sonia were thrilled with her education. "It's the most precious thing in our lives," Sonia told us. It had been different when they lived in Manhattan and sent her to

public schools. There, they couldn't get used to the fact that she was allowed to wear tight pants at school, not the long skirts that were required in Guayaquil; that she was allowed to flirt openly with boys, to debate her teachers, to break schools rules without being beaten. Though she herself was quite demure, she told stories of classmates who habitually used dirty language, or kissed in the corridors, or went out on unsupervised dates, or joined street gangs. Or used drugs.

There were still traces of tension between Teresa and her parents. Carlos criticized her every time she left the house in jeans. She grumbled, with some humor but more irritation, when he railed against American permissiveness and extolled the customs of the middle class in Ecuador, where even university students go out on chaperoned dates.

And in a way, Teresa's mastery of English was an even greater source of tension. It was a necessity—no one denied that—but it also made her strangely superior to her parents, who had trouble learning the language. She was their guide on New York's streets. She could enter the grand, mysterious world of English-language TV. She translated her teacher's comments on her work. So when they insisted she speak Spanish at home, it was because they wished to preserve their authority as well as their language.

Carlos and Sonia were also haunted by a constant, knotting fear that they or Teresa would be the victim of some violent crime—a fear they'd never known in Ecuador. Like most of their Hispanic friends, they believed that American blacks were responsible. They couldn't understand why the United States was so lax with criminals.

As far as they were concerned, this was the land of economic and intellectual opportunity. But it contained a social virus—permissivenes—that terrified them. Happy as they often felt, they were also adrift between two cultures.

Most English-speaking New Yorkers still assume that when they hear a street conversation in Spanish, they're listening to Puerto

Ricans. But the reality is dramatically different. Technology, in the form of television programs and movies that make life in the United States seem idyllic, has spread through Central and South America, acquainting even the poorest *campesino* with the opportunities that exist outside his *pueblo*. And reduced air fares have meant that the long journey to the United States is no longer restricted to the very rich. In the past decade, there has been a vast, new migration, first to Latin-American cities, then—for some people—to the United States. (The current Hispanic population of the United States is estimated at more than 10 million.)

The "continent in the city" is by no means a monolith. Hispanos live in all five boroughs. Though children mingle in the schools and on the streets, many older people retain the class and regional antagonisms they developed at home. For example, in the Jackson Heights-Elmhurst-Corona area of Queens (where the Police Department estimates the Hispanic population has mushroomed from 600 people in 1960 to between 80,000 and 100,000 in 1975) there is a distinct Dominican section, an Ecuadorian section, a Colombian section.

As more Hispanos settle here, as their nationalist rivalries are replaced by a shared New Yorker's self-interest, they are bound to become an increasingly important political and economic force. And, in some ways, they represent a patriotic force, too. For, in an age when most people in this country are haunted with fear for America's future, the influx of Hispanos is a reminder that for millions of people in the world, the United States is still the promised land.

The Espinozas, like most South American immigrants, came from a higher social class than that of most Puerto Ricans and Dominicans in the city. The trip from Santo Domingo or San Juan is cheap enough for *campesions* or the urban poor to afford; but the air fare from Guayaquil to New York is $294, an amount within the reach of only the middle classes. Most Ecuadorian, Colombian and Peruvian immigrants, legal or il-

legal, were social workers, grocers, barbers or mechanics back home. In fact, their standard of living was below that of the average U.S. worker. They couldn't afford cars, for example, or washing machines, or electric stoves, or summer vactions that lasted longer than a day or two at the beach. But, unlike the millions of desperately poor people who crowd Latin America's urban slums, they were able to eat meat most nights. Their houses contained enough space to let adults sleep in separate rooms from their children.

The "continent in the city" is filled with avid consumers who are eager to buy goods that didn't exist (or existed only for the very rich) in their home countries. For example, according to Nelson Lavergne, manager of WADO, one of two Spanish-language radio stations in the city, they spend $66 a week on food—as much as the average New Yorker, though their incomes tend to be lower. They buy three times as many cigarettes and four times as much beer as any other group in the city, according to Lavergne. Goya Foods, a company that specializes in Latin-American foods, grossed $6-million nationally 10 years ago; now it grosses $60-million.

When the Puerto Rican migration accelerated in the nineteen-fifties, most social planners assumed that Hispanos would become mainstream Americans. That never happened. Unlike earlier ethnic groups, they protected their language fiercely—an estimated 70 per cent to 80 per cent of them still speak Spanish at home. In part, that was possible because they were separated from their families by a quick plane ride, not a difficult ocean voyage. Furthermore, their numbers in New York were so large that they didn't have to speak English—they could live comfortably in a totally Spanish *ambiente*.

So far, it is Cubans who have profited most from the Hispanic community's rapid expansion. As political refugees, they have never had to worry about living here legally. Many have held a competitive edge over other Hispanos. They were part of Cuba's middle class. Many had business and professional backgrounds; they had worked for

U.S. firms; they had been educated in the United States.

The have gained influence in decaying towns like Union City, N. J., and turned them into thriving *pueblos,* clean, lively places where multicolored signs jut gaily into the street, where store windows carry notices reading "English spoken here."

Most are extremely grateful to the United States. But, during long conversations, you realize they're apprehensive about this country, too. We interviewed Dr. Julio Forcade, a Cuban refugee who is president of the growing, largely Hispanic-owned United Americas Bank, a few days after he'd learned that the U.S. embargo on Cuba might be lifted. When he talked about financial matters—about how the growth of New York's Latin community was the key to the bank's prosperity—his face was composed. But when we asked him about politics, it became softer, more misty. "I'm an American. I've seen how ironic it is that you don't know what you've got until you lose it. You're not sufficiently proud of what you have. You're spoiled."

The Jackson Heights-Corona-Elmhurst section of Queens is an especially cosmopolitan Hispanic area in the city. During the past decade, immigrants from South America and the Caribbean, and upwardly mobile Puerto Ricans, have settled in the neighborhood. They're replacing an older generation, the Italians who left the crowded Lower East Side for the farmlands of Queens, the Irish who moved from Manhattan in the nineteen-forties, Jews who saw the area as a way station to the suburbs, WASP's who built the nation's first cooperative buildings on its pleasant terrain. For some Hispanos, Jackson Heights is a second stop on their journey to prosperity, a step up from the South Bronx or Washington Heights. For others, the newcomers, it's a safety zone in a strange land.

Roosevelt Avenue, the lifeline of the neighborhood, must look dingy and inhospitable to people whose childhood days were spent in the languid tropical sun. Now their main shopping area is a dark, noisy canyon beneath the unrelenting thunder of the El. The sun's rays rarely reach the people hurrying along the sidewalks. Between the trains and the din of flights from LaGuardia, it is hard to carry on a relaxed conversation, as people love to do in South America.

So much is different here! They can no longer savor the peaceful ceremony of the noon-hour siesta—the gracious family lunch, the refreshing nap that they enjoyed in Quito or Santo Domingo. In Queens, the tiny garment factories give their underpaid employes a fleeting half-hour to digest their lunch before they must bend over their sewing machines once again.

Yet the community has absorbed so very many Hispanic people that by now Roosevelt Avenue has begun to throb with cheerful signs of their culture. The fast beat of a *merengue* or a *cumbia* bouncing from a record store invites passersby to wiggle their hips and dance a few steps.

A Hispano is never far from the latest hometown ball scores or political events. All over Jackson Heights the newsstands are stocked with newspapers from Bogotá, Buenos Aires, Guayaquil, Santo Domingo, all of which arrive in New York a day or two after they are published. Nor is he far from his spiritual roots. There are Catholic and Pentecostal churches all over the neighborhood. Here and there are the tiny shops whose windows are jammed with statues of saints, with paintings of the Blessed Virgin and Christ on the Cross. If you know the owners, you might explore the secrets of Afro-Hispanic mysticism, and sample the small vials of potion designed to restore a flagging love affair or hex an enemy.

The *bodegas* are owned by Dominicans, Cubans and Argentinians. These industrious storekeepers work an average of 110 hours a week, according to a study of *bodegas* by WADO's Nelson Lavergne, and their wives and children often serve as cashiers and clerks. They stock the yucca and the yautia, the Goya rice and beans, the Bustelo coffee, the canned guavas and naranjillas that their customers have been raised to consider the heart of a satisfying meal. They also stock the special kitchen utensils their customers have always used: the *espresso* coffee pots, the wooden *tostoneras* for flattening slice green plantains, the *maté* pipes. They place trays of baked *dulces*—coconut squares, sweet guava-filled cakes—by the cash register to tempt their departing clients. Their prices are higher than those at nearby supermarkets. But the *bodeguero* performs an indispensable service—he speaks his customer's language, knows where to look for jobs, apartments, friendly doctors; he's part of the grapevine of gossip in Jackson Heights. And he extends credit.

Roosevelt Avenue offers a feast to aficionados of Latin-American food. El Inca, its most elegant restaurant, has attracted a large English-speaking clientele by offering bland dishes along with its *arroz con pollo* and its Inca soup. The Illimani is more authentically ethnic, with its menu of juicy Bolivian-style beef *chorryllana* and its plates full of succulent fried pork with hominy corn. On a Saturday night it was crowded with young people who had come to eat, drink and hear an Ecuadorian crooner accompanied by a long-haired partner on a Moog synthesizer. On a Sunday afternoon, its proprietors were busy dispensing meat *empanadas*—stuffed with spiced beef, raisins, hard-boiled eggs, onions and peas—to Bolivians who'd come in from New Jersey for a taste of home.

Besides the restauranteurs and the travel agents, the most visibly successful Hispanic entrepreneurs on the avenue are the realtors—Playa, Latino, Linea. Home ownership is changing rapidly in the area as the Hispanos grow more affluent and the *yanquis* feel more isolated. For some Hispanos one of Jackson Heights' or Elmhurst's attractive two-story frame houses represents an anchor in the community. For others, it's an investment to be cashed in when it's finally time to go back home and start a business there.

The influx of Hispanics has also had an impact on the schools. Nine of the 24 schools in District 24 have bilingual programs, with close to 1,000 students enrolled. At Intermediate School 61, the program started with 18 children three years ago. Now, 350 students, some of whom have never been to school, learn English as a second language and develop their skills in Spanish. Donald Bandel, the coordinator, has established an unusually friendly atmosphere for the students. Still, at first, the parents opposed the bilingual program. They felt their children would be Americans only if all the courses were in English. But now most have accepted it.

Victor Maridueña is an Ecuadorian who has long been active in the Jackson Heights community. His ham radio set makes his house a hub of activity for his *paisanos:* On Sundays, as soon as the *futbol* games end in Guayaquil and Quinto, he receives phone calls from Ecuadorians all over the city who want to know the scores immediately.

Maridueña is proud of the Hispanic contribution to the community. "We've revitalized this neighborhood. You don't see any abandoned housing here—you see buildings going up. No stores are empty—new businesses are opening all the time."

But many of the Irish and Italians who remain in the neighborhood resent the changes Maridueña extols. Sometimes they talk about problems that bother the Hispanos, too, like the crime rate. They all believe that Roosevelt Avenue has become the center of the city's cocaine trade. They're concerned about gang fights, though they're not exactly new in the neighborhood. In the old days, Irish and Italian kids joined the gangs that hung out in their local park—the Woodside Chiefs, the Elmhurst Gaylords, the Corona Dukes. The turf has remained the same, but the names have changed to the Latin Gents, the Latin Tops, the Savage Nomads. According to Inspector Frank Sullivan of the 110th Precinct, though, the gangs are not—and never have been—a serious police problem. He is more concerned about the drug trade. Many cocaine dealers do live in the area, and his force tries to keep them under constant surveillance. But they are relatively discreet in Jackson Heights, where they're known, he says. They do the bulk of their business in other parts of the city.

Though the Anglos talk about crime, about declining property values, about the invasion of illegal aliens, and consider realtors who sell to Hispanos no better than blockbusters, the roots of their anger are deeper and less tangible. They resent the Hispanos for disrupting their way of life, for talking too fast in their alien tongue, for crowding the sidewalks of Junction Boulevard with their stalls of merchandise, for filling the air with loud music and spicy food smells. They fear that they'll soon be abandoned by their English-speaking neighbors who can afford to flee, that they'll be trapped in an overcrowded noisy neighborhood where they'll feel like foreigners.

Some of their politicians, like Assemblyman Joseph Lisa and former Community Board Chairman Patrick Deignan, have attempted to wage a highly publicized campaign against illegal aliens. But more liberal Queens Democratic party politicians like Mike Dowd and John Rowan feel more sanguine about their presence. Since most of them are not citizens, they pose no political threat. "They never vote. I wish I had more of them in my district," Dowd says.

He's right about the past, but he may well by wrong about the future. For Herman Badillo's 1969 and 1973 mayoralty campaigns had the same tonic political effect on New York's Hispanic community as the McCarthy and McGovern campaigns had on the generation of antiwar politicians who were elected to Congress in 1974.

Fausto Gomez, the son of an Ecuadorian tailor, was working as a busboy at Schrafft's, a bartender at the Hotel Taft, a Lower East Side salesman of hair dryers, flashlights and clothes brushes during the late nineteen-fifties and early nineteen-sixties, when Herman Badillo was working his way up through Bronx politics. By 1969 Gomez had moved to Queens Village (he now lives in the more fashionable Briarwood section) and become a real-estate dealer. As a high-school student in Quito, he'd been fascinated by politics, but he never thought he could participate in it here: It was a shock to him to learn that a Hispano could run for Mayor of New York.

In 1973, when Badillo came in second in the Democratic primary, Gomez's business was prospering. He let Badillo's campaign workers use his office as a local headquarters. Last year, he helped form the Jackson Heights United Hispanic American Democratic Club; this year, he was chairman of the club's anniversary banquet, where, last month, 200 people attended a $25-a-ticket dinner for the city's nine elected Hispanic officials. The next time there is a Hispanic candidate for Mayor, the Jackson Heights area with its club is likely to be a significant source of funds.

That would be an important development in the political life of the "continent in the city." For one things, it would be a sign that Latins are able to agree that their community's self-interest is more important than its ethnic rivalries. Since the candidate is likely to represent a more impoverished area than Jackson Heights, the alliance would also involve a kind of political philanthropy. And that is extremely rare in the Hispanos' home countries, where most people assume that aid will come from a powerful, capricious individual—the *patrón,* the *jefe,* the *general*—instead of a grassroots organization.

Most Hispanic politicians believe the Badillo campaigns were auguries, not aberrations—that the city will have a Latin Mayor by the mid-nineteen-eighties. But since the next mayoralty election is two years away [1977], there is little visible jockeying for power. So the community leaders stress voter registration and complain about the apathy and frightened confusion much of their community feels when it must deal with the city's bureaucracies.

(Most of them, off the record, complain that the Anglo-owned El Diario, the city's only wide-circulation Spanish-language newspaper, does little to combat the apathy. Instead, they say, the paper reinforces the Hispanos' negative self-image by constantly emphasizing crime stories with hugh front-page headlines. Moreover, the paper provides only brief wire-service coverage of local and national news. Recently, a group of prosperous Hispanos of several nationalities decided to challenge El Diario's monopoly by publishing *Poder Hispano*—Hispanic Power—a daily paper that will be printed in four colors. Its pilot issue is scheduled for July 4 [1975].)

One reason for political apathy, Badillo says, is that, despite the size of New York's Latin community, not a single Congressional district has a Hispanic majority. The fact that voters are so scattered has made it impossible to build the traditional kind of political machine that serves a particular ethnic group by registering voters, doing them favors throughout the year, then reaping its rewards on election day. He sees registration as an election-by-election chore. And he feels that the Democratic party is uncooperative at best; malevolent at worst. This year, he introduced an amendment to the Federal Voting Rights Act that would send Federal marshals here to make sure registered voters' names are listed on buff-colored cards, that the voting machines function, that the ballots are counted accurately.

Joe Erazo, Director of Special Programs for Mayor Beame, is regarded by many community leaders as Badillo's principal rival in the Hispanic community. His enemies regard him as a somewhat devious machine politician; his supporters see him as a smart man who is forging intra-Hispanic alliances that have never before existed.

He is seeking to register non-Puerto Rican Hispanics by combating what he calls "umbilicalism"—the attachment of Latins to the politics of the countries they left behind.

That attachment is still strong for many. In 1973, 5,000 Colombians voted in their national elections from booths set up on Roosevelt Avenue. Dominican groups—those who support President Joaquin Balaguer, and the faction-ridden group that seeks to oust him—struggle to influence Dominican politics. Some Cuban exiles work to keep the U.S. from establishing relations with Castro. Puerto Rican Socialists organize massive rallies for their island's independence. Several of the Puerto Ricans we interviewed were *independentistas*. Chileans who left after Allende's overthrow lobby constantly for the withdrawal of U.S. aid from the military junta.

"I'm always careful not to take stands on those national issues," Erazo says. "But I insist that since they're here now they have to look out for their self-interest, and their children's. So they have to register to vote—to identify with the Hispanic community in New York."

It's possible, though, to over-identify with that community, Badillo says. Since so much of the city is bilingual now, one can become immersed in the Spanish-language world and forget that Hispanics are still a minority group. Badillo plans to run for Mayor in 1977, and he's convinced that he can win only in the kind of coalition with blacks and white liberals that he tried to establish in 1973. But he's bitterly aware of that coalition's instability. He fears that a machine-supported black or white liberal will shatter it, as he believes Al Blumenthal's candidacy did in 1973. And he's convinced that the coalition can be led only by a black or a Latin: A white liberal just wouldn't inspire the minority vote.

"The reformers think that we should be grateful that they're giving us a break," he says. "They don't realize that I come from Puerto Rico, where we are the powerful as well as the powerless. I refuse to plead with them. That's the source of the famous Badillo arrogance."

Badillo is still the only Hispanic politican with a city-wide following. But he was the only community leader we interviewed who constantly referred to Latins as Puerto Ricans, not Hispanics. And most of the people we interviewed agreed that a less well-known figure—Erazo, Bronx City Councilman Ramon Velez, State Senator Robert Garcia, Brooklyn City Councilman Luis Olmedo, or someone who hasn't yet become visible to the public—could emerge as a commanding figure within the next decade. Right now, they seem more excited by the prospect of a Hispanic Mayor than by any particular candidate.

Increasingly, non-Puerto Rican Hispanics in Jackson Heights are cutting their "umbilical cords" to their homelands. Lilia and Luis Fandino left Bogotá on their honeymoon planning to remain in the United States for two months. That was 16 years ago. Now Mr. Fandino works for an electronics firm, and she is a crossing guard at a local parochial school. They own their own home. They named their children Douglass, Albert and Janet—because the kids are Americans. But the Fandinos have not sought to escape their roots. They fought hard to initiate a Spanish-language mass at Jackson Heights' Blessed Sacrament Church because they saw the mass as a way to protect their people's tradition from the restrictive demands of the staid Irish congregation, which didn't approve of guitars in the service and complained about the Latins' passionate style of singing and praying.

The Lopez family left Cuba for Spain in 1969, then came here last year. When their son, Felipe, arrived, he didn't know any English. This spring he won entrance to Stuyvesant High School. Their daughter has happily adopted blue jeans, and wants to be a journalist. The editor of El Colombiano, a small community newspaper, sends his sons to the Flushing Y.M.C.A. so they'll acquire the discipline and sportsmanship he thinks they'll need to succeed in this country.

Señora Leonora Rivas, an older woman from the small town of Daule, Ecuador's mango center, has worked in New York dress factories and design studios for 20 years. Now she runs a small tailoring shop in her two-story home. "I got here before this passion to come to New York got started," she recalls. "Back then it was lonely to arrive at the airport all by yourself. Now it's different. They say everybody in Guayaquil has a relative in New York." Every Saturday Señora Leonora makes 165 *humitas*—corn tamales—to sell at the weekly dance at the Ecuadorian Social and Cultural Center on Roosevelt Avenue.

Her voice slowed down, then faltered, as she told us about her Ecuadorian-born sons who had worked so hard to become American citizens. The younger died in a car crash. The older was killed in Vietnam. "So you see, this is my country now. My blood is in this earth. I'll never go back to live in Ecuador."

One day Victor Maridueña invited us to the inauguration of a night class he'd organized in the Ecuadorian Center. About 20 students—Colombians, Peruvians, Ecuadorians, Dominicans—had enrolled in the high-school equivalency course.

For us, it was an uncomfortably familiar setting. As Peace Corps volunteers we'd gone to dozens of similar occasions: inaugurations of courses in cake decorating, sewing, hair dressing, where you ate *humitas*, drank warm beer and plastered a courteous smile on your face while you listened to meaningless pep talks. There was no way those courses would help anyone succeed. Ecuador was a closed society, controlled by a tiny, greedy oligarchy.

But—corny as it may seem—the night school in Jackson Heights had just the atmosphere of hopefulness we'd joined the Peace Corps to transmit. Within the limits imposed by a shrinking economy, exploitive employers and the mounting campaign against Hispanic illegal aliens, there was truth to Maridueña's assertion that success in the course could lead to success in the United States. The prospective students certainly felt that way. They nodded as he urged them to practice virtues like industry, self-discipline, courtesy—qualities that seem old-fashioned to many other New Yorkers. With tears in her eyes, a Peruvian who had graduated from the previous class urged the students to study hard "so that you can bring pride to your countries and our Latin America." It was as if we'd stumbled into a Spanish translation of a scene from "The Education of H*Y*M*A*N K*A*P*L*A*N."

We decided to tell our friends Carlos and Sonia Espinoza about the course. The simple knowledge of its existence might be more help to them than all the theories of community development we'd outline during those long classes in Guayaquil.

But when we called, Sonia told us she had bad news. A week before, the immigration police had knocked on the Espinoza's door, looking for a neighbor who was reported to have overstayed his visa. Despite Carlos's years as an illegal alien, he'd never lost his awe of law-enforcement officials. So he answered the door and politely asked them what they wanted. When they saw that he spoke poor English they asked for his papers. Of course he had none. Neither did Sonia. The inspectors forgot the original suspect and seized Carlos instead. After a night in the jail at immigration headquarters, he appeared in immigration court. He and Sonia were given 60 days to leave the country voluntarily.

Sonia told us the story with more relief than anger. She'd never been able to accept the conflicting realities of her satisfying work and her skulking, hunted life as an economic outlaw. Besides, their lawyer said that if she wanted to return, she'd only have to wait two years until her visa came through, for her professional status made her eligible for residency.

We drove them to the airport on a cold blustery day. Though Carlos was angry at his stupidity, he and Sonia kept teasing us about how we'd be shivering while they luxuriated in Guayaquil's warm climate. Only Teresa was genuinely nervous. She had classmates who had returned to South America and found it nearly impossible to readjust to the strict customs there.

As Carlos waited to have his baggage weighed, he began to chat with a Peruvian woman, an importer who was going home on business. She lived in Jackson Heights, too. "You know, we Peruvians don't come in large numbers like you Ecuadorians," she said. "The Peruvian likes a good time. So when he leaves home he works in France or Italy where things are more relaxed."

Carlos paused a minute before answering her. "*Bueno,* I've been here six years, and New York has been good to me. But life was getting too *agitado.* So we decided to go back home." He'd worked out a good cover story. He'd tell his friends in Guayaquil that, though he succeeded in New York, he didn't like the constant fast pace. The story would do until he and Sonia obtained the documents to come here legally.

Black and White in Catholic Eyes

MICHAEL NOVAK

Confrontations between white and black ethnics go back to the pre-Civil War conflicts between recent arrivals and native blacks for casual labor jobs in northern cities. Since World War I, when large numbers of blacks began to move to urban centers, the interaction between the national and racial minorities naturally increased. The relationship between Afro-Americans and other urban ethnic enclaves has been clouded by contention for jobs, living space, resources, and power in this country's deteriorating municipalities. In the essay reprinted below, Michael Novak, a city-bred son of Slavic immigrants and an insightful scholar in ethnic studies, examines the problematical relationship of the black and white ethnic minorities by presenting the perspective of the latter group. "Black and White in Catholic Eyes" gives us a greater appreciation of the problems of the white ethnics and of the tragic consequences that have arisen from the miscalculations and miscomprehensions that the racial and national minorities have of themselves, of each other, and of the real forces that prevent them from attaining harmonious co-existence and a decent life.

In Boston recently, Catholic mothers have said their rosaries in the streets to protest busing, rather like the "flower children" of 1967 protesting war. In Rosedale, Queens, some Catholic hoodlums have twice bombed the home of a brave black man from Trinidad, a despicable method favored by the New World Liberation Front. Protests, demonstrations, riots and civil disobedience continue in the 70's—but not at the same places as in the 60's. They are likely to get worse.

These conflicts are usually presented by the media in terms of simple racism, viewed as they are against the common perception of urban blacks, their problems and their aspirations that has preoccupied opinion makers and politicians in this country for more than a decade. And yet the conflicts between urban Catholics and blacks are far more complicated, for they involve considerations of social class and clashes of genuine interest, as well as race. In fact, there is good reason to believe the proposition that affluent liberals who take a protective attitude towards the black underclass, with little regard for the white-ethnic lower class, are—at the risk of great social turmoil—participating in an unconscious, or perhaps conscious, conspiracy of the upper classes to prevent formation of an inner-city alliance that could function as a major political force.

Certainly, there is much to support the notion that blacks and white ethnics have more reasons for unity than for division. Robert Kennedy was the last politician who knew how to hold the trust of both groups, but another one could emerge (though it will not be his brother, whose record in bringing white ethnics and blacks together is abominable). If one does, the political consequences could be important—in terms of substance as well as style.

For example, no Brookings Institution is at present developing realizable policies on the undramatic issues of jobs and security, protection from migrant corporations, fair treatment from local banks, help in caring for the family's aged, a sense of public dignity in the media and the schools, a fair shot at representation in the higher echelons of power and status, a break in the stranglehold of the top 10 percent of the nation (in terms of education and income)—the "opinion leaders"—upon the definition of political issues. To understand the true importance of these issues, it is necessary to take a look at the Northern cities and their problems from a white-ethnic—which usually means a Catholic—point of view.

One hundred years ago, 90 percent of all black Americans lived in the South, and 90 percent of the nation's present Catholic population had not yet arrived from Europe. In the Northern cities, the 20th century has been largely the story of the fateful meeting of these two migrations, unprepared for each other, not linked through the mystic bond of slavery. In the last 20 years, we have learned a great deal about the black experience, and prejudice against blacks is no longer considered acceptable. But subtle forms of bigotry against Catholics are still respectable.

Catholic politics, highly personal and strictly accountable in its fashion, is called in pejorative terms "machine politics." Elite

Protestant politics, highly impersonal and far vaster in wealth and power, is spoken of in terms of "conscience" and "reform." Catholic favoritism is called graft and nepotism; Protestant favoritism is forgiven as a result of an inevitable "old-boy network." At the top, there is no melting pot. On the boards of the foundations, among appointive judges, on boards of trustees of universities and in other places, white ethnics characteristically have as few token representatives as blacks. In Chicago's top 106 corporations, only 1.9 percent of 1,341 directors are Italian; 0.3 percent are Polish; 0.4 percent are black; 0.1 percent are Hispanic. In the Chicago police department today, at every level, Poles are almost as underrepresented as blacks. In Pittsburgh today, the foreign-stock families with incomes under $3,500 per year outnumber the black poor by more than 2 to 1. At one time or another, various groups have viewed Catholics as social antagonists. Sympathy for Catholic viewpoints requires from some an extra generosity.

One out of four Americans is Catholic in culture and tradition (not counting those who are no longer "practicing" Catholics). The Catholic population in Northern states is sometimes close to 50 percent, as in Massachusetts, and usually at least 30 or 40 percent. Moreover, in the Northern urban centers, practically the only whites left are Catholics and (in Chicago and Detroit) Appalachian migrants. Two out of every three persons in Detroit are black or Polish. Newark is divided by blacks, Hispanics and Italians. In recent decades, an increased urban migration of Hispanics, an influx of Cubans and the migration of many Catholics from the Midwest have raised the percentage of Catholics in Florida and Texas—usually thought of as Protestant states—to more than 20 percent. Catholics are especially highly represented in the 10 states, including California, with the largest electoral votes. Paricularly in the North, urban history in the 20th century may have been more affected by Catholic cultures than by any other.

The black population of the North has increased since 1900 from under one million to over 10 million. The Catholic population there has increased from about 11 million to about 45 million. In all, Catholics in the U.S., North and South, number about 13 million Eastern Europeans, 10 million Italians, nine million Irish, seven million Germans, five million French-Canadians, and (here the figures are more uncertain) 15 million Hispanics.

One out of five Catholics lives in census tracts with blacks, compared to one out of 18 Anglo-Americans. Ethnics are already the most integrated white Americans.

As long ago as blacks were slaves, many among these Catholics had themselves been serfs. Even today in Eastern Europe, the relatives of many of them live under an oppression more severe than in the days of the Czars, and in some respects as bad as any ever known to blacks. In the computation of human sufferings borne upon this planet, many do not consider themselves to have suffered less than blacks during the last 500 or 1,000 years. This is an important self-perception. Torture, imprisonment, grinding poverty, exclusion from education—these have all been visited on Catholic ethnics in Europe as well as on black slaves in America.

Once in America, the white ethnics often experienced the New World's own subtler forms of discrimination, if not oppression. By their names, accents and social links, Catholics have felt clearly identified and vulnerable before the powers-that-be in mills and mines, just as blacks have by their color. Whites still sort each other out by class, culture and kinship; some whites oppress others as they have blacks; many whites feel a burden of oppression, lack of status, and inequality. Blacks are not alone in suffering evil, in feeling self-doubt, in meeting prejudice. Slavic folksongs share with black melodies the melancholy of a long oppression. Nor are rebellion and resistance limited to blacks. Joe Namath and Andy Warhol, Boston's ROAR, Al Capone in Cicero, the long ethnic struggles in the coal fields, steel mills and auto factories, the building of Catholic "ward politics," the role of Slavic women, like Big Mary Septak in Pennsylvania, in pushing their men to rebellion— these suggest the range of Catholic populism, a study that much needs to be written. It is a populism that differs from the populism of Bryan, La Follette and Huey Long, as well as from that of King, Carmichael and Wilkins. A kind of self-hatred and passionate contempt for upper-class hypocrisy often suffuse it.

Blacks and Catholics had almost no cultural preparation for their fateful meeting in the Northern cities of America. They met not as slaveowners and slaves but as competitors in the grim and uncertain business of survival. About 1915, blacks were beginning to migrate North in sizable numbers. When, about 1919, blacks began to be used in large numbers as strikebreakers, as in Pittsburgh, a major change occurred in Catholic-black perceptions. From then on, the ethnic competition became serious, sometimes ugly and occasionally violent.

Many black leaders in the U.S. do not know the experiences of Catholic ethnic cultures, whether in Europe or in America. Hence, they often misjudge motives, interests and political behaviors. Without thinking about it very much, they often assume Protestant upper-class biases and put down the white ethnics. Thus, Stokely Carmichael took the epithet that upper-class nativists had long hurled at Catholic foreigners, "hunkie" (derived from "Hungarian" and connoting stupid, foreign, unworthy) and altered it to "honkie," applying it to all whites. Hearing it, white ethnics heard an old slur. The slur seems especially unfair; white ethnics are not the sole, or even the main, and certainly not the most powerful carriers of racism—a fact that has been publicly acknowledged by some blacks. Whitney Young was in 1971 the first black leader to issue a warning about the strategic danger of the public bias against white ethnic Catholics (and Jews). Recently, Robert Hill, research director of the Urban League, and Vernon

Jordan, executive director, reviewed all the studies of white-ethnic attitdues toward blacks. Hill wrote: "How is it that, despite the overwhelming consensus of these studies, white ethnics are believed to be more racist than white Protestants? Generally, we have found that white Protestants throughout the nation are more likely to hold unfavorable racial attitudes than are white ethnics in similar size communities and regions." Young's Harris survey showed that 22 percent of Anglo-Americans favored racially separate schools, compared with 6 percent of the Irish, 5 per cent of the Italians and 16 percent of the Poles. Studies by Nathan Kantrowitz, Angus Campbell, Norman Nie and other—including a 1971 report in Scientific American by Paul B. Sheatsley and Andrew Greeley—consistently show the same patterns.

Furthermore, some issues—security in jobs and neighborhoods, for example—unite blacks and white ethnics, despite their real differences. Progressive majorities in the North have invariably depended on large majorities in white-ethnic and black neighborhoods together. Few white ethnics would deny that, generally, limiting comparisons solely to the North, Catholics are statistically doing better than blacks. But in terms of gross numbers, there are more white poor than black poor. What helps one can help the other, if programs are so designed.

Certain understandings are telegraphed between Protestants, including blacks, in the public language of such diverse figures as Lyndon Johnson, Sam Ervin, George Wallace, Albert Gore, Ralph Yarborough and also (in a different vein) of John Gardner, Elliot Richardson, Nelson Rockefeller and others. Catholics can only decipher them from the outside: the way America is spoken of as a "covenanted people," for example, and the interplay in Protestant consciousness between morality, guilt, reform and politics. Protestants somehow always manage to seem more high-minded and moral than Catholics,

while not seeming to become less wealthy or less powerful in the process.

In the evangelical tradition, blacks seem to take up this politics of morality by second nature. Many describe racism as a moral failing, about which people should feel guilty and change their ways. (A different tactic would be to treat racism as an unconscious way of perceiving, and work on issues where coalition is possible and mutual loyalties can be built. Guilt divides; shared goals unite.) The first political move of many black politicians, in the media at least, seems to be to make their listeners feel guilty, in order to increase political leverage over them. Nativist Protestants (like Archie Bunker to his Polish son-in-law) used to call Catholics hunkies, dagos, bohunks, wops, micks and greasers; now others, including some blacks, call them racists, Fascists and pigs, terms not any the more affectionate. Or accurate.

Many ordinary Catholics, meanwhile, do judge blacks harshly and unfairly, reacting in some confusion to stereotypes of blacks promoted in the media. Bill Moyers asked a man in Rosedale why he wanted to keep blacks out. The reply: "If you really want to know, they're basically uncivilized. Wherever they go, the crime rate goes up, neighborhoods fall apart, whites have to leave. Well, we don't share their life-style and we're not going to live with them. Rosedale is the last white stronghold in this city and nobody's going to push us out. We're going to keep it crime-free, clean and white. If that's racism, make the most of it." A Ruthenian tool-and-die operator in Pittsburgh may have a grudging respect for the black worker who has worked beside him for several years and get along well with the black family across the street, in terms of wholly personal relations; but he may still dislike intensely the perception of blacks he gets from television and the papers. More to the point, he may hate the schemes of "social engineering" emanating from his hereditary enemies in the Protestant upper class, like busing or bank "redlining" or real-estate "blockbusting." In his eyes, he is being asked to pay the entire price for the injustices done to blacks—he who is living on the margin himself—while those who were enriched pay nothing. He also believes these schemes of forced intervention are both illusory and unfair. Persons of a more "modern" and "enlightened" mentality, by contrast, may have no relations with blacks as personal as his, and think of his resistance to blacks as a group as "prejudice."

The modern category of "prejudice," indeed, is based on an ideal of dubious merit. Instead of noticing differences between cultures and their imprint on personality, the "enlightened" or "nonprejudiced" person tries to see what all humans have "in common," a "universal brotherhood," the ways in which we are all, fundamentally, "the same."

In more highly educated and affluent circles, these attitudes are rather easy to maintain, or to fake, for at least two reasons. First, intimate competitive contact with persons of pronounced cultural difference is neither frequent nor disturbing. Money provides space, privacy, mobility and the ability to choose one's associations. Second, the persons one does meet tend to be highly cultivated and well-tutored in how to avoid unpleasant subjects; they tend to represent the best qualities of their own culture and to proceed in the best qualities or their own culture and to proceed in a manner wholly civil.

Cultural contact between the less privileged members of each group tends, by contrast, to be both deeper and more intimate when it is healthy, and rougher, less civil or even violent when conflicts arise. The Ruthenian tool-and-die worker may esteem his black colleague, drink with him in the bar after work, and talk with him as frankly as Archie Bunker with the Jeffersons. Yet his conflicts with blacks may be real. The bitter struggles for survival at the bottom of America are not merely irrational, and over skin color. They concern real goods; jobs, turf, real-estate values, education, culture.

What we call "lack of prejudice," therefore, is often rather more an aspect of privilege than a profound spiritual accomplishment. What we call "prejudice" *is* sometimes prejudice—that is, an irrational resistance to cultural difference, an attribution of inferiority based on group characteristics rather than on individual performance. On the other hand, it is sometimes also an accurate reading of actual economic and social competition. There *are* fewer jobs than there are job-seekers; there *are* neighborhoods fighting for stability and neighborhoods suddenly swamped by what Kenneth Clark has called a "tangle of pathologies"; there *are* skills structurally more highly developed in one culture than in another, skills of real economic and political effect in competition between groups. Those lower on the economic ladder do not have the money, mobility or freedom of choice to evade the bitter conflicts that result. Their resistance is not "irrational"; it concerns quite "rational" matters like their jobs, their schools, their mortgages.

Most Catholics, I believe, perceive at least three strata among blacks. (Among themselves, they also see the same strata.) First are the highly successful and prominent blacks, from Martin Luther King Jr. to Senator Edward Brooke, to the black athletes, professors, singers, actors and lawyers they see so often in the media (but seldom in real life). Second comes the black middle class, pious and disciplined and hard-working, whom they do see in their neighborhoods or meet in their schools—people very like themselves. Third comes the black underclass: that one-fourth or one-third of the black population that lives in poverty, joblessness and the widely publicized "tangle of pathologies."

It is this third group of blacks that dominates public consciousness, those whose "victimization" by society provides the rationale for special public assistance. Commentators conveniently forget that as much as one-fifth of the white-ethnic population is in similar economic and sometime cultural desperation. Oakland Raider football player George Blanda grew up in the coal fields near Pittsburgh; he and his nine brothers and sisters never saw more than $2,000 a year from their father's work in the mines; even today the average income thereabouts is $6,000 a year. "They don't have to tell me what life is like in a ghetto," Blanda says. "I've heard 'dumb Polack' as often as they've heard 'nigger.'"

This misplaced emphasis and a host of other factors combine in the resentment—documented by writers from Robert Coles to Jimmy Breslin—working-class Catholics tend to feel over the alliance between rich, highly educated and powerful whites and the black underclass. It is as though an alien upper-class society has decreed that advances for the black underclass should come chiefly at the expense of working-class whites, while the privileged give up nothing at all.

The resentment and the resulting conflict with blacks is hardly mitigated by the facts that the black underclass, mostly newer to the impersonality and grimness of the Northern cities, is especially weak in an area to which both middle-class blacks and working-class Catholics give pre-eminent value: a strong, disciplined family life. According to the National Center for Health Statistics, 46 percent of all black births in 1973 were illegitimate, almost half of these (119,800) to girls between 15 and 19 years old. Without making moral judgments—for both Eastern and Southern Europeans have a sexual morality quite different from that of the Irish or Anglo-Saxons—one can estimate that the economic consequences are severe. Sons are normally socialized, both in white-ethnic and in strong black families, by the firm, even harsh, discipline of the father; and they are usually taught job skills in the home. By the time they graduate from high school, white-ethnic children have already had several types of job experience—the jobs usually being found for them by their fathers or their father's friends. Thus, youngsters without fathers suffer a severe economic handicap. Understandably, some members of the highly unemployed black underclass resent this situation, but to white ethnics, the valuing of strong family relationships is an important way to deal with economic adversity.

Many middle-class blacks also share the white ethnics' belief in the value of family life as well as their perception of the black underclass. Jesse Jackson, the Chicago black leader, has voiced it eloquently to Paul Cowan in The Village Voice. Like Catholic working people, they too believe passionately in discipline, hard work, education for their children and in a life of higher security, decency, peace and opportunity than they have known before. This black working class receives little or no attention from the black-militant leadership or from the press. It is considered "square," bourgeois, dull, not admirable.

Instead of trying to bring about an alliance between the black working class and the white working class, based on analogous patterns of attachment to church, school, family and hard work, too many social activists have for 15 years now lionized the black underclass and exulted in its differences from the black and white working class. This is a self-destructive political strategy.

Just as there are several different cultures among blacks so also are there several different cultural systems among Catholics. Symbolically, the Irish dominate the Catholic population, but in fact only 17 percent of American Catholics are Irish. Because they have spent the most time in America, and speak English as a native language, because of their educational and occupational success, their literary self-expression, their dominant roles in the church, in national politics and in other areas, the Irish are at the top of the Catholic ladder. Still, those poor and working-class Irish locked in the old neighborhoods of Boston, Providence, Queens, Philadelphia and other Eastern cities retain the images of oppression they have experienced for 300 years in Ireland and in America. An insular people, they are less accustomed to welcoming foreign elements into their midst than some of the other Catholics. (In Western Pennsylvania, where I grew up, we Slavs and Italians were "foreigners." When we said "the Americans" we meant the Irish.) The high level of economic, forensic, managerial and political skills nourished in their culture for centuries has kept the Irish ahead of the Eastern European Catholics—the largest single family of Catholic cultures.

The Slavs, by and large, went to work in mines, mills and factories, working far more often for others and for weekly wages than, say, the Jews, the Greeks or the Italians, who with high frequency went into business for themselves. The American economic system tends to grant larger rewards to those who follow the latter rather than the former course. In Eastern Europe, the great symbol of winning liberty from serfdom was the ability to own one's own home. Even in the United States, home ownership remains the highest economic priority of Slavic families; higher, even, than education for their children.

The Poles vote more frequently than the other Slavs, and in higher proportion than any other ethnic group in America; but they have developed few highly placed political leaders. So far, the Slavs seem to lack the vivid charismatic and cosmopolitan intellectual and political leadership their numbers warrant. Edmund Muskie is really not very Polish and resisted identifying himself with white working-class immigrants; Mary Anne Krupsak and Barbara Mikulski may represent a new order.

The Italians, by contrast, rival the Irish in forensic and political skills. Sixty-two percent of the Italian immigrants settled within an arc from Providence to Philadelphia, and where they found the Irish dominating the Democratic Party, many of them began to take over the Republican Party. In Hollywood, the arts and the creative departments of advertising firms the Italians may be second to none in talent, visibility and success.

In literature and scholarship, there may soon be a similar explosion. In the great corporations and in banking, they are making their presence known—but barely. Like the Eastern Europeans, the Italians tend to be a highly stable people; like the others, many move to the suburbs, but the old neighborhoods tend to live on longer than most.

More than other groups, they also seem willing to fight for their neighborhoods, to protect them, and to resist outside bullying or outside threats. Thus in Boston, when observers warn that South Boston may have been tough, but busing in the Italian North Ward may be even tougher, they are judging by a common folk wisdom. In New York, the word among other white-ethnic groups is "live next to the Italians, if you want to stay." Rosedale is largely Italian.

Conflicts such as that going on in Rosedale are hardly in the best interests of the city's future, but neither is a likely alternative—a massive exodus of whites from the old neighborhoods. In this sense, the cultural background that leads Italians and Slavs to prefer to stay in their old neighborhoods is one of the few remaining hopes of integrated cities in the North. Why is their willingness to stay not politically and economically reinforced?

First, it must be acknowledged, urban Catholics have often been betrayed by their own leaders. Disastrous Catholic "machines," like Rizzo's in Philadelphia, have won bluster but no real advance for their people; Catholic bishops, concentrating on narrow ecclesiastical issues, have ignored the vast social instability of the cities; Catholic intellectuals have been establishing ideological credentials as "conservative" or "liberal," with little attention to working-class sufferings; local Catholic political leadership, as on the Boston School Committee, has often been disgustingly poor.

Thus, Catholics must blame themselves for their political predicament. However, some share of the blame—and hope for change—rests with the larger, and far more powerful, Protestant Establishment. Banks, investment houses, corporate law firms and realtors—the institutions par excellence of the great Protestant Establishments in every Northern city—give the media beautiful ads about integration. In actual practice they destroy the family businesses, family investments and family morale of neighborhood after neighborhood. Banks "redline" changing neighborhoods; realtors "blockbust." Then the "tangle of pathologies"— undisciplined teen-agers (who commit 70 percent of all crime), other forms of crime, deterioration of housing, the bankruptcy of small businesses, the decline in services— moves in. The pundits then call those who flee "racists." The racism is in the Establishment. The institutions of the Establishment betray a neighborhood, drive people out, destroy their dreams and rob their savings. This is a scandal that cries out to heaven.

Black leaders have made a tragic mistake, strategically and tactically, in choosing white-ethnic neighborhoods as the target, the victim and the hostage of their desperation. Black leaders must know that the white-ethnic schools in Boston—or Philadelphia, or Detroit—are as bad as their own, that less money is often available to them, that the idealistic young teachers from Harvard and Columbia go first to black, hardly ever to white-ethnic schools. But some argue, "We will bus your children to our schools, as hostages to remind you of our plight." Why would black leaders choose their most potent voting allies as their hostages? It defies all rationality.

Black leaders have no closer bloc of political support than white-ethnic voters, who have provided majorities for every piece of progressive economic legislation and civil-rights legislation this nation has had these last 50 years. There is no progressive victory in Pennsylvania without large majorities in the white-ethnic wards of Pittsburgh and Philadelphia to overcome the Protestant, conservative, rural votes; the liberals of Bryn Mawr cannot carry even their own Main Line

constituency. You cannot win Illinois for a progressive victory without huge white-ethnic majorities in Chicago; Michigan without Detroit; New York without Queens, the Bronx and Buffalo; Ohio without Cleveland and Toledo. In 1968, Wallace won 7.7 percent of the Catholic vote but 16 percent of the Protestant vote. White ethnics and black workers have the same economic interests and analogous cultural interests. Why divide them?

The Protestant and Jewish liberals who dominate the media are ignorant about the Catholic working class. Since they define the issues, they would save much grief if they would not divide working-class blacks from working-class Catholics and others, if they would praise the virtues of hard work and family economic wisdom by which parents give their children better opportunities than they received. Black and Catholic leaders share a similar responsibility. The destruction of urban ethnic neighborhoods is the No. 1 domestic tragedy of our time. This is the disease that will kill us all. This is the ecological abuse more fatal than dirty air.

"Redlining" and "blockbusting" must be stopped. There must be some plan of Federal insurance to protect and investments in homes and small businesses that hard-working people have made in their neighborhoods. These are more important social forms of savings than deposits in savings banks. When white-ethnic families can look ahead 20 or 30 years to reasonable prospects of financial security and neighborhood stability, they stay. They integrate. They have long since begun to be integrated. They do not love blacks, any more than Archie Bunker (not a white ethnic) loved the Jeffersons, but they do live next door, speak with the rough truthfulness of the working class, and—given no reason to fear for the future—live together decently.

There must also be greater honesty about the pathologies of the white and black underclass. The white-ethnic poor share the supposedly "black" pathologies—high dropout rates, drugs, cynicism, an upsurge in broken families economically unprepared youths. The white underclass of Boston described in George V. Higgins's novels is threatened by self-destruction. To expect suffering and wounded communities like these to assume, on top of their own, the even more grievous burdens of blacks is a measure of political foolishness that leaves one speechless.

I see on the horizon two possibilities. Either a political leader of the stature of Robert Kennedy will hold the trust of both black and white-ethnic workers and build a politics of human ecology designed to strengthen the cultural and family networks that make urban life faintly possible. Or the political foolhardiness of the sort chosen by the N.A.A.C.P. in Boston—a willingness to destroy a city in order to ''save'' it—will awaken the most enormous political and moral revulsion. Blacks and Catholics can go forward together. If they are pitted against each other, those on the top of the American ladder will rejoice in their own moral superiority—until turmoil and bitterness enshroud us all.